THE RESPONSE TO
PROSTITUTION IN THE
PROGRESSIVE ERA

THE RESPONSE TO

Prostitution

IN THE PROGRESSIVE ERA

MARK THOMAS CONNELLY

THE UNIVERSITY OF NORTH CAROLINA PRESS

CHAPEL HILL

© 1980 The University of North Carolina Press
All rights reserved
Manufactured in the United States of America
ISBN 0-8078-1424-5
Library of Congress Catalog Card Number 79-24038

Library of Congress Cataloging in Publication Data

Connelly, Mark Thomas, 1948–
   The response to prostitution in the progressive era.

   Bibliography: p.
   Includes index.
     1.   Prostitution—United States—History—20th century.
   2.   United States—Moral conditions.   I.   Title.
HQ144.C66   301.41'54   79-24038
ISBN 0-8078-1424-5

TO MY MOTHER

AND THE MEMORY OF MY FATHER

CONTENTS

ACKNOWLEDGMENTS

Many people contributed in many ways to the writing of this book. Members of my family never flagged in their encouragement. My mother, Irene F. Connelly, deserves special recognition in this regard, which is registered on the dedication page. In addition, my aunt, Eleanor C. Williams, proficiently proofread an early draft.

The history department at Rutgers University provided a most congenial environment for scholarly pursuits. Gerald N. Grob read my early attempts at dealing with these issues and used his broad knowledge of American social history to help me in defining my thinking about them. James W. Reed spent more time with these materials than I ever had a right to expect, and his comments and advice were invaluable.

James L. Wunsch read the manuscript with a critical eye and offered numerous suggestions for improvement. Readers who are further interested in the concerns raised here are urged to consult his own fine study of prostitution in American society, which offers numerous original and perceptive insights and observations.

The specialist readers for The University of North Carolina Press each responded with a thorough and trenchant critical appraisal. The support and encouragement of both of these senior scholars was most welcome.

Walter J. Petry, Jr., who first pointed me toward the study of history, supported my efforts at writing the book at every stage of the way. His counsel was greatly appreciated.

Norman Miller, wordsmith extraordinaire, wielded his knowledge of the art of writing to correct and improve several successive drafts of this study. His attention to matters of style and substance was of the highest order.

The staff of The University of North Carolina Press saw the book through the many stages of publication with the highest degree of professional concern and competence. Executive Editor Lewis C. Bateman was constant in his support, Sandra Eisdorfer's supervision of the editing and proofreading was superb, and Janis R. Bolster's skilled and meticulous copy editing improved the manuscript immeasurably.

My greatest intellectual debt is to Warren I. Susman. His insights into the past, and its relationship to the present, influenced to a large degree whatever understanding I possess about American History.

THE RESPONSE TO
PROSTITUTION IN THE
PROGRESSIVE ERA

INTRODUCTION

Tonight I saw some of the whore-house district—from the outside, &
amateurishly.—An enormously long dance hall, Thalia[,] with a free
vaudeville program; a search-spot-calcium light flashing from the rear
thru a dusky 100 feet to fall on the twinkling legs of a soubrette.
Orchestra of 10–12 pieces, but cracked plaster on the wall behind the
stage. Then the lit[e]s turned on for dancing by the great crowd of
muckers, soldiers sailors etc. with whores, who couldn't pass beyond the
bar by the rail. Announcers & waiters w[ith] eye shades. Whores leaning
over the rail coaxing me "Oh you Ginger—long—thin." Free balcony
w[ith] drinks. Long line of gallery booths one side. . . . Reg[ular]
vaudeville program. ——Another dance hall with small stage; whores
leaning over swinging gates only.——
    Sinclair Lewis, San Francisco, 1909[1]

It was hard for anyone, even the most naive visitor from some provincial
hamlet, to miss them. They were known to all, those who cared to know
and those who did not, certain streets and certain blocks in certain parts
of town. During the first two decades of the twentieth century there was
at least one red-light district in virtually every American city with a
population over 100,000 and in many of the smaller ones, too. Chicago
and New York, as befitted their eminence, had several each.

    Many Americans undoubtedly considered prostitution an unfortunate
but inevitable part of social relations; it was, after all, hardly a new
problem. Thus, during much of the progressive era, urban prostitution
was tacitly tolerated, relatively undisturbed, and often tightly woven
into a web of payoffs and corruption involving municipal officials, political machines, the police, and others who filled their pockets with the
profits that prostitution generated. It was a time when the house of
casual pleasure was still almost as much a part of social life as the
cocktail lounge is today, when red-light districts were as fundamental a
part of the urban scene as cobblestones, trolleys, sweatshops, and tenements. The Tenderloin, the Levee, Storyville, and the Barbary Coast—the
famous vice districts in New York, Chicago, New Orleans, and San

Francisco—have become part of our urban folklore, memorialized in novels, memoirs, popular histories, and films.

Less well remembered, but of equal historical importance, is the great national alarm that the open existence of the "social evil" prompted between the turn of the century and World War I. To many vocal and influential individuals and groups, prostitution appeared as an ominous symptom of an unsettling and systemic social crisis. This study offers a reconstruction and interpretation of that intriguing episode in American history.

Concern about prostitution existed, of course, before the progressive era. It is a matter of record, for instance, that by the mid 1650s the "city upon a hill" more commonly known as Boston sported a brothel run by one Dermin Mahoone. The divines, at least in public, did not look upon Mahoone's calling as an auspicious sign for the commonwealth. Throughout the colonial era, American communities were very concerned with enforcing moral codes dealing with a wide range of illicit sexual behavior. In the eighteenth and well into the nineteenth century, this community concern often assumed extralegal dimensions, in the form of whorehouse riots. Annoyed citizens took to the streets to ransack and torch brothels in Boston in 1734, 1737, and 1825; in New York City in 1793 and 1799; in St. Louis in 1831; and in Chicago and Detroit in 1855.[2]

During the early nineteenth century, however, a new approach to the problem of prostitution emerged, influenced both by evangelical and perfectionist notions of social reform and by the rate of urbanization, which made prostitution more noticeable and concentrated in American cities. In the 1820s and 1830s, moral reformers, aroused over what appeared to be rampant immorality in the cities, formed organizations, such as the New York Magdalen Society, dedicated to the moral and social rehabilitation of prostitutes and the prevention of sexual lapses.[3] Consternation about prostitution also prompted Dr. William W. Sanger, the resident physician at the women's detention center on Blackwell's Island in New York, to write his pioneering work of 1858, *The History of Prostitution: Its Extent, Causes, and Effects throughout the World*, which was the first serious American consideration of prostitution and still stands as an impressive contribution to nineteenth-century American social science.[4] But the issue of prostitution was at most a secondary issue in the antebellum years; it was overshadowed by the slavery controversy and its political implications and, to a lesser extent, by the temperance movement.

In the decades after the Civil War, prostitution in the cities continued to be a focus of concern and prompted what has been called a "purity

crusade" for the regeneration of American sexual morality. This movement emerged in the 1860s and 1870s when women's groups, former
abolitionists, temperance organizations, and ministers joined together
to oppose the municipal regulation and medical inspection of prostitutes
in cities including New York, Chicago, and St. Louis. On one side of
the controversy were the "regulationists"—usually municipal officials,
public health officers, the police, and some physicians—who felt that
prostitution would always exist and concluded that medical inspection
was the only way to protect the public from the contagion of venereal
disease. The purity forces totally opposed such a plan and viewed any
official sanction and licensing of prostitutes as an insult to womanhood,
a denial of the civil liberties of the prostitute, an unworkable solution
because most prostitutes would never be registered on the official roles,
and an endorsement of the double standard of morals. For the purity
forces, medical inspection was an immoral compromise with a hideous
evil. The most notable such contest occurred in St. Louis in the early
1870s, where purity forces were able to overturn a city ordinance that
had instituted a system of medical inspection.[5]

Although the campaign against the municipal regulation of prostitution was the mainstay of the purity movement in its early years, by the
mid 1880s purity reform had expanded to include moral education, child
rearing, sex education, social hygiene, book censorship, prohibition, and
almost anything else having to do with moral and physical purity. Prostitution remained a purity issue, perhaps even the most important one, but
it was now one of many. Yet as important as purity reform was in the late
nineteenth century, prostitution remained essentially a local problem and
did not become a national issue comparable in significance to the money
controversy, populism, or the labor question.

Not until the first two decades of the twentieth century did prostitution emerge as a major national issue, precipitating an outburst of concern quite unlike anything before, or, for that manner, since. Persons
as prominent and diverse as Jane Addams, Theodore Roosevelt, Lincoln
Steffens, Emma Goldman, Brand Whitlock, Walter Lippmann, Frederic
Howe, Abraham Flexner, and Raymond Fosdick at one time or another
during the progressive years turned their attention to the problem of
the social evil. The pervasive alarm over prostitution assumed many
forms: state and local vice commission reports; lurid exposés of "white
slavery"; United States Supreme Court decisions; federal and state legislation and reports; the activities of boards of health, medical groups,
and individual physicians; the investigations of muckraking journalists;
best-selling novels; and certain policies of the federal government during
World War I. All of these manifestations of interest and concern consti-

tuted what is referred to in this study as the response to prostitution, or antiprostitution.[6] But although prostitution is the subject of the following chapters, this is neither a social history of prostitution in the progressive years nor an historical analysis of the women who were or became prostitutes. These are important areas of inquiry and have been addressed most admirably by others, but this work is oriented in other directions.[7]

This study sets forth an analysis and interpretation of the cluster of ideas, beliefs, emotions, and fears that propelled antiprostitution in the early twentieth century. The intention is to place the published response to prostitution in its intellectual, social, and cultural setting. The central argument is that antiprostitution had at least as much to do with the anxieties produced by the transformation of American society occurring in the progressive era as with the actual existence of red-light districts. This is not to imply that the issue of prostitution was a red herring. The progressive generation accurately perceived the social evil as one of the grosser manifestations of industrial America, as an embodiment of alienation, force, fraud, oppression, and exploitation. The grim reality of the vice districts and of streetwalkers plying their trade along the thoroughfares was the immediate occasion of the progressive concern over prostitution, and this study is in no way intended to minimize that basic truth.[8] By itself, however, the social reality of urban vice is not sufficient to explain the extraordinary outburst of concern and anxiety over prostitution in the early twentieth century. Such apprehensions existed, after all, throughout the nineteenth century. What produced the full-throated alarm of the progressive years was a new evaluation of prostitution's significance. There was, in short, more to the progressive furor over prostitution than prostitution itself, just as there is often more to an obsession with communism than communism itself.

As a form of illicit sexual behavior, prostitution has always provoked highly charged emotions. During the progressive years, however, its inherent capacity to provoke fear and alarm was greatly expanded. Prostitution became a master symbol, a code word, for a wide range of anxieties engendered by the great social and cultural changes that give the progressive era its coherence as a distinct historical period.

During the tumultuous years between the closing of the landed frontier in 1890 and the end of World War I, the United States was transformed from a predominantly rural-minded, decentralized, principally Anglo-Saxon, production-oriented, and morally absolutist society to a predominantly urban, centralized, multi-ethnic, consumption-oriented, secular, and relativist society. The buckboard was replaced by the Model T; the artisan's tool set gave way to the assembly line; the Protestant values of thrift and austerity were undermined by the new forces of advertising, consumerism, and commercialism; and the verities of the small towns, of the thousands of Winesburg, Ohios, across the nation, were joined in a losing battle with the allure of the new urban life-styles. This extraordinary transformation was not, of course, complete by 1920. Many of its consequences were fought out in the cultural and political battles of the 1920s, and others have not yet been fully resolved. Nor did the transformation start precisely in 1890; it had roots as far back as the first important signs of the industrial revolution in the 1830s. But whereas before the progressive years it was possible to write off the signs of change as aberrations, or as at most changes of degree, by 1915 it was no longer possible to do so. During the progressive years changes of degree became changes of kind, and what were previously perceived as aberrations emerged, slowly, but with the inexorable certainty of a glacier, as the new norm.[9]

This transformation in American society is generally regarded as forward-looking and modernizing. It was accompanied, however, by contrapuntal themes of tension, anxiety, and fear. The response to prostitution constituted just such a theme, for it expressed, and was propelled by, grave misgivings about the manifestations and consequences of that reorientation. Antiprostitution was not uniformly negative, provincial, or backward-looking. Indeed, in one sense antiprostitution was a progressive reform and, like much of the progressive reform impulse, had its optimistic and confident, not to mention self-righteous, strains. Nonetheless, the most salient characteristics of the response to prostitution were confusion and bewilderment; it was an American expression of modernization and its discontents. It is this singular quality that gives antiprostitution in the progressive years much of its historical importance and uniqueness.[10]

The following chapters develop and amplify this interpretation by analyzing the response to prostitution in the context of the troubling social and cultural questions with which prostitution was repeatedly associated, and which gave it much of its identity as a major social problem. They detail how antiprostitution became a psychological clearinghouse for an extraordinary range of troubling issues: the appearance of independent and mobile young women in the cities, widespread clandestine sexual immorality, a conspiracy to flood the nation with alien prostitutes, the catastrophic physical and social consequences of the unchecked contagion of venereal disease, the depersonalization and commercialization of sex in the metropolises, an alien-controlled conspiracy to debauch American girls into lives of "white slavery," and, by 1918, the ability of the nation to wage war for democracy, decency, and civilization.

Collectively, these chapters demonstrate how a deep-seated and profound ambivalence toward the sweeping social and cultural changes of the progressive years shaped the perception of, and response to, prostitution. One especially anxiety-provoking manifestation of the reorientation of American society, the breakdown in nineteenth-century morality, or "civilized morality," was particularly influential in shaping antiprostitution. Indeed, almost every expression of antiprostitution was based on a commitment to this value system and was propelled by the sense of moral crisis that its decline engendered.[11]

Civilized morality was the prescriptive system of moral and cultural values, sexual and economic roles, religious sanctions, hygienic rules, and idealized behavioral patterns that emerged in the Jacksonian period and came to infuse American middle-class life between the Civil War and World War I. At the core of the code were two related propositions. There was, first, a belief in a unified and responsible self that, through the exercise of will and conscience, could (and must) control and repress the unruly and base sexual instincts. Its corollary was that "civilization" and "progress," as well as personal economic and social advancement, depended on this control of the potentially dangerous sexual drive. These beliefs supported a sexual code that strictly prohibited premarital sexual relations, proclaimed monogamous marriage to be the only permissible context for sexual intercourse, and declared that even within marriage the only purpose of sexual relations was reproduction. This sexual code, in turn, drew on a large body of widely circulated medical theorizing on sex that endorsed sexual continence for men and warned against the debilitating effects of the loss of semen through masturbation or excessive intercourse, cautioned that illicit intercourse could lead to incurable venereal disease, and affirmed that women were basically asexual and therefore repulsed by males unable to contain their baser passions.

Adherents of civilized morality believed that the code's viability depended on an unremitting effort to root out all opportunities for moral lapse. This understanding fueled the purity crusade of the late nineteenth century, particularly the shenanigans of Anthony Comstock and like-minded individuals, who were determined to protect American society from salacious books, prostitutes, poker, and other forms of mental or physical licentiousness. In a sense, the purity crusade was an attempt to force the reality of social conditions into line with the dictates of civilized morality. And the merger of state and local purity groups into the American Purity Alliance in 1895 was a signal that civilized morality had become a formally institutionalized force in American life.[12]

In the ideal world of civilized morality all moral values were absolute and timeless, masculine and feminine roles were sharply defined and demarcated, sexuality was seen as a potentially destructive force, and life, in general, was conceived in terms of duty, service, and self-denial. Civilized morality was imbued with the rhetoric of evangelical Protestantism, but for all the God-fearing ministers and physicians who preached it, there was little overt theology in civilized morality. It was repressive and puritanical, but its fears and concerns were distinctly those of this world. In this respect, civilized morality reflected the dominant orientation of American Protestantism in the late nineteenth and early twentieth centuries, which was increasingly coming to focus on secular and nondoctrinal matters, such as alcohol and evolution. Civilized morality was also the moral code of the rising nineteenth-century urban middle class, which would produce the leaders of and spokesmen for many progressive causes; it implicitly decried the enervating idleness of the leisure class, while fearing the "licentiousness" of the lower class. Thus, when the middle-class generation born between 1850 and 1880 achieved power and prominence during the progressive years, so, too, did the tenets of civilized morality.

The triumph would be short-lived. During these same years, a new group of intellectuals, who were born in the 1880s and 1890s and who would come to prominence in the 1920s, were inaugurating a radical critique of nineteenth-century creeds and were disavowing in their work and lives the mandates of civilized morality. There is also growing evidence that in the late nineteenth and early twentieth centuries the sexual attitudes and behavior of significant numbers of middle-class Americans began to move away from the repressive orthodoxy of civilized morality. The decline of nineteenth-century morality and the emergence of a more tolerant attitude toward sexuality was a major manifestation of the transformation of American society in the progressive era. Civilized morality had been the moral ethos of a production-oriented society, and as American society shifted toward a consumption ethic in the early decades of the twentieth century, its authoritative stature began to wane. By the beginning of World War I, at the very time that civilized morality seemed preeminent, it was becoming clear even to its most ardent supporters that it was sagging under its own weight. Its values and ideals would be trumpeted once more during World War I, but, otherwise, it was largely defunct as a dominant cultural force by 1915.[13]

The alarm and confusion precipitated by the crisis and decline in civilized morality influenced almost every aspect of the response to prostitution. Prostitution blatantly defied the prescriptions of the code, specifically the prohibition of extramarital intercourse, the equation of intercourse with reproduction, and the idealization of female purity. This was not, however, a new problem in the progressive years, for it was precisely this awareness that generated the concern about prostitution in the late nineteenth century. The new force in the progressive years was the combination of the older understanding that the existence of prostitution mocked the ideals of civilized morality with the new awareness that the foundation of the system itself was crumbling. Any last attempt to reaffirm the validity of the code had to come at this critical point. Because prostitution had always constituted the most flagrant violation of civilized morality, it is not surprising that the greatest outburst of concern about it manifested itself precisely when civilized morality was in its final stage of decline. Indeed, as this study demonstrates, it could hardly have been otherwise.

One

ANTIPROSTITUTION IN

THE PROGRESSIVE YEARS:

AN OVERVIEW

It would be interesting to know how much of the social conscience of our times had as its first insight the prostitute on the city pavement.
Walter Lippmann, *A Preface to Politics* (1913)

In 1915 the distinguished Chicago sociologist Robert Park observed in his now classic essay "The City" that it was in the very nature of urbanization for a city to develop "moral regions." These were areas where parts of the urban population would segregate itself "not merely in accordance with its interests, but in accordance with its tastes or its temperaments. . . . A moral region is not necessarily a place of abode. It may be a mere rendezvous, a place of resort." The "vice districts which are found in most cities," Park went on, were examples of moral regions, and he urged that society "accept these 'moral regions' and the more or less eccentric and exceptional people who inhabit them, in a sense, at least, as part of the natural, if not the normal life of a city."[1]

Park's remarkably detached analysis did not, to put it mildly, express the dominant view of prostitution in the progressive years. In contrast to his delight in the diversity of urban styles, the progressive generation as a whole regarded prostitution as a most shocking shame of the cities, a failure of traditional institutions—the church, family, school—to enforce civilized morality in the urban milieu. Indeed, the very notion of a plurality of "moral regions," and the moral and cultural relativism it implied, was utterly incompatible with civilized morality. Just five years before the publication of Park's essay, there appeared a more representative approach to the "moral regions" in Park's beloved Chicago in a book entitled *Chicago and Its Cesspools of Infamy.* In the following year, 1911, the Chicago Vice Commission, in its massive report *The Social Evil in Chicago,* stated as its motto: "Constant and Persistent Repression of Prostitution the Immediate Method: Absolute Annihilation the Ultimate Ideal." And the *Independent* summed up contemporary opinion when in 1913 it branded prostitution "the chief of all the evils that both infest and infect society. It blasts more names, it destroys more lives, than does the saloon, or the tyranny of predatory wealth."[2]

Antiprostitution in the progressive era was exceedingly protean. A variety of groups and interests approached the problem from a broad range of positions and with a rich diversity of styles. There was general agreement, however, that the ultimate goal was to abolish prostitution, eliminate the reasons for its existence, or, at the minimum, destroy its most visible and flagrant form—the segregated vice district. The range of efforts to achieve this goal, along with the organizations involved, problems encountered, tactics employed, and solutions advocated, are worth looking at in detail.

Almost every aspect of antiprostitution was somehow related to the stark realities of the American city in the early twentieth century. In the half century between 1860 and 1910, the years in which the progressive generation came to maturity, the larger American cities increased in population nearly sevenfold. In the last two decades of the nineteenth century alone, New York's population doubled, Chicago's tripled, and St. Paul's and Minneapolis's quadrupled. The open and unabashed oppression and disorder in the industrial cities—the teeming slums, the atrocious sweatshops, the child labor, the brazen prostitution—shocked the progressive generation and mocked the self-congratulatory shibboleths about American society that its members had imbibed in their middle-class upbringings. Although the progressives were not, generally speaking, of an antiurban cast of mind and indeed usually accepted the city, as Frederic Howe put it, as the hope of democracy, they also, and understandably, saw in the shocking aspects of urban America a "hideous phantasmagoria of hunger, disease, vice, crime, and despair."[3] In an important sense, antiprostitution in the progressive years was another manifestation of the uneasy peace that has existed for so long between Americans and their cities.

Because prostitution was most concentrated, sophisticated, and visible in the large cities, they became the primary arenas for antiprostitution activity. The New York City Committee of Fifteen, organized by prominent members of the Chamber of Commerce in 1900 to investigate the extent of vice in the city, was the first expression of concern over prostitution in the progressive era. The committee responded to two main influences: a growing anxiety among New York clergymen about the extent of prostitution in the city, and investigations conducted by the state legislature that pointed to connections among the vice districts, Tammany Hall, and the police. Edwin R. A. Seligman, a professor of economics at Columbia University and a member of the committee, co-ordinated the research and writing of its first publication, *The Social Evil: With Special Reference to Conditions Existing in New York City*, issued in 1902.

Most of the report, which was actually researched and written by Alvin Johnson, one of Seligman's graduate students, dealt not with con-ditions in New York but rather with the history of European attempts to regulate prostitution. The committee admitted that regulation and medi-cal inspection was the preferred European policy but argued that it had not worked. In the final pages of the report, Seligman attempted to formulate a policy that would control prostitution and venereal disease without "regulating" it in the European sense. He proposed a vague solution called the "Moral Regulation of Vice." "Such a system," he wrote, "would abandon the task of effecting the impossible, in either morals or hygiene, and would reserve the powers at its command for the bringing about of such amelioration as experience and reason have shown to be possible." The system would be called "the Moral Regula-tion of Vice, since it would never lose sight of the fact that moral con-siderations are of paramount importance." Unfortunately, Seligman did not indicate how such a finely tuned system might be put into practice.[4]

The Committee of Fifteen continuously cooperated with other groups in the city investigating the same problem, most notably the New York State Tenement House Commission created under Governor Theodore Roosevelt in 1900, and provided support for political reform groups dedicated to reducing the political power of Tammany Hall. In 1902, the year after the death of its chairman, William H. Baldwin, Jr., and the election of the reform mayor Seth Low, the Committee of Fifteen dis-banded. Its successor was the Committee of Fourteen for the Suppression of the "Raines Law Hotels" in New York City, organized in 1905. Until 1910, the Committee of Fourteen devoted most of its energies to sup-pressing the so-called Raines Law Hotels (hotels believed to be associated with the practice of prostitution). In that year the research section of the committee published *The Social Evil in New York City: A Study in Law Enforcement*, which called for a much broader attack on prostitution, one that would investigate the relationship of the real estate interests to prostitution, and the connection between women's wages and immo-rality. With this goal in mind, the committee reorganized and expanded its membership in 1912. The reconstituted Committee of Fourteen em-phasized that it would concentrate on only the most commercialized aspects of prostitution and would eschew any attempt at complete re-pression. Its approach promised to be more empirical and realistic than Seligman's vision of the "Moral Regulation of Vice," but the committee was unable to realize even these modest aims. It continued to function well into the 1920s, but its influence after 1910 steadily decreased.

New York City was also the site of another major organizational attempt to deal with prostitution, that of the American Society of Sanitary and Moral Prophylaxis. In the words of its founder, Prince A. Morrow, the society was dedicated to "preventing or diminishing the spread of diseases which have their origin in the Social Evil." More than any other group concerned with prostitution, this one was largely the result of the effort of one man, Morrow, who guided it until his death in 1913.[5]

When Morrow organized the society in 1905, he was already an eminent and well-respected dermatologist. His interest in the etiology of venereal diseases (which were considered dermatological in the nineteenth century) dated back to the 1880s, when he translated into English the *Syphilis and Marriage* of the great French physician Jean-Alfred Fournier. Morrow was shocked at Fournier's delineation of the consequences to marriage and society of undiagnosed and untreated syphilitic infection. In the ensuing decades, he continued his education in the social ramifications of venereal disease, which resulted in his own major work of 1904, *Social Diseases and Marriage: Social Prophylaxis*, in which he advocated a program of public education concerning the consequences of venereal disease.

In 1902, Morrow journeyed to Brussels to attend an international conference on the public health aspects of venereal disease. There he was urged by members of the French Society of Sanitary and Moral Prophylaxis, including Fournier himself, to found a similar organization in the United States. In May of 1904, Morrow published an article calling for such a society, and in February of the next year the first organizational meeting of the American Society of Sanitary and Moral Prophylaxis, attended by twenty-five people, was held in New York City.

At the inaugural meeting, Morrow urged that "the society should be a permanent organization." The problems of prostitution and venereal disease were evils of "vitality and permanence" that could be combated only by "active, continuous, and sustained effort. The emotional waves of excitement which from time to time sweep over the community," he went on, "do little permanent good. Violent measures, which are necessarily spasmodic and intermittent always defeat the object in view."[6] Although membership was open to all, the overwhelming majority of members were physicians who supported an approach to prostitution and venereal disease consistent with the latest advances in venereology. Many opposed the more religious and moral orientation of groups such as the American Purity Alliance, or the Committee of Fifteen's emphasis on the moral rather than the hygienic aspect of prostitution. The society clearly stated that prostitution was the source of venereal diseases, but, unlike the purity groups and the vice commissions, it was not primarily interested in repressing prostitution. Instead, the society's goal was the mass inculcation of the "gospel of continence" among the male population (most specifically the unmarried), which would reduce both the need for prostitution and the rate and spread of venereal infection. To this end the society embarked on a massive educational campaign aimed at replacing the allegedly erroneous belief that sexual intercourse was a physiological necessity for men with a new ethic of the complete compatibility of perfect health and sexual continence.[7]

In its first five years the society grew impressively, both in size and in influence. The membership, just under 350 in 1906, rose to almost 700 by 1910. Local and affiliate branches were established in Philadelphia, Baltimore, Detroit, Chicago, Milwaukee, Indianapolis, St. Louis, Pittsburgh, and Portland, Oregon, and, on a state level, in Texas, West Virginia, California, Indiana, New Jersey, and Connecticut. The society published its own *Transactions*, and within a year of its founding, Morrow could claim that because of its activities, more attention had been focused on prostitution and venereal disease "within the last ten months than in the previous twenty years."[8]

As early as 1907, Morrow saw the need for a more powerful and centralized national organization that could coordinate the activities of the various local social hygiene groups. In 1910 the first meeting of such an organization, the American Federation for Sex Hygiene, was held in St. Louis, and Morrow was elected president. Morrow died in 1913, but his life's work continued. In that year the American Federation for Sex Hygiene merged with the purity-oriented American Vigilance Association to form the American Social Hygiene Association; and from this point on, the social hygiene movement in America had a secure institutional foundation.[9]

The Committee of Fifteen, the Committee of Fourteen, and the American Society of Sanitary and Moral Prophylaxis, notwithstanding their differences in personnel and goals, all embodied an approach to prostitution that was organized and systematic. They stand in marked contrast to earlier expressions of concern, such as the famous Stead crusade in Chicago in 1893 and the Reverend Charles Parkhurst's similar activities in New York City two years later, which, although providing excellent front-page copy, did not contribute significantly to the understanding of prostitution.[10] The progressive generation was a fact-finding one, and this spirit fully informed the response to prostitution. The new approach appeared in full force in the vice investigations organized in twenty-seven cities and three states between 1911 and 1916. Presenting a wealth of information on prostitution in specific localities, the vice commissions self-consciously perceived themselves as marking a new departure in the investigation of prostitution. "We must no longer depend wholly upon volunteer committees of citizens for the study and solution of modern city problems," the Syracuse Vice Commission stated in its 1913 report. "These twentieth century civic evils," it went on, "must be handled by twentieth century methods if we expect to prevent their overwhelming us. They require steady work day by day, and year after year by educated, experienced and paid social workers."[11]

This desire was realized on a massive scale in 1913 with the incorporation of the Bureau of Social Hygiene. The bureau was organized and heavily financed by John D. Rockefeller, Jr., who had first confronted the problem of prostitution in 1910, when he served as foreman of a special New York City grand jury charged with investigating an alleged "white-slave" traffic in the city. This experience impressed the philanthropist with the need for a well-financed, professionally staffed, permanent organization to study prostitution and its effects, which would be similar in form to the Rockefeller Foundation for Medical Research, founded in 1901. Within a few years, the Bureau of Social Hygiene commissioned and supported two important investigations: George Jackson Kneeland's *Commercialized Prostitution in New York City* (1913) and Abraham Flexner's researches into European methods of dealing with prostitution, *Prostitution in Europe* (1914). In the following years the bureau sponsored research on aspects of prostitution such as police systems, the need for women police, legal statutes, and court reform and produced a series of psychological studies of delinquent women. The general response to the creation of the Bureau of Social Hygiene was overwhelmingly favorable. Many commentators remarked on the merits of a future-oriented "bureau" over a present-minded "commission," and the progressive *Survey* summed up most of this opinion when it stated that "we are to have, for the first time, an organization to study not one or a few aspects of vice, but the whole, an organization possessed of ample means, and starting with a thorough survey of conditions." The Bureau of Social Hygiene, which carried on and broadened its work for decades, seemed the perfect answer to the desire for information and organization.[12]

All individuals and organizations concerned about prostitution in the progressive years encountered two basic problems in the course of their endeavors: defining the kinds of behavior that constituted prostitution and deriving aggregate estimates of its extent. The first was very much related to the second, because disparities in definition would necessarily change the basis of the estimate. In one sense, these problems of definition and estimate were typical of almost every progressive attempt to ameliorate a social problem. In the case of antiprostitution, however, these matters had a deeper and more important cultural significance.

What is immediately striking about most of the definitions of prostitution in the progressive years is their imprecision, even vagueness. This is no trivial matter, for as two contemporary scholars of the subject point out, the "lack of a satisfactory definition of prostitution, and the lack of an adequate basis for determining who is a prostitute, lead to grotesque historical errors, mistakes in social policy, and countless individual injustices." There was not, to be sure, a complete lack of definitional rigor. For instance, the eleventh edition of the *Encyclopedia Britannica* (1911), that great storehouse of late-nineteenth-century Anglo-Saxon culture, offered a reasonably precise definition. "Prostitution," the entry began, was "promiscuous unchastity for gain. . . . It has always been distinguished in law and custom from concubinage, which is an inferior state of marriage, and from adultery and other irregular sexual relations, in which the motive is passion." And, in 1916, the Illinois Senate Vice Committee advised at the beginning of its report that, although "in general the remedies for prostitution are likewise the remedies for immorality," the "act of selling oneself, which is prostitution," should not be confused with "the act of giving oneself without pay." These clear definitions, however, stand in marked contrast to the general disinclination to define exactly what constituted prostitution, and which women could be accused of practicing it.[13]

The 1911 Chicago Vice Commission report can serve as a typical example. *The Social Evil in Chicago* began with a clear proposal to "inquire into conditions existing within the limits of the city with reference to vice of various forms." This inquiry took into account, the report went on, "all practices which are physically and morally debasing and degrading, and which affect the moral and physical welfare of the inhabitants of the city." Prostitution was undoubtedly considered one of these "vices" or "practices," but that was the extent of the consideration given to the problem of definition. This confusion was compounded when the commission, in the course of its detailed consideration of practices and activities that could clearly be characterized as prostitution, regularly turned its attention to aspects of urban social life that only the most ecumenical definition of prostitution could include: dance halls where young working women met men, assignation houses where married individuals conducted extramarital affairs, lake boats where adolescents congregated unchaperoned, unsupervised picnics, summer amusement resorts, saloons, and vaudeville halls. In the Chicago report and elsewhere, the sexual activity that purportedly occurred in these situations

often was categorized as "clandestine" prostitution. This designation ostensibly differentiated women who worked as prostitutes sporadically or
on a part-time basis from public prostitutes—streetwalkers and brothel
prostitutes. More often than not, however, this distinction was glossed
over. In addition, clandestine prostitution was taken to include almost
any premarital or nonmonogamous female sexual activity, whether or
not financial exchange was involved. Thus, in the moral world of *The
Social Evil in Chicago*, potentially all sexual activity unsanctioned by
marriage could be characterized as prostitution.[14]

Other definitions of prostitution, offered in all seriousness, were
equally imprecise and similarly all-inclusive. For instance, in 1912 the
Outlook defined prostitution as "the attempt to isolate the sensuous
element in love from the social affectations and family responsibilities it
was meant to support." The next year, T. D. Crothers, the president of
the New York Medico-Legal Society, an organization interested in social
problems such as prostitution, described prostitution as "the direct result
of a widespread delusion and obsession," an "insane impulse for the
unrestrained gratification of the sexual functions of the body," an "obsession that dominates every consideration of duty and obligation and
purpose in life, in which procreation is not considered." Another New
York physician defined a prostitute as a "woman who satisfies the physical side of the sexual desire of man without regard as to whether the
passion is associated with admiration and respect, and insists on receiving money in payment for her effort," *or* any "woman who will
cohabit with any man for the pleasure that it gives her."[15]

The inexactitude and ambiguity of all these definitions are self-evident.
Each could have applied, with rough accuracy, to a professional street-
walker, a sexually active or promiscuous young woman, a married man
or woman in an extramarital affair, or even a married couple practicing
birth control. Also significant was the similarity of the normative words
and phrases: "duty," "obligation," "purpose in life," "procreation," "admiration," and "respect." These words were the linguistic linchpins of
civilized morality. Thus, although the purported focus of antiprostitution
was the segregated vice district, it seems clear that in its fullest meaning, "prostitution" actually included any form of sexual behavior that
violated the moral imperatives of civilized morality.

The lack of an exact definition of prostitution is not, however, as
strange as it at first seems. It has become increasingly evident that during
the progressive years a new sexual ethos emerged, which sanctioned
limited premarital sexual experimentation and a more pleasure-oriented
view of sexual relations. Middle-class attitudes and behavior began to
move away from the demanding prescriptions of civilized morality, and

the traditional reticence about discussing sex and related topics in public was rapidly disappearing. In one sense the open and widespread discussion of prostitution was an important aspect of the breakdown of the conspiracy of silence that formerly surrounded the discussion of sexual matters. In a more important sense, however, it constituted a reaction against it. To adherents of civilized morality, the new attitudes and the behavior they justified amounted to a complete breakdown of moral standards. "Prostitution" was often (but obviously not always) a shrouded reference to this anxiety-provoking change. This explanation accounts for the discussion, under the general rubric of "prostitution," of female sexual activity that today would be more precisely labeled "promiscuity" or "permissiveness." During the progressive years, however, it would have been almost impossible for antiprostitution forces to make such distinctions, for fundamental cultural and even linguistic reasons. One of the great accomplishments of the sex researchers of the twentieth century has been the compilation of a vocabulary of sufficient complexity and subtlety to differentiate among various kinds of sexual behavior; social scientists now even have among their tools a scale so finely calibrated that it can measure fine gradations of sexual permissiveness. Needless to say, no such vocabulary, or methodological apparatus, which would have provided the means to distinguish prostitution from permissiveness or promiscuity, was available to antiprostitution groups. Thus, when confronted with what appeared to be ominous shifts in sexual mores and behavior, progressives often categorized all of what they saw as "prostitution," a historically familiar phenomenon. "Prostitution," in fact, was the only suitable label available to them. These ambiguous definitions of prostitution, then, though nearly useless for the formulation of any social policy, were highly revealing cultural expressions, for they indicate that the emergence of a new sexual ethic which contravened the ideals of civilized morality was as important an impetus to antiprostitution as were the brothels and segregated districts so highly visible in American communities.[16]

Not surprisingly, the imprecision of definition produced a wide spectrum of estimates of the social evil in particular areas. This was not, it should be emphasized, a problem unique to the time. Even today, using techniques far superior to those of the past, it remains exceedingly difficult to ascertain the extent of prostitution in complex and large geographical areas.[17] Thus, what is important is not the failure of antiprostitution groups to produce uniform statistics but, rather, the reasons for some of the wild fluctuations, the meaning of the insistence that statistics on prostitution were necessary, and the larger ends to which it was hoped they could be put.

For New York the estimates of the number of prostitutes plying their trade ranged between 15,000 and 35,000. Chicago, which in 1910 had a population less than half that of New York, presented an even more confusing situation: the estimates fluctuated between a low of 5,000 (the estimate of the Chicago Vice Commission) and a high of 68,000. There was somewhat more agreement on the national level. In 1898, B. S. Steadwell, a Wisconsin native and president of the International American Purity Federation, after contacting mayors, police chiefs, reformers, and ministers in cities with populations over 25,000 (how many he did not reveal), concluded that a "conservative" estimate of the number of prostitutes in the United States was 300,000. In 1912, Stanley W. Finch, chief of the Bureau of Investigation in the Department of Justice, stated that his investigations showed there to be "not less" than a quarter of a million prostitutes in the country. Other contemporary estimates put the figure at 500,000.[18]

The issue of national statistics on prostitution became a focus of controversy at the Fifteenth International Congress on Hygiene and Demography held in Washington, D.C., in 1912. The newly formed American Federation for Sex Hygiene sponsored an exhibit stressing the need for sex hygiene education, complete with charts and photographs illustrating the tragedy and horror of venereal disease. The exhibit, prepared by Robert N. Wilson, a Philadelphia physician who was secretary of the federation, also presented figures on the extent of prostitution in the United States. Wilson's "ultraconservative estimate of the number of public female prostitutes and earnings" was 544,350 prostitutes at a yearly cost to the public of over $272 million. Wilson also estimated there to be three "clandestine" prostitutes for each public prostitute, which brought the total to 1,633,050 at a cost of $408,262,500. "There is every reason to believe," he concluded, that, conservative estimates aside, "we are spending on immorality and the social diseases . . . not less than $3,000,000,000."[19]

The congress cited the excellence of the federation's production, but within months the exhibit was attacked in the *American Journal of Public Health* by John S. Fulton, a physician who had served as secretary-general of the congress. In Swiftian style, Fulton flatly stated that the federation's "statistical misadventures," "numerical confections," and "guesstimates" could not be substantiated; and although he did not himself offer ironclad figures to contradict those of the federation, he did point out some interesting contradictions. "In the light of a few concrete facts," he observed, with reference to the claim that prostitution was a $3 billion a year business, "the Federation might have delayed for a few years at least, the announcement that the molly-coddled males in this country can deliver into the hands of the mollies, every year, one-fourth of all the money in the world, all the money there is in the United States, enough to pay a fourth of the world's total debt, a billion dollars more than enough to discharge the public debt of the United States." As Fulton also pointed out, the federation's statistics indicated that approximately 15 percent of the national urban female population over fifteen years of age were prostitutes. Furthermore, if the federation's contention that 50,000 prostitutes died each year was true, there would be 20,000 more prostitutes than "decent" women in the death roll for those between the ages of fifteen and thirty-five, the years in which prostitutes allegedly expired. Wilson countered Fulton's accusations with an equally polemical repartee, asserted the validity of the federation's estimates, and then launched an ad hominem attack on Fulton's character and motives.[20]

Fulton was not alone in questioning the accuracy of most estimates of the extent of prostitution. J. Ewing Mears, a Philadelphia attorney and physician, wrote in 1913 that the figures of the American Federation for Sex Hygiene were "too general to be accepted as entirely worthy of consideration from a scientific viewpoint." In 1916, I. L. Nasher, a New York physician who claimed familiarity with prostitution in the city since 1886, criticized "hysterical would-be reformers who see vice through magnifying glasses" and "couldn't tell a brothel if they were inside one." The incidence of prostitution, he argued, had actually decreased during the thirty years of his acquaintance with it. In addition, two major investigations by the federal government, one by the Senate on the condition of women and child wage earners, the other by the U.S. Immigration Commission on the importation of alien prostitutes, asserted that it was impossible to estimate the extent of prostitution in the nation accurately. Any such figures were, in the words of the Senate investigation, "the merest guesswork."[21]

At no time during the progressive years, then, was there a consensus on the proportions of prostitution in the United States. What accounted for the statistical variations? To begin with, the absence of a specific definition of prostitution certainly contributed to the striking disparities among the various figures. In addition, the habit of relying on police records also produced vastly different figures, because the number of arrested or incarcerated women would vary according to different administrations or surges in public opinion demanding "cleanups" of vice districts.[22]

The very high estimates also undoubtedly were influenced by the conviction, which gained currency sometime during the eighteenth century, that the life of the prostitute, while perhaps not solitary or poor, was certainly nasty, brutish, and short. Well into the twentieth century it was a dominant belief that a prostitute's fate was a slow physical and mental degeneration to death within five years of beginning "the life." This popular stereotype of the harlot's plight was nourished by nineteenth-century theories on the deleterious effects of sexual excess and was constantly cited in pronouncements on prostitution during the progressive years.[23] The "five-year" theory was never proven, but its general acceptance made it necessary to assume that large numbers of women were needed each year to fill the death-ravaged ranks. Although not solely responsible for the high figures on prostitution, a belief in the five-year theory certainly made prostitution appear a much larger and more dynamic problem than it actually was, and the vision of tens of thousands of women debauched into immorality each year fanned the fires of the more extreme reactions to prostitution, particularly the white-slave panic.[24]

The belief in clandestine prostitution also influenced the estimates. Because clandestine prostitution was so broadly defined, virtually any woman, but particularly any young, single, and mobile woman, could be accused of engaging in it. It is easy to see how this potentially enormous amount of sexual immorality affected the perception of the extent of prostitution in general, which itself was vaguely defined. The American Federation for Sex Hygiene estimated that for each public prostitute there were three clandestine, and estimates ranged from this ratio to that estimated for Cincinnati, which was one to one hundred.[25]

What is most revealing about the commotion over prostitution statistics, however, is not the variations in the estimates but rather the unanimous insistence that such statistical information was necessary. In a way this was simply an expression of a statistically oriented approach to social problems that dated back at least to the 1840s. This statistical vision, first promulgated in the United States by men like Edward Jarvis and institutionalized by 1902 in the National Census Bureau, held that all phenomena, especially social problems, could and should be discussed in quantitative and aggregate terms. In the progressive response to prostitution, however, this positivistic outlook existed in a peculiar tension with the desire that the statistical data on prostitution be addressed to a moral end: the rebuttressing of civilized morality. In a broad sense, anti-prostitution was a national jeremiad, a lamentation on the immorality, licentiousness, and moral decay of the time, and it was hoped that once the enormity of the transgressions against civilized morality was presented in statistical form, the wayward nation would mend its ways. This amalgam of the scientific and moral is the most interesting aspect of the concern for prostitution statistics, and the achievement of such a balance must be regarded as something of an intellectual and emotional victory.

Actually, of course, in the years after 1920 the statistical approach to sexual behavior became increasingly subversive of any rigid or absolute set of moral edicts regarding human behavior, for the bottom line of the statistical vision reveals that "morality" or "normality" are themselves statistical derivations. This principle guided the Kinsey investigations in the 1940s and 1950s and has continued to inform research in sexual behavior. In their collection and use of statistical data, the antiprostitution groups can be said to have made an early contribution to the study of sexual behavior, but, given their moral goals, it is doubtful that they would recognize the modern studies as the legitimate heirs of their own work.[26]

Underlying the concern for statistics, and almost every aspect of antiprostitution, was the guiding conviction that once an evil was made public and exposed, "society" would spring to eliminate it. This was an expression of a tradition dating back to the eighteenth century, which championed the capacity of an aroused republican virtue to crush out evil, corruption, and vice, once they were bathed in the spotlight of public opinion and deprived of the secrecy and darkness in which they flourished. Prince Morrow, for example, urged that the "purifying light of publicity" be turned on prostitution, and the Syracuse Vice Commission began its report by declaring that, "the light having been thrown upon the social evil by the publication of this report," the "Citizens can be relied upon to make Syracuse cleaner, healthier, and more moral."[27]

The belief in the power of publicity was optimistic and utopian; yet, ironically, it was one of the weakest aspects of antiprostitution. It rested on a pre-Freudian view of human nature, behavior, and society, which gave little recognition to an inherent conflict between individual instincts and the requirements of civilization.[28] It was based on an interpretation of man and society rooted in eighteenth-century rationalism and nineteenth-century liberalism: the individual was a potentially rational, reasonable, and calculating being, who, when made aware of correct and reasonable modes of behavior, would then intelligently conform his conduct to them. For antiprostitution forces, this was a guiding principle; they saw prostitution as a violation of civilized morality and believed that once the nature and extent (the statistics) of the evil were publicized, individuals would accordingly and in an enlightened manner change their behavior.

By 1910, though, this view of behavior and society already was under serious challenge. In the 1890s, European social scientists, disenchanted with the various forms of nineteenth-century positivism, began stressing and exploring the role of the irrational in individual and societal behavior. Walter Lippmann was one of the earliest American social critics to steep himself in the heady new theories of Freud, Henri Bergson, and Graham Wallace. This was especially clear in his critique of the Chicago Vice Commission report. Lippmann argued that the commission's belief in the power of publicity and education to change human behavior— especially sexual behavior—was naive and simplistic. He wrote of the "enormous bewildering demand that prostitution answers" and maintained that it could not be easily lessened. "The Commission," he wrote, "did not face the sexual impulse squarely. The report is an attempt to deal with a sexual problem by disregarding its source." The conservative writer Agnes Repplier reached the same conclusion in 1914. Simple publicity of the evils of immorality, she wrote, was of little use. "If knowledge alone could save us from sin," she argued, "the salvation of the world would be easy work. If by demonstrating the injuriousness of evil we could insure the acceptance of good, a little logic would redeem mankind." But, she continued, "the laying of the foundation of law and order in the mind, the building up of character which will be strong enough to reject both folly and vice,—this is no easy task."[29]

One important aspect of antiprostitution indicated a pervasive doubt that the mere publicizing of the extent of immorality would lead directly to a change in behavior: the widespread and continuous demand for legislation to suppress prostitution. This sentiment embodied a strong belief in the value of all laws, along with a liberal vagueness as to how these specific laws were to be implemented. Sometimes it bordered on the absurd. A prominent Chicago minister, for instance, argued in 1913 that laws should be enacted and enforced against prostitution because prostitution was "unconstitutional." But there were also many attempts to deal with prostitution through traditional legal means: tenement house laws; injunction and abatement acts; judicial reforms; public health ordinances; the revisions of the national immigration statutes in 1903, 1907, and 1910; the Mann Act of 1910; and certain provisions in the Selective Service Act of 1917. And these were only the most frequently discussed and debated.[30]

The efficacy of such measures is another matter. Some warned of the "consequences of unenforceable legislation" proposed by those who "hold firmly . . . that there is in a statute a certain alchemy whereby the elements of leaden soddenness and brazen vice . . . may of an instant be transmuted into the pure gold of spirituality." Unenforceable laws passed in haste would only undermine the legal process by encouraging a corrupt alliance among the police, public officials, and the vice interests.[31] Others argued that too many laws produced more heat than light. In 1915, for example, Arthur Spingarn, an attorney working for the New York Probation and Protection Association, concluded after assiduously compiling a list of New York City prostitution laws that they were "ill considered, scattered, inconsistent, and chaotic."[32]

An even more problematic aspect of the drive to suppress prostitution emerged in the often-drawn comparison between antiprostitution and Prohibition. Many in the antiprostitution ranks saw similarities between the goals and tactics of the two movements, which indeed there were. Both had roots in nineteenth-century evangelical reform movements, and both achieved their greatest success in the progressive years. Each blended cultural and political conservatism with perfectionist and utopian visions of moral and social reform. Medical opinion was a major aspect of each movement: Prohibitionists circulated medical evidence demonstrating the poisonous effects of alcohol, and medical men alarmed over the relationship between prostitution and venereal disease were highly visible in the antiprostitution movement. Each group considered that prostitution and liquor were linked. Prohibitionists argued that the saloons and the "liquor trust" were allied with the brothel keepers and that alcoholic excess led to sexual excess. Antiprostitution forces agreed, adding that situations of sexual debauchery—brothels—led to alcoholic debauchery.[33]

Some in the antiprostitution groups, however, saw subtle and important distinctions. To begin with, sexual behavior was harder to control than drinking. "There are hundreds of towns and villages where it is impossible to get a drink of any kind," a vice-district missionary worker observed in 1909, "while on the other hand there is not a single town, hamlet, or community of any size where the evil of impurity does not exist to a greater or less degree."[34]

There was an even more fundamental difference. William Cullen Bryant, a Pittsburgh physician, maintained in 1913 that although "the liquor habit can be eliminated," prostitution presented a different problem: "Since the sexual element in all mankind is a perfectly normal part of his being, having, as it does, so much influence on the propagation and development of the human race, it is hardly reasonable to suppose that we can apply the same rules and regulations in the safeguarding of this particular part of his normal makeup as we would to the protection or elimination of what we may call his unnatural or acquired habits and vices."[35] Prohibitionists could condemn liquor and the saloon, describe the desire to drink as an "acquired habit" lacking any redeeming social value, and go on to demand total suppression. The problem of prostitution was not analogous: the sexual instinct could hardly be referred to as an "acquired habit" at a time when President Theodore Roosevelt was lecturing women on their duty to "breed freely." Indeed, an idealized vision of the sexual instinct as central to the well-being of the family, nation, and race was widely cherished in genteel America. "The sexual instinct," one commentator maintained, " . . . is the most important function of which any man or woman is capable. . . . Did not the desire exist for sexual intercourse, the corporal manifestation of this great instinct, love were a farce, and the home, the basic principle of all civilization and morality, were an impossibility."[36] This belief of course propelled antiprostitution, because prostitution was seen as an awful perversion of that "important function." But, at the same time, this commitment posed a philosophical problem, for the biological instinct that appeared so appalling in the red-light districts was also the foundation of the home, marriage, and the family. This quandary, notwithstanding the demands for the "annihilation" of prostitution, and the proselytizing of the gospel of sexual continence, was never really resolved.

What were the results of the drive to suppress prostitution? Certainly the combination of organized investigations, aroused public opinion, and repressive legal measures contributed to a change in the form of prostitution in American cities in the second decade of the century. In 1922, in one of the first evaluations of the antiprostitution movement in the progressive years, Joseph Mayer argued that these three factors were most instrumental in closing down, between 1912 and 1920, the segregated districts in the two hundred largest American cities, including all those with populations over one hundred thousand. And, by 1920, Americans for the most part had discarded the traditional belief, most forcibly stated in the nineteenth century by the British historian William Edward Hartpole Lecky, that prostitution was a necessity, the "most efficient guardian of virtue" and of the "purity of countless happy homes." Antiprostitution groups contributed to the closing of the segregated districts, just as other groups helped to ameliorate some of the other offensive manifestations of the new urban world, and what some scholars have termed the "Golden Age of the Brothel in America" in general did come to an end by 1920.[37]

Yet it is doubtful that this change, which was one mainly of form, was the result only of publicity campaigns and legislation. Indeed, it is almost certain that other contemporary social and cultural changes—the advent of the automobile, the increased availability of telephone service, shifting neighborhood patterns, the proliferation of apartment buildings, and, most important, changing moral standards—had just as much to do with the waning of the red-light districts. After the red-light districts declined, prostitution changed form, just as did the consumption of liquor following the adoption of the Eighteenth Amendment: the call girl and the speakeasy appeared on the American scene at just about the same time.[38]

Another and more positive result of antiprostitution was the increased attention given in the teens to the prostitute herself, as opposed to the obsession with prostitution as a moral abstraction. The latter of course did not vanish, but the appearance in professional journals of collective and individual studies of prostitutes did mark the beginning of a new approach. Public health officials and physicians in cities as diverse as Boston, Albany, Newport News, Cincinnati, and San Francisco studied groups of prostitutes ranging in size from one hundred to over five hundred and published information concerning the women's ages, races, ethnic groups, places of birth, economic class, familial backgrounds, physical and mental health, and educational levels. Some surveys were conducted in detention centers, some in hospitals, some in military towns, and others in brothels.[39]

In his great 1858 study of prostitution, William Sanger had expressed the hope that knowledge of the prostitute would serve to humanize her in the minds of the citizenry. For half a century, however, his wish was not father, or mother, to the deed. For all the flurry of activity concerning prostitution in the late decades of the nineteenth century, there did not appear a new or compelling investigation or empirical study of prostitution that could stand alongside Sanger's. This lack was remedied during the progressive years, and, at least for those familiar with them, the group studies of prostitutes, along with the state and municipal vice commission reports, brought some order and specificity to the confusion that often marked the approach to prostitution. Thus, by the late teens, serious students of prostitution did not have to confront a dearth of documented and detailed information, and the progressive generation must certainly be given credit for this improved state of affairs.

Yet in a broader sense, the legacy of the antiprostitution forces is ambiguous: they produced an extraordinary amount of information on prostitution and labored diligently to remove its most obvious and obnoxious forms, but they never really confronted the causes of its persistent existence in their own time and in the years after their struggle ended. Possibly Frederic Howe had this shortcoming in mind in 1925 when he wrote, in *The Confessions of a Reformer*: "We are not on the level in our moral crusades; worse still, of their hidden effects we are crudely ignorant." Perhaps, he went on, "this is another by-product of the evangelical-mindedness that seeks a moralistic explanation of social problems and a religious solution for most of them."[40] Howe's suspicions were well founded. But though the "evangelical" and "moralistic" aspects of the progressive response to prostitution appeared troublesome to Howe from the vantage point of the twenties, from that of an even later age these aspects appear the most interesting and historically revealing.

Two

PROSTITUTION AND THE

PROBLEM OF WOMEN IN

INDUSTRIAL AMERICA

Fifty years ago we recognized, roughly speaking, two types of women, the one completely good and the other completely bad,—what we now call the old-fashioned girl and the girl who had sinned and been out-lawed. At present we have several intermediate types,—the occasional prostitute, the charity girl, the demi-virgin, the equivocal flapper, and in addition girls with new but social behavior norms who have adapted themselves to all kinds of work. . . . All of them represent the same movement, which is a desire to realize their wishes under the chang-ing social conditions. The movement contains disorganization and reorganization, but it is the same movement in both cases. It is the release of important social energies which could not find expression under the norms of the past. Any general movement away from social standards implies that these standards are no longer adequate.
William I. Thomas, *The Unadjusted Girl* (1923)

What exactly did a Chicago physician mean when he wrote in 1906 that "Around the sexual life of women . . . are grouped some of the most adverse and perplexing questions of all time, involving the double stan-dard of morals, divorce, prostitution, and the plague of venereal diseases; questions which seem almost as difficult of practical solution as the problem of perpetual motion"? And in what ways did this statement ex-press a sensibility that profoundly shaped and infused antiprostitution?[1]

The progressive era was a time of profound flux and uncertainty in the position and perception of American women. At the turn of the century, the reserved and hourglass-figured eternal feminines wistfully and allur-ingly posing in Charles Dana Gibson's pen-and-ink drawings embodied the dominant vision of American womanhood. Just a generation later, by 1925, the Gibson girl had evolved into the flapper. Placed in the context of a quarter century of social and cultural change, this evolution rep-resented a shift of consciousness of no mean importance; and that the uproar about prostitution peaked at almost exactly the midpoint of that shift was no mere coincidence. To the contrary, antiprostitution was a part of that transformation and mirrored many of the anxieties and preoccupations accompanying it.[2]

The origins of this change can be discerned as far back as the early 1830s, when the first country girls from rural Massachusetts journeyed to Lowell to work in the textile factories. These new occupational endeavors, together with the activities of women in the antislavery and suffragist movements, raised important questions concerning the traditional place of women in society.[3] Although women had secured some important educational and economic gains by 1900, the most dramatic manifestations of their changing position in American society appeared in the opening decades of the twentieth century. Numerous events and controversies were emblematic of this turmoil and confusion: the debate over the rising divorce rate, which often focused on the new and changing social, economic, and moral status of women; the contention surrounding the birth-control movement; the politically oriented suffragist movement; the advent of the more radical Greenwich Village feminists, who called for a restructuring of American society that would result in the equality of men and women; the appearance in 1898 of Kate Chopin's *The Awakening*, a novel about feminine self-consciousness and marital instability; the suppression of Dreiser's *Sister Carrie*, the first great American novel to portray an American woman breaking with convention; the 1908 Brandeis brief in *Muller* v. *Oregon*, the 1909 Shirtwaist workers' strike in New York City, and the 1911 Triangle Fire, each of which drew attention to women's presence in the urban industrial world; and the troubled awareness of all these issues in the popular novels and plays (usually by male writers) of the period.[4]

The cultural sum of these developments was an acute awareness that rapid industrialization and urbanization had profoundly undermined the traditional role and status of women, which for centuries had been perceived in the context of a stable and predetermined sequence: marriage, childbearing and rearing, and homemaking. There emerged a rather widespread sense of the problematical position of women in modern industrial society, which surfaced in both the most sophisticated feminist writing, such as Charlotte Perkins Gilman's *Women and Economics* (1898), and the most retrograde antisuffragist or sexist outbursts.[5]

This sense of the new and problematical position of women was a crucial element in shaping the response to prostitution in the progressive era. The issue of prostitution was invariably reduced to an analysis of the problem of female prostitutes. An extraordinary amount of time was spent determining why women became prostitutes; very little was spent determining which men engaged them and why. Prostitution became a manifestation of female maladjustment and dislocation, even for those who took pains to denounce the double standard and the uncontrolled male sex drive. Antiprostitution was, in fact, consciously based on a historical analysis of the origins of the "woman problem." The 1914 Massachusetts Vice Commission, for instance, went to some lengths to provide the historical context of the subject of its investigation:

> The changes in habits and customs brought about by modern industries and modern urban life must be recognized. In former times girls worked at home under their mothers' watchful eyes, and seldom went abroad unless accompanied by women of mature years. Children were held in strict discipline. The majority of families lived in small communities, and boys and girls helped on the farm, in the household and in other home industries. Until late adolescence, when character and habits were formed, children selected their associates and found their interests and recreations in the home, the church, and the neighborhood, under the watchful eyes of their parents. Religion was a controlling influence over conduct.
>
> Present conditions are vastly different. Modern invention and business methods have transferred industry and its products from the home to the factory, the big store and the office. The great majority of our people live in large towns and cities. . . . The early economic independence of working girls brings temptations, and makes them intolerant of restraint. It has become the custom of young women to go about freely, unaccompanied.[6]

These sentiments also appeared in *The Social Evil in Chicago*, and, at one point, the Chicago Vice Commission thought it necessary to provide quotations from nineteenth-century state and federal investigations, the *Muller* v. *Oregon* decision, the Pittsburgh survey, and British commission reports, to support the argument that prostitution was directly related to the havoc that industrialization had played with traditional women's roles.[7]

The most common and controversial connection drawn between the new position of women in industrial America and prostitution involved women's wages. The low wages paid to young working women, so the argument went, forced many of them to become full- or part-time prostitutes. This argument was based on two widely held beliefs: that the number of single women working outside the home, especially in the new jobs in the cities, had dramatically increased in the recent past and that the remuneration afforded these young women entering the harsh world of industrial work, usually at the lowest level, was disgracefully substandard.[8]

Both of these beliefs embodied an accurate understanding of social and economic reality. The record is exceptionally clear regarding the increase in female employment even when it is stated on the most general statistical level. During the decade 1900–1910 the total number of all female wage earners grew from 5.3 to 7.6 million, a net increase for the period of 43 percent. (During the same years the number of females ten years of age and older increased by 22 percent.) The number of women employed in the newly emerging trade and transportation fields increased 139 percent between 1900 and 1910. In the same decade the number of women employed as stenographers and typists increased 200 percent, female bookkeepers and accountants increased 150 percent, female telephone and telegraph operators 300 percent, and female factory workers 600 percent.[9]

The wages paid to this new army of working women and girls were, even granting the inevitable inexactitude of general figures on this subject, miserable. In 1911, the U.S. Department of Labor, in a summary of the findings of the U.S. Senate's *Report on Condition of Women and Child Wage Earners in the United States*, came to the rather grim conclusion that the large proportion of working women were paid wages "inadequate to supply a reasonable standard of living for women dependent upon their own earnings for support."[10] In 1915, Charles Persons, an economist who had reviewed the various state and local investigations of women's wages, reported that only 23 percent of employed women earned the minimum necessary weekly wage, eight dollars, and that nearly half earned less than six dollars per week. Of special importance to an understanding of the "wages and sin" controversy was Person's assertion that "youth and low earning capacity are found together": one-quarter of the working women in the decade 1900–1910 were between sixteen and twenty years of age, and their lot was characteristically one of few skills and low pay. It was, according to Persons, an "evil combination that is found here: lack of skill, training, and experience, joined together with the irresponsibility of youth, and great congestion in the labor market."[11]

The belief that the mass employment of young women at low wages was causally linked to prostitution was a mainstay of antiprostitution. The vice commissions endorsed the theory; socialists did as well. Jane Addams made it a central argument in her 1912 book on prostitution, *A New Conscience and an Ancient Evil*; and physicians concerned about the causes of prostitution stressed the factor of low wages.[12] The "wages-

and-sin" issue received national attention in 1913, when the Illinois Senate Vice Committee, after public hearings on prostitution and women's wages, concluded that "low wages are to blame for most of the immorality among our young girls."[13]

Much of the controversy centered on the tens of thousands of young women working in the then still somewhat strange and, to many, dangerous institution of urban life, the department store. The big city emporiums were indeed large employers of young women (in 1913, Siegel Cooper and Company employed 6,000 women in New York and Boston, and Marshall Field in Chicago employed 4,222), and it was a general impression that the low wages paid to the saleswomen, in conjunction with the procuresses and other "low" types who supposedly prowled the stores on the lookout for young women in financial hardship, made the department stores a most dangerous enemy of female morality.[14] The same attitude, in various forms, was expressed concerning women working in industry and even those in domestic service, which had traditionally been viewed as a safe and proper position for young women starting out in the urban world.[15]

The responses to the wages-and-sin revelations were diverse. Socialists believed that the vicious connection between sweated labor and prostitution (which they accepted as uncritically as did liberals) laid bare the pernicious workings of the capitalist wage system. "The graft that sends girls into that shameful death in life," maintained the socialist *New York Call*, "is the original of all grafts—the wage system. . . . That delusive wage system, which for generations has appeared, on the whole, fair and just to the working class, is now being stript of its swindling disguise and a considerable portion at least of its nakedness exposed."[16] For socialists the only solution was a radical restructuring of the economy. More typical was the proposal that the problem might be alleviated through the adoption of minimum-wage legislation for working women. In 1913, Henry Rogers Seager, president of the American Association for Labor Legislation, declared that "prostitution in aid of wages" is the "greatest disgrace of our civilization." By 1915 ten states had passed minimum-wage laws for women, and the concern over the connection between low wages and prostitution was a prime consideration in their enactment.[17]

The ways in which young working women on their own in the cities slipped into sin were described in detail and at length, and with great compassion. The context was always economic destitution, and there were various circumstances and villains: young women living alone in sparsely furnished closet-sized rooms; saleswomen "dieting" on ten- and fifteen-cent meals twice a day; long hours of demanding and tedious work, with frequent periods of unemployment; madams on the lookout for girls needing extra money; working companions who were already experienced in the ways of after-hours work; or unprincipled male supervisors who took advantage of the inferior economic position of their female employees. "The unskilled girl is a drug on the labor market," one utilitarian employer was reported to have opined. "We can always get more than we can possibly use. The supply far exceeds the demand."[18] All of these unpleasant incidents undoubtedly occurred untold thousands of times, yet, notwithstanding the emotional sympathy that such a depressing picture of the plight of young working women evokes, the cause-and-effect relationship between low wages and prostitution was more often asserted than proved or fully explained.

It should at once be conceded that the "wages and sin" theory had a certain logic. It was widely understood, for instance, that for at least a number of years a woman could earn more as a prostitute than in almost any other job open to her in 1910. The Syracuse Vice Commission reported in 1913 that an actress earning fifteen dollars a week had made over ten times as much per week when working as a prostitute; a saleswoman increased her weekly income from six to twenty-five dollars in the same way; and a woman who as a maid earned five dollars a week earned forty as a prostitute.[19] This was certainly a rather macabre state of affairs, and it is hardly surprising that it was interpreted as an important cause of prostitution. But was the matter as clear-cut as this? In fact, there was a substantial body of opinion that disagreed, holding rather that the causes of prostitution were more complicated than the wages-and-sin theory implied.[20]

The U.S. Senate's *Report on Conditions of Women and Child Wage Earners in the United States* (1911), for example, found no clear evidence isolating "low wages as a direct and immediate cause of immorality."[21] Several years later, in 1914, Edith Spaulding, the resident physician at a New England reformatory for women, published the results of a group study of 243 prostitutes that also found no clear and simple connection between prostitution and economic deprivation.[22] And in 1916, Maude E. Miner, a distinguished New York City social worker and a founder of Waverly House, reported that on the basis of her general experience and group studies of prostitutes remanded to Waverly House, it was not valid to link prostitution just to economic need. There were, rather, a multiplicity of causal factors involved, among them family background, education, and psychological and emotional conditions. What was interesting to Miner was that so many women from economically disadvantaged backgrounds did not become prostitutes.[23] It should be emphasized that none of these investigations *discounted* economic exploitation as a factor in prostitution; rather, they argued that the wages-

and-sin theory neglected other factors that might explain why some women became prostitutes and others did not.[24]

Hutchins Hapgood, the noted journalist and husband of the writer Neith Boyce, was working for the *New York Globe* in 1913 and offered a subtle refinement of the wages-and-prostitution thesis in the course of recounting a conversation with a young working woman:

> This girl feels, and many girls feel, tho few of them are as self-conscious as she is, that at the root of prostitution is the spiritual demand for a better life than our industrial and social conditions make possible for great numbers of women. They do not go into prostitution for prostitution's sake, but from boredom, from restlessness, from spiritual stagnation and despair. They do not go into it because they are naturally base, nor because they cannot get enough to eat to keep them alive, but because they ignorantly hope that any change may mean something, or because they have lost hope. It is in reality a blind seeking for a better life, or the effect of despair because they have not been able to secure a better life—more amusement, more joy, more love, more pleasure.
>
> High wages and short hours are of great importance because they add to economic independence, to freedom and so to joy and to contentment. It is the starved soul that goes into prostitution.[25]

One does not have to accept Hapgood's somewhat romantic view of the prostitute—similar to the image frequently encountered in American folklore of the "whore with a heart of gold"—to appreciate that his analysis pointed to the complexity of the "causes" of prostitution. The interesting question then becomes why, in the progressive years, the wages-and-sin theory was so widely held and uncritically accepted.

There are several explanations. In general, this theory was very much an expression of the progressive tendency to view social problems in economic and behavioralist terms. From this perspective, the problem of prostitution could be approached in the same ways as were other social ills: through enacting and enforcing humanitarian legislation aimed at alleviating economic injustice. As was often pointed out, and with justification, such an economic approach to prostitution constituted a marked advance over older attitudes imbued with moralistic and theological overtones, or notions of prostitutes as "innately depraved." The belief in low wages as the cause of prostitution also drew on two current Victorian female stereotypes: women as suffering victims (here of the economic injustice of the sweated wage) in need of protection, and women as rather asexual creatures who would therefore never choose—or enjoy —a life of prostitution, who would submit to it only out of dire economic necessity.

The wages-and-sin theory also, and most significantly, expressed a profound anxiety and pessimism about the new position of women in the industrial world. This attitude was evident not only in the clear concern about women's wages but also in the subtly shifting focus of that concern. For in reading through the literature on wages and prostitution, it is difficult to locate an emotional center: the anxiety seems as strongly provoked by the fact that women were working in industrial jobs *at all* as by the low wages they received. This is not to dismiss the very genuine concern over the economic plight of working women expressed by many who addressed the wages-and-sin issue. But much of the concern over the relationship between women's wages and prostitution was also motivated by the fear that the industrial world was subversive of traditional female morality and by the belief that the solution was to discourage women's departures from traditional female roles.

In 1913, Illinois Lieutenant-Governor Barratt O'Hara, chairman of the Illinois Senate Vice Committee, addressed precisely this matter. "There is absolutely no doubt," he asserted, "that the solution of the problem [of prostitution] is the establishment of a minimum wage for women. . . . In entering the business world the seclusion of the home is lost, and girls become more masculine in their ideas and modes of life. By the establishment of the minimum wage the salaries of men ultimately will be increased. This will make it possible for them to provide better for the home, enable young men to marry, and thus, to a great degree, at least, make it unnecessary for women to seek employment."[26] O'Hara's statement clearly expressed the fear that prostitution and its connection with the industrial employment of women were both symbolic of a strange new phase in the history of women in America. In this sense, Hapgood's depiction of the psychology of the prostitute was correct enough, but not everybody was willing to accept its implications.

As O'Hara's comments make clear, the wages-and-sin dispute centered on what was really just one aspect of the more general and problematic issue of the effect of urban and industrial values and life-styles on conventional standards of female morality. For it was obvious and disconcerting that the young and unmarried women who *worked* in the new industrial callings also *lived*, for varying periods of time, in an urban environment radically different from the family-centered, small-town milieu that was, in the popular understanding, the morally safest place for women. It was almost inevitable, then, that antiprostitution forces would see a direct relationship between widespread urban prostitution and the constantly augmenting number of young, single women living apart from their families in the cities.

Two aspects of the general problem attracted the most attention and occasioned the most alarm: the places where young, single working women lived, and the ways they spent their leisure hours. At the time it was commonly held that the clerks, saleswomen, and factory workers who appeared on the streets or the public conveyances twice a day had left their families in smaller cities or rural areas to move to the city, where they lived in boarding houses or single furnished rooms. These living arrangements, the argument went, were unchaperoned and depressingly lonely and therefore were hardly conducive to proper moral habits.[27]

In 1911, *The Social Evil in Kansas City* reported that almost half of the "white girls able to state definitely where they were staying at the time of the first act [of prostitution] . . . traced it to a period when they were living in a rooming or boarding home." A survey of one of the main boardinghouse districts in the city revealed that fewer than one-third of the roominghouses had a parlor for receiving guests, and the report depicted the evils of this situation in no uncertain terms: "When young girls away from home and freed from any restraining influence must meet young men either in the street or in their bedrooms, the first step towards lower moral standards is taken and others may quickly follow."[28] In *A New Conscience and an Ancient Evil*, Jane Addams addressed the problem on a more speculative level. "For the first time in history," she wrote, "multitudes of women are laboring without the direct stimulus of family interest or affection." Who could say, she went on, "how far the superior chastity of woman, so rigidly maintained during the centuries, has been the result of her domestic surroundings, and certainly no one knows under what degree of economic pressure the old restraints may give way."[29]

Of even greater moral peril than the places where young working women lived were the places of recreation and relaxation they frequented: dance halls, amusement parks, excursion boats, inexpensive theaters, and dimly lit moving picture houses. The fear of these amusements was linked to an important nineteenth-century development. A salient aspect of the maturation of the industrial economy in that century was the imposition of a new and rigid time framework on working patterns, and indeed on life itself. The result was the creation of specific blocks of time of which urban dwellers and workers could dispose as they wished or, more accurately, as their financial resources allowed.[30] This new aspect of industrial life, "leisure time," was a catalyst in the formation during the late nineteenth century of numerous evangelically inspired organizations—the purity groups among them—haunted by the specter of "dangerous" or "immoral" lower-class amusements. The upshot was an outburst of campaigns against, among other evils, dance halls, cigarette smoking, and prizefighting.[31]

By the early years of the twentieth century, the problem of "dangerous amusements" took on another ominous dimension as it became clear that the new urban forms of recreation were attracting the young women who lived and worked in the cities. To the antiprostitution forces, all the urban amusements that a young working woman could afford were dangerously linked to prostitution. One commentator, in the course of a disquisition on prostitution, rather luridly suggested that "a reeling quickstep through the open gates to the social evil is spurred by the sensual familiarities of the sexes formulated and practiced by rote in dancing parlors, schools, halls, towed along into late night hours by the suggestive motion-rhythms of beguiling music that rocks mutual desire to the vortex of acute risque, if not also to the kept-house of actual assignation." At other times, dance halls were referred to as "an open door to the social evil," or the "ante room to hell itself."[32]

By the early teens, similar fears for female morality were occasioned by the "dangerous darkness in moving picture shows," "cheap theaters" producing "sordid" plays, "lascivious" novels, mass circulation urban tabloids that were "little more than a vice directory," and the summer amusement parks that had "sprung up within the last decade all over America."[33] An investigator for the Syracuse Vice Commission reported that the dance halls at the amusement parks just outside the city were "loosely managed" and "mostly patronized by working girls seeking amusement." At one of the dance halls he saw a prostitute from the city "dancing and mingling with the girls. While I actually saw only this one prostitute there, I was told in different houses that the girls were off for the afternoon at one of these resorts. It is customary for the girls to go out with companions during the intermissions. Thus an innocent girl may unwittingly be in a party with one or more prostitutes, and follow their lead."[34]

At the source of this anxiety was the conviction that traditional mechanisms of moral control of women had broken down in the cities. This lessening of control in turn was seen as the cause of the alleged breakdown in female moral standards and the rise of prostitution. (Here it is necessary to remember how vaguely and imprecisely prostitution was defined in the progressive years, for much of what supposedly occurred in the rooming houses or dangerous amusements was not prostitution, in any strict sense.) Often this concern shifted from specific urban threats to female morality to a general and puzzled preoccupation with the increasing visibility of young women on the city thoroughfares. These crowds of young women, who for the most part were engaging in what today would be described as late adolescent behavior, seemed symbolic of a larger, but dimly understood, social change. "One of the most disturbing phases of the present situation in Minneapolis, and an alarming social symptom," the Minneapolis Vice Commission warned in 1911, "is the large number of young girls in the streets at night in the downtown sections. . . . They may be found in numbers loitering about the fruit stores, drug stores and other popular locations, haunting hotel lobbies, crowding into the dance halls, the theaters and other amusement resorts; also in the saloon restaurants and the chop suey places and parading the streets and touring about in automobiles with men." Although the vice commission conceded that it would be unfair "to charge that all or a large proportion of these girls are prostitutes," it was nevertheless "perfectly plain . . . that many . . . are on the direct road. . . . The situation," the commission cautioned, "is unmistakably sinister."[35]

The proposed solutions to this problem were diverse, but they shared a common thrust: the demand for new means of moral control that would replicate the atmosphere of small-town and family-centered society. Jane Addams, certainly one of the most advanced social thinkers of her time, devoted the concluding chapter of her book on prostitution (which, on the whole, was not advanced) to a discussion of the task of constructing social forms to fill the urban moral vacuum that so often produced prostitution. Addressing the problem of "thousands of young women whose undisciplined minds are fatally assailed by the subtleties and sophistries of city life, and who have lost their bearings in the midst of a multitude of new imaginative experiences," Addams proposed a "new and more vigorous development of social control . . . reflecting something of that wholesome fear of public opinion which the intimacies of a small community maintain."[36]

The seer of Hull House did not specify what form this "development" might assume, but others of identical sympathies did. There was a range of recommendations, including the municipal licensing and monitoring of rooming and boardinghouses; the establishing of publicly run and noncommercialized forms of recreation (neighborhood councils, parks, and dances) where young women might express their natural, but vulnerable, desire for fun; the encouragement of organizations such as the Girls' Protective Leagues, the YMCA-staffed Travelers' Aid, and the Campfire Girls; the creation of women police units; and the support of wholesome theaters and movies.[37] Special attention was given to devising new living situations. Maude Miner was impressed with the then new idea of apartment buildings—as distinct from the prevalent single room accommodations—where young women could live in some semblance of a familial or communal atmosphere. Another commentator felt that the rooming house itself could be restructured to provide the young, single woman in the city with a sense of belonging and thus arm her against the myriad of immoral temptations the city offered.[38]

Other responses, however, were less positive; some of them show how the sense of the problematical nature of women could lead to a position that was simply, and simplistically, antiwoman. For instance, the New York City Committee of Fourteen, through various forms of political and economic pressure, was able to force many hotels considered to be of dubious moral reputation to sign an agreement "to serve no unaccompanied woman in the rear room of our saloon . . . at any time, and no woman, even if accompanied, after 7 P.M."[39]

For many Americans, then, urban prostitution constituted not only a glaring evil in its own right but also a symptom and consequence of the departure of women from their traditional social and economic roles. The two problems seemed to be marching in unison to a strange and off-key tune. The vast majority of these young women working and living in the city were not conscious feminists or anything approaching it—acute commentators like Charlotte Perkins Gilman understood this distinction quite clearly. But, even though the destiny and goal of most of these women was marriage and child rearing, they nevertheless had achieved a degree of autonomy outside the context of a male-controlled or domestic setting and, at least for several years in their late teens and early twenties, led lives markedly different from their mothers'. And to those investigating prostitution, this change had not gone unnoticed.

The concern for the moral consequences of women living alone in the city is also interesting for the illumination it sheds on the dominant notions of female morality. For what is most striking about the discussions of the dangers of boardinghouses, movies, and amusement parks is the absence of any insistence that women were innately moral. Instead, and quite to the contrary, one encounters the conviction that female morality was dependent on certain social, economic, or institutional contexts that would foster and protect it. This sensibility was a manifestation of the naturalistic assumptions that so influenced American social thought in the late nineteenth and early twentieth centuries, but it is also important to note that it marked a change from older nineteenth-century religiously inspired doctrines of women's inherent moral purity.[40] Such notions were not of course absent in the progressive years. But the great consideration given to the importance of women's wages, living arrangements, and recreational needs as factors in explaining prostitution at least tacitly conceded that female sexual behavior was influenced by forces more complex than the tender heart and pure mind that an all-wise (and male) creator had vouchsafed to all womankind.

The anxiety over the deleterious influence of urban industrial living on female morality also provides the most important context for understanding the vague definition of prostitution and the widespread fear of clandestine prostitution. Both "prostitution" and "clandestine prostitution" often referred to any female sexual activity that violated the norms of civilized morality, and the distinctions among prostitution, clandestine prostitution, permissiveness, and promiscuity were frequently blurred. With respect to clandestine prostitution, the main fear was that many women, uncounted but vividly imagined, might be behaving immorally in secret, sometimes for money, sometimes not.

These apprehensions were especially visible in the vice commission reports. The Newark Vice Commission reported the existence of a "large number of girls and young women who sin sexually in return only for the pleasures given or the company of the men with whom they consort. . . . They have no ethical standards and believe that they have as good a right, as it is generally supposed men have, to lead a double life; that they have a right to the pleasure they can gain from their bodies if they can do so without exposure." The commission warned that "this spirit is growing with alarming rapidity."[41] A Massachusetts investigation complained of "large numbers of young girls who habitually have immoral relations with boys and men without expecting or accepting financial gain. But for the absence of the element of hire, these relations are not to be distinguished from those of professional prostitutes."[42] The same problem was plaguing Syracuse. The Syracuse Vice Commission told of "girls, many in number, who go out with men for an evening of pleasure and drink and intercourse where no money is asked or offered. . . . These girls take into the saloons the men whom they pick up on the streets, and then go to the bed houses, especially to those where they do not have to register. Often this class of girls will go with men entirely for pleasure with no economic pressure responsible for driving them to the life." An investigator for the Syracuse Vice Commission was somewhat shocked when, upon asking a "very pretty" waitress why she "goes out with men while she is working," he received the blunt answer: "I am getting six dollars a week in this joint, and hardly any tips, and what's the difference, it's in the air." Indeed, the fact that it was "in the air" was what made clandestine prostitution so frightening.[43]

The possibility of women behaving "clandestinely" existed, obviously, only when traditional means of moral control were weakened and in a state of flux. Indeed, it is only in a society deeply uncertain and vexed as to the status and behavior of women that discussions and investigations of prostitution would repeatedly speculate on whether large numbers of young women might be clandestine prostitutes simply because they behaved in nontraditional ways. This judgment does no violence to the historical fact that there were indeed women—like the Syracuse waitress —who sporadically engaged in prostitution for any number of reasons and who logically might have come within the purview of investigations of prostitution. But the meaning of "clandestine prostitution," and indeed of prostitution itself, was not limited to these cases; it could, by inference, include any woman who was unchaperoned, mobile, and might be leading a "double life." The emphasis was not so much on actuality as on potentiality. And this rather curious obsession was not without serious consequences, for, as shall be seen in a later chapter, it was an important ideological factor in the incarceration of suspected prostitutes during the mobilization for World War I.

In marked contrast to the aggressively suspicious approach to women embodied in the fear of clandestine prostitution, but equally emblematic of the awareness of women as problematical, was the belief that many women became prostitutes because they were feebleminded. *The Social Evil in Chicago* gave this theory a national and authoritative endorsement when it stated in 1911 that the "mass of prostitutes in this and other countries belong to the defectives."[44]

The linking of prostitution and feeblemindedness was one of many aspects of what has been called the "myth of the menace of the feebleminded," the propelling vision behind the efforts of eugenicists and psychologists during the early decades of the twentieth century to link almost every variety of antisocial behavior to inherited mental defects. Indeed, at precisely the point when antiprostitution was peaking, in 1912, the renowned eugenicist Henry Goddard published *The Kallikak Family*, which purported to demonstrate the role of heredity in producing in one hapless New Jersey family generations of criminals, prostitutes, epileptics, alcoholics, and other so-called degenerates. The alleged menace of the feebleminded was ultimately repudiated in knowledgeable circles, but during the progressive years it exerted a powerful influence on social thought and attitudes toward many social problems.[45]

By the mid-teens, there existed what seemed to be impressive evidence linking prostitution and feeblemindedness. At least seventeen group studies of the mentalities of prostitutes ostensibly showed that from 30 to 98 percent of all prostitutes were feebleminded.[46] These findings were widely promulgated and cited approvingly, and they became a mainstay of antiprostitution.[47] Even the careful and observant Maude E. Miner, who had studied the problem of prostitution as scrupulously as anyone in the period, accepted the feeblemindedness theory, but perhaps as much on faith as anything else. Arguing that accurate data on the extent of feeblemindedness did not exist, she nevertheless believed that "it serves to bring a large number of girls into a life of prostitution."[48]

What is one to make of such studies and of such a theory? Most immediately, the striking differences among the results of the various studies indicate that the categorization itself was not uniformly understood and applied and therefore had no single meaning. And what meaning it did have was more cultural, descriptive, and connotative than scientific. Also, in the light of the revelations attendant on the U.S. Army's use of intelligence testing during World War I—wherein some 47 percent of the inductees tested recorded a mental age of less than thirteen and were thus "feebleminded"—it would be futile to expect the figures on the feeblemindedness of prostitutes to yield any valid insights into the nature of prostitution, a prostitute's life, or the thorny question of why women become prostitutes.[49]

In fact, the emphasis on feeblemindedness as a major cause of prostitution contradicted most of the testimony taken from prostitutes during investigations, for whenever one encounters a prostitute's quoted deposition (presumably accurate), the overall impression is hardly one of mental incompetence. "I am probably of at least ordinary intelligence," one Milwaukee prostitute commented. "You can't be a fool and live in one of these places. That is a mistaken idea that a great many men have. They think sporting people know nothing, that they are idiots."[50] Of course, the women who talked to investigators might not have been typical. Yet, even taking this factor into consideration, it is closer to the historical truth to see prostitutes as women of at least ordinary intelligence, with the ability to make the best of a bad situation at times, and possessed of some awareness of the relationship of their activity to society in general. Prostitution was part of a very complex subculture, with its own patois, customs, history, roles, and modes of perception and feeling. Survival in this culture, as in any, required the exercise of intelligence. To a large extent, the tendency of investigators and testers to designate prostitutes as feebleminded was the result of a failure, or a psychological unwillingness, to understand how this subculture worked. In this sense, the feeblemindedness theory was as much the product of class and cultural biases as of actual value-free intelligence testing. This is not to argue that prostitutes were all normal or free from psychological maladjustments; it simply means that, in the commonly understood meaning of intelligence, they were not markedly or uniformly substandard.[51]

But the most fruitful historical approach to the feeblemindedness theory of prostitution does not lie in attempts to determine whether—or how many—prostitutes were mentally deficient. It lies instead in probing the significance of the general readiness to accept the theory. Indeed, as in many cases of social labeling, the feeblemindedness theory reveals as much about those who endorsed it as about the women it purportedly described. (It is telling that no one proposed testing the intelligence of the men who engaged prostitutes. One is tempted to wonder what the "results" of such tests might have been.)

On one level the feeblemindedness theory of prostitution answered the need for some kind of rationalized procedure by which to treat apprehended prostitutes.[52] Night court judges, social workers, and reformatory matrons were beset with a bewildering mélange of problems in devising workable rehabilitation programs. The intelligence test offered a system of classification that would allow—theoretically—for each woman to be given the exact type of help she needed or, in the light of the test results, was capable of understanding or responding to. For the women of normal intelligence or better, there was hope of reintegration into society; for the women whose test scores relegated them to the feebleminded range, the prognosis was usually pessimistic. "In cases where the mentality is so low as to preclude the possibility of a life other than one of prostitution," one commentator asserted, "it would be an economy and a humanitarian act to commit such individuals to institutional care for life."[53]

Just as the feeblemindedness theory led to a rationalized procedure (which in many ways was deeply irrational) of treating and reforming prostitutes, it also offered a rationalized *explanation* of the whole phenomenon of prostitution. The emphasis on feeblemindedness made a complex and emotionally explosive problem comprehensible on a purely intellectual level. Female prostitution clearly violated civilized morality's definition of womanhood. But, if it were true that most prostitutes were not mentally responsible for their actions, the cultural and psychological threat implicit in these actions would be defused. The feeblemindedness theory asserted that prostitutes were not responsible for their actions and implied that if they had been mentally able to choose to do otherwise, they would have.

This latter point is important, for it indicates that the feeblemindedness theory can be most fully understood only when it is seen within the context of the awareness of women as problematical. The allegedly feebleminded women who became prostitutes were prototypical examples of victimized women, and this was how they were invariably depicted.[54] In societies less complex than the urban industrial behemoth of the early twentieth century—in, say, the small towns of the mid-nineteenth century —women who might have been classified as feebleminded were not really problematical, for they lived their lives within a network of overlapping agencies and structures able and willing to look after their welfare: family, church, community. In the industrial urban age, however, feebleminded women were unable to cope with the strange new forces and problems and, in the absence of traditional mechanisms of social and moral control and support, were easily led astray. These new forces, however, were profoundly influencing the lives of all women, a fact that points to the fullest meaning of the feeblemindedness theory of prostitution. In the moral world of antiprostitution, the problem of feebleminded women succumbing to prostitution was in reality only an extreme manifestation of the new and tenuous position of all women in industrial society.

In addition to profoundly influencing the perception of prostitution, the awareness of the problematical position of women in modern society also informed many of the measures considered central to the amelioration of prostitution. In fact, many of these solutions were aimed as much at resolving the problematical position of women in general as at repressing prostitution and were based, moreover, on the premise that only after such a resolution had been effected could the evils of prostitution be seriously reduced.

One widely supported measure, which had its origins in the late-nineteenth-century purity movement, involved raising the age of consent —the age at which a girl or young woman can legally assent to sexual relations. Well into the last decades of the nineteenth century, that age in many states was fixed as low as ten, the age designated by English Common Law. Purity forces in the 1880s and 90s, by bringing various kinds of political pressure to bear on state legislatures, were able to improve this situation markedly, but as late as 1900 many states still retained low age-of-consent laws.[55]

The age-of-consent controversy assumed added significance in the progressive years. It became increasingly clear that in a complex industrial society many women were separated from protective family surroundings at early ages and thus required more legal protection than in earlier periods. Feminists were especially aware of the relationship between the age-of-consent laws and prostitution. Raising the statutory age of consent, they argued, would provide the basis for legal recourse for young women induced or seduced into lives of prostitution. Because prostitution depended on a steady supply of young women, raising the age of consent would thus attack the evil at its source.[56] What is striking about the age-of-consent issue is that here again the problem of prostitution was linked to the new and uncertain place of women in modern society.

Equally reflective of this conviction was the recommendation that women police units be established in the cities. Policewomen, it was argued, would be able to deal more effectively than policemen with the new problems associated with the growing number of young women working and living in the city. If policewomen were present at the urban danger points for young women—dance halls, excursion boats, beaches, parks, and night courts—they would be able to intervene in situations where young women might be morally threatened or tempted. The vice commissions urged the creation of units of policewomen as an important step in reducing prostitution, and late in the teens the Bureau of Social Hygiene commissioned a full study of potentially effective uses of women police in the cities.[57]

Somewhat related was the argument that prostitution could be most effectively checked only when middle-class women became more concerned with the problem. Two modes of action were most commonly urged: the actual participation of women in antiprostitution movements, usually through the agency of local women's clubs, and the winning of the franchise for all women.[58] The suffrage argument sometimes assumed a utopian mien, as when, for example, the *Independent* intoned: "One of the most blessed results of giving the ballot to women is that it will mean a fight to the finish against the hateful commerce of social vice in our cities." Other suffragists' analyses were more balanced and realistic, and there was indeed a certain compelling plausibility to the argument: the existence and toleration of segregated vice districts in the cities were usually tightly connected with ward and local politics, and the toleration of prostitution was therefore theoretically susceptible to direct political action at the polls.[59]

Both of these tactics—social action and winning the suffrage—were at the same time answers to and manifestations of the problematical position of women in American society. Forward-looking women accurately saw that as their sex became more involved in and affected by the powerful economic and cultural transformations of the industrial revolution, they would need to wield social and political power. In this light, the advocacy of these tactics implied that women must join and, ideally, lead the fight against prostitution because the masses of men could not be trusted to do so.[60] Women's organizations and the vote were seen as the best means to this end. This vision of social and political women as moral redeemers ultimately never materialized. But the very fact that it was articulated indicates how completely, if somewhat contradictorily, the issue of prostitution had fused with the problem of structuring a new definition of women's role and status in the new society.

Even though the progressive era was a time of flux and uncertainty in the perception of women, there nevertheless existed a dominant conception of the ideal woman. Above all, she was a wife and mother and was devoid of the sexual experience and brazenness of the fallen of her sex.[61] The words used to describe her were "reticence," "delicacy," "shyness," and "grace." Her sphere was the home, be it modest or lavish, which she managed with intelligence and efficiency. "I do not underestimate in the young woman the value of culture, education, and refinement," one commentator observed in the course of a medical school commencement speech on "The Social Evil," "but I do maintain that the beauty of the face and form, given in their perfection to woman only during the years when childbearing is possible, indicate that her chief mission is that of the mother and that her most exalted station is that of the wife who makes possible the home which is the cornerstone of our society." This was, of course, the ideal woman of civilized morality.[62]

In discussions of prostitution, this vision of the ideal woman, pristine and unsullied by social reality, served as the cultural foil of the prostitute; almost invariably they were spoken of only in relation to one another. The characteristics of prostitutes that seemed most worthy of mention were those which most dramatically distinguished them from the ideal woman. A vivid illustration is provided by the phrases employed in routine depictions of prostitutes: "excessive vanity," "immature personality," "sensual type," "unable to appreciate and shoulder responsibility," "indolent nature," "craving for excitement," "lazy," "reckless," "lack of shame or remorse," "the desire for immediate pleasure without regard for consequences," "lack of forethought or anxiety about the future."[63] Prostitutes were not (usually) mothers; it was alleged, in fact, that they took all available precautions to frustrate their biological "destiny."[64] They were not good wives; if they had been married at all, the union had failed and did not seem to be a subject of remorse. Prostitutes lacked "reticence in displaying their feelings," smoked, drank, "actually use[d] the same toilet with the men," and "expose[d] parts of their naked body and use[d] vulgar and obscene language."[65] These characteristics collectively constituted a composite portrait of the prostitute—a nightmarish antithesis of the feminine ideal.

This juxtaposition was interpreted in a number of ways. Many women argued that the toleration of prostitution debased the moral position of all pure women, that, indeed, it was the ultimate in hypocrisy for a society to pretend to honor the dignity of womanhood and motherhood while it encouraged the support of a group of women whose very existence blasphemed them.[66] A variant of this argument held that once a man had consorted with a prostitute he would lose all respect and admiration for the ideal woman and what she stood for. "The edge of the prostitute's true feminine modesty," one physician wrote, "is blunted by the continued indecency that necessity causes her to practice." Accordingly, "association with women whose true modesty has been blunted unfits a man for harmonious marriage."[67]

By 1915, however, true feminine modesty was not what it used to be. Many aspects of the prostitute's life-style, such as the practice of birth control, the independence from traditional familial control, the smart and forward language, the aggressive manners, and the suggestive clothing, were also increasingly evident, albeit in less extreme form, in the behavior of large numbers of urban women who were not, even under the broadest definition, prostitutes.[68] In this light, the prostitute was deplored not only because she violated the beliefs and assumptions of civilized morality but also, and perhaps more importantly, because her life-style, attitudes, and behavior were ominous signs of change in the feminine ideal, which would ultimately influence the behavior of all women. The problematical woman would become the new woman. Anti-prostitution forces did not have access to a crystal ball. Nonetheless, they did sense that the end of American feminine innocence was at hand, and many aspects of the prostitute's behavior seemed to offer a disconcerting preview of the future.

Three

AN AMERICAN DILEMMA:

PROSTITUTION AND IMMIGRATION

*This importation of women for immoral purposes has brought into the
country evils even worse than those of prostitution. In many instances
the professionals who come here have been practically driven from their
lives of shame in Europe on account of their loathsome diseases; the
conditions of vice obtaining there have even lowered the standard of degradation of prostitution formerly customary here. Unnatural practices
are brought largely from continental Europe, and the ease and apparent
certainty of profit have led thousands of our younger men, usually those
of foreign birth or the immediate sons of foreigners, to abandon the
useful arts of life to undertake the most accursed business ever devised by
man.*

U.S. Immigration Commission, *Importation and
Harboring of Women for Immoral Purposes* (1910)

During the opening decades of the twentieth century, the reception halls
on Ellis Island stood as mute witness and accessory to one of the most
profound social and demographic transformations in American history.
Over thirteen million immigrants entered the United States between 1900
and 1914. In earlier periods of the republic's history, immigrants had
come mainly from Germany, Scandinavia, and the British Isles. During
the progressive era, however, most immigrants—in some years, 80 percent—came from Italy, Austria-Hungary, Poland, or Russia. Not surprisingly, the "new" immigration (a contemporary reference to the change
in national origins) became a major national issue during the progressive years, both for those who sought to deal with it sympathetically
and for those of nativist opinions who feared it and worked to restrict
it. The issue of immigration also became intricately intertwined with
antiprostitution.

Immigration and prostitution were perceived by many during the progressive years as contiguous pieces in a jigsaw puzzle of social pathology.
Although, in 1858, William Sanger took note of the relationship of Irish

immigration to prostitution in New York City, for the most part the connection between immigration and prostitution received little attention during the next several decades. After 1900, however, this situation changed dramatically. "The importation and harboring of alien women and girls for immoral purposes and the practice of prostitution," the U.S. Immigration Commission warned in 1910, "is the most pitiful and the most revolting phase of the immigration question." Similar concern was widespread, but it appeared most clearly in legislative and legal developments in national immigration policy.[1]

The impetus for the federal government's increased interest in the relationship between immigration and prostitution during the opening decade of the century was the alleged existence of an international white-slave traffic, in which women and girls were moved from country to country for the purposes of prostitution.[2] Purity groups in both Europe and the United States devoted considerable attention to the issue in the 1880s and 1890s and convened a number of international conferences on the problem. This agitation culminated in 1904, when thirteen European countries ratified an agreement pledging international cooperation in suppressing the white-slave traffic. The United States was asked to be a signatory to the treaty. Accordingly, the Senate advised ratification in 1905, and President Theodore Roosevelt declared it by proclamation in 1908.[3]

As is often the case with highly emotional issues, the white-slave traffic was never precisely defined. Sometimes it meant despicable men procuring and transporting young women and girls against their wills, and at other times it referred to professional prostitutes traveling from country to country via a preestablished and somewhat organized network of contacts.[4] Nevertheless, the concern over the evils of the international white-slave trade and over its relationship to prostitution in the United States steadily grew in the first decade of the century. Occurring at a time of unprecedented immigration into the country, this apprehension profoundly influenced national immigration policy. The immigration acts of 1903, 1907, and 1910 and the Mann Act of 1910 were the most salient manifestations of this influence.

The section on prostitution in the immigration act of 1903 provided:

That the importation into the United States of any woman or girl for the purposes of prostitution is hereby forbidden; and whoever shall import or attempt to import any woman or girl into the United States for the purposes of prostitution, or shall hold or attempt to hold, any woman or girl for such purposes in pursuance of such illegal importation shall be deemed guilty of a felony, and, on conviction thereof, shall be imprisoned not less than one nor more than five years and pay a fine not exceeding five thousand dollars.[5]

This was a clear but limited provision. It dealt with "prostitution" and applied not to immigrant women but to agents or procurers who brought women or girls into the country or who held them for "purposes of prostitution . . . in pursuance of such illegal importation."

Immigration officials were soon convinced, however, that the 1903 act was too limited to handle the problem. Accordingly, the prostitution provision in the immigration act of 1907 was much broader in scope. More than double the length of the 1903 provision, it stated:

> That the importation into the United States of any alien woman or girl for the purpose of prostitution, or for any other immoral purpose, is hereby forbidden; and whoever shall, directly or indirectly, import, or attempt to import, into the United States, any alien woman or girl for the purpose of prostitution, or for any other immoral purpose, or whoever shall hold or attempt to hold any alien woman or girl for any such purpose in pursuance of such illegal importation, or whoever shall keep, maintain, control, support, or harbor in any house or other place, for the purpose of prostitution, or for any other immoral purpose, any alien woman or girl, within three years after she shall have entered the United States, shall, in every such case, be deemed guilty of a felony, and on conviction thereof be imprisoned not more than five years and pay a fine of not more than five thousand dollars; and any alien woman or girl who shall be found an inmate of a house of prostitution or practicing prostitution, at any time within three years after she shall have entered the United States shall be deemed to be unlawfully within the United States, and shall be deported.[6]

This was a substantial expansion of the 1903 construction. The imprecise phrase "or for any other immoral purpose" significantly extended the scope of the original prohibition of the importation of alien women "for the purposes of prostitution." The 1907 law also covered indirect as well as direct participation in the importation of alien women. In addition, a prohibition against maintaining or harboring alien women within three years of entry was added to the holding (which implied the use of force) prohibition of the 1903 legislation. And, perhaps most importantly, the 1907 act provided for the punishment of alien women as well as their importers: any alien woman found as a prostitute any time within three years of her entry into the United States (it was not necessary to prove that she had been a prostitute at the time of entry) could be deported.

The rather wide scope of the 1907 act seemed at first to produce its intended effect, for the number of alien women deported for practicing prostitution within three years of their entry into the United States increased in each year after the law took effect.[7] But the broad powers given to the federal government under the 1907 provision did not go unchallenged; by 1909 two cases contesting the application and constitutionality of the act had reached the Supreme Court.

The first case, *United States* v. *Bitty* (1908), focused on the meaning of the phrase "for any other immoral purpose." Bitty, the defendant, was charged with bringing an alien woman into the United States to "live with him as a concubine"; he was indicted for a violation of the 1907 immigration law and tried in a federal circuit court in New York State. Bitty's attorney filed a motion to have the indictment dismissed. The defense admitted that the concubinage was "highly immoral" but argued that under the *ejusdem generis* principle (which holds that when general words follow an enumeration of specific classes of things, the general words shall be construed as applying only to things of the same general kind as those specifically mentioned), the phrase "for any other immoral purpose" could include only activities covered by the phrase "for the purpose of prostitution." Bitty's counsel argued that there was a sharp distinction between a mistress and a prostitute and that therefore the phrase "for any other immoral purpose" did not cover cases of concubinage. The circuit court agreed and dismissed the indictment.[8]

The U.S. attorney immediately brought the case to the Supreme Court. Bitty essentially repeated the argument presented in the lower court. The attorney general argued that the words "for any other immoral purpose" "must be given some meaning" and claimed that the lower court's ruling had given the words a narrow meaning "not contemplated by Congress." He further averred that Congress had enlarged the scope of the 1903 immigration act in order to cover more than "prostitution" strictly defined; therefore, concubinage, "which is generally condemned by the moral sense of all enlightened communities and is assuredly contrary to purity," was surely intended to be prohibited.[9]

Justice John Marshall Harlan, speaking for a unanimous court, found against Bitty and ordered the lower court's dismissal of the indictment reversed. "We must assume," Harlan asserted, "that in using the words 'or for any other immoral purpose' Congress had reference to the views commonly entertained among the people of the United States as to what is moral or immoral in the relations between man and woman." The phrase "for the purpose of prostitution," Justice Harlan stated, referred to "women who for hire or without hire offer their bodies to indiscriminate intercourse with men. The lives and example of such persons," he continued, quoting one of his predecessors on the bench, "are in hostility to 'the idea of the family, as consisting in and springing from the union for life of one man and one woman in the holy estate of matrimony; the sure foundation of all that is stable and noble in our civilization; the best guaranty of that reverent morality which is the source of all beneficient progress in social and political improvement.'" Harlan argued that, although there was "in the popular sense" a distinction between a prostitute and a mistress, concubinage was clearly covered by the clause "for any other immoral purpose" because it was an evil of "the same general class or kind as the one that controls in the importation of an alien woman for the purpose strictly of prostitution." Bitty, therefore, was liable for prosecution under the 1907 act.[10]

In contrast to the ruling in *Bitty*, the Court's second decision concerning the prostitution provision of the 1907 act, rendered in *Keller* v. *United States* (1909), significantly circumscribed the power of federal immigration officials by declaring an important clause of the provision unconstitutional. In 1905, Irene Bodi emigrated from Hungary to the United States; she maintained residence in New York City until October 1907, when she traveled to Chicago and voluntarily entered a house of prostitution, which the defendants, Keller and Ullman, purchased in November. It was clear that the defendants did not know Irene Bodi until that date and therefore had not been involved with her entry into the country. In June of 1908, Keller and Ullman were arrested and indicted for harboring an alien prostitute and found guilty in a federal district court in Illinois. The case was appealed and argued before the Supreme Court in March 1909. The decision was handed down a month later.

The attorneys for Keller and Ullman argued that the clause in the 1907 law under which their clients were convicted—"whoever shall keep, maintain, control, support, or harbor in any house or other place, for the purpose of prostitution, or for any other immoral purpose, any alien woman or girl, within three years after she shall have entered the United States"—was unconstitutional. The enforcement of the clause, they claimed, required an exercise of the police power, which, under the Constitution, was clearly left to the states. Although they conceded that the federal government did have jursidiction over aliens at the point of entry into the United States (which the first clause of the provision covered), they maintained that federal authority gave way to state jurisdiction once entry was effected. Thus, because Keller and Ullman were not involved in Irene Bodi's entrance into the United States, they could not be prosecuted under federal immigration law.[11]

The attorney general's brief skirted serious consideration of the constitutional issue and argued on purely pragmatic grounds. For the government the issue was one of law enforcement, of the need for a way to detect and punish alien prostitutes and those associated with them. In fact, there was no consideration of the complex problem of framing immigration legislation within the context of federal theory. "The validity of the clause in question," the attorney general asserted, "should be maintained because it relates to and materially affects the importation of the class of women mentioned therein." The clause, which did not appear in the 1903 legislation, was added in 1907 for a very specific reason. Because of "the many subterfuges resorted to by those interested in the importation of women and girls for the purpose of prostitution and other immoral purposes," the government argued, "it was necessary to make it conclusive evidence that the importation was for such immoral purpose as she might be found engaged in within three years after her entry, and that he who might be found keeping her for an immoral purpose within such time, should be deemed to do so in pursuance of an unlawful importation."[12]

The government was making a broad but tenuous assertion here. In effect, it argued that because an alien woman found as a prostitute within three years of entry could be "deemed to be unlawfully in the United States" (that is, it could be assumed that she was a prostitute at the time of entry but had disguised the fact), anyone maintaining or harboring her within the same time period could be deemed to have been involved with an illegal entry. The clause in the act prohibiting the *holding* of an alien prostitute did limit federal authority to cases of holding "in pursuance of such illegal importation." The maintaining and harboring clause, under which Keller and Ullman were indicted, did not limit federal jurisdiction to cases of maintaining and harboring in pursuance of an illegal importation: the phrase "in pursuance of such illegal importation," which would have provided clear, but also limited, federal authority, did not appear in the clause. Therefore, because Keller and Ullman had not been involved with Irene Bodi's entry, the government could and had to "deem" them involved with an illegal importation, an action that clearly came under federal jurisdiction. In addition, the government argued that Keller and Ullman came under federal jurisdiction because their actions were conducive to an alien woman's practicing prostitution. She was therefore liable for deportation, and "it is certainly within the power of Congress to provide a punishment for those who thus bring about her expulsion." Keller and Ullman argued that both such action and the law on which it was based were unconstitutional. Their view prevailed.[13]

Justice David J. Brewer, delivering the opinion of the Court, asserted that "the single question is one of constitutionality. . . . The keeping of a house of ill fame is offensive to the moral sense," he stated, "yet that fact must not close the eye to the question whether the power to punish therefore is delegated to Congress or is reserved to the State." Brewer allowed that Congress had the authority, as the government maintained, to control immigration; it did not, however, have the right "to control all the dealings of our citizens with resident aliens." Brewer admitted that Congress might have authority for "punishing wrongs done to an alien," but this issue in any event did not apply to the case; Keller and Ullman were charged with harboring Irene Bodi, not with holding her against her will. And regarding the government's avowal that anyone connected with an alien prostitute within three years of entry should be considered guilty of compliance with an illegal entry, the Court ruled that Congress could not "punish those whose acts furnish evidence from which the Government may determine the question of expulsion." The Court did not gainsay the right of Congress to deport an alien found practicing prostitution within the three-year probation period, but those tangentially connected with such prostitution could not be prosecuted under the federal immigration law. The Court therefore declared the clause unconstitutional and ordered the indictment against Keller and Ullman quashed.[14]

Justice Oliver Wendell Holmes dissented from the majority opinion, holding that Congress had the right to consider the practice of prostitution within three years of entry as retroactive proof of fraudulent entry and therefore had the authority to punish anyone who was connected with the illegal entry or who was in "cooperation with an equally unlawful stay." There were, Holmes stated, precedents in the immigration law to support this interpretation. But what is of special interest in Holmes's dissent was his assertion that "the law can throw the burden of finding out the fact and date of a prostitute's arrival from another country upon those who harbor her for a purpose that presumably they know in any event to be contrary to law." Holmes's comment did not fall on deaf ears: it was later written into the section on immigration in the Mann Act.[15]

In 1910, the year after the *Keller* decision, Congress enacted two additional measures dealing with immigration and prostitution: the immigration act of 1910 and the White Slave Traffic Act (Mann Act). Both pieces of legislation were directly influenced by the work of the U.S. Immigration Commission, the results of which were first made available to Congress in February 1909.[16] The Immigration Commission, commonly called the Dillingham Commission after Senator William P. Dillingham of Vermont, who served as its chairman, was created under a section of the immigration act of 1907. President Roosevelt strongly supported the creation and work of the commission, which comprised three representatives, three senators, three experts appointed by the president, and a research staff of three hundred. In 1910 the commission produced a massive and seemingly authoritative forty-two-volume study of almost every aspect of immigration.

The Dillingham Commission's report and recommendations, however, were not scientific or impartial and indeed were permeated with the contemporary belief in the racial inferiority of the "new" immigration. The volume on immigration and prostitution—*Importation and Harboring of Women for Immoral Purposes*—was at times blatant in this regard. At one point, for instance, the commission warned that the "vilest practices are brought here from Continental Europe, and beyond doubt there have come from imported women and their men the most bestial refinements of depravity. The toleration with which continental races look upon these evils is spreading in this country an influence perhaps even more far-reaching in its degradation than the physical effects which inevitably follow the evils themselves."[17] More important than the nativist mentality that the report reflected, however, was the picture it drew of the white-slave trade, for this was what materially affected later legislation. *Importation and Haboring of Women for Immoral Purposes* was based on a study of conditions in twelve American cities. Some were intensively investigated, whereas others were subject only to rapid surveys. The commission admitted that even after two years of work, it could not ascertain the exact dimensions of the problem. It was impossible, the commission maintained, "to secure figures showing the exact extent of the exploitation of women and girls in violation of the immigration act." Nevertheless, the commission report asserted that the problem was of "large proportions" and that, according to "practically everyone who has had an opportunity for careful judgment, the numbers imported run well into the thousands each year."[18]

The report discussed the traffic in immigrant women in detail: the economic aspects, the methods of recruiting and importing women, and the difficulty in detecting suspects at points of entry. To support the findings of the report, a twenty-five-page appendix was provided, which included testimony from trials of immigrant white slavers, confiscated correspondence between pimps and importers, statements from immigration officials, and personal experiences of the commission's investigators. All of this evidence indicated that the traffic in immigrant women was a serious problem of increasing proportions and that firm remedial action was imperative. The United States, the commission advised, could count on European cooperation in fighting the white-slave trade, but "owing to the difference between the European and American views regarding prostitution," European countries could not be expected to do very much to stop the voluntary travel of prostitutes into the United States. Accordingly, the United States could protect its interests only by stronger legislation dealing with this aspect of immigration.[19]

In March 1910, just eleven months after the *Keller* decision, and after having full access to the early drafts of the Immigration Commission's findings on the traffic in alien women, Congress enacted a new immigration act. The section on prostitution in the 1910 act was almost five times the length of the 1903 provision and more than twice the length of the 1907 language. The Supreme Court's ruling in *Keller* was duly incorporated by the inclusion of the phrase "in pursuance of such illegal importation" in the harboring clause of the 1910 legislation. This addition obviously limited federal jurisdiction in a harboring offense and presumably solved the constitutional problem raised in *Keller*. The 1910 legislation, reflecting the Immigration Commission's advice to strengthen immigration regulations, also increased the fine for the importing, holding, or harboring of an alien prostitute to ten thousand dollars and provided that, in cases concerning alien prostitutes, the testimony of a husband or a wife against a husband or wife was admissible.[20] (The last-mentioned provision was somewhat incongruent with Justice Harlan's peroration on the "holy estate of matrimony" in the *Bitty* decision.)

The most significant aspect of the 1910 act, however, was the new twist given to the clause in the 1907 act prescribing the punishment of alien women found as prostitutes. The 1907 clause had provided that:

> any alien woman or girl who shall be found an inmate of a house of prostitution or practicing prostitution, at any time within three years after she shall have entered the United States, shall be deemed to be unlawfully within the United States and shall be deported.

This prohibition was significantly expanded in the 1910 act:

> Any alien who shall be found an inmate of or connected with the management of a house of prostitution or practicing prostitution after such alien shall have entered the United States, or who shall receive, share in, or derive benefit from any part of the earnings of any prostitute; or who is employed by, in, or in connection with any house of prostitution or music or dance hall or other place of amusement or resort habitually frequented by prostitutes, or where prostitutes gather, or who in any way assists, protects, or promises to protect from arrest any prostitute, shall be deemed to be unlawfully in the United States and shall be deported.[21]

The 1910 construction in effect made guilt by association grounds for arrest, prosecution, and possible deportation. It was worded in such a way as to apply to immigrant women or men (the 1907 wording "alien woman or girl" was changed to "alien") who were found at the wrong place at the wrong time (music halls, dance halls, or other places "frequented by prostitutes, or where prostitutes gather") but who might have had no connection, or only a marginal one, with prostitution. In addition, the 1907 three-year limit of liability for deportation was dropped in the 1910 act. This change meant that aliens could be deported on prostitution or prostitution-related charges anytime between their entry and their acquisition of U.S. citizenship, an interval that could well be longer than three years.

The reasoning behind the three-year rule—that when an alien woman was found practicing prostitution within three years of entry it could be assumed that she was a prostitute at the time of entry and that therefore the entry had been illegal—was gratuitously harsh to begin with.[22] Holmes had observed in his *Keller* dissent that "three years seems to be long" but added that he was not "prepared to say, against the judgment of Congress that it is too long." But what Congress ignored was the relationship between the oppressive and impoverished conditions in which most recently arrived immigrants lived and the existence of immigrant prostitution. There was an extraordinary range of forces—from the psychological to the economic—working on an immigrant woman during her initial years in the strange land, any or all of which could push her toward prostitution. Indeed, it bordered on the irrational to believe that if a woman became a prostitute within three years it was what she had planned to do all along. Yet, although three years was a long time, it was at least a limited period of liability, a limitation that was removed in 1910.

A few months after enacting the immigration act of 1910, Congress passed the White Slave Traffic Act, which quickly came to be known as the Mann Act after its sponsor, Representative James R. Mann of Illinois.[23] Section 6 of the Mann Act empowered the commissioner-general of immigration "to receive and centralize information concerning the procuration of alien women and girls with a view to their debauchery, and to exercise supervision over such alien women and girls, receive their declarations, establish their identity, and ascertain from them who induced them to leave their native countries." Drawing on Justice Holmes's remark in *Keller* that "the law can throw the burden of finding out the fact and date of a prostitute's arrival from another country upon those who harbor her for a purpose that presumably they know in any event to be contrary to law," the Mann Act stipulated:

> Every person who shall keep, maintain, control, support, or
> harbor in any house or place for the purpose of prostitution, or for

any other immoral purpose, any alien woman or girl within three years after she shall have entered the United States from any country, party to the said arrangement for the suppression of the white slave traffic [Agreement between the United States and other powers for the repression of the trade in white women, 1908], shall file with the Commissioner-General of Immigration a statement in writing setting forth the name of such alien woman or girl, the place at which she is kept, and all facts as to the date of her entry into the United States, the port through which she entered, her age, nationality, and parentage, and concerning her procuration to come to this country within the knowledge of such person.[24]

The intent of this provision is clear. Failure to comply could result in federal prosecution, with the possibility of a fine of up to two thousand dollars or imprisonment for up to two years, or both. If, however, keepers of alien prostitutes registered the required information with federal authorities they would be admitting the nature of their livelihood. This admission might have undesired repercussions, such as prosecution under state law. In order to avoid a challenge on Fifth Amendment grounds, the Mann Act provided that no person could be prosecuted under U.S. law on the basis of any such information furnished to federal authorities. Such information, however, could be the basis for prosecution under state laws, and most states had statutes forbidding the harboring of prostitutes or the keeping of houses of prostitution. Thus, in obeying the federal law, keepers of alien prostitutes would be providing information that could be used against them in state courts.

Like the immigration act of 1910, the Mann Act incorporated some of the findings of the Immigration Commission. This indebtedness was clear in the report recommending the bill when it was voted out of the House Committee on Interstate and Foreign Commerce (chaired by Representative Mann) and placed before the entire House for consideration.[25] But regarding one important point—the extent to which the international traffic in women was organized—the committee report greatly exaggerated the findings of the commission. The Immigration Commission took some care to emphasize repeatedly that the "belief that a single corporation is largely controlling this traffic in the United States is doubtless a mistake. The number of women imported by any one person or organization is probably quite limited." However, according to the committee report, the traffic in alien women was conducted by an "organized system, or syndicate" and was "systematic," "continuous," and "not . . . limited to isolated and accidental cases." One reason for this emphasis was the desire to convince Congress that the legislation was necessary, but the committee's emphasis on the extensiveness of the international white-slave traffic was also a reflection of the alarmist mentality sparked by the threat of a domestic white-slave trade, a subject for later and more detailed discussion.[26]

In a sense, Section 6 of the Mann Act complemented the immigration act of 1910: whereas the immigration law pertained most forcibly to alien prostitutes themselves, Section 6 applied only to their importers, procurers, and managers. The Mann Act was, however, a far more powerful piece of legislation. It was designed to allow federal authorities to punish those involved with alien prostitutes in the individual states, but it was worded in such a way, and based on such constitutional reasoning, as to avoid the issue of federal usurpation of state police power, which circumscribed the application of the immigration acts. This goal was accomplished by predicating the enforcement of the Mann Act on two powers expressly granted to the federal government in the Constitution: the power to regulate foreign and interstate commerce and the power to legislate in furtherance of an international treaty to which the United States was a party.

The commerce clause was the basis for the sections of the Mann Act that focused on the interstate (domestic) white-slave trade. Section 6, which empowered federal immigration officials to arrest and prosecute managers of alien prostitutes in the states (action the Court had declared unconstitutional in *Keller*) was based on the duty and the power of the United States to honor its treaty obligations. The treaty involved was the international agreement for the repression of the white-slave trade, which the United States joined in 1908. Justice Brewer, in *Keller*, had considered whether the federal prosecution of Keller and Ullman could be considered as a fulfillment of federal treaty obligations but concluded it could not, because Keller and Ullman were indicted before the United States became a party to the treaty. The Mann committee saw the potential in Brewer's idea and used the authority to enforce treaties as a basis for action against those associated with alien prostitutes. The only limitation on this federal power was that the prostitute must have come from a country that signed the international agreement against the white-slave traffic. The Supreme Court upheld Section 6 of the Mann Act in *United States* v. *Portale* (1914), thus giving the federal government the jurisdiction and authority it had been denied just five years earlier in *Keller*.[27]

By 1910, then, there existed a clearly defined national position on the relationship between prostitution and immigration. This position had important implications. First, the national legislation and supporting reports gave the impression that immigration was the main source of prostitution in the United States, even though no statistical evidence was presented to substantiate this claim. In addition, by viewing immigrant prostitution in the United States as a matter of alien prostitutes fraudulently entering the country, federal policy in effect avoided addressing the relationship between immigrant prostitution and the conditions in which many newly arrived immigrants lived. By focusing on the "importation" of alien prostitutes, federal policy defined immigration prostitution as an attack from without, when, in fact, the problem was rooted in domestic social and economic conditions. That some foreign prostitutes did enter the United States cannot be doubted (it could, of course, be argued that immigration of prostitutes began not long after the *Mayflower* dropped anchor off the Massachusetts coast). But such an interpretation of the complex relationship of immigration and prostitution served only to oversimplify and distort the matter.

Concern about the relationship between prostitution and immigration was not, however, limited to political and legal expressions. Indeed, almost every individual and group concerned about prostitution seems to have been plagued with anxiety about that relationship. On the most general level there were vague mutterings about the "racial" implications of prostitution. "We have got to remove this evil," Charles W. Eliot, former president of Harvard, warned in a 1913 address, "or this country will not be ruled by the race that is now here. The family life of the white race is at stake in its purity, in its healthfulness, and in its fertility."[28] From other quarters similar sentiments were expressed, but in a somewhat more direct manner: "With rare and temporary exceptions, the Teutonic nations have always prohibited, by statute or common law, the keeping of houses of prostitution. . . . Let us not now be betrayed to a Latin or Asiatic laxity of morals, lest we go the way of the great Latin and Asiatic nations that have fallen."[29] Exactly how such a debasement would occur was never clearly spelled out, and often such sentiments were buttressed only by oracular analogies to the moral dissipation that supposedly caused the fall of Rome.[30]

On a more concrete level, there was the belief that most of the prostitutes and those who managed them were immigrants of Eastern or Southern European origin.[31] The Jewish community, especially in New York City and Chicago, came under pointed attack in this regard. In New York in 1894 a state senate investigation of corruption and vice in New York City gave considerable attention to the Max Hochstim Association (otherwise referred to as the Essex Market Court Gang), a lower East Side procurement ring that allegedly recruited immigrant girls and women from the tenement districts into lives of prostitution. This kind of official exposé provided perfect material for those of anti-Semitic views, and in some responses to prostitution, most notably the white-slave tracts, a pronounced anti-Semitism emerged as a significant theme.[32]

This outlook was expressed most fully by the muckraking journalist George Kibbe Turner, in articles published in *McClure's Magazine* in 1907 and 1909. In the first, "The City of Chicago: A Study of the Great Immoralities" (which was a rather intemperate and reformist diatribe against slum politics, boss rule, and the moral dissipation of the urban masses), Turner declared that the group responsible for furnishing women for Chicago prostitution was "largely composed of Russian Jews," who had contrived "a sort of loosely organized association extending through large areas of the country, their chief centers being New York, Boston, Chicago, and New Orleans." Two years later, Turner produced "The Daughters of the Poor: A Plain Story of the Development of New York City as a Leading Center of the White Slave Trade of the World, under Tammany Hall," a detailed expansion of his earlier brief comments on Jews and prostitution. Like "The City of Chicago," "The Daughters of the Poor" was an attack on urban moral and political corruption, but instead of repeating the shotgun approach he used in his first piece, Turner focused on vice and its connection with Tammany Hall. Here he described—without documentation or the mention of sources—the history of the international Jewish white-slavery organization, the way in which it established itself in New York City in the 1890s, and its quick association with the Tammany machine. Turner also discussed the New York Independent Benevolent Association, an organization of Jewish procurers, which allegedly provided death benefits and burial facilities for members and which, once established, spread its trade and methods outward to Newark, Chicago, San Francisco, and St. Louis. Everywhere, Turner implied, the nefarious business of prostitution was run, in the main, by Jews.[33]

Turner's attitudes and reporting were to some extent balanced: he devoted considerable attention to the efforts of prominent Jewish leaders in New York and Chicago to combat organized prostitution in their communities, and he was sympathetic to the plight of unprotected and victimized immigrant women. But he was not, to put it mildly, enlightened on matters of race or immigration. Indeed, his articles describing a Jewish-run national prostitution conspiracy reflected an ever-present American anti-Semitism, which had appeared in the money wars of the 1890s and which would appear during the progressive years in such forms as the report of the U.S. Immigration Commission, the Leo Frank case, and the first American printing of a version of the scurrilous "Protocols of the Elders of Zion" in 1920.

There were, however, more intelligent and realistic approaches to the problem of prostitution and immigration. The Jewish community itself, cognizant that any actual or imagined Jewish involvement in prostitution could be used in anti-Semitic attacks, took rigorous action to ameliorate what it admitted was sometimes a serious problem. But Jewish leaders maintained, in contrast to Turner's allegations, that prostitution in Jewish neighborhoods was more a result of the economic deprivation and social dislocation of tenement district life than of the cabalistic machinations of the caftan-cloaked latter-day Shylocks lurking in Turner's exposés. In addition, organizations such as the National YWCA and the National Council of Jewish Women began to devote considerable energy to a wide range of social programs directed at preventing the sexual exploitation of immigrant women and girls. In this endeavor they were joined by the staffs of settlement houses and immigrant protection leagues in various cities. Such luminaries as Frances A. Kellor, Jane Addams, Grace Abbott, and Lillian Wald lent their names and time to such programs, including the provision of aid and advice to immigrant women in transit and the securing of safe and reputable employment for immigrant women.[34]

The belief in a direct relationship between immigration and prostitution was, then, widely held and acted upon in many areas of American society—from the Supreme Court and congressional corridors to the settlement houses in the immigrant districts. The pertinent question thus becomes, Was there in fact such a relationship, and if so, what were its general dimensions? The sources on which an informed answer might be based are, by nature, imprecise and incomplete, but there is enough material to support some general conclusions.

Although some Americans associated immigration with prostitution at least as early as the 1840s, when the first great numbers of Irish landed on American shores, the relationship between the two issues was not what many in the progressive years thought it to be. For example, in William Sanger's 1858 investigation of some 2,000 New York City prostitutes, 706 (35 percent) were born in Ireland. But in that year the Irish-born constituted almost 30 percent of the New York City population, and Sanger's figure is therefore much less startling than it looks. Similarly, in an investigation of prostitution in New York City in 1912 by the Bureau of Social Hygiene, 31 percent of 1,106 prostitutes studied were foreign-born, and 11 percent were born in either Russia or Austria-Hungary, two countries prominent in the "new" immigration. But this

was at a time when approximately 40 percent of New York City's population was foreign-born, and 14 percent were immigrants from Russia
and Austria-Hungary. Thus, in both categories, immigrants were underrepresented. It is also notable that, by 1912, Irish prostitution had
declined significantly (Eugene O'Neill's opinions notwithstanding) from
the 1858 figure. Correspondingly, Jewish prostitution would virtually
disappear within a few decades. It would seem, then, that immigration
was related to prostitution, but only during the years when an ethnic
group was struggling to overcome the initial years of poverty and dislocation. And to the extent that an ethnic group made headway in that
struggle, its contribution to prostitution declined. In fact, if there was
any group whose representation in the ranks of prostitution increased, it
was native-born Americans: in 1858, 38 percent of Sanger's prostitutes
were native-born women; in 1912 the figure stood at 68 percent.[35]

These computations from investigations conducted fifty-five years apart
do not, of course, deliver the ultimate verdict etched in stone. But they do
indicate, in general, the basic nature of the relationship between immigration and prostitution. And, in fact, there was enough information
available during the progressive years for this relationship to have been
understood. For example, the figures produced by the Immigration Commission on the number of women barred from entry into the United
States as suspected prostitutes—the highest number for a one-year period
was 124—hardly showed the traffic in alien women into the United
States to be of extensive proportions.[36] These figures hardly supported
claims that the traffic involved as many as 15,000 alien women each
year.[37] There were also the reports of vice commissions from Syracuse,
Wisconsin, and Kansas City, which stated that, although prostitution
was flourishing, there was very little involvement by immigrants.[38] From
another perspective, most of the group studies of prostitutes that appeared after 1910 indicated that in very few cases did the ethnic breakdown of the prostitutes deviate very much from that of the general
population in the specific locality. Indeed, in many instances, immigrant
groups were underrepresented.[39] Thus, while commentators, many of
them sympathetic and enlightened, were remarking on the sudden appearance of Jewish prostitution—"Less than a generation ago," the social
worker Maude E. Miner wrote in 1916, "it was rare in New York City
for a Jewish girl to be living a life of prostitution"—most figures showed
Jews to have less involvement in prostitution than other groups.[40] Much
the same was true with the rates of venereal disease, widely held to be
closely associated with prostitution. In 1911, Richard Cabot, a prominent Massachusetts physician and public health official, reported that the
best available information showed that the incidence of venereal disease

was about equal for the native-born, the Irish, and the Italians, whereas among Jewish-Americans, the incidence of syphilis was one-third and the incidence of gonorrhea one-half of that among other groups.[41]

All of this evidence indicates that immigration was a far less important factor in American prostitution than the attention given to it implied. Prostitution, it seems, was able to thrive anywhere, whether or not immigrants were present. To be sure, if one strolled down certain streets in New York, or Chicago, or Philadelphia, or St. Louis in 1910, one would have indeed encountered foreign-born prostitutes. But it would have been unlikely that any foreign-born group, or combination of groups, would have enjoyed a monopolistic or oligopolistic position in the business. The ethnicity and religious affiliation of prostitutes in any given city would have reflected—within a reasonable margin of error—the number of ministers, priests, and rabbis in the local population. Here, perhaps, was an impressive manifestation of the highly reputed American tradition of ethnic and religious pluralism.

Given this rather unremarkable state of affairs, how does one account for the fact that the relationship between immigration and prostitution received so much notice from so many quarters? There was, assuredly, the reality of racial and ethnic prejudice. This took many other forms in early twentieth-century American society, and it is not surprising that it turned up in the response to prostitution. The prurient interest in the alleged sexual depravity of both Jews and Catholics had been, in Europe as in the United States, a salient feature of anti-Semitism and anti-Catholicism. These tendencies were clearly present, and there were undoubtedly those who found psychological release in fantasizing about lascivious immigrant pimps and prostitutes. There was, however, another equally noteworthy aspect to the propensity to connect immigration with prostitution. Simply put, it was evasive. This is not to gainsay the motives of those, and there were many, who were sincerely concerned over the plight of vulnerable immigrant women and girls. Prostitution was a real and ugly aspect of the unconscionable conditions under which many immigrants were constrained to live. Nonetheless, the concern over how many prostitutes were immigrants, how many immigrants were prostitutes, how many alien prostitutes were slinking into the country, and how many Jews were pulling the strings, functioned mainly to shift attention from the basic problem, prostitution in American cities, which existed whether or not immigrant populations were present.

It is worth noting, by way of a brief epilogue, that at the very end of the progressive era the relationship between immigration and sexual immorality and prostitution was finally addressed in a form far superior to anything that preceded it. It came deeply buried in the pages of what has been proven to be one of the masterworks of twentieth-century American social science, William I. Thomas and Florian Znaniecki's *The Polish Peasant in Europe and America*, published between 1918 and 1920. Thomas, a leading figure in the Sociology Department at the University of Chicago, became extremely interested in the enormous immigration into the United States during the first decade of the twentieth century. But unlike many of his countrymen, who were concerned about what immigration was doing to the United States, Thomas focused his attention on what American society was doing to the immigrants. Thus, sometime between 1908 and 1909—just about the time of the *Keller* decision, the appearance of Turner's exposés, the preliminary report of the Immigration Commission on the importation of women for immoral purposes, and the drafting of the Mann Act—Thomas and Znaniecki began collecting material, both in Poland and in Chicago, for an inquiry into the experience of the Polish peasant immigrants.

The *Polish Peasant in Europe and America* presented an almost mythopoeic interpretation of immigration. From a profoundly traditional, pre-industrial, communal, and agricultural society, one anchored in a stable and historical mosaic of familial, religious, class, and economic patterns, the Polish peasant entered a complex, highly urban and technological, secular, fiercely individualistic, and savagely competitive society. The result, as Thomas and Znaniecki phrased it, was widespread "demoralization," the "decay of the personal life-organization of an individual member of a social group." This demoralization assumed a number of forms: the appearance of economic indigence, family pathology and marital problems, crime, and delinquency. These were not totally paralyzing problems, and indeed Thomas and Znaniecki devoted considerable attention to the ways in which the Polish-American community was able to counteract them. But they were, nevertheless, of serious proportions.[42]

In *Sex and Society* (1907), Thomas had written perceptively on the relationship of sex to personality and social organization, and he brought his understanding of this subject to bear at many points in *The Polish Peasant in Europe and America*. It was particularly evident in the analysis of sexual immorality, or "sexual demoralization," among first-generation Polish girls in Chicago. Sexual propriety and chastity in young unmarried women, the authors maintained, had been structurally integrated into peasant society in Poland; it had been an important part of family organization, community stability, kinship patterns, and the general patriarchal order. In the American environment this situation radically changed, and the old patterns of restraint on young women dissolved. The weakening of family solidarity and sexual demoralization among parents in the new urban world was an important aspect of this process. Furthermore, the routine of household responsibilities, which had served as the young woman's connection with family life in the old society, no longer had this significance in America, and was stripped of all meaning. The traditional demand for sexual purity among women was similarly challenged: because the dowry system was weakening, and because the anonymous urban environment encouraged behavior impossible in the tightly knit peasant communities, premarital sexual activity increasingly became only another "incident." In addition, the individualistic American ethos weakened communal restraints and made sexual behavior more a matter of individual gratification and expression than of communal obligation. All of these conditions, Thomas and Znaniecki asserted, enabled and encouraged young Polish-American women to break with, even revolt against, the traditional patterns of sexual control.[43]

Thomas and Znaniecki's work, and the work of the Chicago school in general, have not gone uncriticized. Nonetheless, their intelligent and sympathetic attempt to understand and interpret the problem of sexual immorality among young immigrant women (which they viewed in almost tragic terms) towered above most of the other efforts of the period. But their insights did not enjoy a wide audience. The first two editions of *The Polish Peasant in Europe and America* sold only three thousand copies. Yet even had the book been widely circulated, things would not have been much different: Thomas and Znaniecki's treatment of the question of immorality among young Polish immigrant women was not tailored to the fashion of the time. While many Americans looked at the issue to see how immigration was contributing to the decline of American morality, Thomas and Znaniecki saw that they had cause and effect reversed. For what the two scholars finally said was that sexual immorality among young Polish women, far from being "unAmerican," was often part of a Faustian compact by which immigrants became truly "American."

PROSTITUTION, VENEREAL DISEASE,

AND AMERICAN MEDICINE

*An asylum. Here is a case of general paresis; there a melancholiac; in the
next room a maniac can be heard shrieking. Wild oats a-plenty!
A jail, full of drunks, criminals, bums. Wild oats again!
A foundlings' asylum full of children cursed before they were born, by
society's cruel term "bastard." Poor little wild oats!
A beautiful girl found dead in the river one fine morning. What was she
doing there? Washing the wild oats out of her life!
A pistol shot rings out in a gambling hell—a man falls dead. The gun was
loaded with wild oats!*
    G. Frank Lydston, M.D., 1909

The American medical profession's concern about the physical and social
consequences of venereal disease infused antiprostitution in the progressive years with a particular urgency. Physicians and laymen, to be sure,
had pointed much earlier to the relationship between prostitution and
venereal disease. Dr. William Sanger, for instance, in his 1858 investigation of prostitution in New York City, argued that uncontrolled prostitution made the city a "hotbed where . . . syphilis may be cultivated and
disseminated." During the late decades of the nineteenth century, however, important advances in venereology, which were part of the great
efflorescence of medical research accompanying the rise of bacteriology,
gave venereal disease and, by implication, prostitution a new and more
serious dimension.[1]

    After 1838, the year in which Philippe Ricord demonstrated that
syphilis and gonorrhea were distinctly different diseases, progress in the
understanding of venereal disease came rapidly.[2] In 1854, Pierre Diday
published his account of the symptoms of congenital syphilis. In the late
1860s, Jean Alfred Fournier stressed the fact of latency in syphilis and
traced a variety of serious physical and mental problems to syphilitic
infection. Albert Neisser isolated and identified the gonococcus, the gonorrhea bacterium, in 1879. In 1903, Elie Metchnikoff and Emile Roux

transmitted the syphilis organism to monkeys, thus making possible the experimental study of the disease. Two years later, Fritz Schaudinn and Erich Hoffman discovered and isolated the syphilis bacterium, *Treponema pallidum*. The next year, Karl Landsteiner perfected the dark-field microscopic technique, which allowed researchers to see *Treponema pallidum* clearly and alive.

The advances in the control and treatment of venereal disease were equally impressive. In 1884 the German obstetrician Karl Siegmund Crede discovered that a solution of silver nitrate put into the eyes of newborn babies prevented gonorrheal ophthalmia, a condition often resulting in total blindness in children born of mothers infected with gonorrhea. Working with the principles of the newly discovered complement fixation tests, August von Wassermann and his colleagues in 1906 developed a serological test for determining the presence of the syphilis bacterium in human blood. And in 1910, Paul Ehrlich and Sahachiro Hata discovered that an arsenical compound, later named Salvarsan, could be used to kill the syphilis bacterium. These developments were well known to informed American physicians and stimulated an intense appreciation of both the possibility and the necessity of controlling venereal contagion.

For the American medical community, the prophylaxis of venereal disease became inextricably tied to the issue of prostitution by virtue of the fundamental assumption that prostitution was the major, and to some the only, source of venereal contagion. During the progressive years, any analysis of the issue of venereal disease invariably stressed its relationship to prostitution.[3] The case was succinctly stated by Lavinia L. Dock, a member of the Nurses' Settlement in New York City, who maintained in her 1910 nursing manual for venereal disease that prostitution "is now as certainly the abidingplace and inexhaustible source of . . . venereal disease, as the marshy swamp is the abode of the malaria-carrying mosquito, or the polluted water supply of the typhoid bacillus."[4] By the second decade of the century, this belief rested on two seemingly unassailable bodies of evidence. The first of these, drawn from group studies of prostitutes conducted after 1914, indicated that a large percentage of prostitutes—between 28 and 100 percent—were infected with venereal disease, which they communicated to their patrons.[5] The second body of data, contained in the records of hospitals, clinics, and private practitioners, suggested that most cases of venereal infection in men could be traced to contact with prostitutes.[6]

Whether prostitution actually was responsible for most of the contagion of venereal disease in the progressive years is not easily determined.[7] In recent times, when the venereal disease rate in some areas has been at extremely high levels, only 5 percent of all reported venereal disease cases can be traced to prostitution.[8] This figure contrasts strikingly with the statistics from the progressive years. The low contemporary figure certainly reflects, however, two important changes in sexual behavior that have occurred in the last half century: the decrease in the number of contacts of American men with prostitutes and the concurrent increase in sexual activity not related to prostitution.[9] The continuing progress in the medical control of venereal disease is also an important consideration. During the early decades of the twentieth century, both the etiology and the treatment of venereal disease were in a state of flux. Furthermore, even after Salvarsan and fairly reliable serological tests became available in the teens, it cannot be assumed that prostitutes immediately made use of them. Since 1943, however, when penicillin was first used in the treatment of syphilis, the effectiveness of both personal and professional prophylaxis has improved to a point where a knowledgeable prostitute can achieve a control over venereal infection far superior to that of her counterpart in the early decades of the century.

It was probably the case, therefore, that prostitution played a significant role in the spread of venereal disease during the progressive era; at least it played a more important role then than it does today. But what is finally important about the belief that prostitution was the major source of venereal disease was its implication that venereal disease was a "result" of prostitution and that therefore, by a logical deduction, all the pernicious social and physical effects of venereal disease were also "results" of prostitution. Given these convictions, any attempt to ameliorate the consequences of venereal disease would have to focus on prostitution.[10] This is the point at which the medical community's concern over venereal disease most perfectly dovetailed with antiprostitution.

Though physicians agreed that prostitution was the source of venereal disease, they could not cite any authoritative statistics indicating the extent of venereal infection on a national level. To be sure, data on most diseases in the early twentieth century were incomplete or sketchy, but reliable statistics on venereal disease were virtually nonexistent.[11] There were at least three reasons for this state of affairs: the prudery and conspiracy of silence surrounding discussion of venereal disease, which enlightened elements within the medical profession were only beginning to challenge effectively in these years; the fact that the venereal diseases had not been included in the late-nineteenth-century public health regulations requiring the reporting of other infectious diseases; and the practice by both physicians and hospitals of recording cases of venereal disease under more socially acceptable medical classifications. By 1910, then, there existed a rather ironic situation: although knowledge of the medical and social aspects of venereal disease was steadily progressing, physicians, in the absence of reliable official figures, did not know exactly how extensive venereal infection was.

Physicians were unanimous in bemoaning the lack of official vital statistics on venereal disease, but the dearth of such material did not prevent many practitioners from compiling and publicizing what unofficial figures were available.[12] In 1901, a committee of seven physicians of the Medical Society of the County of New York circulated a questionnaire to 4,750 physicians in the New York City area asking each practitioner to state the number of venereal disease cases he was treating. On the basis of 678 replies, the Committee of Seven estimated there to be 200,000 syphilitics in New York City.[13] Several years later, in 1904, Prince Morrow, the chairman of the Committee of Seven, estimated that 60 percent of the adult male population in the United States contracted either gonorrhea or syphilis at some time in their lives; his figure translated into about 450,000 new infections per year.[14] The next year another physician cited evidence of 50,000 new cases of syphilis in New York City each year.[15] In 1909 still another practitioner calculated that the national rate of venereal infection in the 1860s, 85.11 per 1,000, had grown by 1908 to 194.5 per 1,000.[16] In 1910 it was reported that 80 percent of urban males, and 60 to 75 percent of "marriageable age" men, had gonorrhea.[17] And by the teens there was an extensive medical literature of estimates of venereal infection, all of which pointed to an enormous amount of venereal disease in the United States.[18]

The sources and basis for these high figures were, however, sometimes sharply questioned. For instance, in 1911 the distinguished Massachusetts physician Richard C. Cabot, in delivering the Shattuck lecture before the Massachusetts Medical Society, questioned Prince Morrow's estimate of the extent of gonorrhea in the United States. Morrow had maintained in his book *Social Diseases and Marriage* (1904) that 75 percent of American men contracted gonorrhea, so that it was in his opinion the most widespread disease in the adult male population. Cabot doubted that this was the case. "Many wild guesses about the proportion of adult males afflicted with venereal disease have . . . been published for campaign purposes," he claimed. But he argued that there was "no solid basis" for such estimates and further asserted that "gonorrheal infection ranks very far below . . . tubercular infection in the numbers of persons attacked each year." Hospital records, Cabot insisted, contained the only reliable data on venereal disease, and, on the basis of an examination of the records of 8,031 adult males admitted to the Massachusetts General Hospital over eighteen years, he found that 35 percent had contracted gonorrhea sometime in their lives. The discrepancy between this figure and Morrow's was the result, Cabot felt, of Morrow's wild guessing.[19]

Morrow quickly registered a brief in his own defense: "It may be laid down as a general proposition that the statistics of general hospitals as to the actual or relative frequency of venereal morbidity are absolutely worthless. It would be just as absurd to compute the proportion of prostitutes or drunkards in a community from the census of a church congregation." Most cases of venereal disease, Morrow argued, never reached a hospital, and the ones that did were often admitted under a "respectable pseudonym." A much more accurate body of data, he pointed out, was the statistics on venereal infection in military posts, because they were based on a more representative cross section of the population than were hospital statistics. But no matter how many sets of data were used, he concluded, "It is only by reading between the lines that we can arrive at any adequate conception of the extent of venereal morbidity."[20]

Who was right? There is no way of knowing for sure, but both estimates were probably higher than the actual incidence of the disease among the general population. Yet, with due regard to Cabot's criticism of inflammatory figures, Morrow better understood the social context of venereal disease in 1910 and was absolutely correct in seeing the essential uselessness of hospital records for determining the extent of venereal disease. Morrow was convinced—and rightly so—that any one set of figures on venereal disease would be inaccurate and misleading; an accurate computation of venereal infection could be achieved only by "reading between the lines" of many sets of data in an attempt to account for such irrational factors as fear, shame, ignorance, and deception. This was hardly an exact procedure, and in our own age of labyrinthine data banks and imposing computer technology, it at first appears utterly primitive. But even today, in fact, most countries in the world do not have reliable statistics on venereal disease. In the United States, the Public Health Service concedes that because only a small percentage of venereal disease cases are reported (8 to 12 percent for infectious syphilis and 7 to 11 percent for gonorrhea), it must employ extrapolation techniques, a sophisticated form of reading between the lines, to arrive at a reliable estimate of the national rate.[21]

In 1917 one physician wrote that "the actual number of cases of gonorrhea and syphilis contracted and treated in a large city is a hundred fold greater than is indicated by the official reports."[22] This was undoubtedly an overstatement, but given the low percentage of venereal disease that is reported even today, it was not as irrational as it might first appear. More importantly, it manifestly articulated the contemporary belief that venereal disease was rampant and out of control, a belief just as vital in focusing medical and public attention on the problem of prostitution and venereal disease as the concurrent explosion of new medical knowledge of the nature and consequences of venereal infection.

Even though American physicians believed that the incidence of venereal infection was very high, there was no immediate agreement on how to approach the problem. By the late teens, an influential wing of the medical profession was loosely united in an attitude toward venereal disease that was fundamentally scientific and secular, but this unity was achieved only after more than a decade of conflict of opinion.

The most formidable obstacle to a rational approach was the traditional cultural censorship imposed on any frank discussion of the subject. Medical history is replete with instances where an atmosphere of fear and shame hindered a reasoned approach to certain diseases. The problems surrounding the treatment of cholera and tuberculosis in the nineteenth century are salient examples. But because the venereal diseases were associated in both an actual and an emotional sense with illicit sexual behavior (itself a tabooed subject), any forthright discussion of syphilis and gonorrhea had to confront a conspiracy of polite silence more tenaciously maintained than was the case with other diseases. Thus, around the turn of the century, Howard Kelly, an eminent gynecologist and professor at the Johns Hopkins Medical School, asserted at a meeting of the American Medical Association that the discussion of venereal disease was "attendant with filth and we besmirch ourselves by discussing it in public."[23] And throughout the progressive years, many physicians who supported an open discussion of venereal disease also supported the belief that fear of infection acted as a deterrent to illicit intercourse and that infection, if contracted, constituted the just wages of sin.[24] The American Society of Sanitary and Moral Prophylaxis, although in some respects marking a new departure in the approach to venereal disease, also incorporated much of the older legacy of fear. "The only way to make these diseases effective guardians of virtue," Prince Morrow argued, "is to expose their true significance and real danger, to substitute a wholesome fear, for the ignorant contempt in which they are now held, the fear of infection, the fear of microbes, to appeal to enlightened self interest. After all, fear is the protective genius of the human body, and the basis upon which all hygienic precepts are inculcated."[25]

During these same early years of the century, however, there emerged an increasingly scientific and more socially responsible attitude.[26] There was, to begin with, a growing belief among physicians that the atmosphere of ignorance and misinformation surrounding the venereal diseases could be effectively countered by a program of education in sex hygiene.[27] There was also slow but encouraging growth in the number of clinics, and in particular evening clinics, for the treatment of venereal patients.[28] In 1903 the American Medical Association established a standing committee on venereal disease, and the annual meeting of that association in 1906 held two important symposia. One, on the "Duty of the Profession to Womankind," considered the dire effects of ignorance of the consequences of venereal disease on married women, marriage, and the family. The other, on the venereal diseases in general, centered on the need for the medical profession to take an active role in educating the public on the seriousness of unchecked venereal infection.[29] In 1913 there were three signs of progress: the French playwright Eugene Brieux's *Les Avaries* (translated as *Damaged Goods*), a drama dealing with the marital and social consequences of syphilis, was produced with commercial success in New York, Washington, and Chicago;[30] the morally oriented purity forces merged with the medically oriented groups to form the American Social Hygiene Association;[31] and the Rockefeller-financed Bureau of Social Hygiene formally opened. And in 1914 the first number of the *Journal of Social Hygiene*, a publication devoted to the discussion of venereal disease, prostitution, and related issues, appeared.

All of these developments clearly signaled the emergence of a recognizably modern trend in both attitude and therapy, but the contest with prudery, ignorance, and superstition was not resolved by 1915. Much of the enlightenment that took place within the medical profession never extended beyond it. Throughout the period, physicians complained that quack remedies for venereal infection, sold at drug stores or from the back of a wagon, were still popular and frequently resorted to by the general public.[32] Even the enlightenment within the profession was not complete. For instance, well into the teens, concerned physicians were declaring the state of instruction in venereology in most medical schools to be inadequate and thus productive of practitioners unqualified to diagnose and treat venereal diseases adequately.[33]

There was also the problem of inadequate facilities for the treatment of patients. In New York City in 1905, there were only ninety-six hospital beds available for venereal patients (this in comparison to 960 beds in Paris, a city with only two-thirds the population of New York). In New York City in 1916, only ten of the thirty general hospitals would admit cases of active syphilis, and in Pennsylvania in 1912, a survey revealed that of fourteen major hospitals none would accept venereal disease cases.[34] Throughout the progressive years there were demands that hospital authorities change these restrictive admission policies and enlarge the facilities available for treatment of venereal disease.[35] In some cases it was common practice, again well into the teens, to list admitted patients as having more socially acceptable diseases—an approach that, in addition to reflecting a moralistic attitude, hindered the compilation of accurate statistics on the incidence of venereal infection.[36]

There was, then, tension between old and new modes of thought and attitudes. On the one hand, an older legacy of fear and shame was manifest in a variety of forms. On the other hand, many physicians were beginning to separate the patient from the illness and to treat the venereal diseases without regard to the moral or social character of either the patient or the disease. Because of the unique nature of venereal disease and because it was so closely associated with the emotionally volatile issue of prostitution, this was no easy task.

Most physicians found the venereal infection statistics compelling. Even more alarming, however, were the catastrophic physical and societal consequences of the unchecked spread of syphilis and gonorrhea. By the outset of the twentieth century, medical research had conclusively demonstrated the relationships between syphilis and certain birth deformities (congenital syphilis, commonly called "syphilis of the innocent") and between gonorrhea and infant blindness.[37] At a symposium on venereal disease held in Rhode Island in 1905, for instance, specialists estimated that between 25 and 40 percent of blindness in infants was the result of gonorrheal conjunctivitis. An estimate a decade later was even higher.[38]

Perhaps most horrifying was the relationship between syphilis and general paresis (paralysis and insanity, the final form of tertiary syphilis). Early in his career, Prince Morrow had translated into English the French venereologist Jean Alfred Fournier's work on the correlation between syphilis and paresis; and by the opening decade of the twentieth century, American physicians—at least those who kept up with the medical journals—were well aware of the widespread incidence of syphilis-induced insanity.[39] Some physicians and public health officers estimated that between 8 and 20 percent of insanity cases under treatment could be linked to a syphilitic infection in the patient's past.[40] These were staggering figures, both for the toll in human suffering they represented and for the cost to the public of institutional care, and they were among the most important facts marshalled by physicians concerned with the consequences of venereal disease for American life.[41]

It is important to understand, however, that physicians and laymen perceived the venereal diseases as clearly distinct from other infectious diseases of similar medical seriousness. The venereal diseases were more than an ordinary health problem: they had, and still have today, although to a diminished degree, an emotional dimension that other diseases did not. The spread of syphilis and gonorrhea posed serious threats not only to the public health but also to the integrity of certain conceptualizations of great cultural and psychological value: the "race," marriage, the family, motherhood, womanhood, and manhood. These concepts were key components of civilized morality. The reproductive act, in its proper setting, marriage, was central to the fate of these ideals and values. The venereal diseases, because they were transmitted in this most sacred of acts and because they were so closely associated with prostitution and illicit sexuality, blighted and corrupted the meaning of those ideals and the moral system they represented. The idea of marriage and particularly of the middle-class married woman, stood at the focal point of these ideals, and it was the fate of the married woman that became a master symbol of the disastrous consequences of venereal disease, its transmitters—profligate men—and its source—prostitution.

Physicians argued, albeit with little hard evidence, that venereal disease was responsible for most of the sterility in marriages that many middle-class Americans were finding so alarming. When President Roosevelt introduced the phrase "race suicide" into the public parlance (in reference to the fact that the birthrate of patrician Anglo-Saxon Americans was declining), it was widely assumed that he was referring to the result of voluntary birth control.[42] Physicians disagreed and argued instead that barren marriages, and what Prince Morrow called "one child sterility," were rather the result of the physiological effects of gonorrheal infection in either the husband or, more often, the wife.[43] One physician, writing in 1910, argued that prior to 1850, just 2 percent of "our native born white women" were sterile, whereas by 1900 the ratio had increased to one in five. Venereal disease, he asserted, was behind this disconcerting increase. Other physicians presented figures purporting to show that from 20 to 75 percent of childless marriages were the result of venereal disease-induced sterility.[44] It requires only a sympathetic sensibility to appreciate the emotional impact of such figures on an age and culture in which parenthood and especially motherhood were envisioned as almost sacred roles.

Physicians also pointed to an alarming connection between venereal disease and divorce, namely, the instances in which marriages collapsed after the wife was infected with venereal disease by her husband, who had contracted it from a prostitute. Prince Morrow bemoaned these calamities in his *Social Diseases and Marriage* and, as president of the American Society of Sanitary and Moral Prophylaxis, continued to warn against the "morbid irradiations [of venereal disease] when introduced into married life." "Notwithstanding the conspiracy of concealment between the husband and physician," he asserted, "women often learn the name and nature of their trouble, which not infrequently leads to the breaking-up of the family. The number of applications for divorce from this cause, especially in the middle and upper classes of society is much larger than is commonly supposed. In divorce proceedings, the cause of action usually appears under some non-compromising name, such as 'cruelty,' 'non-support,' 'desertion,' while the true cause is never made public."[45] The same argument, put forth in 1910 by a prominent physician in the widely circulated *Pearson's Magazine*, simply read: "Divorce increasing? Of course; cannot you all see why? Divorce increases in direct ratio to the increase in venereal diseases. We cannot stop the effect until we stop the cause."[46] Here prostitution, venereal disease, and divorce seemed locked in a vicious triangle. The belief that prostitution was the main source of venereal disease, along with the belief that a substantial percentage of the men frequenting prostitutes were married (a fact that most investigations of prostitution regretfully verified), made the connection among prostitution, venereal disease, and divorce a logical, if not irrefutable, proposition.

Another serious result of venereal contagion, related to the issues of sterility and divorce, involved women, invariably depicted as innocent wives, constrained to undergo serious gynecological surgery after being infected with gonorrhea by their husbands. At a meeting of the American Gynecological Society in 1879, the eminent German physician Emil Noeggerath proposed to his American audience that most serious diseases of the female reproductive organs were related to gonorrheal infection. At the time, American physicians were not willing to accept the implications of such a theory.[47] By the opening decades of the twentieth century, however, many of them conceded Noeggerath's case.

Prince Morrow, not known for the flippancy of his remarks, asserted in 1904 that "there is more venereal disease among virtuous wives than among professional prostitutes in this country," a proposition that, although questionable in a purely statistical sense, nonetheless pointed to a most distressing problem.[48] Indeed, numerous physicians argued that gonorrheal infection by husbands stood in the shadows in between 10 and 75 percent of cases of women requiring major gynecological surgery (including hysterectomies or removal of the fallopian tubes because of acute salpingitis).[49] Katharine Houghton Hepburn (mother of the actress), a Hartford, Connecticut, suffragist active in antiprostitution activities in that city, wrote in 1910 that "Seventy-five per cent of all operations peculiar to women are necessary because the husband has infected the wife with one of the diseases which are spread through all ranks of society by means of the social evil."[50] This matter had an emotional as well as a medical impact, for what was at stake was the very sanctity of marriage. "What more distressing picture can be portrayed," asked one physician, "than that of a young wife of but a few weeks, one who, in her youthful innocence of venery and its subsequent possibilities, is looking forward to a future containing all the blessings of married life, being forced to consult her physician, who finds in her a new victim of the insatiable appetite of the venereal spectre."[51]

This was a most serious situation in itself, and was treated as such, but it was also an indication of another less readily verifiable but equally serious problem: the existence of a secret collusion between physicians and male patients, either husbands or prospective husbands, which resulted in unsuspecting women being infected with venereal disease.[52] The "medical secret," as this was called, operated in either of two ways: a physician might treat a male patient for venereal disease without insisting that the patient inform his wife or fiancée; or, if the wife should subsequently be infected and seek medical aid, the physician might attempt to treat her without her learning of the nature or the source of her disease. It is next to impossible to calculate how pervasive was the practice of the "medical secret" within the profession, short of examining the records or the diaries of thousands of general practitioners and specialists. One point, however, merits notice here. The "medical secret," when it was operative, was deeply entangled in the psychology of male power and loyalty, and recent studies have shown that a similar situation prevailed in other areas of medical diagnosis, therapy, and ethics.[53] But whatever the actual extent of this complicity between physician and patient, the medical profession's concern for venereal disease-related surgery for women speaks for itself and for the mental and physical suffering inflicted on untold numbers of women.

The situation was not, however, one of unrelieved gloom, and many physicians pointed to several ways of avoiding these marital disasters. Almost all physicians concerned with the consequences of prostitution and venereal disease felt that some kind of a national or local program of sex hygiene education—especially for adolescents—was an immediate desideratum. The main emphasis of these programs was not, however, on prophylactic techniques—the use of condoms, for example—but rather on the practice of sexual continence for males, or what was often referred to as the single standard of morals. Much of this educational propaganda was aimed at the doctrine of "male sexual necessity," the traditional belief that sexual intercourse was necessary for male physical and psychological health.[54] Social hygienists argued that this belief had no medical basis, that it was one of the root causes of prostitution, that it was the foundation of the double standard of morals, and that it resulted in the spread of venereal disease. Some physicians in the early decades of the century, however, continued to support the doctrine of male necessity or at least to express misgivings about the gospel of continence. One physician, for instance, remarked: "Now, if men could be continent or chaste without women they would not need to marry. It may be inquired if any officer of this model society [the Philadelphia Society for the Study and Prevention of Social Diseases] has not found it more comfortable to cohabit with a wife than to live in absolute chastity as a celibate."[55] To counterbalance this kind of thinking, other social hygienists and physicians loudly proclaimed that sexual continence was absolutely compatible with perfect health.[56]

The repressive nature of the gospel of continence is obvious. So too is the emphasis on male sexuality to the almost total exclusion of female sexuality. And the phrase "sex-hygiene education" is somewhat misleading, because what was advocated was not an open knowledge of sexuality and sexual behavior but rather an enlightened indoctrination in proper and safe sex roles. But, given the belief that prostitution, via the uncontrolled male sex drive, was the main source of venereal infection, the idea of male continence, notwithstanding the psychological problems that can be seen in it today, seemed a logical solution to a serious problem.

Other physicians, particularly those allied with the public health movement, pointed to two other ways to avoid or check the ravages of prostitution and venereal disease: the mandatory reporting of cases of venereal disease, and legislation making an examination for venereal disease a prerequisite for marriage. Although in the nineteenth century numerous states enacted legislation mandating the reporting of cases of various communicable and infectious diseases, venereal disease had not come under the purview of such legislation.[57] Throughout the first decade of the twentieth century, however, more and more physicians argued that compulsory reporting was as necessary for venereal disease as for any other disease. Some physicians were quick to voice their opposition, usually on the grounds that reporting venereal disease would violate the confidentiality of the doctor-patient relationship (which was especially important given the social taboo on venereal disease), that reporting was unworkable because many doctors would refuse, and that many individuals would not seek a physician's aid and might have recourse instead to a quack if they knew that their malady would be reported to public health authorities.[58]

The forces that supported the reporting of venereal disease were, however, clearly dominant.[59] There was, to be sure, disagreement about exactly how such a system should work—for instance, whether cases should be reported by full name or, instead, by a numbered code. But reporting by one method or another was, by the teens, clearly the trend of the future. By 1922 all forty-eight states had enacted some kind of legislation requiring the reporting of venereal disease.[60]

The proposal that freedom from venereal disease be a state-enforced prerequisite for marriage was also widely supported by physicians and public health authorities as a way to safeguard marriage and the family from some of the consequences of prostitution and venereal disease. As with the issue of reporting venereal disease cases, there was some opposition. Prince Morrow, curiously enough, felt that such a measure would not work. "So far as the woman is concerned such examination is entirely unnecessary," he asserted, "as women almost never introduce these infections into marriage; besides, many sensitive, refined women would rather forego marriage than be subjected to a physical examination which they would regard as an outrage upon their modesty, and an indignity to their persons."[61] Other physicians articulated reservations similar to Morrow's, but by the teens, when fairly accurate serological tests for syphilis were available, the medical profession in general was favorable to what one physician termed the "guarantee of safety in the marriage contract."[62]

In 1910, Evangeline Young, a Boston physician, put the matter in clear and certain terms: "The young woman should know the actual conditions in society. . . . It is a crime to marry a clean woman to a diseased man, for her to find out when it is too late that she is sharing the disease of the women of the street; that almost to a certainty she will become sterile, or an invalid, or suffer death itself, an innocent victim to the double standard of morals. At the very least, she should have a choice in the matter." Laws requiring a premarriage examination, in addition to "educating young women to realize the dangers of marrying young men who cannot meet these requirements," would also serve "as a warning to the young men, who will realize as in no other way that venereal disease will disqualify him for honorable marriage."[63] Support for mandatory examinations grew steadily in the following years. Washington passed such legislation in 1909 and Wisconsin in 1913, and by 1921 twenty states had enacted statutes of various kinds declaring freedom from venereal disease a prerequisite for marriage.[64] Sometimes the efforts of physicians and public health authorities to promote these laws received the support of local eugenics groups, which saw such provisions as "eugenical marriage laws." But actually the two movements were quite distinct in orientation and objective; as an authority on the eugenics movement has succinctly observed, "eugenics was concerned with genes, not germs."[65]

One characteristic of many of the early laws requiring premarriage examinations merits special notice: the stipulation that only the prospective husband, not the wife, demonstrate freedom from infection.[66] Though there may have been a medical rationale for this rather peculiar exemption, what seems to have been equally at work was a recrudescence of the Victorian penchant for envisioning women as suffering victims. This was a dominant theme in antiprostitution in general; it was especially visible when the focus was on venereal disease, because it was always an innocent bride or wife who suffered from a male's contaminating association with a prostitute. There was hardly a single reference in the medical literature on prostitution and venereal disease to an innocent husband being infected by his wife.

This point is interesting for the illumination it sheds on the medical profession's perception of women, but it is also important to note that the depiction of brides and wives as innocent victims of venereal infection ran counter to the logic of a key component of antiprostitution: the belief in widespread clandestine prostitution. Because "clandestine prostitution" referred to such a broad range of female sexual activity, there were potentially thousands of women in America in 1915 who were involved in clandestine sexual behavior and were, therefore, possibly infected with venereal disease if and when they married. Thus, according to a basic assumption of antiprostitution and to the reasoning used to support premarriage exams, women should have been covered in the legislation requiring such exams. This situation stands in curious tension with the willingness of medical and nonmedical groups and individuals to support legislation requiring prenuptial examinations only for males. Much of the explanation for this inconsistency lies in the powerful cultural commitment to the idea that, as Morrow put it, "men are the responsible authors of these social crimes—women the victims," and to the vision of married and marriageable women as pure and ethereal mothers, wives, and helpmates who could never transmit the most morally reprehensible diseases into the fundamental relationship of family life.[67]

The advocacy of premarriage examinations is thus a complex matter for interpretation. For, on the one hand, the belief in the efficacy of such exams was forward-looking and educational; as Evangeline Young pointed out, it encouraged young women to "know the actual conditions in society," to be conscious of and exercise some control over an important aspect of their lives. On the other hand, the argument behind the early premarriage exams, in emphasizing only the role of the male in spreading venereal disease, depicted women in the orthodox nineteenth-century manner: as passive victims. This is not to say that women did not suffer under the moral, sexual, and medical conventions of the society in which they lived. They did. And it would be similarly inaccurate to argue that women (excepting prostitutes) were as central to the spread of venereal disease in the early years of the twentieth century as were men, although there is much more work to be done on this subject. But to insist that women could not spread venereal disease simply because they were women embodied an attitude that, even by 1915, was becoming increasingly absurd.

The mandatory reporting of venereal disease and the premarriage exam, topics of sharp disagreement in the progressive era, are now established practices. Another heatedly debated issue pertaining to the control of venereal disease, however, is only vaguely remembered today. This was the question whether the spread of venereal disease could be most effectively and efficiently controlled by the medical inspection and regulation of segregated prostitution districts. Such regulation was the subject of great controversy in both England and America in the nineteenth century, and it is sometimes assumed that the conflict of opinion substantially died out by the end of the century. In part it did. In England the Contagious Diseases Acts (which instituted medical inspection of prostitutes in certain cities) were eventually repealed, and in the United States, after the demise of the 1870 St. Louis experiment in medical inspection, there were only sporadic attempts to repeat it.[68] But on an intellectual and emotional level, the medical regulation of prostitution remained well into the twentieth century an issue which those concerned about prostitution and venereal disease felt constrained to address. Indeed, one of the achievements of antiprostitution in the progressive era was the final resolution of this question.

The controversy stemmed from the medical profession's belief that prostitution was the main source of venereal disease. Given this assumption, there was a certain logic to medical inspection: if prostitution was the principal agent in the spread of venereal disease, one could propose that controlling that agent was a practical objective. Many voices, however, were raised in opposition to this way of thinking, and the cacophonous debate continued throughout the progressive years. It was an exceedingly complicated controversy, and many participants, both physicians and laymen, approached it from points of view that can only be described as perversely idiosyncratic. Then, too, there were some physicians who framed their arguments in such careful wording that it is impossible to place them on one side or the other. Nevertheless, two distinctly opposing positions can be discerned.

Those who supported the medical control of prostitution were usually called regulationists. The regulationists, most of whom were male physicians, argued that the only way to curb the ravages of venereal disease was to confine the practice of prostitution to a certain section of a city (this was already the existing situation in most cities) and to subject it to rigorous medical supervision.[69] The regulationists insisted that the medical profession take a strictly pragmatic attitude toward the problem of prostitution and venereal disease. "As far as the prevention of disease is concerned," one physician wrote, "the physician should be the chaperon of the house of ill fame."[70] Supporters of regulation, conceding that no system could completely control the spread of venereal disease, nonetheless maintained that in American cities where regulation was in de facto operation—in Cincinnati, for example—the spread of venereal disease had been curtailed.[71]

The regulationists allowed that earlier European experiments in medical inspection had not proven very effective but argued that the fault lay not in the concept of regulation itself but in the primitive medical knowledge that prevailed in the nineteenth century. The ever-increasing progress in the diagnosis and treatment of venereal diseases, the regulationists argued, would constantly improve the effectiveness of a system of medical inspection. This view found impressive endorsement in 1916 by Albert Neisser, the German researcher who had first identified the gonococcus in 1879.[72] Many regulationists also pointed to programs in European cities and in the U.S. military as examples of how medical inspection worked to control venereal disease.[73] The regulationists also held that the medical inspection of prostitutes would help to prevent prostitution from spreading throughout the urban community, and, as prostitution would no longer be illegal, the widespread network of corruption involving police and public officials would disappear. In fact, under most proposed systems of medical inspection, implementation would be carried out by professional and disinterested public health officials, rather than the police.[74]

Opposition to the regulation of prostitution came from a broad and disparate collection of groups, interests, and individuals.[75] The Women's Christian Temperance Union and the purity groups held to the antiregulation position they had espoused since the latter decades of the nineteenth century. The social hygiene forces—most notably the American Society of Sanitary and Moral Prophylaxis and later the American Social Hygiene Association—also opposed a system of regulation.[76] So did numerous physicians, both male and female.[77] The vice commission reports and the white-slave narratives declared against regulation in the strongest language, even though these documents were quite different in other respects.[78] Feminists were appalled at the idea of regulation, and local women's clubs and groups also took a rigorous stand against it. Jane Addams, the muckraking journalist George Kibbe Turner, and social worker Maude E. Miner lent their voices to the opposition.[79] Theodore Roosevelt, who had had some experience in dealing with prostitution as police commissioner of New York City, wrote, in characteristic style, that "there should be no toleration of any 'tenderloin' or 'red light' district, and that above all there should be the most relentless war on commercialized vice." In 1912 the *American City*, in an editorial entitled "Shall Chicago Legalize Hell?" answered a resounding "no" to regulation. The following year, in a consideration of the issue of regulation, the *Independent* declared that "Mormon Polygamy is better."[80]

The antiregulationists agreed with the regulationists that prostitution was the source of venereal disease.[81] They argued, however, that the remedy was, not the regulation of prostitution, but rather its repression. The antiregulationists argued that although a system of regulation might control prostitution, it would also centralize and advertise it. In addition, a segregated district would invariably become a magnet for all kinds of criminal elements and could only foster a disrespect for law and order. Even more importantly, the medical inspection of prostitutes would not accomplish its object: the control of venereal disease. Systems of medical inspection had not reduced the incidence of venereal disease in the past and would not do so in the future, not because of any medical technique that was or was not used, but because of a basic flaw in the philosophy of regulation itself, namely, that only the prostitute would be treated, and the "masculine spreader of disease" (in Prince Morrow's words) would be ignored.[82] What would be the good, antiregulationists asked, of a medical document certifying a prostitute's freedom from venereal disease, renewed weekly, when she might be infected by a patron immediately after her examination? Indeed, the false sense of security that such an official certificate would promote would actually lead to an increase in the incidence of venereal disease.[83]

The antiregulationists also insisted that the military example used by the regulationists was inappropriate, because a fluid and mobile group of prostitutes could not be controlled like a military post.[84] In addition, the antiregulationists, especially the feminists and women among their number, warned that any system of regulation and inspection could potentially abuse the rights and personal freedom of many women, prostitute and nonprostitute alike. Lastly, antiregulationist physicians contended that any complicity with a system of medical inspection could only discredit and disgrace the medical profession. Howard Kelly of Johns Hopkins, in a talk given at a 1904 meeting of the American Medical Association, addressed exactly this point. "Consider for a moment, gentlemen," he warned, "what effect the legalization of vice will have on the medical profession. The necessity for examining women licensed to carry on their business will create in our midst a vile and odious specialty, akin and closely allied to the professional abortionist, degrading to our profession and justly bringing it into contempt by making it thus pander to vice. . . . What a lowering of our standards when we come to that!"[85]

Until 1914, the antiregulation position was for the most part diffuse and unintegrated, lacking a central, all-encompassing statement of purpose and philosophy. In that year, however, this problem was remedied by the publication of Abraham Flexner's *Prostitution in Europe*. Indeed, Flexner's book gave the antiregulationist position an authority never to be seriously challenged.

Flexner's career and achievements constitute one of the more impressive twentieth-century American biographies. The son of German-Jewish immigrants, Flexner grew up in Louisville, Kentucky, and graduated from Johns Hopkins University in 1886. He gained national prominence in 1910 with the publication of his *Medical Education in the United States*, the result of an investigation of medical schools conducted under the auspices of the Carnegie Foundation for the Advancement of Teaching. Flexner's detailed description of the appalling state of medical instruction was so compelling, and so damning, that it forced many American "medical schools" out of existence. In 1912, just as he was completing a study of medical education in Europe, Flexner was asked by John D. Rockefeller, Jr., who just recently had financed the founding of the Bureau of Social Hygiene, to conduct an investigation of prostitution in Europe. The bureau had recently commissioned its first study of prostitution, George Jackson Kneeland's *Commercialized Prostitution in New York City*, and, as Flexner later in life recalled, "there were those who believed that America had much to learn from European experience." Flexner accepted the assignment and spent the next two years surveying the sexual underworld of twenty-eight cities in the British Isles, the Continent, and Scandinavia.[86]

Flexner approached his task with characteristic thoroughness. He toured the brothels, bordellos, and shady haunts of the European cities (Theodore Dreiser accompanied him in Paris); conversed with prostitutes, police, and public officials; and watched hundreds of women being examined for venereal disease in those cities where regulation existed. Flexner recounted all of these experiences, including a brief but frank discussion of homosexual prostitution, in sober and clear prose. In addition to his own investigations, he used and indeed seems to have mastered the forbidding body of German, French, and British scholarship on prostitution, including the bewildering and constantly proliferating statistical material on the subject. But *Prostitution in Europe* was much more than a collection of copious citations. It was the high-water mark in the flood tide of progressive fact-finding investigations, even though it was, at least nominally, about Europe.

Its title was, however, somewhat imprecise. For what Flexner set out to investigate, and what he wrote of, was not prostitution in Europe but the various European policies concerning prostitution. It is this overarching emphasis which makes *Prostitution in Europe* a central document in the American controversy over medical inspection. Before leaving for Europe, Flexner remembered some years later, he talked with physicians and social workers who indicated that "on the Continent at least, prostitution was so regulated that the dangers to health were minimized." His experience in Europe did not bear out this claim. In fact, he found that on matters of European regulation, Americans were "completely ignorant."[87]

The major thrust of Flexner's argument was that European systems of medical examination of prostitutes were worthless. He argued that those who held up European systems as models for the United States were in error and that, indeed, the regulation of prostitution did not help maintain public order or control the spread of venereal disease. He was particularly adamant on the latter point. In many of the cities he visited, the prostitutes who were enrolled on the official rosters were compelled to appear at municipal centers, sometimes the police headquarters, where they were examined for venereal infection. This had been the prevailing situation in numerous Continental cities for several decades, and regulationists argued that it effectively controlled venereal contagion. Flexner asserted that this claim was nonsensical. His arguments, all of which were accompanied with appropriate statistical evidence, were many. The regulated prostitutes comprised only a small fraction—perhaps just one-quarter—of the total number of professional and clandestine prostitutes in any city. The actual medical inspection was usually hurried and careless and seldom included microscopic examinations of smears. Accordingly, syphilis in its most infectious forms was usually detected, but chronic gonorrhea was not. Also, experienced prostitutes were able to disguise certain kinds of symptoms of infection and thus escape detection. "The clinical method," Flexner argued, "is utterly incompetent to detect any considerable portion of infectious disease." In fact, he produced figures showing that regulation, by making prostitution seem "safe," actually led to an increase in venereal disease.[88]

Flexner presented evidence showing that cities in which prostitution was not regulated had a lower rate of venereal infection than did regulated cities. European authorities, he reported, were finally understanding this variation, for the number of regulated cities was steadily declining.

Flexner admitted that prostitution was "by far the main factor in the spread of venereal disease," but he argued that the proper remedy was the rational and intelligent repression of prostitution and the provision of clinical treatment for all venereal sufferers, not just prostitutes.[89]

Flexner's study offered the most thorough understanding of European dealings with prostitution available to Americans in the progressive years. But *Prostitution in Europe*, despite its title, was also a book about the United States. For just as Tocqueville analyzed democracy in America with one eye looking back to Europe, Flexner studied prostitution in Europe with one eye focused on his native land. He produced not only a scholarly and informative study but also a treatise on comparative morality. The driving force of *Prostitution in Europe* was a commitment to the belief that America must remain above the moral and political corruption that European systems of regulation both symbolized and embodied. Flexner devoted an entire chapter, "The Real Inwardness of Regulation," to showing that the regulation of prostitution in Europe was a product of social and political conservatism, class distinctions, militarist values, and the vested interests of corrupt police systems.[90] The message to antiprostitution forces in the United States was clear: there was nothing in Europe for a young and virtuous democratic nation to emulate.

What emerges in *Prostitution in Europe* is a familiar picture: a democratic and optimistic American exploring the dark and twisted streets of thousand-year-old European cities—ancient or medieval cities burdened with a history of corruption, superstition, and moral compromise and chained to the atavistic social arrangements and attitudes of a dark and repressive past. Considering the purpose of his journey, Flexner cannot be said to have been an innocent abroad, but, nonetheless, the clash between American innocence and European corruption is the sotto voce theme of his book. European regulation of prostitution was to Flexner what European imperialism was to Woodrow Wilson: an irrational expression of decadent European culture, with which American civilization must have no alliance.[91]

Flexner's work touched a nerve in the United States: it was reviewed and synopsized widely and at length and was seen as a document just as relevant and important to American concern with prostitution as were the vice commission reports, which dealt with the subject on native grounds. Indeed, *Prostitution in Europe* was the last major prewar expression of antiprostitution and seemed to be the definitive resolution to the controversy over regulation.[92]

Because regulationists and antiregulationists often used the same studies and statistics to support their opposite conclusions, the controversy over regulation might at first appear to be only a matter of different interpretations of the same facts. This was not, however, the case, for the two positions were based on fundamentally different social and moral assumptions. The regulationists clearly did not "approve" of prostitution, but they saw prostitution and venereal disease as serious problems that, although insoluble in any total sense, could be rationally and scientifically *managed*. They were aware that the solution they advocated was at profound variance with some of the dominant beliefs of their age, but they felt that the seriousness of the problem made such an accommodation imperative.

There is a quiet irony here. In effect, the regulationists were proposing to deal with prostitution and venereal disease in a fashion well within the parameters of the liberal gradualism that so permeated the progressive political outlook in general. The key goal of the regulationists' program of medical inspection was the imposition of order, stability, control, and predictability on a potential source of irrationality and conflict. Many of the antiregulationists supported this approach when applied to other social problems. For instance, progressive reformers did not often propose that the solution to the problem of poverty was the annihilation of the economic order itself. Quite the contrary, it was the dominant progressive approach that social and economic problems could be gradually controlled and rationalized. Yet many who endorsed this basically ameliorist approach concerning a broad range of social issues— Theodore Roosevelt, for instance—did not apply it to the problem of prostitution but instead called for a total solution: absolute repression and annihilation.

Why such a position? An immediate explanation for the antiregulationists' position lies in the fact that the issues of prostitution and venereal disease, because of their association with illicit sexuality, were so anxiety producing that a "conventional" or "rational" response was simply impossible. But there were deeper and more specific reasons. The antiregulationists saw quite clearly that the idea of the medical inspection of prostitutes, of setting apart a group of women for the sole purpose of sexual service, outrageously violated the vision of the ideal woman as reserved, reticent, and rather asexual. The very thought of lines of outcast women waiting their turn to be probed, inspected, and graded as so many heads of cattle, like the thought of a sanitary, antiseptic, efficiently run, and openly administered medical bureaucracy that would certify certain women as medically safe for sexual use, was a specter to which the antiregulationists could respond only with shock and moral indignation.

But even more fundamentally, the antiregulationists deplored the medical inspection of prostitutes because it would publicly contravene the basic canons of civilized morality, especially those decreeing that sex was meant to serve only the purposes of reproduction, that all sexual activity must take place within the context of marriage, and that male continence prior to marriage was the truest sign of manhood.[93] Abraham Flexner commented, "Regulation implies the absence of any expectation of male self-restraint; it is society's tacit assent to laxity." The feminist Anna Garlin Spencer went even further. "Do we accept monogamic marriage as the only right and wise arrangement for the union of the sexes?" she asked. If so, "then we can no longer tolerate the brothel, with all its vulgar concerns turned over to the police force, while the rest of us shut our eyes." Regulation, she went on, would be "a tacit admission that we do not mean what we say by the marriage laws."[94]

The antiregulationists clearly understood that at the heart of the regulationists' position was the assumption that prostitution was "necessary" —that it was a phenomenon which, no matter how onerous, seemed to be deeply rooted in biological reality and the very structure of social and moral relationships. The medical examination of prostitutes would be a public and symbolic declaration that this assumption was correct. Therefore, those who were fully committed to the ideals of civilized morality had to oppose regulation, for to do otherwise would be tantamount to an admission that civilized morality was not working.

By 1914, however, antiregulation was more than an affirmation of a moral system; it was an affirmation of a moral system in the process of collapse. There was an additional irony here. By 1914 the segregated prostitution districts, which would have been a key component of most systems of medical inspection, were also in a state of decline. This decline was attributable in part to the increase of sexual activity unrelated to prostitution, which was one of the results of the demise of civilized morality. Thus, the crisis in civilized morality, while on the one hand providing much of the fuel for antiregulation, was on the other hand rendering it, willy-nilly, a superfluous position.

This analysis, it should be emphasized, is intended only to put the antiregulationist position in its complete cultural context; it does not invalidate the humanitarian concerns of the antiregulationists. To the contrary: many of the concerns of the opponents of regulation—most importantly their recognition that, as dehumanizing as prostitution was, an official complicity in that dehumanization could only be worse—still have relevance and meaning today.

In the postpenicillin era, much of the progressive concern about venereal disease might at first seem exotic and strangely removed from contemporary experience. Surely we would wince today to hear a physician say, as one did in 1910: "The cough spray of a syphilitic may be more dangerous than the discharge of a gun into a person's face." Today most cases of both syphilis and gonorrhea can be completely cured with a single massive dose of penicillin, and this simple fact has profoundly influenced the general view of venereal disease.[95]

In 1900 the death rate for syphilis was 13 per 100,000; in 1970 it stood at .03 per 100,000.[96] Sir Alexander Fleming's discovery of penicillin was mainly responsible for this extraordinary change, but it has created a problem of historical interpretation. Venereal disease is still a matter of concern, but because of the existence of penicillin and other antibiotics, the problem is no longer primarily one of curing the disease but rather one of reaching the infected person. Physicians in the pre-penicillin era, and particularly in the early decades of the twentieth century, were working under very different circumstances. The fact of this historical divide must be kept in mind in evaluating their performance. The penicillin era is about the length of the atomic age; in contrast, physicians in the progressive years were working at the end of a period that stretched back at least as far as the Renaissance.

The differences between the two eras appear quite clearly. There was not, for all practical purposes, any completely effective cure for syphilis and gonorrhea in the early twentieth century. Salvarsan and the arsphenamines raised hope in this direction (regarding syphilis), but treatment with Salvarsan was an expensive and lengthy procedure. Most could not afford it, and those who could often did not go through with the whole program. During World War I, rigidly enforced programs of prophylaxis were surprisingly effective, but it was widely recognized that such a policy could not work with a civilian population.

This lack of an effective cure had many effects. It can account in part for two of the policies advocated to halt the spread of venereal disease: sexual continence and the repression of prostitution. Notwithstanding the fact that they were related to issues other than venereal disease, they had a certain logic as a prophylactic against venereal disease in the pre-penicillin age. The absence of a completely effective cure also made prostitution much more than morally obnoxious: it was, in fact, a locus of a disease for which there was no sure cure. This factor, in turn, points to another difference between the progressive concern over prostitution and venereal disease and our own. Now, although prostitution is still seen by many as morally reprehensible, it is seldom seen as a serious health problem—largely because of the existence of penicillin.[97]

As striking as these differences are, they ought not to obscure the similarities and common problems regarding venereal disease that span the first three-quarters of this century. Although penicillin is a very effective cure for venereal disease, many of the problems surrounding the control of venereal disease that plagued progressive-era physicians persist today. Some physicians in the progressive years understood an important component of this problem: the rather unique nature of venereal disease. Whereas other infectious and communicable diseases were related to such agents as mosquitoes and impure water sources, or such habits as spitting, venereal disease was connected with something of far greater complexity: human sexual behavior. The streets might be swept, the common drinking cup abolished, spitting educated out of existence, and the pools of stagnant water irrigated away, but the sex instinct, as many psychologists were coming to understand, was not susceptible to such rational approaches. Physicians like Prince Morrow argued that the irrational aspects of sexual behavior might be counterbalanced by education and sexual continence. In this attitude he exhibited the general nineteenth-century belief in reason and education, but in his understanding that individuals might irrationally *choose* to expose themselves to venereal disease, he pointed to a basic conundrum of venereal disease control.[98] And, just as individuals might choose to take a chance on contracting venereal disease, they might also, if infected, choose to stay away from a physician because of the shame associated with illicit sex and venereal disease. For the same reasons, a physician might not report a case of venereal disease under his care. These factors were important in the progressive years, and they still are today.

These considerations should help to put the progressive effort to deal with prostitution and venereal disease in a contemporary and sympathetic perspective. Progressive physicians certainly threw a beam of light on what had been a dark corner of medicine and social policy, and they made an important start in framing a rational approach to venereal disease control. But their attempt was only partially successful, both because of the limitations of their own cultural commitments and, even more importantly, because of the social and cultural dynamics of venereal disease. Unfortunately, the latter still plague us today.

THE SOCIAL EVIL IN

THE CITY: THE CHICAGO VICE

COMMISSION REPORT

[*The Chicago Vice*] *commission made, in fact, a very valuable report . . . but it had determined beforehand the limitations and character of its investigation and results, and excluded the possibility of a new determination of behavior norms in this field.*

A method of investigation which seeks to justify and enforce any given norm of behavior ignores the fact that a social evolution is going on in which not only activities are changing but the norms which regulate the activities are also changing. Traditions and customs, definitions of the situation, morality, and religion are undergoing an evolution, and a society going on the assumption that a certain norm is valid and that whatever does not comply with it is abnormal finds itself helpless when it realizes that this norm has lost social significance and some other norm has appeared in its place.

William I. Thomas, *The Unadjusted Girl* (1923)

American cities were widely and historically known for their propensity to burst forth into frantic bouts of self-congratulatory "boosterism" many years before Sinclair Lewis gave the word such vivid meaning in *Babbitt*. American city pride in the nineteenth century ranged in scope and power from the pathetic hucksterings of struggling midwestern towns to the lofty and stereoscopic urban vision of the "White City" at the 1893 Columbian Exposition in Chicago. Boosterism was an integral aspect of the growth of nineteenth-century American cities; it was a cultural mechanism through which urban dwellers could gain a sense of what their community was and the glorious future that awaited it; it was a means whereby private doubts or anxieties could be assuaged by public acts of affirmation; and it obviously filled the pocketbooks of certain persons and groups. By the end of the nineteenth century, boosterism had been institutionalized in associations such as the Chamber of Commerce and was a hallmark of the American urban middle class.

Strange it is, then, that at the end of the first decade of the twentieth century the major American cities, along with a good number of the smaller ones, should establish vice commissions to probe and publicize the nature and extent of prostitution and sexual immorality within the city limits.[1] In contrast to the booster tradition, which stressed the successes and promises of the urban community, the vice commission delineated the city's moral failings, the fact that it was not living up to the boosters' vision. The Chicago Vice Commission published its massive 400-page report, *The Social Evil in Chicago*, in 1911, beginning what might be termed a collective act of ritual humiliation by urban America.[2] Other cities followed Chicago's lead, so that by 1916 vice investigations had been undertaken in twenty-seven cities. Thus, when Graham Taylor, a member of the Chicago Vice Commission and a prominent social worker, stated that the proliferation of vice commissions represented a "great tidal movement," his metaphor, though hyperbolic, nevertheless captured the nature of this outburst of urban activity.[3]

The Social Evil in Chicago was the preeminent municipal vice commission report of the progressive years.[4] Although atypical by virtue of its thoroughness and wealth of detail, the Chicago report was, for that same reason, the one later vice commissions in other cities unanimously chose as a model. Sometimes this emulation bordered on the slavish; the 1913 Syracuse vice commission, for example, printed the motto of the Chicago commission on its cover. It is this stature which gives *The Social Evil in Chicago* a broader significance than its local origin and focus might otherwise dictate.[5]

The growth and development of Chicago from a small town on the mud banks of Lake Michigan to a great industrial metropolis was one of the most spectacular episodes in American urban history. In 1910, the year of the formation of the vice commission, the population of Chicago stood at just over two million, which made it the second largest city in the land. Only a half century earlier, in the year of Lincoln's election, it had ranked eighth. During those fifty years, as its population swelled twentyfold, Chicago became, as New York had been before and Los Angeles was to become, the preeminent American "shock city." The tone of the city was set in the stockyards and assembly-line slaughter houses of Swift and Armour, where the adaptation of nineteenth-century techniques of mass production to the mechanization of death was first perfected. To supply the labor for the industrial machine there poured into Chicago the great streams of immigrants who by 1900 stitched the city into a patchwork quilt of ethnic and racial communities. By the opening decade of the twentieth century, Chicago had achieved the status of master symbol for all the achievements and excesses of American urban civilization.[6]

Equal in reputation to any of the city's attractions, and of particular pertinence to a discussion of *The Social Evil in Chicago*, was the area of Chicago encompassed by the First Ward, which fronted Lake Michigan and stretched south from the Chicago River to Twenty-ninth Street and west to the south bank of the river and Wallace and Canal streets. The First Ward was, officially, the political and economic center of the city; here were the great wharves of the Port of Chicago, the main commercial and financial districts, and City Hall itself. But the ward's most spectacular attraction was the famous "Levee" district, the private fiefdom ruled by "Bathhouse" John Coughlin and Michael "Hinky Dink" Kenna, two of the most notorious and powerful doyens of the ward's extraordinarily corrupt political machine. The Levee was a Coney Island for the urban (male) id: along with an estimated two hundred brothels, it offered an untold number of barrelhouse saloons, gambling houses, peepshows, bucket shops, pawnshops, hop shops, voodoo doctors, and "low" dance halls. Here also, on South Dearborn Street, was the Everleigh Club, perhaps the most famous, expensive, and luxurious bordello in American history. As in the rest of Chicago, however, the contrast of economic class was glaring; within blocks of the Everleigh mansions were scores of bagnios, with prices as low as twenty-five cents.[7]

Each year the Levee produced the celebrated First Ward Ball, at which the demimondes of Chicago's sexual and political underworld met in open and unrestrained congregation in the Chicago Coliseum, much to the chagrin of other, more decorous, groups in the city. The houses of prostitution in the Levee were clearly prohibited by both state and municipal codes. But Chicago officials, like most of their counterparts across the nation, tended to let the district go undisturbed, partly because there seemed no way to check the steady demand for prostitution and partly because the money received from brothel owners and prostitutes in kickbacks for protection helped keep the political organizations of bosses like Coughlin and Kenna well in the black.[8]

Although Chicago produced some of the most notorious excesses of the industrial city, it also produced the most impressive attempts to understand such cities. Chicago became the location and stimulus for the great chapters in the history of the American social imagination written during the late nineteenth and early twentieth centuries: the work of Louis Sullivan, Frank Lloyd Wright, John Dewey, Jane Addams, Theodore Dreiser, and the members of the Chicago School of sociology. The experience of Chicago prompted all of these persons to search for new forms of art, thought, and architecture that would square with the new conditions of the urban industrial civilization that their home city so supremely embodied.[9]

The emergence of the Chicago School of sociology is of special importance to the background of the Chicago Vice Commission. The University of Chicago's Sociology Department, which dated from the founding of the university in 1892, was one of the main influences in guiding the discipline away from the armchair theorizing of earlier American sociology toward the examination of institutions, urbanization, and urban problems, to cite just the most important areas of work and innovation. Two members of the original department, William I. Thomas and Charles Henderson, were members of the Chicago Vice Commission. Henderson was a former minister with an interest in applied humanitarianism and the use of sociological techniques in social work. Thomas had begun graduate work at the university the year it opened and in 1907 published *Sex and Society*, a volume rich in the use of anthropological methodology, which would be a hallmark of his later and more famous work. This overlapping of personnel should not be overstressed, however, because neither Thomas nor Henderson played a major role in the actual work of the commission, and Thomas did not agree with many of its conclusions and recommendations. What is important, though, is the symbolic meaning of the association of the two groups, for they were, in the large sense, both attempting to build an understanding of the workings of urban society as it was encountered in Chicago.[10]

These, then, are the most relevant cultural landmarks for locating *The Social Evil in Chicago* at its particular point in Chicago's and the nation's development. If the progressive response to prostitution was one aspect of the general confrontation with the new conditions of urban society, then Chicago, by 1910, had become a microcosm for that confrontation. In a way it was only fitting that Chicago possessed the Levee, a vice district commensurate with its other achievements. The members of the vice commission hardly would have attested to such logic, but the massiveness of the report they produced did. It was, in fact, eminently logical that this city, of the twenty-seven that attempted the task, produced the most famous investigation of prostitution in the American city.

The impetus for the creation of a vice commission in Chicago came from religious organizations.[11] In late 1909, Gipsy Smith, an English-born and Salvation-Army-connected revivalist, led a parade of twelve thousand concerned citizens through the Twenty-second Street red-light district of the Levee to publicize the immorality of the city.[12] In early 1910 the Chicago Federation of Churches, under the leadership of Walter T. Sumner, dean of the prestigious Episcopal Cathedral of Saints Peter and Paul (located in the West Side Levee district), petitioned the mayor to create a commission to investigate the extent of prostitution in the city and to recommend measures to bring "relief from the frightful conditions which surround us." As Sumner recalled several years later, "Viciousness and lawlessness, coupled with the fact that four thousand men were rendered service every night, made the problem a most pressing one."[13]

Such a commission was indeed appointed by the mayor two months later. Sumner served as its chairman, and in July the commission retained the services of George Jackson Kneeland, who was to direct several other vice commission probes in the progressive years, to supervise the day-to-day operation of the investigation.[14] The inquiry was conducted during the next eight months, and the final report was delivered to the mayor in April 1911. The commission's total operating budget was eighteen thousand dollars: two municipal appropriations of five thousand dollars and eight thousand from private donations. The 400-page report was printed in an edition of fourteen thousand and distributed nationally by the commission.[15]

The Social Evil in Chicago comprised seven chapters, each devoted to a separate and specific aspect of prostitution in Chicago. Each was copiously documented, with dozens of detailed examples to buttress each description of actual conditions, statement of fact, or point of view. "The filing of documentary evidence to substantiate every statement open to challenge was a fixed policy of the investigation which was strictly adhered to throughout," wrote commission member Graham Taylor. The actual investigation and collection of data was done by seven "expert and trained investigators," both men and women, who at times "made the ways of the underworld their own," and whose written reports were checked and rechecked and occasionally "clinched by affidavits." The result of these procedures, and indeed their aim, was a "correct and unexaggerated idea of conditions." The Chicago report assiduously cultivated and promoted this atmosphere of professionalism, and it is this characteristic, which all the urban vice commissions shared, that most clearly distinguished *The Social Evil in Chicago* from the white-slave narratives.[16]

The subjects of the chapters immediately identify those aspects of the problem of prostitution the commission thought were the most important.[17] The commission was convinced that prostitution and alcohol were invariably connected: "Next to the house of prostitution itself," the commission stated, in a discussion of "The Social Evil and the Saloon," the most important element in prostitution was "the saloon, and the most important financial interest, next to the business of prostitution was the liquor interest. As a contributory influence to immorality and the business of prostitution there is no interest so dangerous and so powerful in the City of Chicago." Saloons were pernicious on four counts: they were places where experienced prostitutes congregated; they were conduits through which young women, usually starting out as waitresses, were lured by easy money to enter the life; they were occasions of vulgar dancing and the singing of "popular ragtime songs with indecent parodies"; and they took "abnormal" profits—180 percent on beer, 300 percent on liquor—on the alcohol sold in connection with prostitution. And at some points, in the commission's opinion, there was very little difference between saloons and brothels. "Instances have been found," the commission reported, "where prostitutes actually live in rooms over the saloon . . . in much the same way as inmates appear in the parlors of regular houses of prostitution. . . . Many saloons are actually houses of prostitution." One of the best ways to combat prostitution, the commission concluded, was "to absolutely divorce the sale of liquor from prostitution."[18]

The chapter entitled "The Social Evil and the Police" addressed what was widely felt to be an important aspect of the problem of prostitution, but it was the weakest in logic and analysis. The commission stated at the beginning of its report that it planned to refrain from any specific criticism of the Chicago police or other municipal officials.[19] It did not wish, it explained, to reduce the problem of prostitution to the problem of a corrupt or inefficient police force, an oversimplification that enjoyed wide currency during the progressive years.[20] Nevertheless, the material presented by the commission portrayed the Chicago police force as indifferent to the enforcement of the antiprostitution statutes and involved in a lucrative network of kickbacks, payola, and graft, although this involvement was not specifically documented.[21]

Actually, the commission's consideration of the problem of police and law enforcement contained a potentially valuable insight into the nature of prostitution, but its full meaning was never grasped. The commission urged that the police department's dereliction of duty be understood within the context of the "peculiar conditions . . . that exist in a city . . . the laws now on the statute books for the protection of society against the Social Evil," the commission explained, "were enacted by legislators, the majority of whom came from the country districts, and who expected them to regulate affairs in large cities as well as in country towns." This system, however, had not worked. "The laws prohibiting houses of ill-fame can be and are enforced in a small community. But the situation is more difficult in a city the size of Chicago. Here an individual may, if he chooses, live any life he pleases, so far as his personal habits are concerned, and no one be the wiser."[22]

This was tantamount to an admission of the impossibility of controlling certain kinds of private and personal behavior in an anonymous urban environment, or of enforcing civilized morality in the city's various "moral regions" (to use Robert Park's phrase). This realization might have led to a new consideration of the efficacy of laws attempting to suppress prostitution. In fact, it did not, and the commission chose instead simply to berate the citizens of Chicago for "the constant evasion of the problem," "their ignorance and indifference to the situation," and "their lack of united effort in demanding a change in the intolerable conditions as they now exist." As a solution to the problem of police inefficiency and public apathy, the commission proposed establishing a "morals commission" to oversee all the city's attempts to control prostitution. The commission did not judge there to be any manifest inconsistency between this recommendation and its own admission of the infeasibility of effectively monitoring sexual behavior in the urban environment.[23]

The commission collected a formidable body of data on Chicago prostitutes themselves, which was presented and discussed in a chapter titled "Sources of Supply." This information, based on a study of the records of 2,420 women, probed the relationship of prostitution to age, place of birth, education, employment, economic class, and family background.[24] In this chapter and in the one immediately following, on the need to protect children from the immoral influences of the urban environment, the commission made what must have been a shocking discovery: intimately connected with prostitution was a jungle of familial pathology. "In a large proportion of cases," Graham Taylor reported, "home conditions contributed to, if they did not cause, the downfall of daughters or wives." A list of sordid examples followed: "Intemperate or vicious parents, or brothers or sisters; deserted, separated, and divorced fathers and mothers; homes which forced upon the children, rather than protected them from, immorality; marriages that were sales into vice." Underlying most of these conditions, the commission believed, were aspects of the industrial economy that promoted family disintegration: unemployment, child labor, and women working in industry. The commission deplored these problems but never proposed how they might be remedied, settling instead for a strenuous, but largely empty, call for a moral regeneration of family control and authority.[25]

The final chapter of The Social Evil in Chicago, "The Social Evil and Its Medical Aspects," discussed the relationship between prostitution and venereal disease, a relationship that the commission put in clear terms at the beginning of the report: "Prostitution is pregnant with disease, a disease infecting not only the guilty, but contaminating the innocent wife and child . . . leaving in its wake sterility, insanity, paralysis, the blinded eyes of little babies, the twisted limbs of deformed children, degradation, physical rot and mental decay." The commission restated many of the ideas promulgated by societies such as the American Society of Sanitary and Moral Prophylaxis and in general called for an enlightened and publicized awareness of the dangers and extent of venereal disease.[26]

The Social Evil in Chicago concluded with eighty-five pages of appendixes, including texts of relevant state statutes, municipal ordinances, tables, and various exhibits. A naturalist of the human species would have been impressed, or depressed, according to temperament, with the variety and variation of prostitution in Chicago as the commission found it. It existed and thrived almost everywhere in Chicago, with a seemingly limitless capacity for adaptation. Given the scope of the problem, and the time limits of the investigation, the commission produced an imposing piece of work. Indeed, *The Social Evil in Chicago* quickly became the authoritative statement of antiprostitution. It was also one of the most revealing documents that antiprostitution produced.

The Social Evil in Chicago is on first impression a rather faceless document. One does not recognize very many—if any—of the names of the members of the commission listed on the first page. Nor, more importantly, can one in reading the report sense the presence of an increasingly familiar human personality, as was the case, for instance, with William Sanger's 1858 investigation of prostitution. The Chicago report was, in this respect, fundamentally different from the white-slave tracts, wherein the emotional and personal component was worn, so to speak, on the sleeve. *The Social Evil in Chicago* also stands in sharp contrast to another American tradition of social investigation—one might mention the efforts of Henry Demarest Lloyd, Upton Sinclair, and Lincoln Steffens—which utilized "facts" and "research" but presented this information within the framework of the individual writer's very present and engaged moral vision. The Chicago report was entirely different; in it we confront the anonymous voice of a *commission*, a voice that presents itself as somehow more than the sum of the wisdom of each individual member, somehow more "objective" and of greater scope and authority than any single human intelligence—that of a muckraking journalist, say—could claim to possess.[27]

The voice of *The Social Evil in Chicago* was, in effect, the voice of the twenty-nine persons who constituted the vice commission. The report emphasized that the commission was a representative group, and several years after the report was issued, the chairman, Walter Sumner, stressed the same point: "A more representative body of men and women could not be found in the City of Chicago," he asserted. "I am giving to you, therefore, not my own opinion, but the opinions of a Commission whose

judgment should have weight. . . . We believe such harmonious una-
nimity on the part of men and women representing so many diversified
callings in life, and so many groups of society, must be a fair indication of
the public mind and conscience of the citizens of Chicago." Such "harmonious unity," Sumner believed, gave *The Social Evil in Chicago* an
authority "it could not have possessed had there been a decided difference of opinion amongst its members with the possible presentation of a
minority report."[28]

A brief look at the composition of the Chicago Vice Commission,
however, reveals that it was not as representative as Sumner proclaimed.
Twenty-five of the twenty-nine individuals represented, essentially, five
major groups: organized religion (three Roman Catholic, two Jewish,
three Protestant); the legal profession (one U.S. district attorney, two
judges, one lawyer); the Chicago medical community (four physicians,
one social hygienist); academics (one college president, three professors);
and the Chicago business community (including the president of Sears
Roebuck). Two of the commissioners were women.[29]

One would expect these groups to be heavily represented in such a
major undertaking in Chicago. The same expectation prevails for the
organizations—such as the Chicago Law and Order League—which appeared before and gave testimony to various subcommittees of the commission.[30] Whether these groups made the commission "representative"
is another matter entirely. The commission was representative only in the
context of American pluralist ideology: it represented economic and political groups and viewpoints that were already established and culturally
sanctioned. The "harmonious unity" was in this sense hardly surprising,
and presentation of a minority report, though certainly remaining a possibility, was rendered highly unlikely by the homogeneous makeup of the
commission.[31]

The voice speaking in *The Social Evil in Chicago* was, then, the voice
of specific, identifiable, powerful, and established groups in Chicago.
There was, for instance, no representation on the commission of that
group in Chicago which might have been most knowledgeable about
prostitution in the city: the intimates of the Levee. *The Social Evil in
Chicago* was, thus, the official version of prostitution in Chicago in the
early twentieth century. This does not in any sense make it a less important source; it simply makes it a certain *kind* of source, a qualification
of no mean importance.

The central message of *The Social Evil in Chicago* was that prostitution
and sexual immorality in Chicago had been commercialized—indeed,
that prostitution was one of the city's most successful business enter-

prises. "The first truth," the report began, "is the fact that prostitution in this city is a *Commercialized Business* of large proportions with tremendous profits of more than Fifteen Million Dollars per year, controlled by men, not women."[32] It was widely believed during the progressive years that prostitution had once been managed and controlled by women, and the "discovery" that men had taken control seemed ominous.[33] Equally disturbing was the realization, based on the examination of account books seized as evidence in raids on brothels, that houses of prostitution were run in a most efficient and businesslike manner, with the bottom line of the balance sheet invariably in the black. There had always been, of course, the knowledge that prostitution involved economic exchange, but the *scope* of the economic activity surrounding prostitution markedly upset the commission.

The Social Evil in Chicago documented the commercialization of prostitution by providing the reader with numerous lists of financial data from various vice districts. A ledger from a South Side district of 119 houses, for instance, read:

Average excess profit of $1,000 per year to owner or lessor	$ 119,000
686 inmates of houses (from police lists) Weekly profit of $50 each, aggregate per annum	1,783,600
Keeper's profit from 686 inmates	1,783,600
143 flats (from police lists) Average excess profit of $600 per year to owner or lessor	85,800
277 inmates of flats (from police list) Weekly profit at $50 each, aggregate per annum	720,200
Keeper's profit from 277 inmates	720,200
Total South Side	$5,212,400[34]

When this total was added to the figures available for two other districts, the "appalling aggregate" was almost seven million dollars. The report also included the records of the earnings of individual women in the houses: the number of customers each day, the amount charged, and the total earned each day. For example:

	Sun.	Mon.	Tues.	Wed.	Thurs.	Total	Av.
Kitty							
No. of Men	24	14	12	9	17	76	15
Florence							
No. of Men	20	23	21	21	45	130	26[35]

One can sense, even in the controlled and neutral format, the psychological impact of this material. It becomes abundantly clear when the information from the account books is compared with a description of sexual intercourse, a representative statement of civilized morality, written in 1911 by an Indiana physician:

> Physically, there should be leisurely interchange of endearments, and natural warmth is kindled into a steady glow, caressing and fondling until the glaze of the altar and not the lurid rage of conflagration, the brilliancy of the arc and not the baleful glare of the lightning's flash; and with it all decent, calm decorum should prevail.
>
> In the act itself the same aplomb should continue with gentleness and consideration. There should be no undue haste, and as it usually happens that one of the pair is more active than the other, that one should exercise such restraint as shall insure that the supreme moment shall be mutual.
>
> There should be no haste in breaking away from the embraces of love, the endearments should continue until the high tension of the physical system relaxes and the waves of transference of magnetic, or electrical, emanation shall have regained perfect balance.[36]

There is a jarring contrast between this extraordinarily ethereal idealization, with its emphasis on moderation and a stylized reticence, and the dollars-and-cents reality of prostitution in Chicago. In effect, what can be seen here in *The Social Evil in Chicago* is the troubled awareness of the "extreme" in sexual behavior.[37] The documented and graphic evidence in the report, with records of women "entertaining" up to sixty men a night, forced the realization that for thousands of people in Chicago the extreme in sexual behavior was in fact the norm. "Commercialized" prostitution, then, denoted not just the commercialization of sexual behavior, but the commercialization of extreme sexual behavior. The one adjective implied the other, and together they formed a frightening antithesis of civilized morality. It was this disparity which to a great extent produced the report's obsession with the commercialization of urban prostitution.

The report's concern about the commercialization of prostitution also reflected that part of the progressive outlook which was hostile to the concentration of almost any kind of power. Although this attitude had deep roots in American social and political thought, it became most visceral in the closing decades of the nineteenth century. By 1890, with the announcement by the superintendent of the census that a frontier line no longer existed, and the enactment of the Sherman Antitrust Act, many Americans were convinced that the cherished vision of America as a dynamic and ever-expanding society would become only a memory if action were not taken to halt the concentration of power. The antitrust movement was the most famous manifestation of this cast of mind in the progressive era, but it took other forms as well, and this general cultural milieu gave the charge that prostitution was "commercialized" a deeply connotative meaning.

This is not to say that prostitution was approved when it existed (or was believed to exist) in an individualistic or open-market situation, but the problem did take on a more threatening dimension as it increased in scale and organizational efficiency. In this context, the Chicago Vice Commission's recommendation to destroy the most blatant manifestation of commercialized prostitution, the segregated red-light districts (interestingly enough, often referred to as "vice trusts"), was an expression of the ideological propensity that found satisfaction in the exposés of writers such as Ida Tarbell and in the various progressive forays to break up the trusts.

The revulsion that the commercialization of prostitution produced was, finally, and in the broadest sense, related to an important discovery of nineteenth-century social thought: the process of "reification," a phenomenon central to the emergence of industrial capitalism. Appearing in the early works of Carlyle, and most systematically developed by Marx, "reification" described the necessity in capitalistic society of turning all relationships into relationships between things, or commodities. Ultimately, even human beings, relationships between human beings, and human attributes become commodities to be exchanged or bought and sold.[38] There is no evidence to suggest that the Chicago Vice Commission was consciously aware of this intellectual construction, but a close reading of *The Social Evil in Chicago* makes it clear that the concern about the commercialization of prostitution reflected a vague recognition of the existence of reification in American society.

Prostitution by its very nature has always entailed depersonalization, but, as *The Social Evil in Chicago* discovered and documented, this characteristic was grossly intensified in the industrial city. Women, who in the moral world of civilized morality were supposed to be the guardians of all the humane values absent in the squalid world of economic and business transactions, were found to be the basic component in the most outrageous example of depersonalized commodity exchange. One can gain some sense of the strangeness of this realization by noting that, when the report referred to a prostitute's working or earning money, the verbs were placed in quotation marks.[39] The very concept of female sexuality as a commodity supporting a multimillion dollar business was so alien that normal language usage could not accommodate it. In the moral world of *The Social Evil in Chicago*, then, prostitution in the industrial city not only negated the ideals of civilized morality but also loomed as an extreme example of the kind of social relationships industrial capitalism was shaping.

The Chicago report's response to the depersonalization that prostitution necessarily entailed, however, was often confused and contradictory. Indeed, the report at times slipped into the very attitude it decried. For instance, *The Social Evil in Chicago* at one point bemoaned the fact that "a girl represents a capitalized value of $26,000 as a professional prostitute, where brains, virtue and all other good things are 'nil,'" an amount "more than four times as much as she is worth, as a factor in the industrial and social economy, where brains, intelligence, virtue and womanly charm should be worth a premium."[40] The references to girls as "capitalized value" or "a factor in the industrial and social economy" were egregious enough to have come from Dickens's Gradgrind. Furthermore, the commission's concern over the commercialization of prostitution did not lead to a critical analysis of the social forces and institutions behind it, as was the case with nineteenth-century conservative and socialist critiques of industrial capitalism. That the Chicago Vice Commission did not adopt such a critical approach should not come as a surprise, however, because *The Social Evil in Chicago* was the voice of those groups most supportive of the social order so accurately mirrored by the commercialization of prostitution.

In a critique of the Chicago report, Walter Lippmann made this same point in a slightly different way. "The Constitution," he wrote, "is a legal expression of the conditions under which prostitution has flourished." Prostitution, he continued, was "rooted in . . . property relations and business practice which have gathered about them a halo of reason and practicality, of morality and conscience."[41] In this respect, *The Social Evil in Chicago* was quintessentially a document of progressive reform, for, as in so many other expressions of social concern in these years, one can sense a deep-seated uneasiness with the fruits of industrial capitalism, but also a point beyond which analysis rarely passed.

Neither this last shortcoming nor, indeed, any of a number of criticisms one might strike off against an investigation so much the product of the reformist middle class, make *The Social Evil in Chicago* a simpleminded whitewash. In fact, although the Chicago report often failed to follow its own line of analysis to its logical conclusion, it was nevertheless, and perhaps as a consequence, a document infused with guilt, compulsion, and doubt. The Chicago Vice Commission published in 1911 not only an account of an investigation of prostitution but also a public confession of moral lapse.

The Social Evil in Chicago was, in this sense, an urban and secular

jeremiad. Like the more theologically oriented expressions of this tradition of American social and moral criticism, the Chicago report can be
considered as a ritualistic or symbolic response to a troubling social and
moral issue. The publication of the report in itself did not solve the
problem of prostitution in Chicago; rather, it served as a culturally
acceptable way of articulating opposition to prevailing (and upsetting)
patterns of social behavior. The report was also a ritual of compulsive
confession; it embodied a recital of the afflictions, an acknowledgment of
the scope of the sin (the extent of prostitution and immorality in statistical terms), and the promise of repentence. The act of publishing the
report was in this sense akin to the older tradition of observing a day of
humiliation. After the sins were publicly admitted, the urban community
could regain its confidence, be lightened of the guilt that the silent knowledge of the extent of prostitution had imposed, and emerge from the
ordeal girded to oppose the evil to the last.[42]

With this comparison in mind, it is interesting to ask why *The Social
Evil in Chicago*, and indeed all the urban vice commission reports, appeared when they did. Why did the specifically urban form of antiprostitution appear in the first several years of the teens? An obvious and
defensible explanation is that, because most antiprostitution activity
took place within the broader framework of urban progressive reform, it
was logical for the municipal vice commissions to produce their reports
at about the time when the spirit of progressive reform was at its peak.

There is, however, a broader and more intriguing explanation. The
first great growth in American industrial cities, which commenced about
1860, ended roughly between 1910 and 1915, the same time period
during which the vice commission reports were issued.[43] This half century of willy-nilly urbanization sealed forever the fate of traditional and
rural America. That a large number of American cities should undertake
a public act of humiliation and confession of moral failure at precisely
this point in the nation's history might well be more than coincidental.
The urban vice commission reports were, in this sense, a manifestation of
profound guilt and urban soul-searching, triggered by the realization of
the vast and irreversible transformation that the triumph of the industrial
city had imposed on traditional American folkways. In this context,
urban prostitution and immorality were the afflictions, as shipwrecks,
plagues, or poor harvests had been in earlier times, which American
society, and particularly American cities, had to endure in penance for
their departure from the sanctioned ways.

Yet for all the moral rigor of the vice commissions, and even given the
noisy motto of the Chicago report—"Constant and Persistent Repression
of Prostitution the Immediate Method; Absolute Annihilation the Ul-

timate Ideal"—the modern reader is equally impressed with another side of these urban jeremiads: the sense of vexation and the acute awareness of the paradoxical. Americans in the progressive era were devoted to the advance of "civilization," but they were greatly bewildered to discover that the more society progressed in "civilization," the more prostitution grew in incidence and complexity. "Prostitution keeps pace with civilization," a Chicago physician wrote in 1909. "As this advances, prostitution increases. The proportion of prostitutes is greater today than formerly. Modern industrial enterprises are peculiarly productive of conditions favoring prostitution."[44]

The Social Evil in Chicago presented ample support for this contention. It became clear, for instance, that the city's thriving real estate business, usually a central point of Chicago's civic pride and regarded as an important index of the city's progress, was in fact intimately tied into the economics of prostitution. Owners of, or agents for, property and buildings used for prostitution enjoyed profit margins vastly exceeding those possible from similar properties used for less exotic (and erotic) purposes. The report further noted that many (unnamed) "so-called respectable citizens" and "wealthy and prominent business men" were "sharing in the increased values from property used to extend the business of prostitution." And an overwhelming majority of the city's real estate agents were willing to handle and rent property used for prostitution. In effect, prostitution was a part of the economic activity usually regarded as an indicator of the city's financial health. The vice commission reluctantly had to reach the conclusion that in this case economic health and progress were going along dollar for dollar with moral decay.[45]

The Chicago Vice Commission, then, was acutely aware that the great economic growth of Chicago in the years 1860–1910, normally the subject of rabid boosterism, had also contributed to the dimensions of the problem it found so disconcerting. In a limited sense, there was a note of primitivism and nostalgia in this attitude; simpler societies, perhaps preindustrial America, had not been so plagued. Yet one does not encounter in the Chicago report a wish for the just-concluded chapter of American historical development, the rise of the great metropolises, to be erased from the national consciousness. It is true that many of the commission's recommendations were intended to buttress traditional morality and behavior patterns, but overriding these was a basic, if uneasy, acceptance of the primary facts of modern urban existence. The commission would proceed to demand and in fact accomplish the closing down of the segregated red-light districts, but the specific urban conditions and forces that had created them were never seriously challenged. In this way, *The Social*

Evil in Chicago fulfilled the main function of the jeremiad; once the transgressions, sins, and guilt were admitted publicly, the city could go forward, accepting, without always approving, the realities of urban America.[46]

The Social Evil in Chicago was widely discussed and, presumably, widely read. "The knowledge of the existence of such a report," one enthusiastic commentator wrote, "has spread to every corner of the United States, and has had more to do, in all probability, than any other single factor, with the crystallizing of public sentiment for the abolishment of what up to that time had been passively accepted by the general public because hidden from their view." The *Survey* magazine immediately and enthusiastically reviewed the report and printed a long article by commission member Graham Taylor, describing in glowing terms the Herculean efforts of the vice commission and the preparation of the report. Later vice commission reports were also reviewed as they appeared, but never as extensively as the Chicago report. Most reviewers agreed that *The Social Evil in Chicago* was the most important American work on prostitution since William Sanger's mid-nineteenth-century investigation, and it immediately became a central text of antiprostitution.[47]

Fortunately, *The Social Evil in Chicago* was commented upon at length by two extraordinary men, one at the peak of a career as the most popular American political leader since Lincoln, the other at the beginning of a career as one of the most informed and thoughtful social commentators in the twentieth century. Theodore Roosevelt and Walter Lippmann were modestly acquainted with one another. Roosevelt was deeply impressed with the remarkably precocious Lippmann and felt an ideological kinship, for a while at least, with Lippmann and the other liberals who founded the *New Republic* in 1914. In 1915, Roosevelt called Lippmann "on the whole the most brilliant young man of his age in the United States." Lippmann in turn saw the ex-president as the most dynamic and progressive politician of his time. Here, then, were two men, each in his own way possessed of extraordinary gifts and a remarkable feeling for the nation's pulse, each feeling a common historical bond with the other. That they felt so differently about what each considered a central document of their age is a statement in microcosm of the contradictory forces shaping the response to prostitution in those years.[48]

Roosevelt immediately saw the importance of the Chicago report: "I know of no volume that has recently appeared which would better repay that kind of careful study which is to result in action, and which the student intends thus to turn to account." He quickly pointed to the more enlightened issues raised in the report: the demand that the prostitute no longer bear society's blame while her male companion was ignored, the need for modern systems of probation for first-time offenders, and the fact that the problem of prostitution was often tied to the inferior economic status of women.[49]

But to Roosevelt these matters did not constitute the chief merit of the report. He found the report noteworthy not for its conclusions, with which he readily agreed, but for its high moral tone and uncompromising dedication to the "annihilation" of prostitution. The logic and method of the report, upon which Lippmann performed surgery without anesthesia, were of little significance. For Roosevelt *The Social Evil in Chicago* was important because it was, above all, a "contribution to the cause of morality and decency." It did not "serve merely to gratify emotions that are foul and base." It was, in short, based on a commitment to civilized morality. The Chicago Vice Commission itself had made this commitment clear, stating at the beginning that its recommendations would be "first, moral; second, reasonable and practical; third, possible under the Constitutional powers of our Courts; fourth, that which will square with the public conscience of the American people." For Roosevelt, this was the only possible priority. The *Survey* had editorialized that *The Social Evil in Chicago* had taken a "stand which is touched with a fine idealism," and this, for Roosevelt, defined its foremost importance.[50]

Roosevelt understood, however, that the publication of such a massive investigation of prostitution was itself a break with the policy of reticence on sexual matters so essential to the coherence of civilized morality: "The spirit in which its report is written would not have been understood even as late as a couple of generations ago." Given the centrality of civilized morality to his own cultural positions and beliefs, it was natural for him to be preeminently concerned that the form of this break with convention be such as would not endanger the moral system as a whole— thus the necessity for *The Social Evil in Chicago* to be, above all else, "moral" and "decent."[51]

Just one year after he penned his comments on the Chicago report, Roosevelt made his famous "Confession of Faith" and prepared for his last great stand for "morality" and "decency" in American life. And when, on that hot August day in 1912, before the Progressive party convention in the Chicago Coliseum (where First Ward dances were held), Roosevelt intoned, "We stand at Armageddon and we battle for the Lord," it was as much a cultural as a political asseveration. It is now clear that civilized morality was in its last encore in 1912, that a new generation of young men and women, with new sensibilities, was waiting impatiently in the wings for the final curtain to drop. Seen in this light, Roosevelt's views on *The Social Evil in Chicago* speak sharply, even a little shrilly, on behalf of that America which was uneasy about the change signaled by the very document whose moral tone it so applauded.

Walter Lippmann agreed with Roosevelt that the publication of *The Social Evil in Chicago* was an important event. The young critic presented a lengthy analysis of the report in *A Preface to Politics*, published in 1913, when he was twenty-four years old. The book was not specifically about prostitution, and Lippmann at one point even declared: "That the report of the Chicago Vice Commission figures so prominently . . . is not due to any preoccupation with Chicago, the Commission, or with vice. It is a text and nothing else," he asserted—one that provided a case in point to illustrate his broader arguments about American society.[52] Yet the fact that Lippmann, who had read so widely in the social commentary of his time, should choose to devote almost a quarter of his first book to this one document gives some indication of its impact on him. Indeed, *The Social Evil in Chicago* seems to have had a special significance to Lippmann. "In casting about for a concrete example to illustrate some of the points under discussion," he wrote, "I hesitated a long time before the wealth of material." He finally narrowed the field to the Pittsburgh Survey and the Chicago Vice Commission Report. The Pittsburgh Survey was clearly "an example of the finest expert inquiry." But, Lippmann recounted, "I was looking for something more representative, and, therefore, more revealing. I did not want a detached study of some specially selected cross section of what is after all not the typical economic life of America. The case demanded was one in which you could see representative American citizens trying to handle a problem which had touched their imaginations."[53]

The Social Evil in Chicago was the "representative" and "revealing" example Lippmann chose to treat, and in the course of his discussion he set down a devastating critique of that report. It immediately became the most penetrating contemporary analysis of antiprostitution in the progressive years.

The dominant theme of *A Preface to Politics* was Lippmann's assertion that there was a manifest and crescive discontinuity between culture and experience in American life. Culture, which he variously referred to as "routine," "taboo," "creeds," "idols," or "ideals," was the "mass of generalizations, abstract ideas, ancient glories, and personal wishes" forced upon the "realities of social life," or experience.[54] Culture was, in other words, the burden of civilized morality. Experience, conversely, was the new, complex, and continually changing urban industrial civilization of 1910. All the confusions, problems, and irrationalities of the new society, Lippmann implied, were traceable to those who bovinely insisted on imposing older and outmoded cultural forms on radically new social conditions, rather than searching for new forms flexible enough to accommodate the accelerating rate of historical change. "Substitution," he declared, was "the essence of statecraft." Many Americans, however, held to the old beliefs even in the face of the new conditions, and Lippmann described the results in a series of ironic cadences: "We pass a law against race-track gambling and add to the profits from faro. We raid the faro joints, and drive gambling into the home, where poker and bridge whist are taught to children who follow their parents' example. . . . Everybody knows that when you close the dance halls you fill the parks. Men who in their youth took part in 'crusades' against the Tenderloin now admit in a crestfallen way that they succeeded merely in sprinkling the Tenderloin through the whole city."[55] Lippmann examined the culture-experience dichotomy throughout *A Preface to Politics*, but he made his most telling use of it in his consideration of *The Social Evil in Chicago*.

Lippmann at once applauded the general concern over the problem of prostitution. It is "the most spontaneous reform enthusiasm of our time," he commented, adding that prostitution was "as far-reaching and real a problem as any that we human beings face." Therefore, the Chicago Vice Commission investigation, creatively executed in the light of modern intelligence, might have led to new understanding and informed action. This, he lamented, did not happen; instead, the only result of the admirable energy the commission put into its work was "an elaborate series of taboos."[56]

At the core of the commission's failure, Lippmann argued, were its outmoded conceptions of how a society functioned and, as a corollary, of how to study a social problem. "The evils of prostitution," he wrote, "are seen as a series of episodes, each of which must be clubbed, forbidden, raided, and jailed." Given this attitude, the commission's recommendation of "Constant and Persistent Repression" and "Absolute Annihilation" made perfect sense. In actuality, though, prostitution could not be surgically removed from the society in which it flourished, any more than could any other social institution of such dimensions. (Lippmann cited the commission's own figures on the extent of prostitution.)[57] In a passage clearly stamped with the Veblenian dispensation, he argued that prostitution could only be understood within the context of the other institutions and norms with which it had a functional and structural relationship. "You cannot look at civilization as a row of institutions each external to the other," he maintained. "They interpenetrate and a change in one affects all the others." The Chicago Vice Commission, however, did not understand this. "The Commission hopes to wipe out prostitution. But it never hints that the success of its plan means vast alterations in our social life. . . . Yet who that has read the report itself and put himself into any imaginative understanding of conditions can escape seeing that prostitution to-day is organic to our industrial life, our marriage sanctions, and our social customs?"[58]

Lippmann further noted the failure of the commission at "tracing vice to its source in the over-respected institutions of American life, and the over-respected natures of American men and women." Lippmann maintained that any serious and fruitful consideration of prostitution must include a rigorous scrutiny of conventional morality and all its social and institutional manifestations: the family, marriage, the position of women, and norms of sexual behavior. The Chicago Vice Commission, however, could not undertake such scrutiny because it started its investigation with a commitment to civilized morality. Roosevelt saw this commitment as the report's greatest strength; for Lippmann, it flawed the commission's procedure from the outset.[59]

Lippmann's reading in the voluntaristic theories of Bergson, Wallas, and Freud (the last of whom he encountered just as he was writing *A Preface to Politics*) was the foundation for another of his arguments against the method of *The Social Evil in Chicago*. "Why," Lippmann asked, "are the sexual problems not even stated?" The answer, he believed, resided in the commission's conception of sexual morality, which precluded it from ever examining the sexual dynamics of prostitution. The commission defined sexual morality, Lippmann argued, in such a way that "sex must be confined to procreation by a healthy, intelligent and strictly monogamous couple. All other sexual expression would come under the ban of disapproval." This view of sex "forced the Commission to ignore the sexual impulse in discussing a sexual problem." The commission had stated at the beginning of its report that "So long as there is lust in the hearts of men it will seek out some method of expression," but the ramifications of that statement were never explored. The commission was therefore unable to see how prostitution functioned, in Lippmann's words, as an "answer to a human need." If the commission had gone on to consider the "enormous and bewildering demand that prostitution answers," it might then have attempted to find "moral equivalents for evil" instead of resorting to repressive taboos.[60]

In pointing to the commission's reluctance to consider the sexual aspects of prostitution, Lippmann identified a most revealing characteristic of *The Social Evil in Chicago* and of the vice commission reports in general. At one point the Chicago Vice Commission reported: "Pervert methods are on the increase in the higher priced houses. The inmates who perform these services earn from two to three times as much money as the so-called 'regular' girls. In one notorious place known all over the country and which caters to a so-called high class trade, these methods are used almost exclusively. The inmates gave testimony before the Commission that they do this on the advice of their physician, who says it prevents disease and other troubles." This was probably an oblique reference to an increase in either oral or anal sex, although how such an increase was measured was not disclosed. The commission never contemplated the possible significance of this information, even though the questions it pointed to seem clear to the modern reader.[61] For example, was the demand for fellatio more characteristic of the "higher priced houses" than of the less expensive ones? If it was, was there a relationship between this pattern of male sexual behavior and the prescriptions of civilized morality, which would have been operative, most likely, in the lives of men patronizing the more expensive houses? Did civilized morality's emphasis on sex for reproduction and on an idealized model of marital sexual behavior in reality support brothels that offered quite opposite forms of sexual behavior? Or, from another perspective, did the less expensive houses generally not specialize in "pervert methods," and, if this was the case, was it a reflection of a class basis for different patterns of sexual behavior?

The Chicago Vice Commission's commitment to civilized morality, as understood and approved by Roosevelt, prevented it from ever considering such questions. Tellingly enough, Lippmann himself did not ask them, even though he sensed that the report was critically deficient without them. This was not the only shortcoming of Lippmann's critique. Notwithstanding the verve and wit of his prose, his instinct for the telling quotation, his ability to marshall the illuminating metaphor, and his impatience with the abstract gentility of the Chicago report, there was a markedly recondite quality to his own comments. He insisted, for example, that substitutes for vice, or "moral equivalents for evil," had to be found, but he never specified what those substitutes would be, and, even in the early period of Freudian thought, his faith in such a wide application of the theory of sublimation was somewhat naive.

Any final assessment, however, will show Lippmann's analysis prevailing over any other of his time. He was the first widely read American to write on prostitution with an awareness and appreciation of the profound insights into social behavior that came in the remarkable outburst of sociological and psychological thought in the 1890s and early twentieth century. He was not a cultural radical, but he accurately perceived, as such a representative American as Theodore Roosevelt did not, the stultifying effects of the Chicago Vice Commission's commitment to civilized morality on its endeavors. In the process, Lippmann performed one of the most important tasks of the creative social critic: transposing dead writing into live writing by probing the inner meaning and implications of official verbiage, statistics, and graphs and, through the vibrant use of language, making them take on newer and larger significance.[62]

Upon reading the celebrated English *Wolfenden Report: Report of the Committee on Homosexual Offenses and Prostitution* (1957), the British psychiatrist Charles Berg was moved to remark drolly, "If one reads page after page of this sort of verbiage, one is apt to be lulled into a more or less acquiescent state of mind, and to forget it is mostly a series of platitudes chosen arbitrarily for the sake of arriving at decisions, worked over and through and through with so much obsessional examination and re-examination that we gain the impression that . . . the conclusions and recommendations framed so smoothly and with such illusion of reasonableness must be the ultimate truth."[63] Modern American history has been so regularly punctuated with commission reports on almost every pressing issue that it is easy to forget that they are products of particular historical periods, written by groups with specific economic positions in society and with identifiable social biases and cultural commitments. Ultimately they are expressive of issues much larger than the specific subject of the investigation. *The Social Evil in Chicago* was no exception, and any final evidence of its significance must be based on an understanding of these characteristics.

During the progressive years, *The Social Evil in Chicago*, and indeed most of the urban vice commission reports, represented the cutting edge of antiprostitution. Lippmann's incisive critique clearly underscored the defective aspects and cultural limitations of the Chicago commission's methodology. But in any judicious appraisal, *The Social Evil in Chicago* and most of the other vice commission reports stood in both form and content as a marked advance from the malarial atmosphere of the Stead and Parkhurst exposés of the 1890s, and as far superior to the revivalistic thrust of the contemporaneous white-slave narratives. One could cite specific and individual pieces on prostitution from these years—found mainly in medical journals—that were more advanced and better informed than the vice commission reports. These studies, however, appeared in diverse and specialized journals and were not widely known or responded to. The two most popular forms of expression of concern over prostitution were the vice commission reports and the white-slave narratives, and though they are equally important for an understanding of the dynamics of antiprostitution, the contribution made by the vice commissions to the study of prostitution was of far greater value than that which the white-slave narratives finally offered.

Within the context of progressive antiprostitution, then, *The Social*

Evil in Chicago merits praise. From a broader historical perspective, however, its meaning becomes more and more contradictory. It embodied a fantastic leap from the potentially fruitful desire to investigate urban prostitution to the dubious conclusion that that which had just been discovered to be so widespread could be annihilated. What was in effect a pioneering investigation of mass sexual behavior in modern American society was unable, because of a blind commitment to civilized morality, to grasp the significance of its own discoveries. The expression of a mature industrial city confident of its ability to solve even its most pressing problems was, simultaneously, a guilt-ridden admission of moral failure and a troubled acknowledgment that the advance of urban civilization had brought with it not only discontent but also (a point that Veblen would have relished) vestiges of human behavior supposed to have been left behind in the less-civilized past. In short, this document, produced in 1911, is at once recognizably modern and as quaint and removed from our own time as the straw boater and the bustle.

One might reasonably choose to fix with greater precision the place of *The Social Evil in Chicago* in American history by emphasizing one or the other of the antagonistic tendencies within it. But an ultimately more satisfying—and more subtle and accurate—conclusion would avoid categorizing the Chicago Vice Commission report as *either* backward-looking or modern; it would instead recognize the report as the result and embodiment of two contradictory visions held in tension, drawing its historical identity and meaning, like the Roman god Janus, from the act of looking in opposite directions at the same time.

Six

SEVENTY THOUSAND INNOCENT GIRLS

A YEAR: THE WHITE-SLAVERY SCARE

This know also, that in the last days perilous times shall come.

For men shall be lovers of their own selves, covetous, boasters, proud, blasphemers, disobedient to parents, unthankful, unholy.

Without natural affection, trucebreakers, false accusers, incontinent, fierce, despisers of those that are good,

Traitors, heady, highminded, lovers of pleasures more than lovers of God;

Having a form of godliness, but denying the power thereof: from such turn away.

For of this sort are they which creep into houses, and lead captive silly women laden with sins, led away with divers lusts.

Ever learning, and never able to come to the knowledge of the truth.

Now as Jannes and Jambres withstood Moses, so do these also resist the truth: men of corrupt minds, reprobate concerning the faith.

But they shall proceed no further: for their folly shall be manifest unto all men, as theirs also was.

2 Timothy 3: 1—9

An exotic literary genre flourished in the United States during the early decades of the twentieth century. Originating mainly in New York and Chicago, but with contributions from locations as diverse as Harrisburg, Pennsylvania, and Los Angeles, a group of books and pamphlets appeared announcing a startling claim: a pervasive and depraved conspiracy was at large in the land, brutally trapping and seducing American girls into lives of enforced prostitution, or "white slavery." These white-slave narratives, or white-slave tracts, began to circulate around 1909. Within five years at least twenty-two had been published, some of which were Gothic tomes of four hundred pages, with titles such as *The Great War on White Slavery; or, Fighting for the Protection of Our Girls: Truthful and Chaste Account of the Hideous Trade of Buying and Selling Young Girls for Immoral Purposes; Startling Disclosures Made by White Slaves during the Trials of Many Procurers and Traders; The Cruel and*

Inhuman Treatment of White Slaves; The Astounding Confession of a Pander; Graphic Accounts of How White Slaves Are Ensnared and a Full Exposition of the Methods and Schemes Used to Lure and Trap the Girls.[1]

The indignation and concern over white slavery was intense, widespread, and often hysterical, and it poured forth from disparate sources. Oscar Strauss, Theodore Roosevelt's secretary of commerce and labor, in his departmental report for 1908 fulminated against the "diabolical traffic." Stanley W. Finch, chief of the Bureau of Investigation of the Department of Justice, spoke out against it at the World's Purity Congress in 1912. Jane Addams excoriated it. The genteel *Woman's World* opened its pages to a series of articles on the traffic in shame; physicians from various parts of the country saw white slavery as the gravest threat to American womanhood; and social workers documented its existence.[2]

By 1912, only two years after its publication, Reginald Wright Kauffman's best-selling white-slavery novel *The House of Bondage* was in its fourteenth edition. Two years later movies such as "The Traffic in Souls" and "The Inside of the White Slave Traffic" were enjoying large audiences.[3] On the political level, the white-slave agitation produced the famous Rockefeller grand jury investigation in New York City in 1910, a U.S. Senate investigation in 1909–10, and the Mann Act in 1910, along with a series of Supreme Court rulings on its constitutionality.[4] By 1913, even the austere Wilsonian presidency, by way of a minor scandal, was involved.[5]

The anxiety over white slavery was expressed most fully and at greatest length, however, in the white-slave tracts. They were concerned, in the broadest sense, with two obvious facts of early twentieth-century American life: the migration of rural and small town young women to the cities in search of jobs and social opportunities, and the existence of open and teeming red-light districts in these same cities. The cutting edge of the white-slave tracts was a question concerning the relationship between these two circumstances: what was happening to the American girl who struck out for the city?

The plotlines were strikingly uniform. Typically, a chaste and comely native American country girl would forsake her idyllic country home and family for the promise of the city. On the way, or shortly after arrival, she would fall victim to one of the swarm of panders lying in wait for just such an innocent and unprotected sojourner. Using one of his vast variety of tricks—a promise of marriage, an offer to assist in securing lodging, or, if these were to no avail, the chloroformed cloth, the hypodermic needle, or the drugged drink—the insidious white slaver would brutally seduce the girl and install her in a brothel, where she became an enslaved prostitute. Within five years she would end up in potter's field, unless she had the good fortune to be "rescued" by a member of one of the dedicated groups fighting white slavery. On the surface it made for rather maudlin melodrama, and the white-slave narratives have often been dismissed as such. Closer analysis, however, reveals much more.[6]

What immediately strikes the reader of these tracts is the strident conspiratorial mentality that permeates them from first page to last. Here, American girls become prostitutes not for the more mundane reasons cited by the vice commission reports but because they are victimized by a huge, secret, and powerful conspiracy, controlled by foreigners, whose evil work is impelled by an incomprehensible fanaticism. American girls were being ruined by a "thoroughly organized, solidly financed system of White Slavery flourishing and growing in America today—a system which controls and ruins hundreds of thousands of women in our midst every year and which requires a constant sacrifice of more than seventy thousand young girls annually to feed its death and disease dealing machinery." Victims seldom escaped. "A girl in the clutches of any one of them has practically no chance of escape, since the agents of all of them are on the lookout. Their eyes are everywhere and upon every girl, including those already fallen as they do the innocent. No Black Hand, no secret organization of any kind is more silent or insidious, or, in the end, more ruthless."[7]

As may be expected, this conspiratorial vision often assumed an apocalyptic tone. The white-slave tracts were filled with catastrophic broodings about the threat to the nation posed by the white-slave conspiracy and sexual immorality. "No apology is needed for this book. We are living in perilous times," began one tract, *The Shame of a Great Nation.* Its author later proclaimed that "we have reached the greatest crisis in the history of our country." The solution was simple: "If the manhood of the nation will assert itself we may be saved from moral decay and civic destruction. If not, we are doomed and the end is not far away."[8]

The white-slave narratives were steeped in a sense of decadence. The immorality of the present generation, the departure from the traditional morality, the craving for luxury and ephemeral things of the world, the indifference of the rich and satisfied, the diminishing power of religion—all were linked to the existence of the white-slave conspiracy.[9] Yet this obsession with moral decay existed in a delicate equipoise with a belief in the possibility of moral regeneration. There was no reluctance to admit the precariousness of the times, but the very vigor of the call for a crusade against the white-slave conspiracy expressed the hope, very much in the progressive spirit, that even this evil might be overcome.

Although the fear of conspiracy was the tradition that most influenced the tone of the white-slave narratives, the captivity experience, an equally old American tradition, shaped the paradigm plot. The colonial Indian captivity narratives were the first American captivity literature, and they have also received the most thorough scholarly treatment. The Indian wars of the seventeenth and eighteenth centuries provided the first and most appropriate literary material for both recording and explaining the colonial experience. The confrontation between colonist and Indian offered a dramatic contest between opposites—the dark, primitive Indian, the denizen of the wilderness, and the fair-skinned, cultured Englishman—and reduced the complexities of the colonization experience to readily comprehensible drama. Many Indian captivities graphically depicted Indians capturing Englishwomen, who, after the ordeal of the captivity, during which they were usually able to stave off a relapse into barbaric customs, either engineered their own escapes or were rescued and returned to civilized society.

The recounting of these experiences served a number of cultural needs. Most generally the Indian captivity narratives provided a means for the early settlers, still insecure about their ability to succeed in the New World, to see their society, values, and beliefs tested and proven. The narratives were also discreetly pornographic; they allowed colonists to witness vicariously primitive and pagan customs that both repelled and fascinated them. Furthermore, the captivity tales expressed the anxiety and guilt engendered in a group when it leaves the geographical location of its loyalties and traditions for a new and strange land. Finally, in repeatedly chronicling the separation of children from parents (the Indians often tearing the child from the mother's arms), the captivities provided a therapeutic expression of familial and generational anxiety.[10]

Like the fear of conspiracy, the captivity experience is a recurrent theme in American history. Nineteenth-century anti-Catholic and anti-Mormon literature, for instance, frequently employed the captivity experience.[11] Moreover, the fear of conspiracy and the captivity experience often merge, because the captivity often takes place within the secret ranks of the conspiracy. In the most general sense, captivity narratives are the expression of a people in desperate need of a dramatic vision which, in times of great social transformation, will explain the events and changes that so bewilder them.

The white-slave narratives were updated versions of the genre inaugurated by the Indian captivity narratives. The Indian captivity narratives' setting in the depth of the forests, the literal wilderness, registered the anxieties of a society attempting to master the frontier. The white-slave tracts, the captivity literature of postfrontier America, reflected rather the anxieties of a rural society facing the new "wilderness" of the twentieth century, the city. The anxieties here were occasioned by the migration of rural and small-town girls to the new urban wilderness. And the white-slave tracts, no less than the Indian captivity narratives, addressed what many were convinced was a crisis the outcome of which would determine the fate of the nation.

The "alien" or "dark" white-slave trader assumed the role formerly occupied by the Indian. The innocent country girls were debauched into the captivity of prostitution by urban denizens invariably identified as Jewish, Italian, or Eastern European. The white-slave traffic, warned the author of *America's Black Traffic in White Girls*, is "carried on and exploited by a foaming pack of foreign hellhounds, . . . the moral and civic degenerates of the French, Italian, Syrian, Russian, Jewish or Chinese races. . . . an American or Englishman conducting such a business is almost entirely unknown." Theodore A. Bingham, a former commissioner of police in New York City, stated flatly that "the majority of the men engaged in the traffic" were foreigners.[12] And Reginald Wright Kauffman, in *The House of Bondage*, described Max Grossman, the white slaver who lures the innocent country girl Mary to her downfall, as "a member of the persistent race" whose speech, with "its quick, thick quality, and its ictus on the vowels, denoted the foreigner; . . . The hair on his head was black and curly. . . . His lips were thick when he did not smile and thin when he did, with teeth very white; and his gray glance had a penetrating calculation about it that made the girl instinctively draw her coat together and button it."[13] Another victim of a "white slave fiend," whose experience was recounted in Clifford Roe's *The Great War on White Slavery*, recalled that the pander was "of foreign parentage, probably a Jew, a Frenchman, an Italian, or perhaps a Greek." When Roe listed the pandering cases that had come under his jurisdiction as assistant state's attorney of Illinois, fifty of the seventy-seven defendants had last names distinctly Jewish, French, or Italian.[14]

This depiction of the white slavers served several functions. The white slaver's racial "otherness" made it psychologically easier and more socially acceptable to direct hatred and aggression against him without violating the conventions of genteel society. "I feel so furious at these devils in human guise," one writer declared, "that I am sure I could not rest comfortable in my grave if I did not take up a good strong cudgel and wield it right lively to help slaughter the evil herd."[15] On a deeper and more emotionally volatile level, the preoccupation with the violation of beautiful native American country girls by alien white slavers might be seen as a projection of native America's deepest sexual fear: immigrant males possessing the daughters of the land while their men stand unable to help or protect. Also involved here was a transference onto the alien white slaver of a sexual violence and intensity—the victimized girls were usually raped—which an opponent of white slavery, or the reader of the narratives, was perhaps unable to confront in his or her own psyche.[16]

In this context it is important to realize that the white-slave narratives, like most expressions of the captivity genre, provided readers with an experience that was vicariously titillating and pornographic. One cannot read them without noticing their obsessional nature and the lurid and detailed descriptions of that which was supposedly so repulsive. Brothels were described in detail: "Red plush chairs and sofa were there. Glaring red rugs were on the floor, and bright red curtains hung at the windows. Even the light-shades were red which reflected a somber glow through the room. All this red . . . typified blood of victims sacrificed upon the altar of lust and sin."[17] The red-light districts were described as places "where young men buy insanity cheap"; brothels were "a slaughter house for girls" or "Red mills, red with the heart's blood of mothers, red with the blood of murdered babies." The brothels were depicted as places of unnatural acts and forbidden lusts, charnel houses with coffins streaming out the back doors to potter's field. Yet the expected revulsion does not occur. Instead the reader is led through the districts street by street, page by page ("Come with me for a walk through the Twenty-Second Street Soul Market—That great human stockyard for girls and boys," one author invites), to peep in the doors and peer through the windows.[18]

As one analyzes these pages it becomes impossible to escape the conclusion that the white-slave narratives served as vicarious "tour guides" to the red-light districts for individuals who would never go there in person. These thick volumes offered a proper, religious-minded, middle-class reader a glimpse, figuratively speaking, into the id of American society, into a sexual underworld that was at the same time repulsive and attractive.

This aspect of the white-slave narratives becomes even clearer when they are compared to the vice commission reports. The vice commissions presented their reports as the result of scientific, thorough, and focused investigations. Each report dealt with conditions in only one city. The reports were replete with tables, statistics, and documentary evidence. They were, in a word, boring to the average reader.

The white-slave narratives served as the spicy cultural counterpart to the stuffy vice commission reports. It was often a very consciously cultivated relationship. Indeed, all the white-slave narratives published after the famous Chicago Vice Commission report of 1911 included some of the data and findings of that report, but in a tone and context that was provocative, lurid, emotionally overwrought, and misleading. The Chicago Vice Commission, for example, had estimated, after "careful deliberation," that at any one time there were five thousand prostitutes in Chicago. In one white-slave narrative, this became, "Each year Chicago alone exacts the ghastly toll of five thousand (see Report of Chicago Vice Commission) of these girls to fill the decaying gaps of our great army of twenty-five thousand lost women."[19] The vice commission reports were written in a detached tone, usually in the third person, and often in the past tense. The white-slave tracts frequently slipped into a highly personal tone, first person, and present tense. The appeal for the reader to become emotionally involved was quite evident. It can of course be argued that anything written on prostitution might have been pornographic for some persons. There may well have been those who were sexually aroused by *The Social Evil in Chicago*. By any objective standards, however, the white-slave tracts offered readers a prurient depiction of prostitution and illicit sexuality that most would not have been able to read into a vice commission report. Many Americans may have read both a vice commission report and a white-slave narrative, but with fundamentally different lasting impressions, and, ultimately, for fundamentally different psychological reasons.

Diametrically opposed to the depravity of the white-slave conspiracy, the brothels, and the panders were their innocent victims, the country and village girls who were taking part in an internal migration about which we still know very little. During the progressive years it was widely accepted that most of the prostitutes so increasingly visible in the cities had come from the rural districts.[20] This belief, although more often asserted than proved, was the dominant obsession of the white-slave narratives and, when carefully analyzed, reveals the outline of a significant crisis in American social history.

The first chapter of Clifford Roe's *The Great War on White Slavery*, entitled "Home Sweet Home," recounts the "heart rending story" of Mildred Clark. Mildred, "still but a child," meets Clarence in Nashville, Tennessee, where she is staying with friends. After working his wiles on the girl for several days, Clarence proposes marriage, and Mildred readily accepts. Clarence arranges for their elopement to Chicago, whereupon he immediately sells the naive country girl to "the best house on the line." Mildred's street clothes are taken from her. She is kept locked in a room and forced to submit to the life of a prostitute. Through her ordeal, Mildred, "clothed in soft filmy lingerie, silk stockings and satin slippers," is haunted by the "vision of home," which often appears as she gazes into the looking glass: "She saw the face of her loving father and felt once more the kindly hand of her tender mother . . . she saw those other things that went to make for happiness in childhood; there was the sitting room in the old homestead; she saw the big log burning in the fireplace and her brothers and sisters playing near the fire." Within a short time, Mildred is rescued by members of a revival meeting being held in the red-light district; she cooperates with the prosecution of Clarence and returns to the family homestead. "Once more the family circle is complete, and the heart-aches and sorrows are gone, and instead the pulse of each member of the family beats in magnificent rythm [sic] and harmony." As the tale ends—"The Lost is found"—the prodigal daughter has returned.[21]

Another white-slave narrative, *Fighting the Devil's Triple Demons: The Traffic in Innocent Girls*, opens with the story of Helen, "the golden haired child in the garden," in a chapter entitled "One Innocent Life's Appalling Wreck." Helen, "a little child" (she is eighteen), lives in a "pleasant country town" where she basks in the love of two adoring parents. "There are a thousand such," the author wrote, " . . . but none, surely, could surpass in charm and loveliness and promise this of the little girl in the garden, a child of beauty, developing in such a home, under tenderest protection and devoted care into what charming young girl-hood and perfect womanhood might bring. . . . That both her parents were absorbed in the life of their only child was not a thing to wonder at. She was all they had!"

Helen, however, has different feelings about the small town and makes up her mind to go to "the great city" in search of better opportunities. Her parents are loath to have her go but finally accede to their daughter's wishes. Her father accompanies Helen to the city, where he sees that she is settled safely in a respectable boarding house. She quickly finds a job as a clerk in a music store and success seems to be hers: "She would demonstrate to them at home that she had been right in leaving the little town." Helen soon meets Mr. Laurier, who has already singled out the beautiful country girl as his victim. He introduces the innocent Helen to new experiences—liquor, theater, and "late suppers." Helen soon falls victim to the "deadly patience and ingenuity" of Laurier; he sells her into a brothel, where she becomes "the chattel of the city."

Helen cuts off contact with her acquaintances in the city but continues for a while to send letters, "pitiful, false letters," home to her parents. Soon even these stop, and her parents never hear from their daughter again. "The little home in the country town now shelters a swiftly failing man and woman of middle age, whose life has been made desolate. The mystery, so far as they are concerned, has never been solved." In her "gaudily furnished room of infamous happenings, . . . choking in the foul atmosphere about her," Helen often sees "in her mental vision the loving father and mother, the little house, the garden and all the pure and fair surroundings." Finally she goes mad. "She was relieved forever from the horror about her, but, though a living, breathing creature, she was henceforth to be, as uncomprehending as are the unknowing dead. She was a hopeless lunatic." Helen spends the rest of her days in a state asylum, where she imagines "that she is a little child again and often that she is playing in a garden where are flowers and bees, and birds with which she chatters." In this tale the prodigal daughter does not return.[22]

The clearest message of the country-girl-to-white-slave theme was that young women ought to stay where it was safe and secure: in the rural areas and small town communities. By the turn of the century the countryside, the freehold farm, and the quiet village were the settings of a sentimentalized vision of American life, preindustrial and preurban, completely antithetical to the burgeoning America of boulevards, factories, and tenements. The most popular songs of the first decade of the century—"In the Good Old Summertime" (1902), "In the Shade of the Old Apple Tree" (1905), "School Days" (1907), "Down by the Old Mill Stream" (1910)—celebrated the simplicities and innocence of rural America, and in his campaign speeches of 1912, Woodrow Wilson urged his audiences to remember the time "when America lay in every hamlet, when America was to be seen in every fair valley."[23]

These sentiments, of course, were part of a pastoral tradition that had its beginnings centuries before. But during the early years of this century a new emphasis appeared. The country girl, the feminine and adolescent embodiment of the "agrarian myth," emerged as a preeminent symbol of all that was pure and innocent in American society, a position formerly held by the yeoman farmer. During these years the fate of the country girl became progressively entwined with the fate of rural America. It was this conviction that infused the white-slave tracts with their portentous tone and note of urgency.

Many of these fears and anxieties found expression in *The American Country Girl*, a scholarly panegyric to rural girlhood, written in 1915 by Martha Foote Crow, which offers valuable insights into the moral world of the white-slave narratives. Dedicating her book to the "Seven Million Country Life Girls of America—with the hope that they may see their great privilege and do their honorable part in the New Country Life Era," Crow urges country girls not to "run away to build their homes and rear their children in the hot, stuffy, unsocialized atmosphere of the town." Instead, they should remain and run the farms of the nation: "Shall I say, to *man* them? No, let us say to *woman* them, to *lady* them, to *mother* them, and so to make them centers of wholesome interesting life that, if the girls do their part, shall be the very heart and fiber of the nation." This hope, however, was in peril: country girls were "following their brothers . . . to take up some industrial fortune in the city." The only remedy for this problem was a revitalization of the role of the country girl, which would keep her on the farm. "The young woman on the farm," Crow urged, "must grow up with the idea that she is essential to the progress of country life and therefore of the national life, and that a career is before her just as much as if she were aiming to be an artist or a writer or a missionary. This purpose makes her life worth while. She must conserve her health for this; she must develop her powers for this. She must train herself heroically for this." But, Crow ominously asks, if country girls should be "estranged irrecoverably from the countryside, what is to become of the countryside in the days that are to come?"[24]

Here, then, was the crisis that so terrified the writers and readers of the white-slave tracts: the fate of rural America was the fate of American country girls, and the country girls seemed to be ending "on the line" or on the streets after they left the country. The response to this situation was a siege mentality regarding the movement of young women away from home and family. "Stay rather at home where all is pure, beautiful and really grand," one narrative declaimed, "for no artisan can build forests and mountains like the great Creator has given you; . . . The crowded smelling car can not supplant the good old horses and carriage. Nor is love so sweet in the gilded drawing room as in the winding shady lane where the moon mellows the heart and fills the soul with joy." Another tract warned that "In this day and age of the world no young girl is safe!" Girls breaking loose from family ties "are in imminent and deadly peril." "The country girl is in greater danger from the 'white slavers' than the city girl," wrote a contributor to *War on the White Slave Trade*, adding that "the best and surest ways for parents of girls in the country to protect them from the clutches of the 'white slavers' is to keep them in the country." The city was referred to as "a forest haunted by wolves," "a marketplace where girls are sold and bought," or a place where white slavers "prowl . . . from end to end . . . and the harvest they reap is plentiful both in numbers and damnation."[25]

This sense of the city as a moral snare for innocent girls is related to a tradition that one historian calls "The Evil City in American Fiction."[26] But there is one crucial difference: the white-slave narratives repeatedly emphasized that what they were exposing was fact, not fiction, that they were documenting not isolated incidents but rather a crisis striking at the very foundations of rural America. Martha Foote Crow's greatest fear, country girls deserting the farms, seemed to have been realized, and in this sense the white-slave tracts constitute an allegory of the passing and debasing of rural America. The almost hysterical injunctions to young women to stay down on the farm embodied the poignant hope that such a decline might be forestalled. By 1910, however, such a hope was only wild fantasy.

A second meaning of the country-girl-to-white-slave theme resides in the recurring presence in the white-slave narratives of distraught fathers and old-before-their-time mothers back in the small town or on the farm, mourning for the "loss" of their daughters. These sentimental and maudlin scenes of hearth and home, grieving parents, broken rural families, and lost children had roots deep in the idealized vision of rural family life that emerged in the mid-nineteenth century.[27] The white-slave tracts were clearly in this tradition, but they also served notice of a new concern: the prodigal *daughter*. The sentimental stories about the rural family in the last half of the nineteenth century mainly bemoaned the son's apostasy and embodied the anxiety and ambivalence occasioned by the emigration of young men, the sons, from the rural districts to the cities. This sentiment is clear in Thomas Hovenden's beautiful and popular painting of the 1890s, "Breaking Home Ties," which depicts, with a restrained and eerie sadness, a rural mother's farewell to her son as he prepares to strike out for the city. More optimistic, but not less complex, reflections of the male migration to the city were the Horatio Alger novels. The important point here is that most of the nineteenth-century depictions, whether optimistic or guilt- and anxiety-ridden, mark the passage of the sons of the land to the cities, but very rarely the daughters.

The white-slave narratives appeared at precisely the time when it was becoming clear that many young women had recently left, or were leaving, the small towns and rural areas for the cities. Certainly the proliferation of the new urban occupations that required an ever-expanding pool of young female workers (stenographers, sales clerks, and telephone operators, for example) had only recently occurred. With their themes of lost daughters and broken rural families, the white-slave tracts expressed the generational and familial stress that this migration provoked in the lives of rural-minded Americans, anxieties that had formerly centered on the sons.[28]

In this context the alternative conclusions of the white-slave captivities, either family reunion or a nameless grave in potter's field, take on special significance. The happy ending, the prodigal daughter's rescue from the captivity of white slavery, can be read as a projection of rural America's deepest hope: the return of the "lost" daughters, the reaffirmation and reunification of the rural family, and the alleviation of the sorrow and guilt occasioned by the daughter's departure from the family. The injunction to young women to stay in the country was an attempt to achieve a rural timelessness, to freeze a state of innocence, to stop history.

The hope that the city-wise prostitutes—rural innocence corrupted—might return to hearth and home and parents was the next logical step into fantasy: if history could not be stayed, then it might someday be reversed.

The disastrous ending of the white-slave captivity narrative—the daughter never heard from again and presumed dead or in the clutches of the white slavers—addressed a very different problem. Many young women leaving the country districts might well have lost contact, for any number of reasons, with their parents and family. In modern parlance they would be "missing persons." It is possible that the tragic endings of the white-slave captivities offered an explanation, admittedly macabre, to parents who had lost contact with their daughters. One white-slave narrative recounted that after a young white slave had been rescued from a brothel, "a simple announcement of the fact in a morning paper brought inquiries from five hundred parents whose daughters had recently disappeared. Where were the other 499 girls?" Another tract related the story of a girl killed in a trolley car accident. A notice was sent to the newspapers in the hope of identifying the young woman: "The most terribly sad feature of the tragedy was the number of men and women who flocked to the morgue—fathers and mothers and relatives of girls who had 'disappeared.' They had read in the newspapers of the accident, and despite disparities in the printed description and the appearance of their own lost one, they came to the morgue in the fearful hope of finding her."[29] These statements, of course, must be considered in the light of the other excesses and exaggerated fears of the white-slave narratives. Nevertheless, it still seems possible that the calamitous endings of the white-slave captivities, in whatever irrational way, answered to a situation as real as an empty mailbox or a missing place setting at the family table.

But if it is conceivable that many young women left the rural districts and small towns and dropped out of sight, it cannot be immediately assumed that they were all kidnapped into white slavery. Indeed, such cases of missing girls might have been a manifestation of a larger social problem that urban social workers dealt with on a daily basis: runaways from unpleasant home conditions. The white-slave tracts sometimes hinted at this problem, when they berated the decline of the moral authority of the family or expressed misgivings about "stage struck" country girls.[30] But the white-slave narratives never really openly confronted the issue of runaways, for the obvious reason that the existence of the problem hardly supported the sentimental version of rural contentment.

Other treatments of prostitution, however, specifically those by sociologists, social workers, and journalists with an urban cast of mind, underscored the familial pathology that pervaded the case histories of prostitutes with rural and small-town origins. "On the very brink of the stream of prostitution," wrote Maude Miner, "are the incorrigible and difficult girls who, in a moment of protest, anger, or adventure, have run away from home." These young girls, "in the dangerous period from fourteen to sixteen years of age," came to the cities, purposely hid their identities by adopting new names, and managed to escape detection.[31]

Thus, if it is not surprising that the white-slave narratives skirted any serious consideration of generational strife, it is illuminating. These tracts portrayed the rural family as a helpless victim of the alien forces of debauchery and, by emphasizing the enormous power of the white-slave conspiracy, by imputing to it the power to ruin any country girl, neatly avoided the unpleasant matters of runaway and rebellious daughters. The implication of this outlook, that the obliteration of the conspiracy would miraculously assuage the griefs of grayed and bent parents and make the countryside safe for family bliss, seems today more pathetic than laughable. Yet it was neither for those who felt that a way of life was passing into history and who could not but balk at facing such bitter truth.

The most curious aspect of the country-girl-to-white-slave theme was the persistent tendency to characterize white slaves in juvenile terms, as ruined children or childish victims. For the most striking example of this propensity, it is instructive to turn briefly from the white-slave narratives to a different medium, sculpture, where the conception of the white slave as a child received its most graphic expression in a work by the American sculptress Abastensia St. Leger Eberle.

Eberle, well known for her depictions of daily life in the tenement districts of New York's East Side, first worked out the composition for *The White Slave* in 1909 but did not actually model and execute it until 1913, when it was shown at the International Exhibit of Art in New York.[32] *The White Slave* then caused a minor controversy when it appeared as the cover illustration of the 3 May 1913 issue of the *Survey*, a liberal magazine concerned with social issues. Two later issues included seven pages of letters to the editor, debating the propriety of featuring the sculpture on the cover of a national periodical. The *accuracy* of Eberle's depiction of prostitution, however, was not challenged or discussed, and this absence of disagreement at least implies that *The White Slave* accurately represented the popular conception.[33]

What is most revealing about the sculpture is the depiction of the white slave-prostitute as a barely pubescent child-woman. The girl's body is shapeless, her breasts hardly developed, her silky haired head bowed in shame, and her facial expression more that of an asexual angel with a dirty face than that of an alluring harlot. Her hands are bound behind her back, and she is being "sold" by a grotesque and cruel-looking hawker of decidedly non-Anglo-Saxon physique and physiognomy. The sentimentalization is overwhelming, and though one critic saw in Eberle's interpretation a quality that "links it as a social force with, say, the dispassionate but terrible report of the Chicago Vice Commission," the sculpture was really more in the tradition of the white-slave tracts. In fact, it perfectly synthesized some of the basic themes of those narratives: the "lost" daughter, the obsession with lost innocence, and the alien character of the white slaver.[34]

This depiction of the white slave becomes even more interesting when compared to the findings on age and appearance of prostitutes in the vice commission reports and other group studies of prostitutes. The Chicago Vice Commission, for instance, presented a study of a group of thirty prostitutes which showed that the average age was 23.5 and that twenty-four of the women became prostitutes after the age of 18. A Massachusetts investigation reported that in a sample group of three hundred prostitutes, only sixty-seven were under eighteen years of age.[35] Other surveys found most prostitutes to be fully developed women in their early twenties.[36] Certainly most of the prostitutes so memorably photographed by Ernest J. Bellocq between 1912 and 1917 in Storyville, the New Orleans red-light district, appear to be at least in their late teens.[37] Some women, of course, did become prostitutes at an earlier age. Nevertheless, at any given time the reality of prostitution on the streets and in the houses was fundamentally different from the way in which it was presented in the white-slave tracts.

Why did the depiction of white slaves as ruined children enjoy such wide currency? To begin with, the portrayal of the white slave as a child-woman reduced the complexities of urban prostitution to the problem of victimized children, a drastic oversimplification highly effective in terms of melodramatic and sentimental appeal but of little worth as a contribution toward a rational understanding of a serious social problem. A concern with actual child prostitution and exploitation is admirable; the belief that all prostitutes are ruined children is something quite different. On a deeper level, this interpretation of prostitution reflected an inability or an unwillingness, perhaps both, to confront prostitution as a manifestation of *adult* sexuality totally outside the prescriptions of civilized morality. Childish victims were perhaps easier to deal with psychologically than libidinous men and women.

Because the white-slave conspiracy allegedly operated across the entire United States, there was agreement among those concerned with the problem that only national action could effectively halt the traffic in

American girls. The White Slave Traffic Act, or Mann Act, enacted by Congress in 1910, was based on just such a premise.

Although a lengthy section of the Mann Act dealt with the international traffic in alien white slaves, the rest of the act clearly addressed the domestic and interstate white-slave traffic. Based on the power of Congress to regulate interstate commerce, the Mann Act provided that any person who in any way knowingly aided or enticed a woman or girl to travel in interstate commerce "for the purpose of prostitution or debauchery, or for any other immoral purpose," was guilty of a felony and could be punished by a fine of up to five thousand dollars or by imprisonment for up to five years. If the woman or girl involved was under eighteen years of age, the fine and imprisonment were doubled.[38] Although some members of Congress felt that the act usurped the police powers of the states, or that scheming women might use it to blackmail hapless male companions who paid their way for an out-of-state tryst, most were persuaded of the act's necessity.[39] "Whenever I think of a beautiful girl taken from one State to another," declared a congressman from Tennessee, " . . . and drugged, debauched, and ruined, instead of being murdered, which would be a mercy after such treatment . . . I can not bring myself to vote against this bill or any similar measure."[40] Clifford Roe, the author of several white-slave narratives and an attorney in Representative Mann's home state of Illinois, delivered more than one hundred speeches in support of the White Slave Traffic Act. He was joined in this endeavor by fellow anti-white-slavery crusaders Ernest A. Bell and O. Edward Janney, and by others who regarded the act as a confirmation of their views.[41]

The turgid legal prose of the Mann Act at first seems far removed from the flamboyant rhetoric and overwrought style of the white-slave tracts, but the differences are more apparent than real. In a purely technical sense, the Mann Act simply empowered federal agents to attack the interstate traffic in exploited women and girls. A deeper reading, however, reveals that the great body of interpretive theory that had grown up around the commerce clause was being used to address one of the fundamental fears of the white-slave panic—the fear that the ever-expanding accessibility to the means of geographical mobility was undermining traditional methods of controlling sexual behavior. In the white-slave narratives, the locus of proper and safe morality was the family in the small community, outside the reach of urban influences. But in a time of widespread interstate train and trolley service, it was becoming progressively easy to frustrate the social constraints imposed in small and isoated communities. (It was perhaps more than coincidence, and it is surely symbolic, that the Mann Act was passed in the year following the first mass production of the Model T.) Mobility and morality—many Americans in the early twentieth century felt that the two were incompatible; and the Mann Act expressed the hope that the control of the former, under the aegis of the commerce clause, would lead to the safeguarding of the latter.

The Mann Act was of course tested in the courts, and several cases reached the U.S. Supreme Court. The court's first ruling on the White Slave Traffic Act, *Hoke and Economides* v. *United States* (1913), upheld the statute's constitutionality under the commerce clause. In *Athanasaw and Sampson* v. *United States*, decided on the same day as *Hoke*, the court ruled that the word "debauchery" in the act did not have to refer to actual sexual intercourse but could include actions or advances that might lead to sexual intercourse. In *United States* v. *Holte* (1915), the court held that a woman who was a willing participant in her own interstate travel for the purposes of prostitution could be convicted under the act. The court ruled in *Caminetti* v. *United States* (1917) that the Mann Act applied to the case of two defendants who had paid for the interstate transportation of two willing women as paid concubines, even though no organized prostitution was involved. None of these cases, it should be noted, involved the victimized white slaves that figured so dramatically in the white-slave narratives.[42]

Of course, most of the convictions under the Mann Act were never appealed to the Supreme Court. By 1913, the Department of Justice had produced 633 convictions, and by 1918 the total stood at 2,198. There had been only 323 acquittals. During the same years, many of the states enacted legislation, based on the Mann Act, outlawing intrastate transportation of women for immoral purposes. To those concerned about white slavery, all this seemed to constitute an impressive victory.[43]

The complete truth about the existence and extent of a white-slave conspiracy and a white-slave traffic will perhaps never be known. Historically, prostitution has almost always been a manifestation of the broader system of male dominance, and there can be no doubt that the organized sexual exploitation of women, often of a most brutal sort, was a prominent characteristic of prostitution in the progressive years. No one can fault the white-slave tracts for expressing outrage over such inhumanity. However, many of the other the basic assumptions of the white-slave narratives, the Mann Act, and the white-slave scare in general did not go unchallenged. Indeed, during the ten years or so that the specter of white slavery haunted certain parts of the American imagination, there were many who met the accusations and excesses of the white-slave narratives with skepticism or scorn.

An immediate point of disagreement concerned the relationship between white slavery and prostitution. Without any supporting evidence, the white-slave narratives argued that between 40 and 100 percent of prostitutes in the United States were white slaves; in other words, the problem of prostitution was the problem of white slavery.[44] Other treatments of prostitution, however, maintained that there was a sharp distinction between the two problems. The *Chatauquan*, whose readership was hardly soft on immorality, stated in 1909 that "it is important to bear in mind that the war on the white slave traffic is not a war on the social evil, prostitution itself, which presents a much more difficult and perplexing problem."[45] The implication was that the hullabaloo over white slavery was an oversimplification of a complex problem. Ada Eliot Sheffield elaborated on this point the next year in one of the more penetrating analyses of prostitution written in the progressive years. Without dismissing out of hand the existence at some times of some kinds of organized prostitution, Sheffield claimed that the "danger to society lies in prostitution itself and not merely in the 'white slave' traffic." Her own impression, based on "a dozen years in philanthropic work," was that "the majority of girls in this life could not be considered victims, except in the sense that one may be called a victim of poor environment and injudicious training." Prostitution, she wrote, "has deeper sources than the white slave traffic. It is more serious, because it is the cause, of which the traffic is one shocking effect, and most of all because it is a menace that extends through all ranks and grades of society."[46]

Other critics went further than drawing distinctions and concluded that there was no such thing as white slavery at all. In 1910 a special grand jury investigation under the foremanship of John D. Rockefeller, Jr., reported that it found no evidence of an organized white-slave traffic in the New York City area.[47] Several years later two California physicians, who conducted a detailed investigation of 320 prostitutes during working hours in San Francisco brothels, reported that none of the women mentioned a white slaver or white-slave traffic when asked to state their reasons for becoming prostitutes.[48] Another San Francisco physician, Ethel Watters, who was involved in the medical treatment of venereally infected prostitutes, discovered that many prostitutes moved from one locality to another at their own discretion, a finding that hardly substantiated the version of prostitution as actual slavery presented in the white-slave narratives.[49] Other investigations in St. Paul, Seattle, Illinois, Wisconsin, Massachusetts, Minneapolis, and Syracuse also reported that no evidence of white slavery was uncovered.[50]

One of the most telling critiques of the white-slave scare came from the pen of an Englishwoman, Teresa Billington-Greig, whose opinions, because they concerned a British law similar to the Mann Act, were well known and discussed in the United States. Billington-Greig scorned the stories of the abductions of girls by white slavers, tales "which suggested that the girls reported as trapped must be either limbless cripples or mental deficients." Of the eighteen speakers and writers prominent in the anti-white-slavery societies she surveyed, only five could assert that they knew that a white-slavery conspiracy existed, and just two provided information on three specific cases of white slavery, none of which would bear up under close scrutiny.[51]

Most impressive, however, was Billington-Greig's presentation of information pertaining to missing males and females collected from chief constables of seven British cities. The chief constables all emphasized that "missing persons are invariably found," and all but one of the officials agreed that "no missing girls have been found in the hands of procurers. In every place except Edinburgh, the actual number of men and boys missing and untraced exceeds the number of girls and women, and the percentage of traced females is equal to or greater than the percentage of traced males. One may fairly deduce that there is no abnormal cause of disappearance acting in the case of girls and women alone." The truth was, she argued, that "there are hundreds of feasible reasons why girls and women should desire to leave their homes, and dozens that will explain why, having left home, they may desire to remain undiscovered." The white-slave scare, "this campaign of sedulously cultivated sexual hysterics" conducted by "neuropaths and prudes," did not, she concluded, stand up under analysis. Such activity only inflamed emotions on a sensitive topic and oversimplified a complicated problem.[52]

Billington-Greig's study was the most thorough analysis of the white-slave anxiety and really the only one to offer a methodology to refute systematically the contentions of the anti-white-slavery zealots. Clifford Roe included a reference to her views in his 1914 white-slave tract *The Girl Who Disappeared*, in which he referred to her as a "cynical bystander" who could not appreciate the "toil and sweat and fight for the public welfare" of the anti-white-slavery groups. It is revealing that this brief comment was the extent of his consideration and that he did not attempt to refute Billington-Greig's logic or evidence, for if there was anyone who should have had the facts and figures to do so, it was Roe.[53]

The most reputable American to attack the contentions of the white-slave tracts was Brand Whitlock, who in 1913 was a newly appointed minister to Belgium and a former reform mayor of Toledo. Though he approvingly cited Billington-Greig's critique, most of his stinging analysis was directed at the obsessive mentality of the movement, which he described as "the present recrudescence of that puritanism which never had its mind on anything else" except illicit sex. Whitlock called the white-slave narratives "precisely the sort of pornography to satisfy the American sense of news." It could appeal only to "neuropathic women," "prurient and sentimental men," or "minds starved and warped by puritanism." While he was mayor of Toledo, Whitlock had assigned detectives to investigate the validity of alleged white-slavery cases, but no evidence was found to substantiate the "silly tale." The real harm, he felt, stemmed from the mentality of the white-slave crusader, whose world was "made up of wholly unrelated antitheses. There are no shades of shadows, no gradations, no delicate and subtle relativities. A thing is either white or black, sweet or sour, good or bad. A deed is either moral or amoral, a virtue or a crime. It is all very simple." Although Whitlock's piece lacked the analytical and methodological rigor of Billington-Greig's essay, it more astutely probed the temperament that found release in the crusade against white slavery.[54]

One final voice, which came from experience as well as reflection, deserves to be included among the criticisms of the white-slave scare. In 1919, Harper and Brothers published *Madeleine: An Autobiography*, written by an anonymous reformed prostitute and madam whose career had spanned almost twenty years. Toward the conclusion of her memoir, Madeleine tells how a "woman who devotes much time to social uplift" had "wasted a perfectly good evening" in an attempt to convince her "benighted mind" of the reality of the white-slave traffic. Madeleine is not convinced: "I do not know anything about the so-called white slave trade, for the simple reason that no such thing exists. . . . It was left for the enlightened twentieth century to create the Great American Myth. 'White slavery is abroad in our land! Our daughters are being trapped and violated and held prisoners and sold for fabulous sums (a flattering unction, this), and no woman is safe. . . . In the great city in which I live it is almost impossible to pick up a daily paper," Madeleine continues, "without seeing, in glaring headlines, the announcement that some girl has disappeared and is supposed to be held by white-slavers. Often times a brief item in an obscure part of a later issue states that the girl has been found to have gone here or there of her own free will; but those who read the first article seldom see the second, and so the belief in this myth has become a fixed delusion in the minds of many otherwise sane persons." Like the writers of the white-slave tracts, Madeleine offers no convincing proof of her assertions. Yet, because they come from one privy to the workings of prostitution, and because they confirm the contentions of other critics, it does not seem injudicious to grant to her comments an attention they would not otherwise immediately command.[55]

When one considers together the excesses of the white-slave narratives and the contemporary critical assessments of them, it is difficult to avoid the conclusion that they served only to oversimplify a very complex issue. What Americans needed in 1910 was an analysis of prostitution in light of the new advances in venereology, social work, sexual hygiene, and public health.[56] Some of the attempts to grapple with prostitution, most notably those of the medical profession and the urban vice commissions, gave the impression that these complexities were at least appreciated if not always fully comprehended. The white-slave tracts, however, reduced the problem of prostitution to the cardboard dimensions of a modern-day morality play, with beautiful country girls debauched by swarthy immigrants, lurid descriptions of brothels, and last-minute rescues from a fate worse than death. It was an Armageddon with the fate of American womanhood at stake.

This is not to dismiss the real anxieties expressed in the white-slave tracts. There *were*, for instance, dangers and problems facing the young women, largely untutored in the ways of the urban world, who quit the hamlets, farms, and streets of their birth to make their faltering way to the cities. Many of the warnings to girls and instructions for bewildered parents made sense, and in this way the white-slave narratives acted as guide books, or manuals for acculturation to urban living, much as the Horatio Alger novels did for young men a generation earlier. These instructional parts of the white-slave narratives, notwithstanding their hysterical tone, provided useful information for girls heading for the city: where to go, how to find safe lodging, how to get a job, whom not to trust, and where to go for help.[57] Nevertheless, the lasting impression that the white-slave narratives left with their readers was an overblown and paranoid presentation of the problem of prostitution.

The white-slave scare left its mark on the period. One might cite, for instance, the 1915 description of that new creature, the flapper: "She has a clear and detailed understanding of all the tricks of white slave traders, and knows how to circumvent them. . . . She has a keen eye for hypodermic needles, chloroform masks, closed carriages. She has seen all these sinister machines of the devil in operation on the screen. She has read about them in the great works of Elizabeth Robins, Clifford G. Roe, and Reginald Wright Kauffman. She has followed the war upon them in the newspapers." Or one might mention the scene in F. Scott Fitzgerald's *This Side of Paradise* (1920) where Amory Blaine is almost arrested for a violation of the Mann Act, or the fact that the same law was used to hound and harass persons as different as the boxer Jack Johnson and the architect Frank Lloyd Wright.[58]

Yet as strange and sometimes perverse as the white-slave scare was, it was not a cultural aberration. Indeed, the concept of the prostitute as white slave was completely logical for a culture that had sanctified the ideal of the woman-mother-wife. "The popular conception of well-organized recruiting agencies" for prostitution, Wayland Young argues, "is a mistaken one. The motive for entertaining the illusion," he goes on, "is fairly clear; the more a respectable man idealizes women, and the higher the value he sets on the merits of conventional society, the less will he be willing to believe any girl capable of abandoning it except under pressure or devious corruption."[59] Civilized morality held that women were not subject to the grosser sexual passions and drives that plagued men. The behavior of prostitutes in the teeming vice districts in the cities, however, glaringly challenged the validity of this belief. The white-slave conspiracy and the image of the prostitute as white slave provided a ready and convenient explanation: the white slaves had been caught and violated against their will and were literally held prisoners in the brothels. Only force and outrageous fraud kept them within the ranks of prostitution. The white-slave tracts thus defined prostitution in such a way as to conform with the tenets of civilized morality.

Ironically enough, the white-slave narratives and the publicity given to the white-slave scare actually contributed to the collapse of the moral code they so clearly supported. One of the cardinal rules of civilized morality was that a deliberate reticence was to be observed in confronting anything regarding sex. If a discussion of sexual matters should become necessary, it was to be conducted on an ethereal plane. The white-slave agitation was an embodiment of this morality, but the often lurid white-slave narratives and movies and the publicity in general contributed to what one commentator identified as a "Repeal of Reticence." "The doors of the brothel have been flung hospitably open," warned the conservative writer Agnes Repplier in 1914, "and we have been invited to peer and peep (always in the interests of morality) into regions that were formerly closed to the uninitiated. . . . to excite in youth a curiosity concerning brothels and their inmates, can hardly fail of mischief." Repplier, along with only a few other critics, saw the dangers to conventional morality in the publicity surrounding the white-slave scare, but her warning, coming as it did in 1914, was like a straw in the wind.[60]

Thus, in the broadest context, the white-slave tracts stand as self-contradictory expressions of an equally contradictory age. They clearly embodied many of the humane concerns of the progressive era. Yet they also expressed some of the more sinister tendencies of those years: the ethnocentrism and racial fears of the nativists; the emotional excesses, illogic, inaccuracies, and authoritarianism of the Prohibitionist crusade; and the conspiratorial mentality that often permeated even the most serious reforms. The white-slave tracts cried out in defense of the dignity of womanhood but portrayed women as helpless and passive stooges.

The narratives idealized the countryside and characterized the city as a cavalcade of fleshpots, yet they provided information and instructions to aid the migration of young women to the city that was so feared and decried. These contradictions, this confusion at the core, are what make the white-slave excitement seem so strange today. Many of the social problems posed by prostitution still persist, yet a serious student will look in vain for lessons and guidance in the thousands of pages the white-slave panic produced. These narratives, though well intended, misperceived the problem they were addressing and ended up tilting at a windmill which they could never prove existed, and which critics professed that they could not even see.

ANTIPROSTITUTION, PURITY, AND WAR

Unless their use is redeemed by necessity or by some human cause, arms are merely cruel and mischievous. The sentiments and symbols associated with war are ways of recognizing its inherent hatefulness. They are the means of concealing the ugly truth that arms are devised to kill with. If the use of arms can be judged even tolerable it must be because of the soldier's code and the soldier's cause.
  Ralph Barton Perry, *The Free Man and the Soldier* (1916)

Woodrow Wilson's evangelical call to arms in April 1917 set the stage for the culmination of the progressive response to prostitution. Antiprostitution flowed almost without interruption into the war effort and assumed a central role in the republic's participation in the war for civilization, decency, and democracy. Indeed, antiprostitution became, for the war's duration, one of the purest forms of Americanism.

Most Americans, including most of those who sat in the joint session of Congress to bear witness to Wilson's war message, were only vaguely aware of how the president's finely polished phrases could be translated into the actual raising up of an army capable of fighting a modern war of European scale. Many knew, however, that it would be a prodigious task. In 1917, notwithstanding the groups of college men who had spent summer vacations at military preparedness camps such as Plattsburgh, the nation was not prepared for war. The army numbered only about 128,000 officers and men. In addition, there were about 180,000 National Guardsmen. By the end of the war, the U.S. army numbered four million, half of whom went to Europe as the American Expeditionary Force. The Selective Service Act of 1917, the first compulsory U.S. draft since the Civil War, made possible this quantum leap in size. Conscription ultimately produced an army able to fight on the European continent, but it also created the staggering task of training huge numbers of young men for from five to seven months before they embarked for Europe. There were, naturally, many problems associated with the training camps for the U.S. troops, ranging from construction and maintenance to sanitation and supply. Preeminent, however, was the task of safeguarding the moral and sexual purity of the citizens becoming soldiers.[1]

The challenge of keeping the American soldier sexually pure and "fit to fight" was taken up by Secretary of War Newton D. Baker and his assistant Raymond Fosdick.[2] Both men had experience with antiprostitution activity before the war. Baker, a graduate of Johns Hopkins, had been mayor of Cleveland, Ohio, and like most mayors in the progressive years was familiar with prostitution as a pressing urban social problem. Fosdick, a native of upstate New York, transferred from Colgate to Princeton in 1904, where he first met Woodrow Wilson, then president of the university. After completing a year of graduate work at Princeton and earning a law degree from New York University, Fosdick served several years in government in New York City and, briefly, as Wilson's auditor of the Democratic National Committee.

In 1912, Fosdick was asked by John D. Rockefeller, Jr., to conduct a study of European police systems for the Bureau of Social Hygiene. The bureau was interested in how European municipal police systems were organized and how they dealt with prostitution. Rockefeller had in mind a study that would be a companion to Abraham Flexner's *Prostitution in Europe*, and Fosdick consented to the assignment. He spent two years crisscrossing Europe and in 1914 completed *European Police Systems*. Upon his return to the United States, he served as editor of the *American Journal of Crime and Criminology* and also completed a study of American police systems. By 1915, at the age of thirty-two, Fosdick was a man of wide experience. He had been a resident of the Henry Street Settlement in New York, where he had come to know Lillian Wald and her great achievements in social work; he had seen the operation of a huge city, New York, from the inside; he had traveled and investigated extensively in Europe and America; and he was well informed on urban and social issues.

Baker and Fosdick began what was to be a long friendship in 1916. One of Baker's first problems as newly appointed secretary of war was the skirmishes between U.S. troops and Francisco Villa along the Mexican border. Early in the summer of 1916, reports from the southwest began filtering into Washington, telling of a high venereal disease rate among the American troops, of rampant prostitution surrounding the encampments, and of widespread drunkenness. Knowing of Fosdick's investigative skills, Baker called him to Washington to propose that he visit the border camps and towns and write a first-hand report on conditions, including suggestions and recommendations. Fosdick assented and, upon arriving at the border, found the situation as appalling as the reports and rumors had implied. In his confidential report to Baker, he related that the red-light districts "were crowded with soldiers. . . . In some houses the rooms were so full that admittance was refused to soldiers at the front door and they were told to 'come back in fifteen minutes.' Most of the soldiers whom I saw were young boys. Some of them were quite drunk." Upon talking to some young recruits, he found that their "first real knowledge of the ways of red-light districts was obtained from what they saw in merely walking through the 'crib' sections of Douglas and El Paso. Such a sight," he went on, "not only demoralizes if the opportunity to renew it is continually and immediately at hand, but it leaves a scar on a man's life which he can never efface."[3]

By virtue of his studies of European and American police forces, Fosdick was no stranger to prostitution. Thus, what he found most disturbing was not the immoral conditions themselves but the fact that the army had no formal policy or program for dealing with the problems of prostitution and venereal disease. "Under present conditions," he wrote to Baker, "every general deals with the situation as he sees fit without relation to anything that any other division is doing." What was necessary, Fosdick advised, was a committee of "Army officers, physicians of modern training and scientific spirit, and perhaps civilians who have had experience with the problem," which would formulate a program "applicable to the future as well as the present handling of the prostitute in her relation to the Army."[4]

Fosdick urged Baker to issue an order for the control of the saloons and the repressions of prostitution near the camp, which Baker did immediately. Fosdick returned to Texas shortly thereafter and found that conditions had improved markedly, but he also saw that purely repressive measures were not enough. As he later recalled, "There were no moving shows and no pool tables; there was no place where they could read or write letters; . . . there wasn't even a newstand where they could purchase a magazine or a newspaper. The only attractions in town were a few disreputable saloons and a red light district. These institutions had the field all to themselves; there was nothing to compete with them."[5]

Fosdick and Baker continued through the winter of 1916–17 to formulate a new approach to military morality, and, as it became increasingly probable that the United States would enter the war, Baker saw such a program as an absolute necessity. "All of this seems to me especially important," he confided to a high-ranking general in early 1917, "in view of the possibility of our shortly having to undertake the training of large bodies of men—men selected probably from the youth of the country, who have not yet become accustomed to contact with either the saloon or the prostitute, and who will be at that plastic and

generous period of life when normal and wholesome outlets for exuber-
ant physical vitality will be readily accepted as a substitute for vicious
modes of indulgence, if the former be made accessible." Thus, when the
nation entered the war in April, both Baker and Fosdick were convinced
that an important part of the national war effort had to be a crusade
against prostitution and venereal disease in the army raised up to make
the world safe for democracy.[6]

Shortly after the declaration of war, the Commission on Training
Camp Activities (CTCA) was created by the federal government to deal
with the sexual and morale aspects of the training camps. Fosdick was
appointed chairman. The purpose of the CTCA was, in Baker's words,
that of "rationalizing as far as it can be done the bewildering environment of a war camp." This would prove to be no small task, for by 1918
there were sixteen training camps (or "Soldier Cities," as they were
called) in the United States, with an average population of forty-eight
thousand men. The CTCA directed its efforts toward five major objec-
tives: suppressing prostitution in the cities and towns adjacent to the
training camps; curtailing the operation of saloons in the same areas;
treating soldiers infected with venereal disease; planning and promoting
recreation programs in the camps; and educating the troops in certain
values and ideals. All of this activity was based on what Baker saw as the
basic philosophy of the work of the CTCA. "We will accept as the
fundamental concept of our work," he wrote to Fosdick, "the fact which
every social worker knows to be true, that opportunities for wholesome
recreation are the best possible cure for irregularities in conduct which
arise from idleness and the basic temptations."[7]

The CTCA's authority to suppress prostitution in the communities
surrounding the training camps was based on Section 13 of the Selective Service Act, which outlawed any form of prostitution within zones
around each camp, which usually included all areas within five, and
sometimes ten, miles. "I am determined that these camps," Baker wrote,
"as well as the surrounding zones within an effective radius, shall not be
places of temptation and peril." Investigators from the Legal Education
Division of the CTCA surveyed prostitution in cities near the canton-
ments and were able (as the earlier vice commissions were not) to bring
federal pressure to bear in eliminating the most visible aspects of prostitution: red-light districts and street solicitation. The threat of moving the
training camp to another location was often sufficient to make local
officials comply with the CTCA's desire for "pure" surroundings for the
new American army. This was often the tactic used in the South, most
notably in Louisiana.[8]

The Social Hygiene Instruction Division of the CTCA, headed by

Walter Clarke, a former official of the American Hygiene Association, implemented the CTCA's venereal disease program. Assuming that prostitution and red-light districts were "venereal disease swamps," the CTCA took pains to instill this belief in the U.S. troops. Thus, one CTCA pamphlet, entitled "Keeping Fit to Fight," warned: "You wouldn't eat or drink anything that you knew would weaken your vitality, poison your blood, cripple your limbs, rot your flesh, blind your eyes, destroy your brain. Why take the same chance with a whore?" Freedom from venereal disease was equated to patriotism, whereas contracting venereal disease was tantamount to aiding the enemy. "How could you look the flag in the face if you were dirty with gonorrhea?" asked one pamphlet; another declared, "A Soldier Who Gets a Dose Is a Traitor."[9]

In addition to this moral exhortation—and in tension with it—the army and navy instituted a rigorously scientific and modern program of venereal prophylaxis, which, for the prepenicillin era, was highly effective. Soldiers who had intercourse while on leave were required to report to a prophylactic station (located in the training camps and nearby cities) within eight hours of exposure. No penalty would result from reporting for treatment, but if a soldier contracted venereal disease and did not report for prophylaxis he could face court-martial proceedings. It is hard to tell how successful the moral indoctrination regarding venereal disease was, but the medical program showed outstanding results. For example, a study conducted in 1919 showed that for the preceding year, of all the new cases of venereal disease reported in five large camps (forty-eight thousand cases), all but 4 percent had been contracted prior to the recruit's entry into the army.[10]

The CTCA's program of recreation and "education," in which such organizations as the YMCA, the Knights of Columbus, and the Jewish Welfare Board played an important part, was directed toward keeping the soldier away from prostitutes, alcohol, and the possibility of contracting venereal disease. The educational program, which relied on a series of lectures, stressed the healthful aspects of sexual continence, the evils of alcohol, the value of personal cleanliness, patriotism, uplifting reading, veneration for women and motherhood, and industry and thrift. The recreational programs promoted athletics, group singing, wholesome movies and plays, and the establishing of "Hostess Houses," places in the camps where trainees could meet mothers and girl friends in a quiet and homelike atmosphere. And at every possible point, the CTCA presented its programs as microcosms of the moral meaning of the war. "The Hostess House idea is stamped 'made in America,'" a CTCA spokesman asserted, "and America is the land where women are partners, not chattels. In carrying this atmosphere of chivalry toward women into the training camps of the army and navy, the Government is fostering one of the basic principles of a well ordered democracy—the sanctity of the home."[11]

What is immediately striking about the philosophy and activity of the CTCA is how little of it was actually new in 1918. In fact, almost all of what the CTCA attempted to do was only an extension of the concerns and ideas engendered in the previous fifteen years of grappling with the problem of prostitution and venereal disease. The CTCA's repressive approach to prostitution was identical to that of the municipal vice commissions of 1911–16, and indeed the CTCA did little more than carry out the recommendations of those commissions. It is often assumed that the CTCA shut down the segregated districts in American cities during the war, but this assumption is only partially accurate.[12] In all of the cities that published vice commission reports and acted upon their repressive recommendations, activity in the segregated districts had been sharply curtailed by 1917; therefore, though it is accurate to say that the CTCA administered the coup de grace, it must be remembered that the vice commissions had paved the way in the preceding decade.[13] In this, as in all of its activities, the CTCA operated within a well-established cultural milieu.

In fact, many of the prewar antiprostitution groups simply adopted the war rhetoric and continued with their activities. The American Social Hygiene Association is a case in point. This organization (established in 1913) was itself a major expression of prewar antiprostitution and, after 1917, was able to channel its activities, with the consent of the CTCA, into the war effort. Walter Clarke and Bascom Johnson, both prewar officials in the association, were active in the work of the CTCA, and one of the most widely circulated (among the civilian population) pamphlets of the war, "Smash the Line," was prepared by the association and approved by the CTCA. It stated a basic prewar objective in the new context of the war effort:

> There are two vitally important reasons why *you* must accept a commission, as a citizen, to fight the Segregated District—to "Smash the Line":
>
> 1—Because the elimination of the Segregated District and consequent suppression of Prostitution will be mighty factors in winning the war!
>
> 2—Because in this way, only, can the finest civilization be promoted, the highest ideals and the greatest economic efficiency be developed—after the war is won![14]

Had it been in existence in 1918, the Chicago Vice Commission would hardly have put it differently.

The CTCA's approach to prostitution was also an extension, and in a sense a resolution, of the prewar debate over regulation and medical inspection. Before the war, some generals, along with many physicians, felt that prostitution was a "necessity" for the army. This attitude became clear in Fosdick's investigations of conditions along the Mexican border in 1916. Baker and Fosdick, however, were typical of the antiregulationist progressives (Fosdick was a personal friend of Abraham Flexner) who rejected the older theory of male "sexual necessity." Indeed, Fosdick's arguments against the regulation and medical inspection of prostitutes around the training camps were identical to those used by antiregulationists throughout the progressive years in their opposition to municipal systems of regulation.

The CTCA's endorsement of sexual continence for the U.S. troops was also a reiteration of a basic argument of prewar antiprostitution. In 1918, Bascom Johnson proclaimed, "No other government in the history of the world has taken the stand on this question that the United States government has taken." The American policy of "continence for the armies and navies" was "revolutionary"; it marked "an epoch in the history of the governments in the world." The only new touch was, of course, that in 1918 the CTCA could argue that sexual continence and purity would contribute to the winning of a war for the future of civilization and democracy.[15]

The CTCA's approach to prostitution and venereal disease was most dramatically expressed once the American Expeditionary Force was actually in France. For in France the U.S. attitude came into direct conflict with that of the French High Command, which sanctioned regulated brothels for French troops. Though Premier Clemenceau graciously offered to aid the American Command in setting up special accommodations for U.S. troops, the Americans rejected any compromise of the sexual purity of their men. Throughout the war in Europe, red-light districts were off limits for American soldiers and were tightly picketed by military police. In addition, the stateside policy of mandatory prophylaxis after a sexual contact was maintained in France. The result of both of these programs was an astonishingly low venereal disease rate among the American troops in France. One can see here the clash between American democratic idealism and European "decadence" regarding the regulation of prostitution, which was the tacit theme of Abraham Flexner's *Prostitution in Europe*. In fact, the CTCA's approach to prostitution both in the United States and in France can be seen as the end of the prewar controversy over the regulation of prostitution, a solution backed by federal authority.[16]

The CTCA's program of recreation and education, like its approach to prostitution and venereal disease, was also an expression of prewar ideas on dealing with prostitution. The CTCA's emphasis on the value of planned recreation was based, at least in part, on Fosdick's experience at Lillian Wald's Henry Street Settlement House, where the theory of the moral value of play and recreation in the urban environment was vigorously developed. One member of the CTCA, Joseph Lee, had been the preeminent figure in the progressive playground movement. The CTCA emphasized that the athletic programs contributed to the soldier's fighting potential, but, in a wider context, the CTCA's program of sports and planned recreation was, in effect, the institutionalization of what Walter Lippmann had called, several years earlier in A *Preface to Politics*, the "moral equivalents for evil."[17]

The most significant extension of prewar antiprostitution into the war effort, however, was the CTCA's policy pertaining to women suspected of being prostitutes. The CTCA faced a problem similar to that which the municipal vice commissions confronted several years earlier: what to do about the prostitutes and suspected prostitutes in the cities and towns surrounding the encampments. But here the similarity ended, for, unlike the vice commissions, the CTCA had federal authority to implement a broad repressive policy. Thus, whereas the vice commissions had rhetorically called for the "repression" or "annihilation" of prostitution or expressed concern over the extent of clandestine immorality, the CTCA participated in a program of arresting, detaining, and incarcerating women suspected of prostitution who were found in the zones surrounding the training camps. It was, like many of the more onerous aspects of the war effort, an efficiently administered program; by the end of the war some thirty thousand women had been so apprehended and incarcerated, often without the benefit of due process, trial, or legal representation.[18]

The legal basis for the program was what came to be known as the Chamberlain-Kahn Act, enacted by Congress in July 1918 as a part of the Army Appropriations Act. The Chamberlain-Kahn Act created the Interdepartmental Social Hygiene Board, consisting of, among others, representatives of the secretary of war, secretary of the navy, and secretary of the treasury. The board was empowered to oversee a national program of venereal disease control. The act also created a new Division of Venereal Disease in the Bureau of the Public Health Service, which, under the supervision of the Interdepartmental Social Hygiene Board, was directed to devise a program to decrease the rate of venereal disease in the military and to enforce quarantine regulations against the interstate travel of venereally infected persons. In addition, the Chamberlain-Kahn Act authorized the secretary of war and secretary of the navy to "adopt measures for the purpose of assisting the various States in caring for civilian persons whose detention, isolation, quarantine, or commitment to institutions may be found to be necessary for the protection of the military and naval forces of the United States against venereal diseases." One million dollars was appropriated for the implementation of this provision by the Interdepartmental Social Hygiene Board, and, although the provision used general terms, the "civilian persons" it referred to were predominantly prostitutes, or women who might be prostitutes.[19]

Three months before the enactment of the Chamberlain-Kahn Act, in April 1918, the CTCA created a new subdivision, the Section on Women and Girls (with a budget of $250,000), for the administration of facilities for the rehabilitation of women apprehended as prostitutes during the war. By 1919, with the help of federal funds provided by the Chamberlain-Kahn Act, thirty states had constructed at least minimally adequate facilities for the detention and treatment of venereally infected women. Women suspected as prostitutes were stopped, brought to detention centers, inspected for venereal disease, hospitalized and treated if necessary, and placed in rehabilitation programs. The CTCA, the Department of Justice, the Bureau of the Public Health Service, and the Interdepartmental Social Hygiene Board all participated in this program.[20]

It should be emphasized immediately that this policy embodied sound military logic. Uncontrolled venereal disease could decimate an army as surely as casualties in battle. By the time of the U.S. entry into the war, rumors of the high incidence of venereal disease in the European armies were rife in the United States. One report alleged that since the beginning of the war, Germany had temporarily withdrawn from active service the equivalent of sixty divisions because of syphilis. In 1917 the British had twenty-three thousand men in sick bay with venereal disease; the French had sustained over a million cases of gonorrhea and syphilis since 1914. General Pershing did not want the American Expeditionary Force to emulate either its allies or its enemies in this regard. Thus, once the Americans were in France, Pershing demanded daily reports on venereal disease and took strict measures to keep it to a minimum.[21] The government's stateside policy of detaining and, if necessary, quarantining women found to be venereally infected was an important aspect of this military objective. The policy was also highly effective. One medical officer even proclaimed, "A man is safer in the Army than in civil life."[22]

There was, however, something in addition to military logic at work here. Under the Chamberlain-Kahn Act, the government could quarantine for the "protection of the military and naval forces of the United States" any woman suspected of having venereal disease. The discovery of venereal infection upon medical examination could constitute proof of prostitution. In effect, during the war any American woman could legally be detained and medically examined if, in the opinion of officials of the CTCA or the Interdepartmental Social Hygiene Board, her life-style or observed or rumored sexual behavior indicated that she might be venereally infected. The similarity between this policy and the prewar control with clandestine prostitution and immorality is clear. Indeed, with its murky and ambiguous meaning—in its implication that any woman who was mobile, unchaperoned, and outside traditional contexts of moral control was a potential prostitute—the prewar concern about clandestine prostitution was perfectly suited to merge with the war hysteria. Both thrived on the same elements: guilt by association, half truth, innuendo, and oversimplification. In a sense, the wartime detention of women suspected of venereal infection was the ultimate solution to the anxiety occasioned during the previous decade by clandestine female immorality.

Who were the thirty thousand women who were detained? Some were undoubtedly professional prostitutes. The CTCA and the Interdepartmental Social Hygiene Board, with the cooperation of local officials and committees, were able to identify public prostitutes and apprehend them for medical examination and, if necessary, rehabilitation. Others, however, were probably women in their late teens and early twenties who either lived near or had migrated to the area adjacent to the training camps and who were seen or found near bars, movie houses, roadhouses, or other places that soldiers on leave might frequent. Often referred to as "uniform crazy," many of these women most likely were unemployed or seasonably unemployed; they gravitated to the camp areas perhaps in search of employment, perhaps to meet soldiers or prospective husbands, perhaps to make some money by part-time prostitution, or perhaps out of ordinary boredom and restlessness. Many dated the soldiers and may have entered into sexual arrangements with them. All these women, prostitute and nonprostitute, were liable to detention and incarceration.[23]

There was in all this a complicated issue of civil rights. Venereally infected women were as much a threat to public health in 1910 as to military health in 1918. Prior to the war, however, suspicion of venereal infection was not widely advanced as constituting sufficient grounds for detention and quarantine of prostitutes or women suspected of being prostitutes, even though the U.S. Supreme Court had ruled in a number of cases that, under certain circumstances, a state's duty to safeguard the public health could take precedence over individual civil rights. Certainly there was no authority for a broad-based, nationally coordinated crackdown on women suspected of prostitution or venereal infection.

With the raising up of the war machine in 1917, however, this situation changed dramatically. Women suspected of carrying venereal disease were treated, in effect, as subversives, and their legal predicament was similar to that of radicals and critics of the war who were caught up in the patriotic frenzy. This is not to argue that the women picked up in the wartime dragnet were in any sense political opponents of the war; they were victims of governmental action, not defiant dissenters. Some Americans did sense that something was wrong, and in several communities near training camps individual citizens and groups publicly objected to the arrest and detention of suspected women and took action to have them released by appealing to the right of habeus corpus. But, for the most part, the detention of suspected women seems to have bothered very few—so few, in fact, that by 1918 the *Survey* could approvingly state that "legal control is now generally accepted without challenge."[24]

In a speech delivered in October 1917, just as the first U.S. troops were leaving for Europe, Secretary Baker made what would become a famous statement:

> These boys are going to France; they are going to face conditions that we do not like to talk about, that we do not like to think about. They are going into an heroic enterprise, and heroic enterprises involve sacrifices. I want them armed; I want them adequately armed and clothed by their Government; but I want them to have invisible armor to take with them. I want them to have an armor made up of a set of social habits replacing those of their homes and communities, a set of social habits and a state of social mind born in the training camps, a new soldier state of mind, so that when they get overseas and are removed from the reach of our comforting and restraining and helpful hand, they will have gotten such a set of habits as will constitute a moral and intellectual armor for their protection overseas.[25]

Baker's "invisible armor" was forged of the alloy of values and ideals imposed on the American troops during their stay in the training camps: cleanliness, order, sobriety, sexual purity and continence, and the idealization of women. This invisible armor was, in other words, civilized morality. Indeed, the phrase "invisible armor" was a perfect description of the functional reality of civilized morality, referring as it did to an internalized prophylaxis against a world of excess and temptation.

It was here, in the CTCA's fundamental commitment to civilized morality, that prewar antiprostitution most perfectly merged with the war effort. Prewar antiprostitution had been the preeminent expression of the values of civilized morality. The rhetoric justifying the American participation in the war was also, in large part, based on the ideals of civilized morality. The CTCA fused antiprostitution rhetoric with the war rhetoric; it allowed antiprostitution to become an integral part of the war effort. The training camps in turn institutionalized civilized morality, both as it applied to antiprostitution and sexual purity and as it applied to the war in defense of democracy and civilization.

Whether the CTCA accomplished its goals is hard to determine. Its propaganda presented the doughboys as the finest specimens of moral and physical purity that any nation had ever sent forth to fight and die under its banner. And no less serious a progressive voice than the *Survey* called the work of the CTCA "the most stupendous piece of social work in modern times."[26] But when has war ever been waged by men who might have stepped out of a J. C. Leyendecker illustration?

In fact, there was another side to the story. Frank Tannenbaum, who was to become a famous historian at Columbia University in later years, was twenty-five in 1918 and spent some time in a training camp. His impressions of military life during the war, published in the *Dial* in 1919, cast an interesting light on the CTCA's boasts. "The talk in some quarters to the effect that military discipline has made a moral saint of the American soldier," Tannenbaum observed, "emanates from sources that would place a wish above a fact. And the fact is that the soldier is very much more unmoral than when he entered the army." The attitude toward women fostered in the camps was

> shorn of modesty, morals, sentiment, and subjectivity. . . . Men will sit till late at night in a darkened tent, or lie on their cots, their faces covered with the pale glow of a tent stove that burns red on cold nights, and talk about women—but this talk is of the physical rather than the emotional, of the types, the reactions, the temperaments, the differences and the peculiarities of moral concepts, the degrees of perversity, the physical reactions, the methods of approach—in fact, as if it were a problem in physics rather than morals. . . . After being accosted a number of times one evening by some of these youngsters [soliciting for prostitution], I made some remark offensive to one young huckster, and in reply he avowed, "Look a'here, Soldier, I tell you it is clean, fresh, and good." These were the very adjectives, and others like them, which are on the lips of the men in camp when discussing the problem of sex—an attitude applicable not only to the public woman, but to all women in general.[27]

Although Tannenbaum conceded that the incidence of venereal disease was lower in the army than in civilian life, he argued that this difference was owing not to "greater voluntary abstinence" or "higher morality" among the soldiers, as the CTCA proclaimed, but rather to the military's efficient program of venereal prophylaxis. In fact, the repression of prostitution around the camps was more myth than reality. "In the town near my camp," Tannenbaum wrote, "the public woman has been driven from the street. Some hundred of them are now in jail. But prostitution has prevailed."[28]

One wonders how Newton Baker or Raymond Fosdick would have responded to Tannenbaum's ungloved treatment of life in the training camps and of the work of the CTCA. For what Tannenbaum said was that the CTCA's program, the imposition of civilized morality upon the recruits, had backfired. Life in the training camps, as Tannenbaum saw it, did not produce men who embodied the traits of civilized morality —responsibility, restraint, decorum, gentility, and respect for women. To the contrary, the training camps, notwithstanding the efforts of the CTCA to have the men read, sing, play, and meet their sweethearts at the Hostess Houses, were the catalysts for the disintegration of any traces of the moral code that the recruits may have brought with them into the army.

Some years before the outbreak of the First World War, Rudyard Kipling observed, on the basis of some knowledge of the subject, that men living alone in barracks do not become plaster saints. American military leaders had historically accepted (if somewhat tacitly) this aspect of their livelihood, an aspect that, if Tannenbaum was anywhere near correct, was not much different during World War I than before. The dichotomy between the grosser actualities of life in the army, chronicled so well, for instance, in John Dos Passo's *Three Soldiers* (1921), and the repeated protestations of the CTCA that the American soldier was, if not exactly a plaster saint, something close to it, thus seems at best absurd, at worst duplicitous.

There was also a macabre undertone in much of the CTCA's work. "The Federal Government has pledged its word," Woodrow Wilson proclaimed in 1918, referring to the role of the CTCA, "that as far as care and vigilance can accomplish the result, the men committed to its charge will be returned to the homes and communities that so generously gave them with no scars except those won in honorable combat."[29] In translation, this meant that although men might come back from the trenches limbless, paralyzed, or disfigured, every effort would be made to see that they would not be morally scarred or diseased in the arms of a prostitute. The act of sex would lead to disease and moral depravity. The mass slaughter of mechanized war, "honorable combat," presumably would not. A decade later, Ernest Hemingway would pillory this view of the war in the famous passage in *A Farewell to Arms* where Frederic Henry reflects on the obscenity of the use of words such as "sacred," "glorious," "sacrifice," "in vain," "glory," "honor," "courage," or "hallow" to mask meaningless death and destruction. For Hemingway this disingenuousness was a monstrous joke. Thus Frederic Henry's affirmation of a view of life—and, implicitly, of the war—directly antithetical to the values and ideals for which the war was waged: "I was not made to think. I was made to eat. My God, yes. Eat and drink and sleep with Catherine."[30]

In 1918, however, it was ideologically necessary for the American government, through the CTCA, to assert beyond doubt that the American army was morally pure, even, if need be, in the face of an indomitable reality. The rhetoric and vision of the U.S. involvement in World War I was in large part a grand and planetary extension of the progressive emphasis on purity and morality in American life. Woodrow Wilson framed the goals of U.S. intervention in sublime terms, and, because the instrument of these goals was to be the great American army of democracy, it was necessary to claim that this instrument was as pure as its cause. The CTCA was created as the means of purifying this army, which would in turn purify the world. The French entertained no such ideas concerning the meaning of the war and were thus puzzled at the U.S. commitment to keeping the doughboys away from prostitutes. The Americans, of course, saw their position as consistent and essential; antiprostitution had to be an important component of the war effort.

In a sense, the incorporation of antiprostitution into the meaning and rationale of the war constituted a kind of final resolution of many of the issues that antiprostitution had raised in the previous decade and a half. (The case is analogous to that of the Prohibition movement, which was also able to link its cause with wartime patriotism, although antiprostitution obviously did not produce a constitutional amendment.) In 1910 those who supported a federal attack on prostitution had to settle for the Mann Act, which covered only those aspects of prostitution that came under the federal government's authority to regulate interstate commerce. The war emergency and the need to safeguard the sexual morality of the troops, however, allowed the federal government to strike at prostitution in ways that peacetime standards forbade. The anxiety about clandestine sexual immorality among young single women, the fear of the contagion of venereal disease, the desire to shut down and annihilate the urban vice districts, the belief in the value of sexual continence, the debate over the regulation of prostitution, the alarm at the breakdown in civilized morality—all these issues of prewar antiprostitution were dramatically resolved in the arrest and incarceration of suspected prostitutes and the indoctrination of the troops in the values of civilized morality.

In a perverse way, the wartime program was the closest the nation came to a national and centralized policy on prostitution. It consisted, however, of measures that only the fever of war would allow and sustain, and it stemmed from a commitment to a value system already in the process of collapse, a collapse that the outcome of the war itself would hasten. In the summer of 1914, there were probably few in the antiprostitution movement who knew exactly where Serbia was. But what transpired in that small Balkan nation set in motion a chain of events which ultimately presented antiprostitution with an opportunity few moral reforms ever get: the chance to step off with the flag at the head of the line, to become, for a moment, part of a patriotic groundswell of staggering proportions. But when the soothing breezes of peace finally cooled the heat of the war frenzy, they also extinguished the nationalistic fervor that propelled antiprostitution in its last phase. How ironic, then, that the national anthem, even as it became antiprostitution's victory chorus, also became its swan song.

EPILOGUE

To-day there is little risk in letting fly at the red light. What an easy mark is the "tenderloin"! Rare is the clergyman, teacher, or editor who can be unseated by banded saloon-keepers, gamblers, and madames. Their every "knock" is a boost. If you want a David-and-Goliath fight, you must attack the powers that prey, not on the vices of the lax, but on the necessities of the decent.
    E. A. Ross, *Sin and Society* (1907)

In 1918, in *Hammer v. Dagenhart*, the U.S. Supreme Court addressed the issue of whether Congress, under its constitutional authority to regulate interstate commerce, could prohibit the transportation across state lines of products manufactured under conditions that violated the recently enacted child-labor law. Many Americans hoped that the court would uphold the act, using the logic it had employed five years earlier when it upheld the Mann Act. In *Hoke and Economides v. United States*, the court ruled in sweeping language that Congress could use the commerce clause to "promote the general welfare, material and moral," and therefore had the authority to ban the interstate traffic in women for immoral purposes. The Court was not to be second-guessed. In *Dagenhart* it resurrected the already outmoded theory that Congress could prohibit commerce only when the subject articles were themselves inherently evil. The Court declared the Keating-Owen child-labor law unconstitutional, asserting in effect that Congress could not force manufacturers who shipped their products out of state to treat their juvenile employees with a minimum degree of decency.[1]

The inconsistency of the rulings did not escape the acute legal eye of Justice Holmes. In his eloquent and sometimes disdainful *Dagenhart* dissent, Holmes pointed out that in previous decisions concerning lotteries and adulterated food, the court had affirmed Congress's right to use the commerce clause to attack social ills if "the transportation encourages the evil." And if Congress could prohibit the transportation of women for immoral purposes, as the court said it could in *Hoke*, then it was incongruous, even capricious, to deny the power to ban the interstate transit of the products of "ruined lives."[2]

Ruined virtue and "ruined lives"; exploited women and exploited children—the similarity between them, the fact that they were often part of the same problem, was too obvious for the court to miss. The court's different treatment of them under the law constituted a telling commentary on antiprostitution. Indeed, the incompatible decisions expressed in microcosm the contradictions, limitations, and possibilities of the cultural context in which antiprostitution flourished.

Given the ultimate class and economic structure of early twentieth-century America, the opposition to child labor would be vigorously resisted. Prostitution, on the other hand, was something everyone could be against. Antiprostitution was a safe position. Businessmen could easily support the investigations of vice commissions. Rockefeller assistance could readily be given to research on prostitution and venereal disease. All might fulminate against the horrors of white slavery. Large corporate interests did not argue in court against the Mann Act as they did against the child-labor law. As Walter Lippmann observed wryly, "Magazines that will condone a thousand cruelties to women gladly publish series of articles on the girl that goes wrong."[3]

Antiprostitution was a safe position, however, only because the social and psychological issues it raised were in large part ignored. There were, to be sure, perceptive insights into the dynamics of prostitution in the writings of feminists like Charlotte Perkins Gilman, but these were oblique and fragmentary and escaped wide attention. The dominant tendency, the easier tendency, was to view prostitution as the result of feeble-mindedness, a liberal immigration policy, or white slavery—anything, that is, that did not betray the contradictions of American life itself.

To give the antiprostitution forces their due, they did perceive that widespread prostitution betokened something very wrong in their society, and they attempted to confront and publicize a problem that had formerly been shielded by a cocoon of shame and hypocritical silence. And, in the course of attempting to deal with the problem, they produced an impressive and useful body of information, statistics, and related data. Who can doubt that here was the possibility of a unique and historic insight into American social relations?

It was a promise that was never fulfilled. The problem of prostitution too often was reduced to the most culturally palatable slogans. The slogans reflected, unfortunately, not only intellectual and cultural rigidity, but also confusion and at times desperation. Part of this resulted from the sense of great and unsettling social change, and the plethora of large and sweeping issues with which prostitution seemed connected. Most of the confusion and desperation, however, arose from the inability of the antiprostitution forces to understand their own place in history, to see that their concern was an expression of a much larger cultural transformation and that it was propelled by a commitment to moral and intellectual values which that transformation was seriously undermining.

In the years after World War I, concern about prostitution dissipated almost as rapidly as it had emerged two decades earlier. From time to time prostitution became the stimulus of public excitement, often in the context of municipal politics, as was the case with the Seabury investigations of the New York City Woman's Court in the 1930s. Prostitution and venereal disease attracted public attention again during World War II, as during World War I. But after 1920 prostitution never again became the dominant national issue it had been during the progressive years. In part this change was the result of the triumph of a secular and more technical approach to social problems, which supplanted the older moralistic approach. Then, too, the economic crisis of the 1930s provoked a reordering of the priority of social problems. As one historian has remarked, "While the Progressive grieved over the fate of the prostitute, the New Dealer would have placed Mrs. Warren's profession under a code authority."[4]

The most compelling explanation for the eclipse of concern about prostitution after 1920, however, is that the cultural crisis of which antiprostitution was so preeminently an expression was largely over by this date. The alarming national issues with which prostitution was identified abated, or assumed less prominent forms, in the 1920s and the years after. Prostitution, which had seemed such an ominous symptom and symbol, lost most of its capacity to provoke fear and alarm.

Like the heated debate over the relative merits of a gold or silver monetary system in the late nineteenth century, or the drive to free America from the tyranny of the saloon, antiprostitution has about it the aura of a museum piece. But for all its archaic qualities, and for all the absurdities we can easily (perhaps too easily) see in it today, it was an important and illuminating expression of a truly extraordinary time in American history. And if it can be charged that antiprostitution was a failure, and is not among the enduring legacies of the progressive years, might not its failure be precisely why it reveals so much about American society in that time?

NOTES

Citations of periodical primary source material will contain the title of the journal in abbreviated form and the year of publication. Citations of primary source books or pamphlets will contain the year of publication. Citations of secondary sources will appear in short form. All references are listed in complete form in the bibliography.

Abbreviations

AAAPS	*Annals of the American Academy of Political and Social Science*
AC	*American City*
AJCM	*American Journal of Clinical Medicine*
AJDGUD	*American Journal of Dermatology and Genito-Urinary Diseases*
AJI	*American Journal of Insanity*
AJN	*American Journal of Nursing*
AJO	*American Journal of Obstetrics and Diseases of Women and Children*
AJPH	*American Journal of Public Health*
AJPHy	*American Journal of Public Hygiene*
AJRM	*Atlanta Journal-Record of Medicine*
AJS	*American Journal of Sociology*
AJUS	*American Journal of Urology and Sexology*
ALLR	*American Labor Legislation Review*
AM	*American Magazine*
AMAB	*American Medical Association Bulletin*
AMd	*American Medicine*
ARR	*American Review of Reviews*
AtM	*Atlantic Monthly*
BAAM	*Bulletin of the American Academy of Medicine*
BMJ	*Buffalo Medical Journal*
BMSJ	*Boston Medical and Surgical Journal*
Ch	*Chautaquan*
CJM	*California State Journal of Medicine*
CMJ	*Cleveland Medical Journal*
CMR	*Chicago Medical Reporter*
CO	*Current Opinion*

D	*Dial*
DHG	*Dietetic and Hygienic Gazette*
DMJ	*Detroit Medical Journal*
ER	*English Review*
F	*Forum*
HahM	*Hahnemannian Monthly*
HM	*Hampton's Magazine*
I	*Independent*
IJE	*International Journal of Ethics*
IMJ	*Indianapolis Medical Journal*
IoMJ	*Iowa Medical Journal*
ISMJ	*Interstate Medical Journal*
JAIC	*Journal of the American Institute of Criminal Law and Criminology*
JAMA	*Journal of the American Medical Association*
JCD	*Journal of Cutaneous Diseases Including Syphilis*
JCL	*Journal of Criminal Law*
JSH	*Journal of Social Hygiene*
JSM	*Journal of Sociological Medicine*
KMJ	*Kentucky Medical Journal*
LC	*Lancet-Clinic*
LD	*Literary Digest*
LIMJ	*Long Island Medical Journal*
MB	*Medical Brief*
MCMMS	*Medical Communications of the Massachusetts Medical Society*
Md	*Medicine*
MdR	*Medical Record*
MH	*Medical Herald*
MLJ	*Medical Legal Journal*
MM	*McClure's Magazine*
MMd	*Modern Medicine*
MMJ	*Massachusetts Medical Journal*
MN	*Medical News*
MPCG	*Medico-Pharmaceutical Critic and Guard*
MR	*Missionary Review of the World*
MRR	*Medical Review of Reviews*
MS	*Military Surgeon*
MT	*Medical Times*
N	*Nation*
NEMG	*New England Medical Gazette*
NM	*Northwest Magazine*
NYMJ	*New York Medical Journal*
NYSJM	*New York State Journal of Medicine*
O	*Outlook*
PaMJ	*Pennsylvania Medical Journal*

PAPS   *Proceedings of the Academy of Political Science*
PASA   *Publications of the American Statistical Association*
PHR   *Public Health Reports*
PM   *Pearson's Magazine*
PMJ   *Pacific Medical Journal*
PNCSW   *Proceedings of the National Conference of Social Work*
PR   *Psychological Review*
PrMJ   *Providence Medical Journal*
PtMJ   *Pittsburgh Medical Journal*
QJE   *Quarterly Journal of Economics*
RIMJ   *Rhode Island Medical Journal*
S   *Survey*
SLMR   *St. Louis Medical Review*
SPMJ   *St. Paul Medical Journal*
SS   *Smart Set*
TAGS   *Transactions of the American Gynecological Society*
TMJ   *Texas Medical Journal*
UCR   *Urologic and Cutaneous Review*
VMM   *Vermont Medical Monthly*
VMSM   *Virginia Medical Semi-Monthly*
WMJ   *Woman's Medical Journal*
WsMJ   *Wisconsin Medical Journal*
WVMJ   *West Virginia Medical Journal*
YMJ   *Yale Medical Journal*

Introduction

1. Quoted in Mark Schorer, *Sinclair Lewis*, p. 155.

2. Darrett B.. Rutman, *Winthrop's Boston*, p. 242. For the whorehouse riots see Richard Hofstadter and Michael Wallace, eds., *American Violence*, pp. 447–50; and David J. Pivar, *Purity Crusade*, pp. 21–22.

3. For antiprostitution activities in the antebellum period see the full study by Larry Howard Whiteaker, "Moral Reform and Prostitution in New York City, 1830–1860"; Carroll Smith Rosenberg, *Religion and the Rise of the American City*, pp. 97–124; and Carroll Smith-Rosenberg, "Beauty, the Beast and the Militant Woman," pp. 562–84.

4. The best treatment of Sanger is in James L. Wunsch, "Prostitution and Public Policy," pp. 7–22.

5. See Pivar, *Purity Crusade*, for a full treatment of purity reform. For the controversy over regulation and inspection, see ibid., pp. 13–73; Wunsch, "Prostitution and Public Policy," pp. 38–100; John C. Burnham, "Medical Inspection of Prostitutes in America in the Nineteenth Century," pp. 203–18; and John C. Burnham, "The Social Evil Ordinance," pp. 203–17. For other aspects of prostitution in the nineteenth century see Jacqueline Baker Barnhart, "Working

Women"; Yuji Ichioka, "Ameyuki-san," pp. 1–21; and Claudia D. Johnson, "That Guilty Third Tier," pp. 575–84.

6. Because virtually no one publicly advocated or supported prostitution in the progressive era (although some endorsed looking the other way), in this study the phrases "the response to prostitution," "antiprostitution," and "concern about prostitution," and variations thereof, are used synonymously.

7. Older but still valuable studies of antiprostitution in the progressive era include Willoughby Cyrus Waterman, *Prostitution and Its Repression in New York City, 1900–1931*; Howard B. Woolston, *Prostitution in the United States* (1921); Joseph Mayer, *The Regulation of Commercialized Vice* (1922); and Walter C. Reckless, *Vice in Chicago*. More recent work includes Ruth Rosen, "The Lost Sisterhood"; Ruth Rosen, Introduction to *The Maimie Papers*, pp. xiii–xliv; Roland Richard Wagner, "Virtue against Vice"; Paul Boyer, *Urban Masses and Moral Order in America, 1820–1920*, pp. 191–219; Wunsch, "Prostitution and Public Policy," pp. 101–61; James F. Gardner, Jr., "Microbes and Morality"; Roy Lubove, "The Progressives and the Prostitute," pp. 308–30; Egal Feldman, "Prostitution, the Alien Woman and the Progressive Imagination, 1910–1915," pp. 192–206; Jeremy Felt, "Vice Reform as a Political Technique," pp. 24–51; R. G. Walters, "Sexual Matters as Historical Problems," pp. 157–75; Daniel J. Leab, "Women and the Mann Act," pp. 55–65; Elizabeth C. MacPhail, "When the Red Lights Went Out in San Diego," pp. 1–28; Kay Ann Holmes, "Reflections by Gaslight," pp. 83–101; James R. McGovern, "'Sporting Life on the Line,'" pp. 131–44; and Eric Anderson, "Prostitution and Social Justice," pp. 203–28.

8. For some insights into the bleaker aspects of prostitution in the progressive era, see the recollections of life in Storyville, the red-light district in New Orleans, compiled in Al Rose, *Storyville, New Orleans*, pp. 147–65.

9. See Robert Wiebe, *The Search for Order*; Richard Hofstadter, *The Age of Reform*; Samuel P. Hays, *The Response to Industrialism, 1885–1914*; Henry F. May, *The End of American Innocence*; Morton White, *Social Thought in America*; and Clyde Griffen, "The Progressive Ethos," pp. 120–49. For historiography and criticism, see Peter Filene, "An Obituary for 'the Progressive Movement,'" pp. 20–34; and David Kennedy, "Overview: The Progressive Era," pp. 453–68.

10. For a treatment of some of the more extreme of these tendencies in other areas of American life, see Frederic Cople Jaher, *Doubters and Dissenters*.

11. The concept of civilized morality is most fully developed and brilliantly explored in Nathan G. Hale, Jr., *Freud and the Americans*, pp. 24–46. Hale's starting point is Freud's important polemical essay of 1908, "'Civilized' Sexual Morality and Modern Nervousness." In the discussion that follows, I have drawn upon, in addition to Hale's work, Whiteaker, "Moral Reform and Prostitution in New York City, 1830–1860," pp. 157–200; Steven Marcus, *The Other Victorians*; James Reed, *From Private Vice to Public Virtue*, pp. 3–63; Milton Rugoff, *Prudery and Passion*; R. Christian Johnson, "Anthony Comstock"; Peter Gabriel Filene, *Him-Her Self*, pp. 5–115; John S. Haller, Jr., and

Robin M. Haller, *The Physician and Sexuality in Victorian America*; and Peter T. Cominos, "Late Victorian Sexual Respectability and the Social System," pp. 18–48, 216–50. For a discussion of the historical pitfalls inherent in assuming a direct correlation between the prescriptions of civilized morality and actual sexual behavior, see Carl N. Degler, "What Ought To Be and What Was," pp. 1476–90; and Howard I. Kushner, "Nineteenth-Century Sexuality," pp. 35–36.

12. See Pivar, *Purity Crusade*, pp. 78–121; and Paul Boyer, *Purity in Print*, pp. 1–22.

13. See May, *The End of American Innocence*, pp. 219–329; Daniel Scott Smith, "The Dating of the American Sexual Revolution," pp. 321–35; Reed, *From Private Vice to Public Virtue*, pp. 54–63; William L. O'Neill, *Divorce in the Progressive Era*, pp. 89–167; and James R. McGovern, "The American Woman's Pre-World War I Freedom in Manners and Morals," pp. 315–33.

Chapter 1

1. Robert E. Park, "The City," *AJS* (1915), pp. 610, 612.

2. Samuel Paynter Wilson, *Chicago and Its Cesspools of Infamy* (1910); Chicago, *The Social Evil in Chicago* (1911), p. 25; "United against Social Vice," *I* (1913), p. 509.

3. John Spargo, *The Bitter Cry of the Children* (1906), p. xlii.

4. New York City, *The Social Evil: With Special Reference to Conditions Existing in the City of New York* (1902), pp. 146–47. Johnson's memory of his role in preparing the report can be consulted in his *Pioneer's Progress* (1952), pp. 138–43. My discussion of the Committee of Fifteen and Committee of Fourteen is based on Roland Richard Wagner, "Virtue against Vice," pp. 85–145; and James F. Gardner, Jr., "Microbes and Morality," pp. 46–84, 146–55. Both of these studies draw on the manuscript records of the minutes of the committees' meetings. Also important are Jeremy P. Felt, "Vice Reform as a Political Technique," pp. 24–51; and Willoughby Cyrus Waterman, *Prostitution and Its Repression in New York City, 1900–1931*, pp. 90–118.

5. Prince A. Morrow, "A Plea for the Organization of a Society of Sanitary and Moral Prophylaxis," *MN* (1904), p. 1073. There are detailed discussions of Morrow and the society in Gardner, "Microbes and Morality," pp. 106–54; and John C. Burnham, "The Progressive Era Revolution in American Attitudes toward Sex," pp. 890–97. Factual material on Morrow's career is drawn from Gardner, pp. 106–9, and Burnham, pp. 892–96.

6. Morrow, "The Society of Sanitary and Moral Prophylaxis," *AM* (1905), p. 321.

7. Gardner, "Microbes and Morality," pp. 109, 116, 156; Burnham, "The Progressive Era Revolution in American Attitudes toward Sex," p. 896. For a thorough discussion of the doctrine of male sexual necessity, see James L. Wunsch, "Prostitution and Public Policy," pp. 101–21. For sex hygiene instruc-

tion, see Gardner, "Microbes and Morality," pp. 117–23; and Byran Strong, "Ideas of the Early Sex Education Movement in America, 1890–1920," pp. 129–61.

8. For membership, see Gardner, "Microbes and Morality," p. 156. For the growth of affiliate branches, see Morrow, "Results of the Work Accomplished by the Society of Sanitary and Moral Prophylaxis," *NYMJ* (1907), pp. 1108– 13; Morrow, "Results Achieved by the Movement for Sanitary and Moral Prophylaxis," *MdR* (1909), pp. 1061–65; and Morrow, "Report of Progress in Sanitary and Moral Prophylaxis," *NYMJ* (1912), pp. 577–82. For the sense of accomplishment, see Morrow, "Sanitary and Moral Prophylaxis," *BMSJ* (1906), p. 677; and Morrow, "Social Prophylaxis and the Medical Profession," *AJDGUD*(1905), pp. 271–72.

9. Morrow, "Results Achieved by the Movement for Sanitary and Moral Prophylaxis," *MdR* (1909), pp. 1061–62; Gardner, "Microbes and Morality," p. 180; Burnham, "The Progressive Era Revolution in American Attitudes toward Sex," pp. 897–98.

10. William Stead, a British editor and reformer, claimed to have discovered a "white-slave" traffic in young girls for prostitution in England in 1885, and his exposé in the *Pall Mall Gazette* fueled an evangelical crusade against prostitution in England. In 1893, Stead came to Chicago, to the Columbian Exposition, and there conducted a widely reported vice crusade that resulted in his famous book *If Christ Came to Chicago* (1894). For Stead see Joseph O. Baylen, "A Victorian's 'Crusade' in Chicago, 1893–1894," pp. 418–34. The Reverend Charles Parkhurst conducted a similar, highly emotional, vice crusade in New York City in 1892, emphasizing the graft-ridden relationship among the vice interests, police, and Tammany Hall. See David J. Pivar, *Purity Crusade*, pp. 207–8; Wagner, "Virtue against Vice," pp. 44–57; Gardner, "Microbes and Morality," pp. 46– 105; and Pamela Ann Roby, "Politics and Prostitution," pp. 72–84.

11. Syracuse, *The Social Evil in Syracuse* (1913), p. 83. See also Chicago, *The Social Evil in Chicago* (1911), p. 3; Minneapolis, *Report of the Vice Commission of Minneapolis* (1911), p. 14; Newark, *Report of the Social Evil Conditions of Newark* (1914), p. 64; A. Leo Weil, "In the Hands of the Police," *S* (1913), pp. 203–4; George Kibbe Turner, "The Strange Woman," *MM* (1913), p. 32; "'Daughters of the Poor' One Year After," *MM* (1910), p. 120; Anna Garlin Spencer, "Josephine Butler and the English Crusade," *F* (1913), p. 708; Joseph H. Greer, *The Social Evil* (1909), pp. 61–62; Robert N. Wilson, *The American Boy and the Social Evil* (1905), p. 153; and C. E. Smith, Jr., "Some Observations on Public Health and Morality," *SPMJ* (1912), p. 199. Physicians interested in social issues were equally strong on this point, usually in the context of advocating a purely sanitary approach to the problem of prostitution. See V. G. Vecki, "Can We Abolish, Shall We Ignore, or Must We Regulate Prostitution?" *AJDGUD* (1910), p. 217; F. H. Hancock, "Regulation of Prostitution in the City of Norfolk, Virginia," *VMSM* (1912), p. 560; George B. H. Swayze, "Social Evil Dilemma," *MT* (1906), p. 226; J. Ewing Mears, "The Problem of the Social Evil Considered in Its Social and Medical Aspects and in Its Relation to the Problem of Race Betterment," *MR* (1913), pp. 235–36; J. Rosenstirn, "Should the Sani-

tary Control of Prostitution Be Abandoned?" *MR* (1914), pp. 1067–71; A. L. Wolbarst, "The Problem of Venereal Prophylaxis," *BMSJ* (1906), p. 282; and Rheta Childe Dorr, "Reclaiming the Wayward Girl," *HM* (1911), p. 73.

12. For the Bureau of Social Hygiene, see Gardner, "Microbes and Morality," pp. 222–80. The bureau was established in 1911 but did not incorporate until 1913. For favorable attitudes toward it, see "Supreme Court Upholds the 'White Slave' Law," *S* (1913), p. 802; Graham Taylor, "The War on Vice," *S* (1913), p. 811; "The Bureau of Social Hygiene," *O* (1913), p. 288; "Needed: A Scientific Study of Prostitution," *CO* (1913), p. 6; and "Mr. Rockefeller, Jr.'s War on the Social Evil," *LD* (1913), p. 284.

13. Harry Benjamin and R. E. L. Masters, *Prostitution and Morality*, p. 28; "Prostitution," *Encyclopedia Britannica*, 11th ed. (1911); Illinois, *Report of the Senate Vice Committee* (1916), p. 24. The standard legal definition of a prostitute was "a woman who indiscriminately consorts with men for hire." See *Black's Law Dictionary*, 2d ed. (1910), p. 959. However, an early student of prostitution in the period wrote: "A study of decisions made up to this time [1918] shows that in some cases the element of gain was considered an essential ingredient of prostitution, and that in others this was not the case. Dictionary definitions, whether those of Webster or of Law Dictionaries, are equally confusing. In Webster the definition varies according to the edition." See Howard B. Woolston, *Prostitution in the United States* (1921), p. 35.

14. Chicago, *The Social Evil in Chicago* (1911), p. 6.

15. "The Social Evil," *O* (1912), p. 246; T. D. Crothers, "Some Scientific Conclusions concerning the Vice Problem," *TMJ* (1913), p. 381; Sprague Carleton, "The Prostitute," *HahM* (1908), p. 824. For an awareness that the "social evil" had no single meaning, see William Cullen Bryant, "The Social Evil," *PtMJ* (1914), p. 36.

16. For the change in moral values, see James Reed, *From Private Vice to Public Virtue*, pp. 54–63. Other studies of changing mores include James R. McGovern, "The American Woman's Pre-World War I Freedom in Manners and Morals," pp. 315–33; Burnham, "The Progressive Era Revolution in American Attitudes toward Sex," pp. 885–908; and Daniel Scott Smith, "The Dating of the American Sexual Revolution," pp. 321–35. For a modern view of permissiveness, see Ira L. Reiss, *The Social Context of Premarital Sexual Permissiveness*.

17. See Vern Bullough, "Problems and Methods for Research in Prostitution and the Behavioral Sciences," pp. 244–46.

18. For New York City see William W. Sanger, *The History of Prostitution* (1895 Appendix), p. 678; James Bronson Reynolds, "Procuring and Prostitution in New York," in Clifford G. Roe, *The Great War on White Slavery* (1911), p. 215; "The Problem of Vice and Graft," *LD* (1913), pp. 61–62; and George Jackson Kneeland, *Commercialized Prostitution in New York City* (1913), p. 111. For Chicago see G. Frank Lydston, *The Diseases of Society* (1904), p. 308; Wilson, *The American Boy and the Social Evil* (1905), p. 90; H. M. Lytle, *Tragedies of the White Slave* (1909), p. 3; Reginald Wright Kauffman, *The House of Bondage* (1910), p. 256; Chicago, *The Social Evil in Chicago* (1911) pp. 70, 71; Jean Turner Zimmermann, *America's Black Traffic in White Girls* (1912),

p. 5; Walter T. Sumner, "General Considerations on the Vice Problem," *CMR* (1913), p. 100; and Harry A. Parkin,"Practical Means of Protecting Girls," in Ernest A. Bell, ed., *War on the White Slave Trade* (1909), p. 327. For national estimates, see B. S. Steadwell, Introduction to Roe, *The Great War on White Slavery* (1911), pp. 15–16; Stanley Finch, *The White Slave Traffic* (1912), p. 7; Lavinia L. Dock, *Hygiene and Morality* (1910), p. 152; and Walter D. Bieberbach, "Venereal Disease and Prostitution," *BMSJ* (1915), p. 203.

19. Wilson is quoted in John S. Fulton, "The Medical Statistics of Sex Hygiene," *AJPH* (1913), pp. 661–64. There is a brief discussion of the congress in Gardner, "Microbes and Morality," pp. 184–86.

20. Fulton, "The Medical Statistics of Sex Hygiene," *AJPH* (1913), pp. 661, 663, 668, 670; Robert N. Wilson, "Judge Not, That Ye Be Not Judged! Does the American Federation for Sex Hygiene Speak the Truth?" *AJPH* (1913), pp. 874–81.

21. Mears, "The Problem of the Social Evil Considered in Its Social and Medical Aspects and in Its Relation to the Problem of Race Betterment," *MdR* (1913), p. 235; I. L. Nasher, "Prostitution in 1886 and in 1916," *AJUS* (1916), p. 541 (Nasher estimated that there were five thousand prostitutes in the city, a figure one-tenth of that usually cited; unfortunately, however, he did not divulge how he had arrived at his "estimate"); U.S. Senate, *Report on Conditions of Women and Child Wage Earners in the United States*, vol. 15, *Relation between Occupation and Criminality of Women* (1911), p. 11; U.S. Senate, Reports of the Immigration Commission, vol. 19, *Importation and Harboring of Women for Immoral Purposes* (1910), pp. 60, 64 (hereinafter cited as U.S. Senate, *Importation and Harboring*).

22. See Bullough, "Problems and Methods for Research in Prostitution and the Behavioral Sciences," pp. 244–45.

23. This belief enjoyed wide currency during the progressive years. See Theodore A. Bingham, "The Girl That Disappears," *HM* (1910), pp. 562, 569; George Kibbe Turner, "The Daughters of the Poor," *MM* (1909), p. 59; Greer, *The Social Evil* (1909), pp. 25–26; Dock, *Hygiene and Morality* (1910), p. 153; Wilson, *The American Boy and the Social Evil* (1905), pp. 99–100; Herr Glessner Creel, *Prostitution for Profit* (1911), p. 29; Zimmermann, *America's Black Traffic in White Girls* (1912), pp. 47, 77; Lytle, *Tragedies of the White Slave* (1909), p. 4; Roe, *The Great War on White Slavery* (1911), p. 171; Clifford G. Roe, *The Girl Who Disappeared* (1914), pp. 25–26; Virginia Brooks, *My Battles with Vice* (1915), p. 18; Robert J. Moorehead, *Fighting the Devil's Triple Demons* (1911), pp. 59, 122, 167; Bell, *War on the White Slave Trade* (1909), pp. 59, 75, 141, 158, 443; Ralph Beaton, *The Anti-Vice Crusader and Social Reformer* (1918), pp. 113, 147; Kauffman, *The House of Bondage* (1910), pp. 155, 255; Robert N. Wilson, "The Eradication of the Social Diseases in Large Cities," *JAMA* (1912), p. 926; Denslow Lewis, "The Prophylaxis and Management of Prostitution," *PaMJ* (1906), p. 25; Maude Glasgow, "On the Regulation of Prostitution with Special Reference to Paragraph 79 of the Page Bill," *NYMJ* (1911), p. 1323; Vecki, "Can We Abolish, Shall We Ignore, or Must We Regulate Prostitution?"

AJDGUD (1910), p. 216; and U.S. Senate, *Importation and Harboring* (1910), p. 75.

24. William Acton, the nineteenth-century British authority on prostitution, considered the five-year theory ludicrous and argued that prostitutes were in as good health as their purer sisters: "By far the larger number of women who have resorted to prostitution for a livelihood, return sooner or later to a more or less regular course of life" (William Acton, *Prostitution* [1857], p. 72). In America, Acton's counterpart, William Sanger, supported the five-year theory. See Sanger, *The History of Prostitution* (1858), p. 676. Several of the more thorough vice investigations in the progressive years concluded that the five-year theory was contrary to the evidence. See Chicago, *The Social Evil in Chicago*, p. 168; Paul H. Hass, "Sin in Wisconsin," p. 146; and Fred Robert Johnson, *The Social Evil in Kansas City* (1911), p. 6. The New York physician I. L. Nasher, in "Prostitution in 1886 and in 1916," *AJUS* (1916), pp. 503–4, offered an interesting insight into this controversy. He believed that in 1886 there was a high mortality rate among prostitutes, but he argued that it was related not to sexual excess but to the primitive and dangerous medical, health, and hygienic practices prostitutes then followed.

25. M. L. Heidingsfeld, "The Control of Prostitution and the Prevention of the Spread of Venereal Diseases," *JAMA* (1904), p. 308. The writer states that, in addition to the five hundred prostitutes regularly inspected, there were ten thousand clandestine prostitutes. The issue of clandestine prostitution will be further discussed in Chapters 2 and 7.

26. See John Madge, *The Origins of Scientific Sociology*, pp. 333–76; and, in general, Wardell B. Pomeroy, *Dr. Kinsey and the Institute for Sex Research*.

27. Prince Morrow, "Prophylaxis of Social Diseases," *AJS* (1907), p. 25; Syracuse, *The Social Evil in Syracuse* (1913), p. 6. See also Chicago, *The Social Evil in Chicago* (1911), pp. 25–26; "The Slave Traffic in America," *O* (1909), p. 529; George Cosson, "Why an Injunction and Abatement Law?" *AC* (1917), p. 44; Bingham, "The Girl that Disappears," *HM* (1910), pp. 560, 569; Lewis, "The Prophylaxis and Management of Prostitution," *PaMJ* (1906), pp. 24–30; E. G. Ballenger, "The Social Evil," *AJRM* (1907), p. 8; Eric C. Hopwood, "The Opportunity of the Press as a Moral Educator," *JSH* (1915), pp. 21–36; Abram W. Harris, "The Social Evil," *JAIC* (1913), pp. 804–5; Edmund Alden Burnham, "Abatement of the Social Evil" (1909), pp. 481–82; Maude Miner, *Slavery of Prostitution* (1916), pp. 154–55; Moorehead, *Fighting the Devil's Triple Demons* (1911), p. 46; and Roe, *The Great War on White Slavery* (1911), p. 332.

28. See Nathan G. Hale, Jr., *Freud and the Americans*, p. 347; and Clyde Griffen, "The Progressive Ethos," p. 145.

29. Walter Lippmann, *A Preface to Politics* (1913), pp. 98, 105; Agnes Repplier, "The Repeal of Reticence," *AtM* (1914), p. 300. For the intellectual background, see H. Stuart Hughes, *Consciousness and Society*, pp. 36–66.

30. For the "unconstitutionality" of prostitution, see Sumner, "General Considerations on the Vice Problem," *CMR* (1913), p. 101. For general approval of repressive legislation, see "United against Social Vice," *I* (1913), p. 510; "The

Social Evil: The Immediate Remedies," O (1913), p. 298; G. E. Norcross, "The Regulation of Prostitution," *MMJ* (1905), pp. 335–40; T. H. Mulvy, "The Report of the Louisville Vice Commission," *KMJ* (1916), p. 497.

The New York Tenement House Act of 1901 imposed a fine of one thousand dollars on the owner of a tenement who failed to evict a tenant guilty of prostitution. The Committee of Fifteen was responsible for putting this section into the act. See Waterman, *Prostitution and Its Repression in New York City, 1900–1931*, p. 94. The injunction and abatement law (which Iowa pioneered in 1907) provided that all buildings had to bear the name of the owner on the exterior. Any citizen could bring action against the owner of the premises in which prostitution took place and procure an order placing the property under a court injunction. See Cosson, "Why an Injunction and Abatement Law?" *AC* (1917), pp. 44–45; "California Women and the Abatement Law," *S* (1914), pp. 739–40; Roe, *The Great War on White Slavery* (1911), pp. 358–70; and Wilson, "The Eradication of the Social Diseases in Large Cities," *JAMA* (1912), p. 927. For judicial reforms see Waterman, *Prostitution and Its Repression in New York City, 1900–1931*, pp. 43–80. The public health aspect of the response to prostitution is discussed below in Chapter 4. For the immigration aspect see Chapter 3. The Mann Act is discussed in Chapters 3 and 6 and the Selective Service Act in Chapter 7.

31. Howard S. Gans, "Some Consequences of Unenforceable Legislation," *PAPS* (1911), p. 563. See also Greer, *The Social Evil* (1909), pp. 30, 33–34, 62; William Trufant Foster, ed., *The Social Emergency* (1914), pp. 20–21; U.S. Senate, *Importation and Harboring* (1910), p. 74; "Chicago's 'Morals Court,'" *LD* (1913), p. 1229; Rudolph I. Coffee, "Pittsburgh Clergy and the Social Evil," *S* (1913), p. 815; Ada Eliot Sheffield, "The Written Law and the Unwritten Double Standard," *IJE* (1910), p. 482; and Howard A. Kelly, "The Protection of the Innocent," *AJO* (1907), p. 478.

32. Arthur B. Spingarn, *Laws Relating to Sex Morality in New York City* (1915), pp. xi–xiii.

33. For the Prohibition movement I have relied on Andrew Sinclair, *Era of Excess*; James H. Timberlake, *Prohibition and the Progressive Movement, 1900–1920*; Norman H. Clark, *Deliver Us from Evil*; Jack S. Blocker, Jr., *Retreat from Reform*; and Jon M. Kingsdale, "The 'Poor Man's Club,'" pp. 472–89. The similarities between Prohibition and the antiprostitution movement are stressed in Maury Klein and Harvey A. Kanter, *Prisoners of Progress*, pp. 405–17; and Paul Boyer, *Urban Masses and Moral Order in America, 1820–1920*, pp. 191–219. For contemporary comparisons between Prohibition and antiprostitution, see "No Dirty Compromise," *I* (1913), p. 1117; Anna Garlin Spencer, "A Word More on the Page Bill," *S* (1910), p. 514; "Social Vice," *I* (1910), p. 110; D. T. Atkinson, *Social Travesties and What They Cost* (1916), pp. 87–88; Beaton, *The Anti-Vice Crusader and Social Reformer* (1918), pp. 46, 82; and Winfield Scott Hall, "Intoxicants and the Social Evil," *MR* (1919), p. 336. See Waterman, *Prostitution and Its Repression in New York City, 1900–1931*, pp. 95–118, for the cooperation between the New York City Committee of Fourteen and the Prohibitionists.

34. Bell, *War on the White Slave Trade* (1909), p. 102.

35. Bryant, "The Social Evil," *PtMJ* (1913), p. 40.

36. Roosevelt is quoted in Mark H. Haller, *Eugenics*, p. 79; the other quotation is from Denslow Lewis, "The Need of Publicity in Venereal Prophylaxis," *MdR* (1906), pp. 863–65. For similar sentiments see "The Social Evil," *Md* (1906), p. 750; "United against Social Vice," *I* (1913), p. 510; Denslow Lewis, "What Shall We Do with the Prostitute?" *AJDGUD* (1907), pp. 487–88; Denslow Lewis, "The Social Evil," *BMJ* (1906), p. 251; A. Ravogli, "Education and Instruction in Sexual Relations as a Prophylaxis against Venereal Diseases," *NYMJ* (1910), p. 1218; Marion Craig Potter, "Venereal Prophylaxis," *WMJ* (1908), p. 241; Evangeline W. Young, "The Conservation of Manhood and Womanhood," *WMJ* (1910), p. 52; and C. R. Zahniser, "A Constructive Program of Sex Control," *HahM* (1918), p. 552.

37. Joseph Mayer, *The Regulation of Commercialized Vice* (1922), p. 91; William Edward Hartpole Lecky, *History of European Morals* (1870), 2: 299; Benjamin and Masters, *Prostitution and Morality*, p. 76.

38. Some of these trends are discussed in Walter C. Reckless, *Vice in Chicago*, pp. 99–163. For a full discussion of the drive to close the segregated districts, see Wunsch, "Prostitution and Public Policy," pp. 140–61.

39. These studies include W. R. Draper, "The Detention and Treatment of Infected Women as a Measure of Control of Venereal Diseases in Extra-Cantonment Zones," *AJO* (1919), pp. 642–46; C. C. Pierce, "The Value of Detention as a Reconstruction Measure," *AJO* (1919), pp. 624–36; V. V. Anderson, "The Immoral Woman as Seen in Court," *BMSJ* (1917), pp. 899–903; Clinton P. McCord, "One Hundred Female Offenders," *JAIC* (1915), pp. 385–407; D. E. Robinson and J. G. Wilson, "Tuberculosis among Prostitutes," *AJPH* (1916), pp. 1164–72; Jane Deeter Rippin, "Municipal Detention of Women," *PNCSW* (1918), ppp 132–40; and Jau Don Ball and Hayward G. Thomas, "A Sociological, Neurological, Serological and Psychiatrical Study of a Group of Prostitutes," *AJI* (1918), pp. 647–66. An earlier investigation of this kind is Frances A. Kellor, "Psychological and Environmental Study of Women Criminals," *AJS* (1900), pp. 527–43, 671–82. It will be noted that several of these studies were conducted in connection with domestic measures during World War I, a matter that will be discussed in Chapter 7.

40. Frederic C. Howe, *The Confessions of a Reformer* (1925), p. 55.

Chapter 2

1. Albert H. Burr, "The Guarantee of Safety in the Marriage Contract," *JAMA* (1906), p. 1887.

2. For interesting comments on this change see Kenneth A. Yellis, "Prosperity's Child," pp. 44–64.

3. See Gerda Lerna, "The Lady and the Mill Girl," pp. 5–15; Aileen S. Kraditor, *Means and Ends in American Abolitionism*, pp. 39–77; Eleanor Flexner, *Centuries of Struggle*; and William O'Neill, *Everyone Was Brave*, pp. 3–145.

4. See William O'Neill, *Divorce in the Progressive Era*; David Kennedy, *Birth Control in America*; James Reed, *From Private Vice to Public Virtue*, pp. 34–63; Linda Gordon, *Woman's Body, Woman's Right*, pp. 159–245; Aileen S. Kraditor, *The Ideas of the Woman Suffrage Movement, 1890–1920*; June Sochen, *The New Woman in Greenwich Village, 1910–1920*; Peter Gabriel Filene, *Him-Her Self*, pp. 5–68; James R. McGovern, "The American Woman's Pre-World War I Freedom in Manners and Morals," pp. 315–33; James R. McGovern, "David Graham Phillips and the Virility Impulse of Progressives," pp. 334–55; Christopher Lasch, *The New Radicalism in America, 1889–1963*, pp. 38–68; Joan N. Burstyn, "Images of Women in Text Books, 1880–1920," pp. 431–40; and Lois C. Gottlieb, "The Perils of Freedom," pp. 84–98.

5. There were, of course, different interpretations of this problem. Traditionalists and antifeminists argued that women would cease to be problematical if they would remain in their traditional roles. Feminists, on the other hand, welcomed the new problematical status of women and saw it as the first step out of the bondage of traditional roles and positions. There is also a problem of periodization here. The sense of women as problematical existed in the 1840s and was still current a century later (see for instance David Brion Davis, *Homicide in American Fiction, 1798–1860*, pp. 179–209; and William H. Chafe, *The American Woman*, pp. 199–225). This sense had a continuity over two centuries and was never limited to a specific group of years; each age found the problem more acute than it had been in the previous generation. During the first decade of the twentieth century, however, there were qualitative and quantitative changes that marked a new stage, and an intensified one, in the continuing belief that women were problematical.

6. Massachusetts, *Report of the Commission for the Investigation of the White Slave Traffic, So Called* (1914), p. 66. For a similar view see Syracuse, *The Social Evil in Syracuse* (1913), p. 81.

7. Chicago, *The Social Evil in Chicago* (1911), pp. 199–203. See also William Trufant Foster, ed., *The Social Emergency* (1914), pp. 45–69; and Maude E. Miner, *Slavery of Prostitution* (1916), p. 274.

8. There are discussions of the economic position of women in the early twentieth century in Harold Underwood Faulkner, *The Quest for Social Justice, 1898–1914*, pp. 153–76; and Robert Bremner, *From the Depths*, pp. 230–43.

9. Figures drawn from U.S. Senate, *Report on Conditions of Women and Child Wage Earners in the United States*, vol. 15, *Relation between Occupation and Criminality of Women* (1911), pp. 9–10 (hereinafter cited as U.S. Senate, *Relation between Occupation and Criminality of Women*); and Charles E. Persons, "Women's Work and Wages in the United States," *QJE* (1914), pp. 201–6.

10. U.S. Department of Labor, *Summary of the Report on Condition of Women and Child Wage Earners in the United States*, cited in Faulkner, *The Quest for Social Justice, 1898–1914*, p. 154.

11. Charles E. Persons, "Estimates of a Living Wage for Female Workers," *PASA* (1915), pp. 567–77; and Persons, "Women's Work and Wages in the United States," *QJE* (1914), pp. 208, 213–16. Full earning capacity for women, Persons argued, did not come until after the age of twenty-one.

12. Minneapolis, *Report of the Vice Commission of Minneapolis* (1911), p. 115; Chicago, *The Social Evil in Chicago* (1911), p. 42; Clifford G. Roe, *The Great War on White Slavery* (1911), p. 164; Reginald Wright Kauffman, *The House of Bondage* (1910), p. 257; Robert J. Moorehead, *Fighting the Devil's Triple Demons* (1911), pp. 80, 112, 139, 154, 163; Jane Addams, *A New Conscience and an Ancient Evil* (1912), pp. 55–94; Herr Glessner Creel, *Prostitution for Profit* (1911), pp. 34–39. The medical literature includes Foster, *The Social Emergency* (1914), pp. 16, 45–69; D. T. Atkinson, *Social Travesties and What They Cost* (1916), pp. 58–62; John Hund, *The Physician and the Social Evil* (1911), pp. 24–25; A. L. Wolbarst, "The Problem of Venereal Prophylaxis," *BMSJ* (1906), pp. 281–82; F. H. Gerrish, "A Crusade against Syphilis and Gonorrhea," *BMSJ* (1910), p. 5; G. Frank Lydston, "The Social Evil and Its Remedies," *AJCM* (1909), pp. 22–23; H. A. Kelly, "The Best Way to Treat the Social Evil," *MN* (1905), p. 1162; Denslow Lewis, "The Social Evil," *BMJ* (1906), p. 257; G. L. Eaton, "Venereal Prophylaxis in Large Cities," *PMJ* (1911), p. 666; George B. Swayze, "The Social Evil," *MT* (1906), p. 195; J. Ewing Mears, "The Problem of the Social Evil Considered in Its Social and Medical Aspects and in Its Relation to Race Betterment," *MdR* (1913), p. 234; S. A. Knopf, "Some Thoughts on the Etiology, Prophylaxis, and Treatment of the Social Ill," *NYMJ* (1908), p. 823; Evangeline W. Young, "The Conservation of Manhood and Womanhood," *WMJ* (1910), pp. 51–53; and C. E. Smith, Jr., "Some Observations on Public Health and Morality," *SPMJ* (1912), p. 196.

13. Four wide-circulation American magazines carried prominent articles on the problem of prostitution and low wages in the spring of 1913. See "Wages and Sin," *LD* (1913), pp. 621–24; "Are Low Wages Responsible for Women's Immorality?" *CO* (1913), p. 402; "A Living Wage for Women," *I* (1913), p. 851; and "Nation-wide Attention to Vice and Low Wages," *S* (1913), pp. 897–98. The quotation is from "Wages and Sin," p. 621. For the relevant passages on women's wages in the published report, see Illinois, *Report of the Senate Vice Committee* (1916), pp. 23–38, 52.

14. See Miner, *Slavery of Prostitution* (1916), pp. 68–70; G. Frank Lydston, *The Diseases of Society* (1904), pp. 308, 326–27; Addams, *A New Conscience and an Ancient Evil* (1912), p. 64; George Jackson Kneeland, *Commercialized Prostitution in New York City* (1913), p. 105; Chicago, *The Social Evil in Chicago* (1911), pp. 203–13; Robert O. Harland, *The Vice Bondage of a Great City* (1912), p. 68; Ralph Beaton, *The Anti-Vice Crusader and Social Reformer* (1918), p. 92; Clifford G. Roe, *The Girl Who Disappeared* (1914), pp. 112–27, 140–42; Ernest A. Bell, ed., *War on the White Slave Trade* (1909), p. 112; Theodore A. Bingham, "The Girl That Disappears," *HM* (1910), p. 567; Hund, *The Physician and the Social Evil* (1911), p. 40; Richard Barry, "Who Betrays the Working Girl?" *PM* (1911), pp. 175–81; Henry Rogers Seager, "The Theory of the Minimum Wage," *ALLR* (1913), pp. 83–84; and Creel, *Prostitution for Profit* (1911), p. 12.

15. The relationship between prostitution and domestic service was first documented in 1900 by Frances Kellor, "Psychological and Environmental Study of Woman Criminals," *AJS* (1900), pp. 675, 676. See, in addition, Chicago, *The*

Social Evil in Chicago (1911), p. 282; Fred Robert Johnson, *The Social Evil in Kansas City* (1911), p. 5; Addams, *A New Conscience and an Ancient Evil* (1912), p. 176; and Illinois, *Report of the Senate Vice Committee* (1916), pp. 38–41.

16. The *Call* is quoted in "Wages and Sin," *LD* (1913), p. 623. See also *The Masses'* view of prostitution as discussed in June Sochen, *The New Woman in Greenwich Village, 1910–1920*, pp. 80–81. The standard contemporary socialist analysis of prostitution was in August Bebel, *Women under Socialism* (1904), pp. 146–66, originally published in German in 1883, and translated into English in 1904 by the American socialist Daniel De Leon.

17. Seager, "The Theory of the Minimum Wage," *ALLR* (1913), p. 88. See also Margaret Dreier Robins, "One Aspect of the Menace of Low Wages," *JSH* (1914), pp. 358–63. For state legislation, see Charles E. Persons, "Estimates of a Living Wage for Female Workers," *PASA* (1915), p. 568; and Bremner, *From the Depths*, p. 239.

18. Quoted, anonymously, in Barry, "Who Betrays the Working Girl?" *PM* (1911), p. 176.

19. See Syracuse, *The Social Evil in Syracuse* (1913), p. 79 and the detailed tables on pp. 105, 107. The same imbalance in earning potential is documented in Miner, *Slavery of Prostitution* (1916), pp. 36–39.

20. See, in general, "Nostrums for Vice," *I* (1900), pp. 2942–43; George Kibbe Turner, "The Strange Woman," *MM* (1913), pp. 25–27; J. H. Landis, "The Social Evil in Relation to the Health Problem," *AJPH* (1913), p. 1074; F. Bierhoff, "The Problem of Prostitution and Venereal Diseases in New York City," *NYMJ* (1911), p. 559; J. L. Nascher, "Prostitution," *NYMJ* (1908), p. 260; and I. L. Nasher, "Prostitution in 1886 and in 1916," *AJUS* (1916), pp. 502, 504.

Businesses involved in hiring young women also (and predictably) rejected any connection between low wages and prostitution. For the National Retail Dry Goods Association's response, see "Minimum Wage Discussed by Retail Associations," *S* (1913), pp. 260–61. For Macy's Department Store's own investigation into the matter, see Roland Richard Wagner, "Virtue against Vice," pp. 141–43; and "Gaining Control over Vice in New York," *S* (1914), p. 572.

21. U.S. Senate, *Relation between Occupation and Criminality of Women* (1911), pp. 30–31, 55, 96, 41, 47, 82. The women engaged in "trade and transportation" occupations contributed less than one-third of their proportional representation to prostitution.

22. Edith L. Spaulding, "Mental and Physical Factors in Prostitution," *WMJ* (1914), p. 135.

23. Miner, *Slavery of Prostitution* (1916), pp. 36–38, 74–77. Miner cited a study of one thousand prostitutes, in which only nineteen specifically pointed to low wages as the "cause" of their becoming prostitutes.

24. For a discussion of this point in the context of the history of the study of prostitution, see Vern Bullough, "Problems and Methods for Research in Prostitution and the Behavioral Sciences," pp. 246–47.

25. Quoted in "Are Low Wages Responsible for Women's Immorality?" *CO* (1913), p. 402.

26. Quoted in "Wages and Sin," *LD* (1913), pp. 621–22.

27. There is some evidence to indicate that many young women working in the cities did not live alone but rather with families (although not always their own). The census of 1900 included a study of 1,232,000 working women in twenty-seven cities and reported that 35.2 percent were boarding alone and that the rest were living with families. See Persons, "Women's Work and Wages in the United States," *QJE* (1914), pp. 222–23. The recognition that not all prostitutes began their careers while living alone was implicit in the discovery that many entered the life while living at home. See Syracuse, *The Social Evil in Syracuse* (1913), p. 78; U.S. Senate, *Relation between Occupation and Criminality of Women* (1911), p. 48; Clinton P. McCord, "One Hundred Female Offenders," *JAIC* (1915), pp. 394–406. This finding leads to the question, Why was so much attention given to the problem of women living alone in the city, if the women who actually lived alone in fact represented only a minority of working women? The answer lies, I believe, in the symbolic meaning of the women who did live alone and the realization that they were the advance signs of a social change of greater significance than their absolute numbers indicated.

28. Johnson, *The Social Evil in Kansas City* (1911), p. 4. This material was cited by Jane Addams in *A New Conscience and an Ancient Evil* (1912), p. 90. See also Massachusetts, *Report of the Commission for the Investigation of the White Slave Traffic, So Called* (1914), p. 14.

29. Addams, *A New Conscience and an Ancient Evil* (1912), pp. 56–57. See also Kneeland, *Commercialized Prostitution in New York City* (1913), p. 43.

30. For the historical background of this development, see E. P. Thompson, "Time, Work-Discipline, and Industrial Capitalism," pp. 56–97.

31. Paul Boyer, *Urban Masses and Moral Order in America, 1820–1920*, pp. 67–187; Paul Boyer, *Purity in Print*, pp. 1–22; David J. Pivar, *Purity Crusade*, pp. 233–38. The relationship between vice reform and the reform of dangerous amusements in Chicago during the progressive years is discussed in Mark H. Haller, "Urban Vice Reform and Civic Reform," pp. 290–305; and Kathleen D. McCarthy, "Nickel Vice and Virtue," pp. 37–55.

32. Swayze, "The Social Evil," *MT* (1906), p. 195; Mrs. Belle Lindner Israels, "Regulation of Public Amusements," *PAPS* (1912), pp. 597–600; Bell, *War on the White Slave Trade* (1909), pp. 112, 282–83. See also Kneeland, *Commercialized Prostitution in New York City* (1913), pp. 67–73; Chicago, *The Social Evil in Chicago* (1911), pp. 185–98, 266–67; Minneapolis, *Report of the Vice Commission of Minneapolis* (1911), p. 78; Massachusetts, *Report of the Commission for the Investigation of the White Slave Traffic, So Called* (1914), p. 19; George Kibbe Turner, "The Daughters of the Poor," *MM* (1909), pp. 55–57; and N. E. Aronstam, "The Prevention of the Venereal Peril," *IMJ* (1912), p. 192.

During the progressive years, the urban dance halls existed somewhere in the twilight zone between official urban culture and the subculture of which prostitution was a part. The vast majority of young women who frequented dance halls did not become prostitutes, but, judging from contemporary evidence, prostitutes and pimps also went to these places. The dance halls, therefore, probably did constitute the occasion—as distinct from the cause—of some young women's becoming prostitutes; and the association perceived between dance halls and prostitution had some basis in fact. One commentator wrote: "The backward trail of the prostitute leads *through* these places. It does not originate there." See Creel, *Prostitution for Profit* (1911), p. 14.

33. For the movies, see Theodore A. Bingham, "The Girl That Disappears," *HM* (1910), p. 568. The movie "problem" was of no mean proportions. The Minneapolis Vice Commission estimated that there were thirty-two movie houses in Minneapolis with a total seating capacity of ten thousand, and that thirty thousand people per day attended them (*Report of the Vice Commission of Minneapolis* [1911], p. 129). For other dangerous amusements, see Atkinson, *Social Travesties and What They Cost* (1916), pp. 63–64; Aronstam, "The Prevention of the Venereal Peril," *IMJ* (1912), p. 192; Roe, *The Girl Who Disappeared* (1914), p. 224; "A Vicious Use of Frankness," *I* (1913), pp. 604–5; J. N. Upshur, "The Limitation and Prevention of Venereal Disease," *AJDGUD* (1910), p. 349; Illinois, *Report of the Senate Vice Committee* (1916), p. 55; and Bell, *War on the White Slave Trade* (1909), p. 110.

34. Syracuse, *The Social Evil in Syracuse* (1913), p. 43. See also Chicago, *The Social Evil in Chicago* (1911), pp. 213–15; Bell, *War on the White Slave Trade* (1909), p. 111; Addams, *A New Conscience and an Ancient Evil* (1912), pp. 110–11; and Newark, *Report of the Social Evil Conditions of Newark* (1914), p. 15.

35. Minneapolis, *Report of the Vice Commission of Minneapolis* (1911), pp. 76–77. For similar statements see Syracuse, *The Social Evil in Syracuse* (1913), p. 54; Chicago, *The Social Evil in Chicago* (1911), p. 265; and Massachusetts, *Report of the Commission for the Investigation of the White Slave Traffic, So Called* (1914), p. 43.

36. Addams, *A New Conscience and an Ancient Evil* (1912), pp. 215–16, 206–7. For a discussion of this general theme, see Lasch, *The New Radicalism in America, 1889–1963*, pp. 141–80.

37. For the supervision of rooming houses, see Minneapolis, *Report of the Vice Commission of Minneapolis* (1911), p. 110; Massachusetts, *Report of the Commission for the Investigation of the White Slave Traffic, So Called* (1914), pp. 78–79; Jean Turner Zimmermann, *America's Black Traffic in White Girls* (1912), pp. 48–49; Syracuse, *The Social Evil in Syracuse* (1913), pp. 33, 91; Kneeland, *Commercialized Prostitution in New York City* (1913), pp. 33, 35; Newark, *Report of the Social Evil Conditions of Newark* (1914), p. 51; Chicago, *The Social Evil in Chicago* (1911), p. 34; and Arthur B. Spingarn, *Laws Relating to Sex Morality in New York City* (1915), p. xii. For supervised recreations, see Israels, "Regulation of Public Amusements," *PAPS* (1912), pp. 597–600; Chicago, *The Social Evil in Chicago* (1911), p. 64; U.S. Senate, *Relation between Occupation and Criminality of Women* (1911), p. 91; Miner, *Slavery of Prostitution* (1916), pp. 79–86, 261–66; Foster, *The Social Emergency* (1914), pp. 19, 70–83; and Roe, *The Girl Who Disappeared* (1914), pp. 240–41, 261–62. For young women's organizations, see Clark W. Hetherington, "Play Leadership in Sex Education," *JSH* (1914), p. 41; Miner, *Slavery of Prostitution* (1916),

pp. 283–304; and Minneapolis, *Report of the Vice Commisssion of Minneapolis* (1911), p. 116.

38. Miner, *Slavery of Prostitution* (1916), p. 276; Foster, *The Social Emergency* (1914), pp. 163–64. See also Lydston, *The Diseases of Society* (1904), p. 149; and Virginia Brooks, *My Battles with Vice* (1915), pp. 62–69.

39. Cited in Willoughby Cyrus Waterman, *Prostitution and Its Repression in New York City, 1900–1931*, p. 106.

40. Some of these ideas are explored in detail in Barbara Welter, "The Cult of True Womanhood," pp. 151–74.

41. Newark, *Report of the Social Evil Conditions in Newark* (1914), pp. 12–13; see also pp. 75–87.

42. Massachusetts, *Report of the Investigation of the White Slave Traffic, So Called* (1914), p. 43.

43. Syracuse, *The Social Evil in Syracuse* (1913), pp. 67, 57.

44. Chicago, *The Social Evil in Chicago* (1911), p. 305.

45. The "myth of the menace of the feebleminded" is discussed in Mark H. Haller, *Eugenics*, pp. 95–110, 111–23. See also Donald K. Pickens, *Eugenics and the Progressives*. The rise and fall of the feeblemindedness theory of prostitution among social hygienists and psychologists at the New York State Reformatory for Women at Bedford Hills during the teens is charted in James F. Gardner, Jr., "Microbes and Morality," pp. 291–301.

46. The following studies of prostitutes are summarized in Walter Clarke, "Prostitution and Mental Deficiency," *JSH* (1914), pp. 364–87; and Paul A. Mertz, "Mental Deficiency of Prostitutes," *JAMA* (1919), pp. 1597–99:

	No. Prostitutes Examined	Percentage Feebleminded
State Board of Charities & Corrections, Richmond, Va.	120	83.3
Chicago Morals Court	639	62.0
Chicago Morals Court	126	85.8
Illinois Training School for Girls	104	97.0
Mass. State Vice Commission	300	51.0
Mass. State Women's Reformatory	243	49.0
New York State Reformatory for Women	193	29.8
Bureau of Social Hygiene	100	29.0
New York Probation and Protective Association (delinquents)	500	37.0
New York Probation and Protective Association (prostitutes)	111	35.0

The other important group studies of prostitution that emphasized feeblemindedness were Jau Don Ball and Hayward G. Thomas, "A Sociological, Neurological, Serological and Psychiatrical Study of a Group of Prostitutes," *AJI* (1918), pp. 647–66; D. E. Robinson and J. G. Wilson, "Tuberculosis among Prostitutes,"

AJPH (1916), pp. 1164–72; Spaulding, "Mental and Physical Factors in Prostitution," *WMJ* (1914), pp. 133–36; Frederick W. Sears, "The Wayward Girl," *VMM* (1912), pp. 7–9; Maude E. Miner, "The Problem of Wayward Girls and Delinquent Women," *PAPS* (1912), pp. 604–12; and McCord, "One Hundred Female Offenders," *JAIC* (1915), pp. 385–407.

47. See Spingarn, *Laws Relating to Sex Morality In New York City* (1915), p. xiii; Foster, *The Social Emergency* (1914), p. 14; Charles W. Birtwell, "Sex Hygiene," *S* (1912), pp. 525–26; T. H. Mulvy, "The Report of the Louisville Vice Commission," *KMJ* (1916), pp. 493–99; F. H. Hancock, "Regulation of Prostitution in the City of Norfolk, Virginia," *VMSM* (1912), p. 561; C. R. Zahniser, "A Constructive Program of Sex Control," *HahM* (1918), p. 553; Mabelle B. Blake, "The Defective Girl Who Is Immoral," *BMSJ* (1917), p. 492; Ethel M. Watters, "The Problem of the Woman Venereal Disease Carrier," *CJM* (1919), p. 285; W. Healy, "Contributory Causes of Social Vice," *CMR* (1913), pp. 85–89; George W. Goler, "The Municipality and the Venereal Disease Problem," *AJPH* (1916), p. 359; and Mrs. William Falconer, "The Relation of the Graduate Nurse to the Problem of Social Hygiene," *AJN* (1917), p. 1075.

48. Maude E. Miner, "Report of Committee on Social Hygiene," *JSH* (1914), p. 83. For contemporary criticism of the feeblemindedness theory, see Clarke, "Prostitution and Mental Deficiency," *JSH* (1914), p. 387; and Jean Weidensall, "Psychological Tests as Applied to Criminal Women," *PR* (1914), pp. 370–75. For further discussion, see Gardner, "Microbes and Morality," pp. 291–301.

49. The U.S. Army's attempt to use intelligence testing is discussed in Fred Davis Baldwin, "The American Enlisted Man in World War I," pp. 67–78; and Daniel J. Kelves, "Testing the Army's Intelligence," pp. 565–81.

50. Cited in Paul H. Hass, "Sin in Wisconsin," p. 148.

51. This is what most modern studies of prostitutes indicate. For instance, a 1957 British study of four hundred young prostitutes found most of the women to be of normal intelligence, with about the same incidence of psychological difficulties as nonprostitutes. See T. C. N. Gibens, "Juvenile Prostitution," pp. 3–12.

52. The rationalization of social work in general during this period is treated in Roy Lubove, *The Professional Altruist*.

53. W. F. Draper, "The Detention and Treatment of Infected Women as a Measure of Control of Venereal Diseases in Extra Cantonment Zones," *AJO* (1919), p. 645.

54. There was a basic difference in the way feebleminded men and women were conceptualized. Usually, men who were supposedly feebleminded were seen as aggressive enemies of society: criminals, murderers, alcoholics, etc. They victimized society. Feebleminded women, on the other hand, were themselves victims. This difference did not always hold (an exception might be Lombrosso's theories on female criminology), but when it did, it illustrated how sexual stereotypes influenced even the most "scientific" of theories and classifications.

55. For the nineteenth-century background of the age-of-consent controversy, see Pivar, *Purity Crusade*, pp. 139–46. The age-of-consent laws for the states in 1900 are listed in Lavinia L. Dock, *Hygiene and Morality* (1910), pp. 116–22. In

1900 sixteen states still fixed the age of consent at fourteen years or lower. For a stimulating critique of the drive to raise the age of consent in England in the 1870s and 1880s, which sees in reformers' efforts not only a desire to protect young working-class women but also a desire to control their sexual behavior, see Deborah Gorham, "The 'Maiden Tribute of Modern Babylon' Re-Examined," pp. 362–68.

56. See the well-developed statement by Anna Garlin Spencer, "The Age of Consent and Its Significance," *F* (1913), pp. 406–20. See also Miner, *Slavery of Prostitution* (1916), pp. 128–29; Miner, "Report of Committee on Social Hygiene," *JSH* (1914), p. 85; Dock, *Hygiene and Morality* (1910), pp. 116–22; Maude Glasgow, "Side Lights on the Social Peril," *NYMJ* (1911), pp. 1186–90; Denslow Lewis, "What Shall We Do with the Prostitute?" *AJDGUD* (1907), p. 487.

57. For the demand for "police matrons" made by the purity groups in the 1880s and 1890s, see Pivar, *Purity Crusade*, pp. 153–54. For support of the idea of women police, see Louise de Koven Bowen, "Women Police," *S* (1913), pp. 64–65; Dock, *Hygiene and Morality* (1910), p. 161; and Atkinson, *Social Travesties and What They Cost* (1916), pp. 125–26. For the vice commissions, see Chicago, *The Social Evil in Chicago* (1911), p. 62; Syracuse, *The Social Evil in Syracuse* (1913), p. 91; and Newark, *Report on the Social Evil Conditions of Newark* (1914), p. 22. The Bureau of Social Hygiene study was Chloe Owings, *Women Police* (1925).

58. See "Anti-Vice Program of a Woman's Club," *S* (1914), p. 81; Illinois, *Report of the Senate Vice Committee* (1916), p. 17; and Addams, *A New Conscience and an Ancient Evil* (1912), p. 196. For full statements on the efforts of women and women's groups in antiprostitution, and the reasons for their involvement, see Mary Ritter Beard, *Woman's Work in Municipalities* (1915), pp. 97–130; and Rheta Childe Dorr, *What Eight Million Women Want* (1910), pp. 183–249.

59. "No Dirty Compromise," *I* (1913), p. 1117. See also the arguments of the Hartford, Conn., suffragist Katharine Houghton Hepburn: "Communications," *S* (1910), pp. 637–38, and "The Page Bill," *S* (1910), pp. 79–80; and also Addams, *A New Conscience and an Ancient Evil* (1912), pp. 192–97, 212; Atkinson, *Social Travesties and What They Cost* (1916), pp. 119–35; Robert N. Wilson, *The American Boy and the Social Evil* (1905), p. 145; and Walter T. Sumner, "General Considerations on the Vice Problem," *CMR* (1913), p. 106.

60. The social hygiene reformers strongly supported this position, because they believed that women suffered most from the relationship of prostitution and venereal disease. See Prince Morrow, "Results of the Work Accomplished by the Society of Sanitary and Moral Prophylaxis," *NYMJ* (1907), p. 1112; Prince Morrow, "Prophylaxis of Social Diseases," *AJS* (1907), pp. 21–22; Dock, *Hygiene and Morality* (1910), pp. 157–58, 159; R. N. Wilson, "The Relation of the Medical Profession to the Social Evil," *JAMA* (1906), p. 32; Robert N. Wilson, "The Eradication of the Social Diseases in Large Cities," *JAMA* (1912), p. 928; and Atkinson, *Social Travesties and What They Cost* (1916), p. 128.

61. Throughout the antiprostitution literature, it was generally argued that

women were by nature less sexually oriented than men, if indeed they had any sexual drive at all. This position clearly differentiated pure women (wives and mothers) from prostitutes. Carl Degler, in "What Ought to Be and What Was," pp. 1476–90, has presented evidence indicating that this sexual ideology did not reflect the reality of female sexuality and that middle-class women in the late nineteenth century may have enjoyed normal and healthy sex lives. If Degler is correct, the dichotomy between what may have been the reality of the middle-class woman's sex life and the public (and usually male) insistence that she was devoid of sexual desire points to an important area of inquiry. Degler's views are critiqued in William G. Shade, "'A Mental Passion,'" pp. 13–29.

62. Lewis, "The Social Evil," *BMJ* (1906), p. 251.

63. These phrases are drawn from descriptions of prostitutes in Edith L. Spaulding, "Mental and Physical Factors in Prostitution," *WMJ* (1914), p. 135; Miner, *Slavery of Prostitution* (1916), p. 42; and Massachusetts, *Report of the Commission for the Investigation of the White Slave Traffic, So Called* (1914), p. 29.

64. It was discovered that prostitutes had recourse not only to various forms of birth control but also to abortion. See Chicago, *The Social Evil in Chicago* (1911), pp. 223–27, 277–78; Lydston, *The Diseases of Society* (1904), pp. 267–72; Wilson, *The American Boy and the Social Evil* (1905), p. 134; Moorehead, *Fighting the Devil's Triple Demons* (1911), p. 97; M. L. Heidingsfeld, "The Control of Prostitution and the Prevention of the Spread of Venereal Diseases," *JAMA* (1904), p. 308; and E. G. Ballenger, "The Social Evil," *AJRM* (1907) p. 12.

65. Turner, "The Strange Woman," *MM* (1913), p. 28; Chicago, *The Social Evil in Chicago* (1911), p. 140. This perception of the prostitute was influenced by class and ethnic biases, which are important and usually obvious. The major consideration, however, was the extent to which the prostitute deviated from the norm of the ideal woman, which was, of course, a middle-class creation.

66. Jane Addams, "A Challenge to the Contemporary Church," *S* (1912), p. 197; Roe, *The Great War on White Slavery* (1911), pp. 92–94; Young, "The Conservation of Manhood and Womanhood," *WMJ* (1910), p. 53.

67. Sprague Carleton, "The Prostitute," *HahM* (1908), pp. 826–27.

68. See, in general, McGovern, "The American Woman's Pre-World War I Freedom in Manners and Morals," pp. 315–33.

Chapter 3

1. U.S. Senate, Reports of the Immigration Commission, vol. 19, *Importation and Harboring of Women for Immoral Purposes* (1910), p. 57 (hereinafter cited as U.S. Senate, *Importation and Harboring*). For a general overview of the reaction to immigration in the late nineteenth and early twentieth centuries, see John Higham, *Strangers in the Land*, pp. 106–93; Barbara Miller Solomon, *Ancestors and Immigrants*; and Thomas Kessner, *The Golden Door*, pp. 24–43.

2. An earlier law, the immigration act of 1875 (dealing with Oriental immigra-

tion), included sections on the importation of alien prostitutes. See U.S., *Statutes at Large*, vol. 18 (1875), pp. 477–78, for the text of the act.

3. See James F. Gardner, Jr., "Microbes and Morality," p. 339, for a brief discussion of the background of this treaty.

4. The domestic aspect of the white-slave trade is discussed in Chapter 6.

5. U.S., *Statutes at Large*, vol. 32 (1903), p. 1214.

6. Ibid., vol. 34 (1907), pp. 899–900.

7. The barring from entry and deportation of alien women and procurers increased substantially in 1908, after the passing of the 1907 law:

Alien women barred from entry: 1904: 9; 1905: 24; 1906: 30; 1907: 18; 1908: 124

Alien procurers barred from entry: 1904: 3; 1905: 4; 1906: 2; 1907: 1; 1908: 43

Alien prostitutes deported: June 1907–June 1908: 65; June 1908–June 1909: 261

Alien procurers deported: June 1907–June 1908: 2; June 1908–June 1909: 30

Figures are from U.S. Senate, *Importation and Harboring* (1910), pp. 60–61.

8. *U.S. v. Bitty*, 208 U.S. 393, 395–97 (1908); *Black's Law Dictionary*, 4th ed. rev., s.v. *ejusdem generis*.

9. *U.S. v. Bitty*, 208 U.S. 394–95.

10. Ibid., 397–401.

11. *Keller v. United States, Ullman v. United States*, 213 U.S. 138, 140–41 (1909).

12. Ibid., 138.

13. Ibid., 142.

14. Ibid., 143, 143–49.

15. Ibid., 149–51.

16. An early draft of the report became available to Congress in February 1909. In December 1909 the commission published its preliminary statement on the white-slave traffic, and the final report was presented in December 1910. Quotations in the following discussion are from the final version, which differed very little from earlier ones. The contents of the preliminary report were discussed in "White Slaves," *O* (1910), pp. 131–32.

17. U.S. Senate, *Importation and Harboring* (1910), p. 86. For the racial biases of the report see Oscar Handlin, *Race and Nationality in American Life*, pp. 74–110.

18. U.S. Senate, *Importation and Harboring* (1910), pp. 60, 57, 60.

19. Ibid., p. 89.

20. The complete text of the section on prostitution in the 1910 law was:

That the importation into the United States of any alien for the purpose of prostitution or for any other immoral purpose is hereby forbidden; and whoever shall, directly or indirectly, import, or attempt to import, into the United States, any alien for the purpose of prostitution or for any other immoral purpose, or whoever shall hold or attempt to hold any alien for any such purpose in pursuance of such illegal importation, or whoever shall keep, maintain, control, support, employ, or harbor in any house or other place, for the purpose of prostitution or for any other immoral purpose, in pursuance of such illegal importation, any alien, shall, in every such case be deemed guilty of a felony, and on conviction thereof be imprisoned not more than ten years and pay a fine of not more than five thousand dollars. Jurisdiction for the trial and punishment of the felonies hereinbefore set forth shall be in any district to or into which said alien is brought in pursuance of said importation by the person or persons accused, or in any district in which a violation of any of the foregoing provisions of this section occur. Any alien who shall be found an inmate of or connected with the management of a house of prostitution or practicing prostitution after such alien shall have entered the United States, or who shall receive, share in, or derive benefit from any part of the earnings of any prostitute; or who is employed by, in, or in connection with any house of prostitution or music or dance hall or other place of amusement or resort habitually frequented by prostitutes, or where prostitutes gather, or who in any way assists, protects, or promises to protect from arrest any prostitute, shall be deemed to be unlawfully within the United States and shall be deported in the manner provided by sections twenty and twenty-one of this Act. That any alien who shall, after he has been debarred or deported in pursuance of the provisions of this section, attempt thereafter to return to or to enter the United States shall be deemed guilty of a misdemeanor, and shall be imprisoned for not more than two years. Any alien who shall be convicted under any of the provisions of this section shall, at the expiration of his sentence, be taken into custody and returned to the country whence he came, or of which he is a subject or a citizen in the manner provided in sections twenty and twenty-one of this Act. In all prosecutions under this section the testimony of a husband or wife shall be admissible and competent evidence against a wife or a husband. [U.S., *Statutes at Large*, vol. 36 (1910), pp. 264–65]

21. U.S., *Statutes at Large*, vol. 34 (1907), p. 900; ibid., vol. 36 (1910), p. 265.

22. On the three-year limit, see U.S. Senate, *Importation and Harboring* (1910), p. 91. The commission's comment was, "The evils of the traffic are ordinarily not lessened with the length of time the criminal or prostitute remains in the country."

23. The text of the act is in U.S., *Statutes at Large*, vol. 36 (1910), pp. 825–27. House debate is in U.S., *Congressional Record*, 61st Cong., 2d sess., 1910, 45, pt. 1: 801–23, pt. 2: 1030–41 (hereinafter cited as *Congressional Record*). There is biographical information on Mann in the *Dictionary of American Biography*, 12: 244. Sections 2–5 of the Mann Act and the litigation they generated pertained primarily to the interstate traffic in women and are discussed in Chapter 6. Section 6 of the Mann Act, which pertained to the foreign traffic in women, is discussed here. The treatment of the Mann Act in this study is not exhaustive, and a full-dress work on the origin and enforcement of the act would be a welcome addition to American social history.

24. U.S., *Statutes at Large*, vol. 36 (1910), p. 827. See also *Congressional Record* (1910), pt. 1, pp. 805–8.

25. See the report accompanying the Mann Act, U.S. House of Representatives, Committee on Interstate and Foreign Commerce, *White Slave Traffic* (1909) (hereinafter cited as U.S. House of Representatives, *White Slave Traffic*). References to the work of the Immigration Commission can be found on pp. 12–13 of the report.

26. U.S. Senate, *Importation and Harboring* (1910), pp. 80, 81; U.S. House of Representatives, *White Slave Traffic* (1909), p. 12.

27. For Brewer's comment see *Keller v. United States*, 213 U.S. 138, 147 (1909). For the committee's appreciation of Brewer's suggestion see U.S. House of Representatives, *White Slave Traffic* (1909), pp. 8–9. See U.S., *Statutes at Large*, vol. 35 (1908), pp. 1979–84, for the text of the treaty. The treaty covered all immigrant groups in America except those from Austria-Hungary, which did not sign the agreement. It should be noted that a minority report did accompany the Mann Act when it was recommended to Congress. The minority on the Mann Committee argued that the Mann Act, despite its good intentions, gave to the federal government powers which only the states could possess, and claimed that the issues raised in *Keller* were still valid. See U.S. House of Representatives, *White Slave Traffic* (1909), pt. 2.

28. Quoted in "New Methods of Grappling with the Social Evil," *CO* (1913), pp. 308–9.

29. Clifford G. Roe, *The Great War on White Slavery* (1911), p. 306. See also Ernest A. Bell, ed., *War on the White Slave Trade* (1909), p. 262; and William Trufant Foster, ed., *The Social Emergency* (1914), pp. 140–41, 147.

30. See D. T. Atkinson, *Social Travesties and What They Cost* (1916), p. 93; Lavinia L. Dock, *Hygiene and Morality* (1910), pp. 129, 133, 135; Robert J. Moorehead, *Fighting the Devil's Triple Demons* (1911), p. 119; E. Norine Law, *The Shame of a Great Nation* (1909), p. 9; Roe, *The Great War on White Slavery* (1911), p. 46; J. H. Hager, "Cost of Venereal Infection," *KMJ* (1910), p. 1172; E. G. Ballenger, "The Social Evil," *AJRM* (1907), p. 7; and N. E. Aronstam, "The Prevention of the Venereal Peril," *IMJ* (1912), p. 197.

31. See, in general, Roe, *The Great War on White Slavery* (1911), pp. 63, 196–202; Bell, *War on the White Slave Trade* (1909), pp. 16, 71–72, 145, 187–89, 260; Robert N. Wilson, *The American Boy and the Social Evil* (1905), p. 212; William Lee Howard, "The Havoc of Prudery," *PM* (1910), p. 598; Clifford G. Roe, *The Girl Who Disappeared* (1914), pp. 211–17; Jean Turner Zimmermann, *America's Black Traffic in White Girls* (1912), pp. 7–8, 12–13, 24, 26, 29, 50–52; Theodore A. Bingham, "The Girl That Disappears," *HM* (1910), pp. 561, 566; and Reginald Wright Kauffman, *The House of Bondage* (1910), p. 145.

32. For the Max Hochstim Association, see Moses Rischin, *The Promised City*, p. 91. For the white-slave narratives see Zimmermann, *America's Black Traffic in White Girls* (1912), pp. 12–13, 21, 37; Kauffman, *The House of Bondage* (1910), pp. 18–19; and Roe, *The Great War on White Slavery* (1911), pp. 100–102. This point is further discussed in Chapter 6.

33. George Kibbe Turner, "The City of Chicago," *MM* (1907), pp. 581–82; George Kibbe Turner, "The Daughters of the Poor," *MM* (1909), pp. 45–61. Although the report of the Immigration Commission was written in a more restrained manner, it came to many of the same conclusions regarding the role of Jews in the international white-slave trade. See U.S. Senate, *Importation and Harboring* (1910), pp. 62–65, 77–78. There is a distinct possibility that members of the commission were familiar with Turner's articles.

34. See Charlotte Baum, Paula Hyman, and Sonya Michel, *The Jewish Woman in America*, pp. 170–75; Irving Howe, *World of Our Fathers*, pp. 96–98; Egal Feldman, "Prostitution, the Alien Woman and the Progressive Imagination, 1910–1915," pp. 197–204; Allen F. Davis, *Spearheads for Reform*, pp. 135–38; and Lucille O'Connell, "Travelers' Aid for Polish Immigrant Women," pp. 15–19. For Jane Addams's concern for the plight of the immigrant woman, see Allen F. Davis, *American Heroine*, pp. 176–84.

35. See William W. Sanger, *The History of Prostitution* (1858), pp. 456–63; and George Jackson Kneeland, *Commercialized Prostitution in New York City* (1913), p. 101 (this is only one of several groups of prostitutes examined in Kneeland's investigation). The figures on New York City's population are drawn from Rischin, *The Promised City*, p. 271. On the relationship of prostitution and ethnicity see also Vern Bullough, "Problems and Methods for Research in Prostitution and the Behavioral Sciences," pp. 246–47.

36. See note 7 to this chapter for the figures from the immigration report.

37. See the statement by Edwin W. Sims, U.S. district attorney for Chicago, in Bell, *War on the White Slave Trade* (1909), p. 49.

38. See Syracuse, *The Social Evil in Syracuse* (1913), pp. 77, 103 (of a sample of fifty prostitutes, only 3–6 percent were foreign-born); Paul H. Hass, "Sin in Wisconsin," p. 146; and Fred Robert Johnson, *The Social Evil in Kansas City* (1911), p. 4.

39. See particularly D. E. Robinson and J. G. Wilson, "Tuberculosis among Prostitutes," *AJPH* (1916), p. 1165; Jane Deeter Rippin, "Municipal Detention of Women," *PNCSW* (1918), pp. 133–34; and Jau Don Ball and Hayward G. Thomas, "A Sociological, Neurological, Serological and Psychiatrical Study of a Group of Prostitutes," *AJI* (1918), p. 655.

40. Maude E. Miner, *Slavery of Prostitution* (1916), p. 35. For a similar comment see I. L. Nasher, "Prostitution in 1886 and in 1916," *AJUS* (1916), pp. 543–44. Miner, who was a well-known and professional social worker, probation officer, and founder of Waverly House in New York City, offered in her studies of prostitutes an interesting insight into the relationship of immigration and prostitution. She found that many prostitutes (as many as 33 percent of a group of one thousand) were American-born young women of foreign-born parents. For these women, prostitution may have been connected with the clash between Old and New World cultures. See Miner, *Slavery of Prostitution* (1916), p. 32; and Miner, "Report of Committee on Social Hygiene," *JSH* (1914), p. 82.

41. Richard C. Cabot, Observations regarding the Relative Frequency of the Different Diseases Prevalent in Boston, and Its Vicinity," *BMSJ* (1911), pp. 158–61. See Abraham L. Wolbarst, "The Prevalence of Venereal Disease among Re-

cently Arrived Immigrants, with Special Reference to Intermarital Infection," *NYMJ* (1909), pp. 739–41, for a fuller treatment. Most physicians felt that the relatively low rate of both prostitution and venereal disease among Jews was the result of the "excellence of their sanitary laws" and the strength of familial morality. See, for instance, John Hund, *The Physician and the Social Evil* (1911), pp. 9, 41; J. L. Nascher, "Prostitution," *NYMJ* (1908), p. 261; and C. E. Smith, Jr., "Some Observations on Public Health and Morality," *SPMJ* (1912), p. 195.

42. Peasant society in Poland is discussed in vol. 1, pp. 87–302, of William I. Thomas and Florian Znaniecki, *The Polish Peasant in Europe and America* (1918–20). The disorganization of peasant society in America is discussed in vol. 2, pp. 1647–1830. A discussion and evaluation of *The Polish Peasant in Europe and America* is given in John Madge, *The Origins of Scientific Sociology*, pp. 52–87.

43. Thomas's early important writings on sex are collected in *Sex and Society: Studies in the Social Psychology of Sex* (1907). Thomas and Znaniecki's discussion of immorality among Polish American girls is in *The Polish Peasant in Europe and America*, 2: 1800–1821.

Chapter 4

1. William W. Sanger, *The History of Prostitution* (1858), p. 633.

2. For a general overview of the history of medical research on venereal disease, see Owsei Temkin, "Therapeutic Trends and the Treatment of Syphilis before 1900," pp. 309–16; Kenneth M. Flegel, "Changing Concepts of the Nosography of Gonorrhea and Syphilis," pp. 571–88; Theodor Roseaury, *Microbes and Morals*; R. S. Morton, *Venereal Diseases*, pp. 21–34; William Allen Pusey, *The History and Epidemiology of Syphilis*; H. Goodman, *Notable Contributors to the Knowledge of Syphilis*; Stewart M. Brooks, *The V.D. Story*; and Harry F. Dowling, *Fighting Infection*, pp. 82–104. The factual material in this and following paragraphs is drawn from these works.

3. Today, in direct contrast, one can pick up any recent textbook on venereal disease and find at most only a passing reference to prostitution. For instance, in his *Textbook of Venereal Diseases and Treponematoses*, R. R. Wilcox devotes several pages (423–25) to the relationship between prostitution and venereal disease and concludes that prostitution is not an important factor in the spread of venereal disease. The U.S. Public Health Service, in its 1968 *Syphilis: A Synopsis*, does not mention prostitution at all.

4. Lavinia L. Dock, *Hygiene and Morality* (1910), p. 35. See also Prince Morrow, "A Plea for the Organization of a 'Society of Sanitary and Moral Prophylaxis,'" *MN* (1904), p. 1073; Prince Morrow, "The Society of Sanitary and Moral Prophylaxis," *AMd* (1905), p. 320; Abraham L. Wolbarst, "The Problem of Venereal Prophylaxis," *BMSJ* (1906), p. 280; V. G. Vecki, "Can We Abolish, Shall We Ignore or Must We Regulate Prostitution?" *AJDGUD* (1910), p. 215; J. Rosenstirn, "Should the Sanitary Control of Prostitution Be Abandoned?" *MdR*

(1914), p. 1070; A. J. McLaughlin, "Pioneering in Venereal Disease Control," *AJO* (1919), p. 639; George Jackson Kneeland, *Commercialized Prostitution in New York City* (1913), pp. 134–35; Minneapolis, *Report of the Vice Commission of Minneapolis* (1911), pp. 45–46; Anna Garlin Spencer, "Social Nemesis and Social Salvation," *F* (1913), p. 433; and Massachusetts, *Report of the Commission for the Investigation of the White Slave Traffic, So Called* (1914), p. 45.

5. See Jau Don Ball and Hayward G. Thomas, "A Sociological, Neurological, Serological and Psychiatrical Study of a Group of Prostitutes," *AJI* (1918), pp. 647–65 (of 320 prostitutes, 74 percent had a positive Wassermann reaction, and 23 percent admitted having had syphilis or were under treatment for it); Jane Deeter Rippin, "Municipal Detention of Women," *PNCSW* (1918), pp. 132–40 (of a group of 750 women detained at the Court and House of Detention for Girls and Women in Philadelphia, 259—34 percent—had either syphilis or gonorrhea or both); W. R. Jones, "Prostitution in Seattle," *NM* (1918), pp. 239–42 (of 384 prostitutes examined by the Seattle Health Department, 60 percent had syphilis, 37 percent had gonorrhea, and 17 percent had both); W. F. Draper, "The Detention and Treatment of Infected Women as a Measure of Control of Venereal Diseases in Extra-Cantonment Zones," *AJO* (1919), pp. 642–46 (of a group of 208 prostitutes, all had gonorrhea, and 40 had both syphilis and gonorrhea); Edith L. Spaulding, "Mental and Physical Factors in Prostitution," *WMJ* (1914), pp. 133–36 (of a group of 243 prostitutes studied, 99.5 percent had either gonorrhea or syphilis, and 55.8 percent had both); and Massachusetts, *Report of the Commission for the Investigation of the White Slave Traffic, So Called* (1914), pp. 45–46 (of 80 prostitutes examined at the Suffolk County House of Correction in Boston, 87.5 percent had either syphilis or gonorrhea). Although all these studies were conducted after 1914, there is no evidence to indicate that the incidence of venereal infection among prostitutes would have been much different if such studies had been made, say, in 1905.

6. Figures from a New York City venereal disease clinic (given in William F. Snow, "Occupations and the Venereal Diseases," *JAMA* [1915], p. 2055) revealed the following:

Source of Infection	Percentage of Patients
Street prostitutes	36.3
House prostitutes	18.9
Domestic servants	10.0
Friends	10.0
Working women	7.7
Wives	1.5
Unknown	14.7

These figures show that some 55 percent of the venereal disease cases could be linked with prostitution. In 1910, Frederick Bierhoff, a New York City physician, presented figures from his private practice and from three hospital dispensaries in New York City, dealing with male patients who were infected with gonorrhea. Of a group of 1,429 such patients, 1,056, or 74 percent, traced the origin of their infection to public prostitutes. See Bierhoff, "Concerning the Sources of Infection in Cases of Venereal Diseases in the City of New York," *NYMJ* (1910), pp. 949–51. These figures—and any like them from other studies—are not absolutely conclusive. One would have to know, for instance, the economic class of the patients, their age spread, and approximately what percentage, of the estimated total number of venereal disease cases in New York City, these *reported* cases of venereal disease constituted.

7. Some physicians, however, argued that the public and professional full-time prostitute was *not* the main source of venereal contagion and that ordinary promiscuous sexual intercourse was the real problem. Professional prostitutes, the argument went, were sufficiently experienced and well informed to avoid venereal disease or to seek a cure for it. See A. H. Powers, "Prostitution and Venereal Disease," *NEMG* (1905), pp. 559–61.

8. See Charles Winick and Paul M. Kinsie, *The Lively Commerce*, p. 64; Harry Benjamin and R. E. L. Masters, *Prostitution and Morality*, p. 406; and "Is Prostitution Still a Significant Health Problem?" p. 42.

9. This point was made in both of the Kinsey reports. The studies indicated that for the post–World War I generation (men born after 1900), the percentage of males who had experiences with prostitutes was roughly the same as for the pre-1900 generation, but the *frequency* with which American males went to prostitutes was, for the postwar generation, about half of that for the pre-1900 generation. Kinsey argued that the frequency of intercourse with nonprostitute women increased markedly for the younger generation. See Alfred B. Kinsey et al., *Sexual Behavior in the Human Female*, p. 300; and Alfred B. Kinsey et al., *Sexual Behavior in the Human Male*, p. 411. The problems with the Kinsey data are well known; here the difficulty is the bias in the sample of males.

10. By 1920 a change in emphasis was appearing. Discussions of venereal disease were focusing almost exclusively on the disease itself, with little consideration of prostitution. This attitude would have been highly exceptional just a decade earlier. See, for instance, Jules Schevitz, "Are We Controlling Venereal Disease?" *MMd* (1920), pp. 507–9. See in general Odin W. Anderson, *Syphilis and Society*.

11. See, on this subject, James H. Casidy, "The Registration Area and American Vital Statistics," pp. 221–31.

12. For complaints about the lack of statistics, see Prince Morrow, "Prophylaxis of Social Diseases," *AJS* (1907), p. 22; L. Chargin, "The Reporting and Control of Venereal Diseases," *AJPH* (1915), p. 298; F. H. Baker, "The Control of Venereal Diseases by Health Departments," *AJPH* (1915), p. 293; and Henry D. Holton, "The Duty of the State toward Venereal Diseases," *JAMA* (1906), p. 1249.

13. For the Committee of Seven see James F. Gardner, Jr., "Microbes and Morality," pp. 85–91. Gardner sees the activities of the committee as the beginning of social hygiene agitation in New York State and argues, persuasively, that the high figures on venereal infection were used, at least in one sense, to scare other physicians and the general public into action. The 200,000 figure for New York City was stated again in 1913 by Hermann M. Biggs, an eminent public

health authority. See Biggs, "Venereal Diseases," *NYMJ* (1913), p. 1011.

14. Morrow, "A Plea for the Organization of a 'Society of Sanitary and Moral Prophylaxis,'" *MN* (1904), p. 1074. For similar figures see R. N. Wilson, "The Relation of the Medical Profession to the Social Evil," *JAMA* (1906), p. 29; and Dock, *Hygiene and Morality* (1910), p. 49.

15. L. Duncan Bulkley, "Syphilis as a Disease Innocently Acquired," *JAMA* (1905), p. 682.

16. J. Van R. Hoff, "Is There a Venereal Peril for Us?" *MdR* (1909), p. 897. For other statements on an increase in venereal disease, see L. T. Wilson, "A Few Remarks on the Prevalence of Venereal Disease," *AJPHy* (1907), p. 39; and McLaughlin, "Pioneering in Venereal Disease Control," *AJO* (1919), p. 638.

17. J. H. Hager, "Cost of Venereal Infection," *KMJ* (1910), p. 1172; Evangeline W. Young, "The Conservation of Manhood and Womanhood," *WMJ* (1910), p. 52. See also Wilson, "A Few Remarks on the Prevalence of Venereal Disease," *AJPHy* (1907), p. 39.

18. For two general summaries of the statistical information on venereal disease, each of them based on more than twenty sources, see J. Patterson, "An Economic View of Venereal Infections," *JAMA* (1914), pp. 668–71; and G. V. R. Merrill, "Supervision of the Venereally Diseased," *NYSJM* (1911), pp. 136–38.

19. Richard C. Cabot, "Observations regarding the Relative Frequency of the Different Diseases Prevalent in Boston and Its Vicinity," *BMSJ* (1911), pp. 155–57. Cabot's findings on the incidence of syphilis were close to Morrow's: Morrow believed that from 5 to 18 percent of males suffered from the disease; Cabot placed the figure at either 11 or 14.8 percent.

20. Morrow, "The Frequency of Venereal Diseases," *BMSJ* (1911), pp. 521, 522–25.

21. Rosebury, *Microbes and Morals*, p. 208. The actual number of Americans infected with venereal disease in the progressive years is still not known. The U.S. Public Health Service estimates that 10 percent of the population had syphilis. However, during World War I, about 5.6 percent of the draftees had either syphilis or gonorrhea. Both of these figures, needless to say, could be very inaccurate. See U.S. Public Health Service, *Syphilis: A Synopsis*, p. 13; and Fred Davis Baldwin, "The American Enlisted Man in World War I," p. 66.

22. M. Scholtz, "The Problem of Social Evil in a Large Municipality," *JSM* (1917), p. 104.

23. Kelly is quoted in Denslow Lewis, "The Need of Publicity in Venereal Prophylaxis," *MdR* (1906), p. 863. Kelly's attitude became more tolerant during the first decade of the century. See his "The Protection of the Innocent," *AJO* (1907), pp. 447–81; "The Best Way To Treat the Social Evil," *MN* (1905), pp. 1157–63; "The Regulation of Prostitution," *JAMA* (1906), pp. 397–401; and "What Is the Right Attitude of the Medical Profession toward the Social Evil?" *JAMA* (1905), pp. 679–81.

24. See, for instance, J. N. Upshur, "Venereal Diseases as a Social Menace," *VMSM* (1904), p. 294; H. J. Scherck, "Venereal Disease and the Social Evil," *SLMR* (1910), pp. 39–41; M. L. Heidingsfeld, "The Control of Prostitution and the Prevention of the Spread of Venereal Diseases," *JAMA* (1904), p. 306;

A. L. Wolbarst, "The Venereal Diseases," *AJDGUD* (1910), p. 268; H. A. Brann, "Social Prophylaxis and the Church," *MN* (1905), pp. 74–75; E. W. Ruggles, "The Physician's Relation to the Social Evil," *NYMJ* (1907), pp. 159–60; A. Williams, "The Anti-Venereal Campaign," *DMJ* (1909), p. 40; and T. D. Crothers, "Some Scientific Conclusions concerning the Vice Problem," *TMJ* (1913), p. 386.

25. Morrow, "The Society of Sanitary and Moral Prophylaxis," *AMd* (1905), p. 320.

26. This point is also made in John C. Burnham, "The Progressive Era Revolution in American Attitudes toward Sex," pp. 885–908.

27. A. Vanderveer, "In the Relation We Bear to the Public, What Use Shall We Make of Our Knowledge of the Evil Effects of Venereal Disease?" *AJO* (1911), pp. 1033–42; R. H. Everett, "Publicity and the Campaign against Venereal Disease," *AJPH* (1919), pp. 854–58; Lewis, "The Need of Publicity in Venereal Prophylaxis," *MdR* (1906), pp. 863–65; F. W. Tomkins, "Sanitary Science and the Social Evil," *PaMJ* (1909), pp. 172–74; L. D. Bulkley, "Should Education in Sexual Matters Be Given to Young Men of the Working Classes?" *ISMJ* (1906), pp. 300–304; George R. Dodson, "The Black Plague and the Educational Remedy," *BAAM* (1910), pp. 490–95; M. Call, "A Plan for the Prevention of Venereal Disease," *VMSM* (1904), p. 295.

28. W. R. Jones, "Seattle Prostitution from inside the Quarantine," *NM* (1919), p. 237; W. R. Jones, "A Successful Venereal Prevention Campaign," *JAMA* (1918), p. 1297; A. N. Thomson, "Attacking the Venereal Peril," *LIMJ* (1916), p. 144; Michael M. Davis, Jr., "Evening Clinics for Syphilis and Gonorrhea," *AJPH* (1915), pp. 310–11; M. M. Davis, "Efficient Dispensary Clinics a Requisite for Adequate Coping with Venereal Diseases," *JAMA* (1915), pp. 1983–86; M. F. Gates, "The Prophylaxis of Venereal Disease," *PaMJ* (1910), p. 258; W. B. Bieberbach, "Venereal Disease and Prostitution," *BMSJ* (1915), p. 208; J. Rosenstirn, "The Municipal Clinic of San Francisco," *MdR* (1913), pp. 467–76; Scholtz, "The Problem of Social Evil in a Large Municipality," *JSM* (1917), pp. 109–10.

29. See "Duty of the Profession to Womankind," *JAMA* (1906), pp. 1886–96, 1947–49; and "Symposium on Venereal Diseases," *JAMA* (1906), pp. 1244–58. There were no women physicians at either of these symposiums. See also "Symposium on the Venereal Peril," *PrMJ* (1905), pp. 59–78; and "Symposium on the Social Evil," *KMJ* (1910), pp. 1163–78.

30. See Burnham, "The Progressive Era Revolution in American Attitudes toward Sex," pp. 905–7. For a typical medical endorsement of the play see "Damaged Goods," *LC* (1913), p. 450.

31. The American Purity Alliance (1895) and the National Vigilance Committee (1906) merged in 1912 to form the American Vigilance Association. The American Society for Sanitary and Moral Prophylaxis (1905) merged with other social hygiene groups to form the American Federation for Sex Hygiene in 1910, which merged with the American Vigilance Association to form the American Social Hygiene Association in 1913.

32. See Wilson, "A Few Remarks on the Prevalence of Venereal Disease,"

AJPHy (1907), pp. 41, 45; C. F. Bolduan, "Venereal Diseases," *AJPH* (1913), pp. 1087–93; Chargin, "The Reporting and Control of Venereal Diseases," *AJPH* (1915), pp. 297–304; M. M. Davis, "Efficient Dispensary Clinics a Requisite for Adequate Coping with Venereal Diseases," *JAMA* (1915), pp. 1983–86; A. N. Thomson, "Methods of Controlling Venereal Disease," *AJN* (1917), pp. 1069–70; Thomson, "Attacking the Venereal Peril," *LIMJ* (1916), pp. 141–46; Scholtz, "The Problem of Social Evil in a Large Municipality," *JSM* (1917), pp. 110–11; and H. G. Giddings, "The Evils of Drug Store Prescribing in Venereal Diseases," *RIMJ* (1917), pp. 154–58.

33. This finding is not really surprising, given the conclusions of the famous Flexner Report (1910), which documented the inadequate training and preparation offered in most medical schools at the time. For comments on the sorry state of instruction in venereal disease, see D. E. Gardner, "The Relation of the General Practitioner to the Treatment of Venereal Diseases," *AJDGUD* (1910), pp. 263; C. L. Demeritt, "Venereal Prophylaxis from a Practical Standpoint," *AJDGUD* (1910), p. 425; Abner Post, "What Should Be the Attitude of Boards of Health toward Venereal Diseases?" *AJPHy* (1907), p. 48; Prince Morrow, "Education within the Medical Profession," *MN* (1905), pp. 1153–56; J. M. Anders, "The Role of the Medical Profession in Combatting the Social Evil," *Md* (1906), pp. 824–25; and T. N. Hepburn, "Demand for an Open Change of Attitude toward the Social Evil," *YMJ* (1907), p. 167.

34. Prince Morrow, "The Sanitary and Moral Prophylaxis of Venereal Diseases," *JAMA* (1905), pp. 675–79; J. H. Stokes, "Hospital Problems of Gonorrhea and Syphilis," *JAMA* (1916), p. 1960; H. M. Christian, "The Social Evil from a Rational Standpoint," *PaMJ* (1912), p. 790.

35. J. M. Baldy, "The Most Effective Methods of Control of Venereal Diseases," *TAGS* (1918), p. 198; G. M. Muren, "A Contribution to the Prophylaxis of Venereal Diseases," *AMd* (1903), p. 481; Merrill, "Supervision of the Venereally Diseased," *NYSJM* (1911), p. 138; Scholtz, "The Problem of Social Evil in a Large Municipality," *JSM* (1917), pp. 106–8; Morrow, "The Frequency of Venereal Diseases," *BMSJ* (1911), p. 525; Spaulding, "Mental and Physical Factors in Prostitution," *WMJ* (1914), pp. 133–36; S. A. Knopf, "Some Thoughts on the Etiology, Prophylaxis, and Treatment of the Social Ill," *NYMJ* (1908), p. 825; Bolduan, "Venereal Diseases," *AJPH* (1913), p. 1091. By the end of the teens, some progress had been made, according to one physician, in changing the admission policies of hospitals. See E. R. Kelley, "The State Clinics for the Treatment of Venereal Diseases," *BMSJ* (1919), p. 311.

36. Williams, "The Anti-Venereal Campaign," *DMJ* (1909), p. 41; Prince Morrow, "Health Department Control of Venereal Diseases," *NYMJ* (1911), p. 131; Prince Morrow, "Publicity as a Factor in Venereal Prophylaxis," *JAMA* (1906), pp. 1244–45; Atkinson, *Social Travesties and What They Cost* (1916), pp. 33–34; G. Frank Lydston, *The Diseases of Society* (1904), p. 311.

37. See Pusey, *The History and Epidemiology of Syphilis*, pp. 59–64; and William Trufant Foster, ed., *The Social Emergency* (1914), pp. 32–44.

38. "Symposium on the Venereal Peril," *PrMJ* (1905), pp. 71–72. The later

estimate (60–80 percent) is in Atkinson, *Social Travesties and What They Cost* (1916), p. 41. Atkinson noted that only an estimate could be given because of the lack of accurate records in the United States. There is some evidence to indicate that these estimates were probably too high. For example, in 1914 the Massachusetts Commission for the Blind informed a Massachusetts state commission investigating prostitution that 10 percent of the cases of blindness treated at three Boston hospitals were the result of venereal disease. See Massachusetts, *Report of the Commission for the Investigation of the White Slave Traffic, So Called* (1914), p. 47.

In the white-slave narratives, gonorrheal blindness in babies took on the emotional and melodramatic tone that permeated these documents as a whole. See Ernest Bell, ed., *War on the White Slave Trade* (1909), pp. 283–85, where it is claimed that there are *"half a million blind"* in the world (ten to twelve thousand in the United States) from venereal disease. The text is accompanied by a pathetic picture of a "blind baby in a poor house."

39. John C. Burnham, "Medical Inspection of Prostitutes in America in the Nineteenth Century," p. 212, especially n. 31; Burnham, "The Progressive Era Revolution in American Attitudes toward Sex," pp. 890–94.

40. The 8 percent figure is from a study of 1,698 cases admitted to the psychopathic department of the Boston State Hospital. See B. H. Mason, "Compulsory Reporting and Compulsory Treatment of Venereal Diseases," *BMSJ* (1919), p. 36. The 20 percent figure was supported by F. T. Simpson, neurologist to the Hartford Hospital, Hartford, Conn. See his "The Extent and Importance of the Venereal Diseases in the Social Body," *VMSM* (1909), p. 128. A Massachusetts commission investigating prostitution in 1914 reported similar figures: for the first 2,600 admissions to all insane hospitals in the state in 1912, 8.65 percent; for Boston Psychopathic Hospital, 6.8 percent; for Danvers State Hospital for the Insane, 20 percent; for the State Hospital for Epileptics, 10.63 percent. See Massachusetts, *Report of the Commission for the Investigation of the White Slave Traffic, So Called* (1914), p. 47. For similar statements on the prevalence of insanity owing to syphilis, see Walter T. Sumner, "General Considerations on the Vice Problem," *CMR* (1913), p. 103; N. E. Aronstam, "The Prevention of the Venereal Peril," *IMJ* (1912), p. 190; Hepburn, "Demand for an Open Change of Attitude toward the Social Evil," *YMJ* (1907), p. 172; G. H. Bogart, "The Menace of Clandestine Prostitution," *MH* (1911), p. 495; E. G. Ballenger, "The Social Evil," *AJRM* (1907), p. 8; William Lee Howard, "The Havoc of Prudery," *PM* (1910), p. 591; Chicago, *The Social Evil in Chicago* (1911), p. 25; and Syracuse, *The Social Evil in Syracuse* (1913), p. 82.

The white-slave narratives presented the relationship between syphilis and insanity in statements such as *"The red mills grind out men's brains,"* or *"The red mill destroys the spinal cord,"* giving testimonies from physicians that 75 percent of insanity was the result of syphilitic infection. See Clifford G. Roe, *The Great War on White Slavery* (1911), pp. 310–12.

41. See, for instance, the figures for the state of Massachusetts, in J. H. Cunningham, "The Importance of Venereal Disease," *BMSJ* (1913), p. 80. Cunning-

ham estimated that the cost for institutional care in state institutions for the unquestionably syphilitic insane was just under $110,000 per year. Counting inmates in institutions for remote effects of syphilis, the figure was $300,000.

42. The "race suicide" alarm is discussed, from different points of view, in David M. Kennedy, *Birth Control in America*, pp. 42–44; Mark H. Haller, *Eugenics*, pp. 79–81; Peter Gabriel Filene, *Him-Her Self*, pp. 36–38; and Linda Gordon, *Woman's Body, Woman's Right*, pp. 136–58. Physicians concerned with the problem saw "race suicide" in a much broader context than that of the birth-control controversy and related it not only to the birth rate (which could be consciously controlled) but to the ravages of various diseases on the population. Two of these were, of course, hereditary syphilis and gonorrhea. See D. Clinton Guthrie, "Race Suicide," *PaMJ* (1912), pp. 855–59; Emory Lanphear, "Gonorrhea and Race Suicide," *MPCG* (1907), pp. 7–8; Simpson, "The Extent and Importance of the Venereal Diseases in the Social Body," *VMSM* (1909), pp. 126, 129; Upshur, "Venereal Diseases as a Social Menace," *VMSM* (1904), p. 293; C. F. Hodge, "Instruction in Social Hygiene in the Public Schools," *BAAM* (1910), p. 515; Hager, "Cost of Venereal Infection," *KMJ* (1910), p. 1175; Bieberbach, "Venereal Disease and Prostitution," *BMSJ* (1915), pp. 202–3; Ballenger, "The Social Evil," *AJRM* (1907), p. 8; Merrill, "Supervision of the Venereally Diseased," *NYSJM* (1911), p. 137; D. E. Stannard, "The Crime of Sexual Ignorance, Showing Why the Doctor Is to Blame," *AJCM* (1910), p. 1172; A. L. Wolbarst, "The Venereal Diseases," *MR* (1913), pp. 269, 271; "The Deeper Reason," *TMJ* (1913), p. 394; and Prince Morrow, "Venereal Diseases and Their Relation to Infant Mortality and Race Deterioration," *NYMJ* (1911), pp. 1315–17.

43. Morrow, "Venereal Diseases and Their Relation to Infant Mortality and Race Deterioration," *NYMJ* (1911), p. 1317. Morrow was referring to instances where a woman gave birth to one child but a subsequent venereal infection rendered her sterile.

44. F. C. Walsh, "Venereal Diseases and Marriage," *AJDGUD* (1910), p. 225. See also the following statements on the percentage of childless marriages caused by venereal infection: Upshur, "Venereal Diseases as a Social Menace," *VMSM* (1904), p. 292 (70 percent); Cunningham, "The Importance of Venereal Disease," *BMSJ* (1913), pp. 79–80 (67 percent); Albert Burr, "The Guarantee of Safety in the Marriage Contract," *JAMA* (1906), p. 1887 (75 percent); and Prince Morrow, "Eugenics and Venereal Diseases," *DHG* (1911), p. 15 (17–25 percent).

45. Prince Morrow, "Social Prophylaxis and the Medical Profession," *AJDGUD* (1905), p. 269; Prince Morrow, "The Relation of Social Diseases to the Family," *AJS* (1909), p. 629.

46. Howard, "The Havoc of Prudery," *PM* (1910), p. 591. For similar sentiments see Wilson, "The Relation of the Medical Profession to the Social Evil," *JAMA* (1906), p. 30; J. C. Irons, "The Social Evil," *WVMJ* (1907), p. 347; Ballenger, "The Social Evil," *AJRM* (1907), p. 8; Upshur, "Venereal Diseases as a Social Menace," *VMSM* (1904), pp. 292–94; Call, "A Plan for the Prevention of

Venereal Disease," *VMSM* (1904), p. 294; and Young, "The Conservation of Manhood and Womanhood," *WMJ* (1910), p. 51.

47. See the recollection by G. W. Potter, in "Symposium on the Venereal Peril," *PrMJ* (1905), p. 66.

48. Morrow, "A Plea for the Organization of a 'Society of Sanitary and Moral Prophylaxis,'" *MN* (1904), p. 1075. Morrow at another time pointed out the irony that prostitutes, who were usually experienced in matters of venereal disease, normally got swifter and better treatment for venereal diseases than did a middle-class wife. Here it seems that prostitutes were far more advanced in knowledge of their own physiology than were most other women in early twentieth-century American society.

49. See the obstetricians' and gynecologists' figures cited in Wilson, "The Relation of the Medical Profession to the Social Evil," *JAMA* (1906), p. 31; and Bieberbach, "Venereal Disease and Prostitution," *BMSJ* (1915), p. 204. Prince Morrow cited a statement of the president of the American Gynecological Society in 1907 to the effect that "70 per cent of all the work done by specialists in diseases of women in this country was the result of gonococcus infection" (Morrow, "The Relations of Social Diseases to the Family," *AJS* [1909], p. 626). These statements also asserted that from 30 to 70 percent of married women seeking medical treatment for venereal disease had been infected by their husbands. For general statements on the plight of "innocent wives," see W. A. Newman Dorland, "The Social Aspect of Gonococcal Infection of the Innocent," *BAAM* (1910), p. 469; Walsh, "Venereal Diseases and Marriage." *AJDGUD* (1910), p. 225; Stannard, "The Crime of Sexual Ignorance, Showing Why the Doctor Is to Blame," *AJCM* (1910), pp. 1167–68; Bransford Lewis, "What Shall We Teach the Public regarding Venereal Diseases?" *JAMA* (1906), p. 1255; Hepburn, "Demand for an Open Change of Attitude toward the Social Evil," *YMJ* (1907), p. 172; D. C. Brockman, "What Can We Do to Prevent the Sacrifice of the Innocents?" *IoMJ* (1904), pp. 431–36; A. Ravogli, "Education and Instruction in Sexual Relations as a Prophylaxis against Venereal Diseases," *NYMJ* (1910), p. 1221; G. Frank Lydston, "The Social Evil and Its Remedies," *AJCM* (1909), pp. 156–57; Robert N. Wilson, *The American Boy and the Social Evil* (1905), p. 106; and Atkinson, *Social Travesties and What They Cost* (1916), pp. 19, 20.

50. See Katharine Houghton Hepburn, "Communications," *S* (1910), pp. 637–38.

51. Walsh, "Venereal Diseases and Marriage," *AJDGUD* (1910), p. 225.

52. Morrow mentioned this collusion in his comment on venereal disease and divorce, quoted above (n. 45), although he did not elaborate on it elsewhere. One can find condemnations of the "medical secret," implying that it was a widespread phenomenon, in Edmund Alden Burnham, "Abatement of the Social Evil" (1909), p. 480; and Dock, *Hygiene and Morality* (1910), pp. 145–46.

53. See Ann Douglas Wood, "The Fashionable Diseases," pp. 1–22; and, in general, John S. Haller, Jr., and Robin M. Haller, *The Physician and Sexuality in Victorian America*; and G. J. Barker–Benfield, *The Horrors of the Half-Known Life*.

54. For an overview of the general subject of sex education, see Bryan Strong, "Ideas of the Early Sex Education Movement in America, 1890–1920," pp. 129–61. The doctrine of male sexual necessity is discussed in James L. Wunsch, "Prostitution And Public Policy," pp. 101–21.

55. G. B. H. Swayze, "Social Evil Dilemma," MT (1906), p. 228. For similar attitudes, see C. E. Lack, "The Physician's Duty regarding the Prophylaxis of Venereal Diseases," MT (1909), p. 47; Wolbarst, "The Problem of Venereal Prophylaxis," BMSJ (1906), p. 285; F. Bierhoff, "Venereal Diseases," NYMJ (1912), p. 1012; and E. H. Williams and J. S. Brown, "Venereal Diseases and Practical Eugenics in Small Communities," MdR (1913), p. 1020.

56. The belief in the value of sexual continence permeated the medical literature on prostitution and venereal disease. For some examples, see F. H. Gerrish, "A Crusade against Syphilis and Gonorrhea," BMSJ (1910), pp. 5–6; J. N. Upshur, "The Limitation and Prevention of Venereal Disease," AJDGUD (1910), p. 349; Demeritt, "Venereal Prophylaxis from a Practical Standpoint," AJDGUD (1910), p. 424; Lydston, "The Social Evil and Its Remedies," AJCM (1909), pp. 158–59; Ravogli, "Education and Instruction in Sexual Relations as a Prophylaxis against Venereal Diseases," NYMJ (1910), p. 1219; E. L. Keyes, "The Sexual Necessity," MN (1905), pp. 73, 74; J. H. Landis, "The Social Evil in Relation to the Health Problem," AJPH (1913), p. 1076; Lewis, "What Shall We Teach the Public regarding Venereal Diseases?" JAMA (1906), p. 1253; W. F. Snow, "Public Health Measures in Relation to Venereal Diseases," JAMA (1916), p. 1006; William Cullen Bryant, "The Social Evil," PtMJ (1913), pp. 37–40; Hepburn, "Demand for an Open Change of Attitude toward the Social Evil," YMJ (1907), pp. 170–71; Young, "The Conservation of Manhood and Womanhood," WMJ (1910), p. 52; Ballenger, "The Social Evil," AJRM (1907), pp. 11–12; Sprague Carleton, "The Prostitute," HahM (1908), p. 825; Maude Glasgow, "On the Regulation of Prostitution with Special Reference to Paragraph 79 of the Page Bill," NYMJ (1910), pp. 1321–22; Ruggles, "The Physician's Relation to the Social Evil," NYMJ (1907), p. 159; P. B. Brooks, "The Relation of the General Practitioner to Prevention of Venereal Diseases," NYSJM (1913), p. 102; Call, "A Plan for the Prevention of Venereal Disease," VMSM (1904), p. 296; "Sowing Wild Oats," TMJ (1913), pp. 410–11; C. E. Smith, Jr., "Some Observations on Public Health and Morality," SPMJ (1912), p. 201; W. J. Herdman, "The Duty of the Medical Profession to the Public in the Matter of Venereal Diseases, and How To Discharge It," JAMA (1906), p. 1247; Foster, The Social Emergency (1914), pp. 28–31, 98, 130, 142, 145; Dock, Hygiene and Morality (1910), pp. 60–62; Rabbi Rudolph I. Coffee, "Pittsburgh Clergy and Social Evil," S (1913), p. 815; "Is It Crime As Well As Sin?" I (1913), p. 176; Clara E. Laughlin, "A Single Standard," PM (1914), pp. 737–38; Howard, "The Havoc of Prudery," PM (1910), p. 597; Minneapolis, Report of the Minneapolis Vice Commission (1911), p. 9; and Newark, Report of the Social Evil Conditions of Newark (1914), p. 133.

57. See Barbara Gutmann Rosenkrantz, Public Health and the State, pp. 110–12.

58. N. P. Rathbun, "The Control of Social Disease," LIMJ (1908), p. 22;

Baldy, "The Most Effective Methods of Control of Venereal Disease," *TAGS* (1918), pp. 196–97; E. L. Keyes, "The Prenuptial Sanitary Guarantee," *NYMJ* (1907), p. 1203; W. M. L. Coplin, "Departmental Influence in the Suppression of Social Disease," *NYMJ* (1907), p. 1206; Demeritt, "Venereal Prophylaxis from a Practical Standpoint," *AJDGUD* (1910), pp. 423, 424. The heavy opposition of New York physicians to a New York reporting regulation is discussed in Gardner, "Microbes and Morality," pp. 307–8.

59. This proreporting sentiment was widespread in the medical literature, and, although journal opinion cannot be taken as an absolute indication of physicians' opinions, it clearly indicated an atmosphere, or a set of attitudes, that looked to the future. See, for some examples, Smith, "Some Observations on Public Health and Morality," *SPMJ* (1912), p. 200; "Symposium on the Venereal Peril," *PrMJ* (1905), pp. 65–66; Lack, "The Physician's Duty regarding the Prophylaxis of Venereal Disease," *MT* (1909), p. 48; Young, "The Conservation of Manhood and Womanhood," *WMJ* (1910), p. 53; Ballenger, "The Social Evil," *AJRM* (1907), p. 10; Merrill, "Supervision of the Venereally Diseased," *NYSJM* (1911), pp. 138–39; C. C. Pierce, "Progress of Venereal Disease Control," *JAMA* (1919), p. 421; W. Elder, "The Reporting of Venereal Diseases by Physicians," *JAMA* (1920), p. 1764; Brooks, "The Relation of the General Practitioner to Prevention of Venereal Diseases," *NYSJM* (1913), p. 103; J. Rosenstirn, "The Notification of Venereal Disease," *MdR* (1914), p. 343; Bolduan, "Venereal Diseases," *AJPH* (1913), p. 1088; Gerrish, "A Crusade against Syphilis and Gonorrhea," *BMSJ* (1910), pp. 10–12; Post, "What Should Be the Attitude of Boards of Health toward Venereal Diseases?" *AJPH* (1907), p. 47; and W. A. Purrington, "Professional Secrecy and the Obligatory Notification of Venereal Diseases," *NYMJ* (1907), p. 1209.

60. See, in general, Biggs, "Venereal Diseases," *NYMJ* (1913), pp. 1009–12; S. L. Strong, "A Symposium on the Reportability and Control of Venereal Diseases," *BMSJ* (1913), pp. 903–7; Kelley, "The State Clinics for the Treatment of Venereal Diseases," *BMSJ* (1919), p. 310; Mason, "Compulsory Reporting and Compulsory Treatment of Venereal Diseases," *BMSJ* (1919), pp. 37–38; H. G. Irvine, "The Venereal Disease Campaign in Retrospect," *JCD* (1919), p. 750; and Joseph Mayer, *The Regulation of Commercialized Vice* (1922), pp. 31–32. The anti-venereal disease campaign during World War I gave an important boost to the demand for reporting laws. See Thomas Parran, *Shadow on the Land*, pp. 80–88; Baldwin, "The American Enlisted Man in World War I," pp. 31–49; 111–15; and below, Chapter 7.

61. Morrow, "The Relations of Social Diseases to the Family," *AJS* (1909), p. 632. It is interesting here to compare Morrow's conception of feminine modesty in 1909 with the sensibility of Mencken's 1915 essay "The Flapper," a famous sentence of which reads: "She has been converted, by Edward W. Bok, to the gospel of sex hygiene. She knows exactly what the Wassermann reaction is, and has made up her mind that she will never marry a man who can't show an unmistakable negative" ("The Flapper," *SS* [1915], p. 1).

62. For positive attitudes, see Burr, "The Guarantee of Safety in the Marriage Contract," *JAMA* (1906), p. 1888; "Marriage Laws and Wisconsin's Experi-

ence," *TMJ* (1913), pp. 395–96; Patterson, "An Economic View of Venereal Infections," *JAMA* (1914), p. 671; G. B. H. Swayze, "Shall Social Evil Infections Be Legally Repressed?" *MT* (1906), p. 257; Smith, "Some Observations on Public Health and Morality," *SPMJ* (1912), p. 201; M. Lederer, "The Value of the Gonorrheal Complement Fixation Test and the Wassermann Reaction in Determining the Fitness of a Person to Marry," *LIMJ* (1913), pp. 102–4; Williams, "The Anti-Venereal Campaign," *DMJ* (1909), p. 45; C. D. Lockwood, "Venereal Diseases in Children," *BAAM* (1910), p. 482; W. F. Snow, "The Preventive Medicine Campaign against Venereal Diseases," *AMAB* (1914), p. 193; Mason, "Compulsory Reporting and Compulsory Treatment of Venereal Diseases," *BMSJ* (1919), p. 38; Sumner, "General Considerations on the Vice Problem," *CMR* (1913), p. 103; Aronstam, "The Prevention of the Venereal Peril," *IMJ* (1912), p. 196; Irons, "The Social Evil," *WVMJ* (1908), p. 348; Knopf, "Some Thoughts on the Etiology, Prophylaxis, and Treatment of the Social Ill," *NYMJ* (1908), p. 822; Gardner, "The Relation of the General Practitioner to the Treatment of Venereal Diseases," *AJDGUD* (1910), p. 265; F. H. Gerrish, "A Crusade against Syphilis and Gonorrhea," *MCMMS* (1910), pp. 723–60; and Wolbarst, "The Problem of Venereal Prophylaxis," *BMSJ* (1906), pp. 280–86.

The vice commission reports also supported premarriage medical tests. See, for example, Newark, *Report of the Social Evil Conditions of Newark* (1914), p. 134; Minneapolis, *Report of the Vice Commission of Minneapolis* (1911), p. 2; Chicago, *The Social Evil in Chicago* (1911), pp. 56, 68, 292; and Syracuse, *The Social Evil in Syracuse* (1913), pp. 64, 82.

63. Young, "The Conservation of Manhood and Womanhood," *WMJ* (1910), p. 53.

64. This matter deserves some elaboration. By 1914 seven states had passed legislation dealing with venereal disease and marriage. The Michigan (1899) and Utah (1909) laws declared it unlawful for infected men to marry but provided for no means of enforcement. The Pennsylvania (1913) statute required males applying for marriage licenses to sign affidavits indicating freedom from venereal disease. The Washington (1909), North Dakota (1913), Wisconsin (1913), and Oregon (1913) legislation required males to present physicians' certificates (but *not* the results of serological tests) certifying the absence of venereal infection. In 1914, Edward L. Keyes, a leading physician in the social hygiene movement, commented: "No state requires the physical examination of the prospective bride. We may admit the impracticality of requiring such an examination. Yet its omission nullifies the intent of the law" (Keyes, "Can the Law Protect Matrimony from Disease?" *JSH* [1914], p. 10). In 1917, New York State stipulated that both applicants for a marriage license must sign affidavits; and in 1919, Alabama called for males to present physicians' certificates. By 1922 twenty states had provisions concerning venereal disease and marriage on the books, but none of them required serological tests. See Michael F. Guyer, "Review of Wisconsin's 'Eugenics Legislation,'" *AJO* (1918), pp. 485–92; J. S. Lawrence, "Recent Legislation in New York State, Relating to the Control of Venereal Disease," *MdR* (1919), pp. 669–70; "AnteNuptial Examination of Males for Venereal Infec-

tion," *PHR* (1920), p. 1401; Hugh Cabot, "Syphilis and Society," *JSH* (1915), pp. 347–51; Bernal C. Roloff, "The Eugenics Marriage Laws of Wisconsin, Michigan, and Indiana," *JSH* (1920), pp. 227–54; Mayer, *The Regulation of Commercialized Vice* (1922), p. 31; and Fred S. Hall and Elizabeth Brooke, *American Marriage Laws in Their Social Aspects* (1919).

By 1936 the situation was only somewhat improved. Twenty-eight states had passed legislation, but ten states still required only affidavits from males, and four states (Del., N.Y., Nebr., and Pa.) required affidavits from both parties. Only Connecticut required the results (from both male and female) of serological tests. See Parran, *Shadow on the Land*, pp. 251–52.

By 1939 some progress had been made. Sixteen states (Calif., Colo., Conn., Wash., W.Va., Ill., Ind., Ky., Mich., N.H., N.J., N.Y., Pa., R.I., S.Dak., Tenn.) required male and female to present the results of serological tests. But nineteen states (Ariz., Ark., Fla., Ga., Idaho, Iowa, Kans., Maine, Md., Mass., Minn., Miss., Mo., Mont., Nev., N.Mex., Ohio, Okla., S.C.) had no legislation dealing with venereal disease and marriage. Seven states (Ala., La., N.C., Oreg., Tex., Wis., Wyo.) still required only physicians' certificates from both parties, and three (Utah, Vt., Va.) stated that persons with venereal disease could not marry but set up no means of enforcement. Figures from Bascom Johnson, ed., *Digest of Laws and Regulations Relating to the Prevention and Control of Syphilis and Gonorrhea in the Forty-eight States and the District of Columbia.*

65. Haller, *Eugenics*, p. 142. A distinction between the eugenics orientation and the campaign against venereal disease is made in Snow, "Public Health Measures in Relation to Venereal Diseases," *JAMA* (1916), p. 1008.

66. See note 64 to this chapter.

67. Morrow, "The Relations of Social Diseases to the Family," *AJS* (1909), p. 633.

68. For the nineteenth-century controversy over regulation, see Wunsch, "Prostitution and Public Policy," pp. 38–100; Burnham, "Medical Inspection of Prostitutes in America in the Nineteenth Century," pp. 203–18; and David J. Pivar, *Purity Crusade*, pp. 50–77.

69. See W. E. Harwood, "A Practical Lesson in Reglementation," *JAMA* (1906), pp. 2076–78; Frederic Bierhoff, "The Page Bill and Regulation of Prostitution," *MPCG* (1910), pp. 437–42; F. Bierhoff, "The Problem of Prostitution and Venereal Diseases in New York City," *NYMJ* (1911), pp. 557–61, 618–22; Vecki, "Can We Abolish, Shall We Ignore, or Must We Regulate Prostitution?" *AJDGUD* (1910), pp. 213–20; F. H. Hancock, "Regulation of Prostitution in the City of Norfolk, Virginia," *VMSM* (1913), pp. 559–61; Landis, "The Social Evil in Relation to the Health Problem," *AJPH* (1913), pp. 1073–86; Bryant, "The Social Evil," *PtMJ* (1913), pp. 42, 45–48; J. Huici, "The Necessity of Isolating Prostitutes Who Suffer from Syphilis," *AJPH* (1910), pp. 523–30; Christian, "The Social Evil from a Rational Standpoint," *PaMJ* (1912), pp. 789–90; Bieberbach, "Venereal Disease and Prostitution," *BMSJ* (1915), p. 206; A. W. Herzog, "A Plan to Regulate Prostitution," *MB* (1905), pp. 381–83; Denslow Lewis, "What Shall We Do with the Prostitute?" *AJDGUD* (1907), pp. 485–93;

Aronstam, "The Prevention of the Venereal Peril," *IMJ* (1912), pp. 192–93, 196; J. C. Wood, "The Social Evil," *HahM* (1912), p. 573; and George B. H. Swayze, "Shall Social Evil Infections Be Legally Repressed?" *MT* (1906), p. 257.

70. Lewis, "What Shall We Do with the Prostitute?" *AJDGUD* (1907), p. 491.

71. For Cincinnati see D. E. Robinson and J. G. Wilson, "Tuberculosis among Prostitutes," *AJPH* (1916), pp. 1164–65, 1171–72; and J. H. Landis (Cincinnati health officer), "What Departments Can Do to Solve the Venereal Problem under Existing Conditions," *MRR* (1915), pp. 535–38. For some brief comments on the system of medical regulation in Cincinnati, see Zane L. Miller, *Boss Cox's Cincinnati*, pp. 98, 177–78, 218. For Cleveland and Toledo see Theodore A. Bingham, "The Girl That Disappears," *HM* (1910), p. 570.

72. A. Neisser, "Is It Really Impossible to Make Prostitution Harmless As Far As Infection Is Concerned?" *AJUS* (1916), pp. 289–99.

73. For European cities, see F. Griffith, "Observations upon the Protective Value of the Inspection of Public Women as Carried Out in Paris," *MdR* (1904), pp. 651–52; Frederic Bierhoff, "Police Methods for the Sanitary Control of Prostitution in Some of the Cities of Germany," *NYMJ* (1907), pp. 298–305, 354–59, 400–406, 451–56 (Bierhoff admitted that the German system, for a number of reasons, was not effective, but argued that the faults could be remedied); H. P. deForest, "Prostitution: Police Methods of Sanitary Supervision," *NYSJM* (1908), pp. 516–35 (deForest, a police surgeon in the New York City police department and a professor of obstetrics, was somewhat unique among regulationists in that he advocated, along with the inspection of prostitutes, the inspection of their male customers); and Wilhelm Dreuw, "The Modern Examination of Prostitutes," *UCR* (1914), pp. 182–91 (this is a detailed and illustrated article describing the procedure, instruments, and techniques used in examining prostitutes in Berlin, Germany; it was, in short, a specific model for U.S. physicians to follow).

The military analogy was two-sided. First, it was contended that military programs which required prophylaxis for men after sexual contact (shore leave, etc.) reduced the rate of venereal disease and thus showed that similar programs applied to prostitutes would also work. See E. O. J. Eytinge, "A System of Venereal Prophylaxis and Its Results," *MS* (1909), pp. 170–71; Gates, "The Prophylaxis of Venereal Disease," *PaMJ* (1910), pp. 255–59; and Robert A. Bachman, "Venereal Prophylaxis: Past and Present," *PrMJ* (1913), pp. 231–44. It was also argued that in military areas where prostitution was under medical supervision, the rate of venereal infection for military personnel was decreased. See H. Goodman, "Prostitution and Community Syphilis," *AJPH* (1919), pp. 515–20.

74. An exception was the program advocated by Theodore A. Bingham, former chief of the New York City police, who argued that a system of medical inspection should be run by the police, in cooperation with the public health authorities. See Bingham, "The Girl That Disappears," *HM* (1910), pp. 572–73.

75. The opposition to the regulation of prostitution was not organized in the progressive years, and it cannot be assumed that the individuals and groups mentioned in this paragraph worked together or even were entirely aware of

what the others were doing. Their activities are presented simply as expressions of a particular pattern of response to the idea of regulation. It should also be emphasized that these groups did not share the same outlook on many other social issues and, indeed, were many times on opposite sides of particular questions.

76. For a typical statement by Prince Morrow opposing the regulation of prostitution, see his "The Sanitary and Moral Prophylaxis of Venereal Diseases," *JAMA* (1905), p. 675. In its first major publication, George Jackson Kneeland's *Commercialized Prostitution in New York City* (1913), the Bureau of Social Hygiene concluded that a policy of regulation was useless (p. 9).

77. Glasgow, "On the Regulation of Prostitution with Special Reference to Paragraph 79 of the Page Bill," *NYMJ* (1910), pp. 1320–23; Maude Glasgow, "Side Lights on the Social Peril," *NYMJ* (1911), pp. 1186–90; Kelly, "The Regulation of Prostitution," *JAMA* (1906), p. 398; Lydston, "The Social Evil and Its Remedies," *AJCM* (1909), p. 279; Call, "A Plan for the Prevention of Venereal Disease," *VMSM* (1904), p. 295; Crothers, "Some Scientific Conclusions concerning the Vice Problem," *TMJ* (1913), p. 391; Gerrish, "A Crusade against Syphilis and Gonorrhea," *MCMMS* (1910), pp. 732–36; Post, "What Should Be the Attitude of Boards of Health toward Venereal Diseases?" *AJPHy* (1908), pp. 47–48; Chargin, "The Reporting and Control of Venereal Diseases," *AJPH* (1915), p. 298; Ballenger, "The Social Evil," *AJRM* (1907), p. 9; P. F. Rogers, "The Sociologic Aspect of the Venereal Diseases," *WsMJ* (1909), p. 256; George W. Goler, "The Municipality and the Venereal Disease Problem," *AJPH* (1916), p. 357; J. M. Mabbot, "The Duties of the Gynecologist in Relation to the State Control of Vice," *AJO* (1911), pp. 227–37; Heidingsfeld, "The Control of Prostitution and the Prevention of the Spread of Venereal Diseases," *JAMA* (1904), p. 308; Hepburn, "Demand for an Open Change of Attitude toward the Social Evil," *YMJ* (1907), pp. 167–73; "Symposium on the Venereal Peril," *PrMJ* (1905), p. 64; Ruggles, "The Physician's Relation to the Social Evil," *NYMJ* (1907), p. 160.

78. See Chicago, *The Social Evil in Chicago* (1911), p. 26; Syracuse, *The Social Evil in Syracuse* (1913), pp. 87–88; Minneapolis, *Report of the Vice Commission of Minneapolis* (1911), pp. 34–36, 37, 52, 53; Massachusetts, *Report of the Commission for the Investigation of the White Slave Traffic, So Called* (1914), p. 45; and Illinois, *Report of the Senate Vice Committee* (1916), pp. 42–45.

For the white-slave narratives see Bell, *War on the White Slave Trade* (1909), pp. 257–60; Roe, *The Great War on White Slavery* (1911), p. 362; E. Norine Law, *The Shame of a Great Nation* (1909), p. 183; and Clifford G. Roe, *The Girl Who Disappeared* (1914), pp. 302, 306–11.

79. See the statements by Anna Garlin Spencer: "State Regulation of Vice and Its Meaning," *F* (1913), pp. 587–606; "The Scarlet Woman," *F* (1913), pp. 276–89; and "A World Crusade," *F* (1913), pp. 182–95. See also Jane Addams, *A New Conscience and an Ancient Evil* (1912), pp. 45–49; Jane Addams, "A Challenge to the Contemporary Church," *S* (1912), pp. 195–98; George Kibbe Turner, "The Strange Woman," *MM* (1913), p. 33; and Maude E. Miner, *Slavery of Prostitution* (1916), pp. 138–42, 155–61. Much of the opposition to regula-

tion drew inspiration from the efforts of Josephine Butler in opposing the medical inspection of prostitutes in England in the nineteenth century. See Anna Garlin Spencer, "Josephine Butler and the English Crusade," *F* (1913), pp. 703–16.

80. Theodore Roosevelt, *Autobiography* (1913), p. 237; "Shall Chicago Legalize Hell?" *AC* (1912), pp. 405–6; "California Dux," *I* (1913), pp. 1064–65.

81. This acceptance of the same basic assumption sometimes took amusing forms. For instance, the Minneapolis Vice Commission was at pains to show that prostitution was the major source of venereal disease and that therefore prostitution ought to be repressed and not regulated. The commission used some figures gathered by Frederick Bierhoff, a New York City physician, which showed that three-quarters of venereal disease cases could be traced to prostitution. What is interesting is that Bierhoff had presented these figures in the course of an article in support of a policy of medical regulation. See Minneapolis, *Report of the Vice Commission of Minneapolis* (1911), p. 46, for the citation of Bierhoff's figures. For Bierhoff's presentation, see his "Concerning the Sources of Infection in Cases of Venereal Diseases in the City of New York," *NYMJ* (1910), pp. 949–51.

82. Morrow, "The Sanitary and Moral Prophylaxis of Venereal Diseases," *JAMA* (1905), p. 675.

83. M. L. Heidingsfeld, a private practitioner in Cincinnati, argued that during the years 1900–1903, when Cincinnati had a system of medical inspection, his volume of venereal disease cases *increased*, and that a high percentage of these cases could be traced to "inspected prostitutes." See Heidingsfeld, "The Control of Prostitution and the Prevention of the Spread of Venereal Diseases," *JAMA* (1904), pp. 305–9. (Other Cincinnati officials came to the opposite conclusion. See the citations in note 71 above.) A Cleveland physician, a superintendent of a community dispensary, also presented figures showing that regulation did not work. He argued that during the eight months before the closing of the segregated district in Cleveland, the dispensary handled 112 cases of venereal disease, whereas in the first eight months *after* the closing of the district, there were only 53 cases. See A. R. Warner, "The Result of Closing the Segregated Vice District upon the Public Health of Cleveland," *CMJ* (1916), pp. 171–73.

84. See Demeritt, "Venereal Prophylaxis from a Practical Standpoint," *AJD-GUD* (1910), pp. 422–23; Lydston, *The Diseases of Society* (1904), p. 407; and Dock, *Hygiene and Morality* (1910), pp. 131–32. Pivar, *Purity Crusade*, discusses earlier nineteenth-century American opposition from purity reformers to military programs for the regulation of prostitution (pp. 218–24).

85. Kelly, "What Is the Right Attitude of the Medical Profession toward the Social Evil?" *JAMA* (1905), p. 681.

86. Flexner, *I Remember* (1940), p. 186. For Flexner's early life, see pp. 3–184. There is some material on Flexner's relationship with Rockefeller and the Bureau of Social Hygiene in Gardner, "Microbes and Morality," pp. 248–49.

87. Flexner, *I Remember* (1940), p. 188.

88. Abraham Flexner, *Prostitution in Europe* (1914), p. 231.

89. Ibid., pp. 12, 286–394.

90. Ibid., pp. 265–85.

91. For this interpretation of Wilson's approach to European imperialism, see N. Gordon Levin, Jr., *Woodrow Wilson and World Politics*, pp. 1–10.

92. For reviews, see "A Hopeful Book on the Social Evil," O (1914), pp. 293–94; James Bronson Reynolds, "Prostitution in Europe," AC (1914), pp. 155–56; "A Real Social Evil Treatise," N (1914), pp. 75–76; "Prostitution in Europe," S (1914), pp. 471–73; and C. V. Carrington, "An Analysis of the Report of Abraham Flexner on the Regulation of Prostitution in Europe," VMSM (1916), pp. 11–16. These were all laudatory reviews, but for one that questioned Flexner's interpretation, see D. C. McMurtrie, "A Study of Prostitution in Europe," MdR (1914), pp. 325–28.

93. Although most physicians subscribed to civilized morality, its rhetoric, especially the belief in sexual continence, was most strenuously espoused by the physicians and others who were against regulation. Those who supported regulation were not, usually, proselytizers for the gospel of continence. And those who supported the belief in continence usually were strongly against the regulation of prostitution. One can see this breakdown in a crude sense by noting that the physicians listed in note 69 above as regulationists do not appear in note 56, with the proponents of continence. And, the physicians listed in note 55 as critics of the gospel of continence do not appear in note 77, with the antiregulationsts. There were, of course, some exceptions. For instance, J. H. Landis supported both the regulation of prostitution and the theory of continence (see "The Social Evil in Relation to the Health Problem," AJPH [1913], pp. 1073–86).

94. Flexner, *Prostitution in Europe* (1914), p. 219; Spencer, "State Regulation of Vice and Its Meaning," F (1913), p. 600. Spencer's article is one of the fullest analyses of the significance of the regulation of prostitution to be found in the progressive years.

95. Hodge, "Instruction in Social Hygiene in the Public Schools," BAAM (1910), p. 515.

96. Brooks, *The V.D. Story*, p. 22.

97. The physicians interviewed in "Is Prostitution Still a Significant Health Problem?" basically agreed that prostitution is no longer as important a factor in venereal disease control as it once was but argued that it is a problem in terms of drug abuse and diseases such as hepatitis.

98. Morrow, "The Sanitary and Moral Prophylaxis of Venereal Diseases," *JAMA* (1905), p. 677.

Chapter 5

1. City booster groups were often proponents of reform and good-government movements and frequently supported vice investigations. See, for instance, Zane L. Miller, *Boss Cox's Cincinnati*, pp. 113–28. There was, however, a fundamental distinction in tone and mood between a typical booster publication and a vice commission report, which will be made clearer in this chapter.

2. Technically, *The Social Evil in Chicago* was not the first vice commission report published in the progressive years. The New York City Committee of Fifteen published *The Social Evil* in 1902, and the same city's Committee of Fourteen published *The Social Evil in New York City: A Study of Law Enforcement* in 1910. The great outburst of urban vice commission reports, however,

came after 1910. The production of vice commission reports in the years immediately after 1910 became something of a vogue, of which a minor indication is that the 1902 report of the New York Committee of Fifteen was reissued in 1912, with a new introduction. The vice commission reports after 1910 were published in the following order (see bibliography, under the city or state of publication unless otherwise noted, for full titles): 1911: Chicago, Minneapolis, Kansas City (listed in the bibliography under the name Fred Robert Johnson), Cleveland; 1912: Atlanta; 1913: Little Rock, Denver, Hartford, Lafayette (Ind.), Grand Rapids (Mich.), New York City (listed under George J. Kneeland), Elmira (N.Y.), Syracuse, Portland (Oreg.), Lancaster (Pa.), Philadelphia, Pittsburgh, Charleston; 1914: Baton Rouge, Portland (Maine), Massachusetts, Bay City (Mich.), Newark, Wisconsin; 1915: Lexington (Ky.), Louisville (Ky.), Shreveport (La.), Rockland County (N.Y.), Lancaster (Pa.); 1916: Bridgeport (Conn.), Illinois, Paducah (Ky.), Cleveland.

3. Graham Taylor, "Police Efficiency the First Test of Vice Inquiries," *S* (1912), p. 141.

4. Although *The Social Evil in Chicago* will be the text for this chapter, most of its themes and preoccupations were present in reports from other cities. For summaries of other vice commission reports, see Roland Richard Wagner, "Virtue against Vice," pp. 111–229.

5. Syracuse, *The Social Evil in Syracuse* (1913). See also Fred Robert Johnson, *The Social Evil in Kansas City* (1911), pp. 1, 11–12.

6. For the history of Chicago, see in general Harold Mayer and Richard Wade, *Chicago*; Ray Ginger, *Atgeld's America*; Hugh Daziel Duncan, *Culture and Democracy*, pp. 196–200; and Zane L. Miller, *The Urbanization of America*, pp. 124–46.

7. There is no history of the First Ward and the Levee that treats them in sophisticated terms as a "subculture" of official Chicago and probes the functional and structural relationship between the two. For popular accounts, see Lloyd Wendt and Herman Kogan, *Lords of the Levee*; Charles Washburn, *Come into My Parlor*; Emmett Dedmon, *Fabulous Chicago*, pp. 135–57; and Herbert Asbury, *Gem of the Prairies*.

8. See *The Social Evil in Chicago*, pp. 309–10, for the texts of the laws. The relationship between sexual corruption (prostitution) and political corruption was a main theme of antiprostitution. George Kibbe Turner, the prominent muckraker, made this connection in his sensational exposé of Chicago, "The City of Chicago: A Study of the Great Immoralities," *MM* (1907), pp. 575–92.

9. See in general Ginger, *Atgeld's America*, and Duncan, *Culture and Democracy*.

10. Robert E. L. Faris, *Chicago Sociology, 1920–1932*. The connection between the Chicago Vice Commission and Chicago sociology continued after the commission's work was completed. Walter Reckless, a graduate student in the University of Chicago Sociology Department, wrote a dissertation entitled "Natural History of Vice Areas in Chicago" (1925), which was the basis for his *Vice in Chicago* (1933). He built on the work of the commission, and his work is still the best sociological study of urban prostitution in the early decades of the century.

11. The important role of the clergy in Chicago distinguished vice reform in this city from that in other cities, especially New York. See Wagner, "Virtue against Vice," pp. 177–78. The published vice commission reports of the various cities, however, do not vary significantly in tone or content.

12. Walter C. Reckless, *Vice in Chicago*, p. 3. For a detailed analysis of the origin of the Chicago Vice Commission and the dynamics of vice reform in Chicago in general, see Eric Anderson, "Prostitution and Social Justice," pp. 203–28.

13. *The Social Evil in Chicago*, p. 1; Walter T. Sumner, "General Considerations on the Vice Problem," *CMR* (1913), p. 97.

14. Kneeland directed vice commissions in New York City; Paducah, Ky.; Newark; Lancaster, Pa.; Elmira, N.Y.; and Syracuse. His most famous report, after his Chicago work, was that on prostitution in New York City, conducted under the auspices of the Bureau of Social Hygiene and published as *Commercialized Prostitution in New York City* (1913).

15. Sumner, "General Considerations on the Vice Problem," *CMR* (1913), pp. 97, 99. The report at first circulated untroubled through the mails. Then, after John D. Rockefeller, Jr., decided to send several thousand copies through the mail to libraries and individuals throughout the country, the Chicago Post Office censors began excluding the volume from the mail. See "Discussing the Social Evil," *N* (1911), pp. 308–9.

16. Graham Taylor, "The Story of the Chicago Vice Commission," *S* (1911), pp. 240–41; *The Social Evil in Chicago*, pp. 28, 31, 69.

17. The chapters in the report were as follows: 1, Existing Conditions in Chicago; 2, The Social Evil and the Saloon; 3, The Social Evil and the Police; 4, Sources of Supply; 5, Child Protection and Education; 6, Rescue and Reform; 7, The Social Evil and Its Medical Aspects.

18. *The Social Evil in Chicago*, pp. 119, 134, 139, 130, 132. Most vice commissions came to the same conclusion. See, for instance, Syracuse, *The Social Evil in Syracuse* (1913), pp. 33–42; Minneapolis, *Report of the Vice Commission of Minneapolis* (1911), p. 25; and Paul H. Hass, "Sin in Wisconsin," pp. 138–51.

19. The commission added the rather confusing distinction of condemning the police "system" but not the "personnel of the police as a whole" (*The Social Evil in Chicago*, p. 29).

20. See, for instance, Lyman Beecher Stowe, "Vice, Crime, and the New York Police," *ARR* (1913), pp. 74–76; Turner, "The City of Chicago," *MM* (1907), pp. 588–90; George Kibbe Turner, "The Strange Woman," *MM* (1913), p. 33; G. Frank Lydston, "The Social Evil and Its Remedies," *AJCL* (1909), p. 280; N. E. Aronstam, "The Prevention of the Venereal Peril," *IMJ* (1912), pp. 193–94; Maude E. Miner, *Slavery of Prostitution* (1916), pp. 134–38; Lavinia L. Dock, *Hygiene and Morality* (1910), pp. 100–101; and U.S. Senate, Reports of the Immigration Commission, vol. 19, *Importation and Harboring of Women for Immoral Purposes* (1910), pp. 84–85.

21. *The Social Evil in Chicago*, pp. 150–58.

22. Ibid., p. 143.

23. Ibid., pp. 28–29.

24. Ibid., pp. 163–74.

25. Taylor, "The Story of the Chicago Vice Commission," *S* (1911), p. 244.

26. *The Social Evil in Chicago*, p. 25.

27. The following discussion of the Chicago Vice Commission draws on Anthony M. Platt, ed., *The Politics of Riot Commissions, 1917–1970*, a volume of critical essays on American riot commissions; and Charles J. Hanser, *Guide to Decision*, a study of the evolution of the British Royal Commission, the preeminent model for modern investigations by commission. The similarities between race riot commission reports and the vice commission reports are clear, and an interesting study could be made comparing the official response to prostitution in Chicago in 1911, *The Social Evil in Chicago*, to the official response to the race riot of 1919 by the Chicago Commission on Race Relations, *The Negro in Chicago: A Study of Race Relations and a Race Riot* (1922).

28. *The Social Evil in Chicago*, p. 32; Sumner, "General Considerations on the Vice Problem," *CMR* (1913), p. 98. See also Taylor, "The Story of the Chicago Vice Commission," *S* (1911), p. 239. For similar examples of the projection of this self-image, see Syracuse *The Social Evil in Syracuse* (1913), p. 10; and Minneapolis, *Report of the Vice Commission of Minneapolis* (1911), p. 13.

29. For the names and occupations of commission members, see *The Social Evil in Chicago*, p. 2.

30. The groups testifying before the commission were the Anti-Cigarette League, Anti-Saloon League, Baptists Ministers' Union, Chicago Deaconess' Home, Citizens' Association, Chicago Law and Order League, Central Howard Association, Congregational Ministers' Union, Catholic Abstinence Union of Illinois, Chicago Refuge for Girls, Chicago Rescue Mission, Douglass Neighborhood Club, Brewers' Exchange, South Park Improvement Association, Florence Crittenton Anchorage, Hull House, Immigrant Protective League, Juvenile Court, Juvenile Protective Association, Legal Aid Society, Lincoln Center, Law Enforcement League of the Northwest Side, Methodist Brotherhood of Chicago, Midnight Mission, Northwestern University Settlement, Salvation Army Maternity Home, Retail Liquor Dealers' Protective Association (*The Social Evil in Chicago*, p. 9).

31. See Platt, *The Politics of Riot Commissions*, p. 18, for commissions' tendencies to present unanimous reports.

32. *The Social Evil in Chicago*, p. 32. The fear of the "commercialization" of prostitution was widespread in the period and not limited to the vice commission reports. The white-slave narratives, for example, dwelled on this aspect of prostitution at great length. The vice commissions, however, supplied the original data—facts and figures—which showed the extent to which prostitution was "commercialized." Roy Lubove, in "The Progressives and the Prostitute," pp. 328–30, notes briefly the perception of prostitution as commercialized but does not explore in any detail the reasons for or the meaning of this fear.

33. See, for example, Turner, "The Strange Woman," *MM* (1913), pp. 30–31. This alleged shift from female control to male control was of great importance to the arguments of the white-slave tracts, as the alleged white slavers were of course men. See Ernest A. Bell, ed., *War on the White Slave Trade* (1909), p. 262;

Clifford G. Roe, *The Girl Who Disappeared* (1914), p. 72; and Theodore A. Bingham, "The Girl That Disappears," *HM* (1911), p. 566. The importance of this belief is made clear in Chapter 6.

34. *The Social Evil in Chicago*, p. 102.

35. Ibid., p. 98.

36. G. Henri Bogart, "One Bane of Prudery," *TMJ* (1911), pp. 170–71.

37. Steven Marcus, in *Engels, Manchester, and the Working Class*, pp. 44–45, 192–93, 219, discusses the growing awareness of the extreme in social existence in the early decades of English industrialism, an awareness prompted by the discovery of the unbelievable squalor in which the industrial proletariat lived. A similar point can be made concerning prostitution. Prostitution always involved sexual behavior that might be called extreme; but the consciousness of the extreme in sexual behavior obviously depends on that with which it is compared. In the eighteenth century, when a tolerant sexual ethic seems to have prevailed, prostitution did not provoke notions of the extreme. With the rise of civilized morality in the nineteenth century, however, a much stricter sexual code was in operation, and within the framework of this code, prostitution came to be seen as an example of the extreme.

38. Marcus, *Engels, Manchester, and the Working Class*, pp. 102–12; Herbert Marcuse, *Reason and Revolution*, p. 279.

39. *The Social Evil in Chicago*, pp. 98, 104.

40. Ibid., p. 104.

41. Walter Lippmann, *A Preface to Politics* (1913), p. 123.

42. For the American jeremiad in its classic religious form, see Perry Miller, *The New England Mind: From Colony to Province*, pp. 19–52; and Alan Heimert, *Religion and the American Mind*, pp. 62, 284–86, 423–26, 478–91. There was, of course, a great difference between the highly theological nature of the early jeremiads and the basically secular nature of the Chicago Vice Commission report. The emphasis here is on the jeremiad as a cultural form of expression and response to events, which has remained fairly consistent throughout American history.

43. See, for instance, Blake McKelvey, *The Urbanization of America, 1860–1915*, pp. 17–72, 231–86; Blake McKelvey, *The Emergence of Metropolitan America, 1915–1966*, pp. 3–30; and Charles N. Glaab and A. Theodore Brown, *A History of Urban America*, pp. 107–66.

44. Lydston, "The Social Evil and Its Remedies," *AJCM*, (1909), p. 21.

45. *The Social Evil in Chicago*, pp. 87–88, 89–101. For the background of the land and real estate business in Chicago, see Homer Hoyt, *One Hundred Years of Land Values in Chicago*, pp. 128–231.

46. For the ambiguity of the jeremiad, see Miller, *The New England Mind: From Colony to Province*, p. 26.

47. W. A. Evans, "The Attack upon Venereal Diseases through Education and Publicity," *MRR* (1915), p. 539; "Report of Chicago Vice Commission," *S* (1911), p. 99; "The Chicago Vice Commission," *S* (1911), pp. 215–18; Taylor, "The Story of the Chicago Vice Commission," *S* (1911), pp. 239–47. Another commission member, Edward M. Skinner, published a similar account, "The

Work of the Vice Commission," *CMR* (1913), pp. 90–93. For other vice commission reports, see Eugene T. Lies, "Minneapolis Vice Commission's Report," *S* (1911), pp. 694–95; Rudolph I. Coffee, "Pittsburgh Clergy and the Social Evil," *S* (1913), pp. 815–16; "The Vice Problem in Philadelphia," *S* (1913), p. 259; "Gaining Control over Vice in New York," *S* (1914), p. 572; "Closing a Vice District by Strangulation," *S* (1915), p. 229; "How Atlanta Cleaned Up," *LD* (1913), pp. 1012–13; and "Pittsburgh's Housecleaning," *LD* (1913), p. 1232.

48. Charles Forcey, *The Crossroads of Liberalism*, pp. 88–89 and, in general, pp. 88–108.

49. Theodore Roosevelt, "The Cause of Decency," *O* (1911), pp. 569, 570. For additional comments by Roosevelt on the problem of prostitution, see his *Autobiography* (1913), pp. 235–39; and Elting E. Morison, ed., *Letters of Theodore Roosevelt* (1911), 7: 207–8.

50. Roosevelt, "The Cause of Decency," *O* (1911), pp. 569–70; *The Social Evil in Chicago*, p. 25; "Report of Chicago Vice Commission," *S* (1911), p. 99.

51. Roosevelt, "The Cause of Decency," *O* (1911), p. 570.

52. Lippmann, *A Preface to Politics* (1913), p. 121. For the background of the writing of the book, see Forcey, *The Crossroads of Liberalism*, pp. 88–118.

53. Lippmann, *A Preface to Politics* (1913), pp. 95–96.

54. Ibid., p. 129. For the general background, see Henry F. May, *The End of American Innocence*, pp. 121–329; Morton White, *Social Thought in America*; and Claire Sprague, ed., Introduction to *Van Wyck Brooks: The Early Years*, pp. vii–xxix.

55. Lippmann, *A Preface to Politics* (1913), pp. 107, 33.

56. Ibid., pp. 96, 97, 112.

57. Ibid., p. 108.

58. Ibid., pp. 104, 103–4.

59. Ibid., p. 146.

60. Ibid., pp. 136, 133, 100, 98, 105; *The Social Evil in Chicago*, p. 27. Lippmann's interest in "moral equivalents for evil" was clearly influenced by William James's famous 1910 essay on the need to find moral equivalents to war.

61. *The Social Evil in Chicago*, p. 73. The commission's lack of attention to the sexual dynamics of prostitution might account for the great attention it gave to the relationship between alcohol and prostitution. Of the twenty-five suggestions for the repression of prostitution the commission offered to Chicago authorities, twelve focused on repressing the operation of saloons and the consumption of alcohol. Although this approach might at first appear as a neat sidestepping of the problem, it was actually perfectly consistent with the commission's view of sex: without the biologically and psychologically uninhibiting effects of alcohol, sexual behavior would remain rational. See *The Social Evil in Chicago*, pp. 55–65.

62. On this important writer's function, see Marcus, *Engels, Manchester, and the Working Class*, p. 108.

63. Charles Berg, *Fear, Punishment, Anxiety and the Wolfenden Report*, pp. 44–45.

Chapter 6

1. There is an early but generally uncritical discussion of the white-slave scare in Howard B. Woolston, *Prostitution in the United States* (1921), pp. 159–78. An early perceptive analysis is in Walter C. Reckless, *Vice in Chicago*, pp. 32–68. For more recent discussions, see Paul Boyer, *Urban Masses and Moral Order in America, 1820–1920*, pp. 191–219; James L. Wunsch, "Prostitution and Public Policy," pp. 122–29; Peter Gabriel Filene, *Him-Her Self*, pp. 86–90; and Daniel J. Leab, "Women and the Mann Act," pp. 55–65. Sporadic concern over white slavery in the late nineteenth century, much of it prompted by William Stead's exposé of white slavery in England in 1885, is covered in David J. Pivar, *Purity Crusade*, pp. 135–39, 207–8; Joseph O. Baylen, "A Victorian's 'Crusade' in Chicago, 1893–1894," pp. 418–43; Roland Richard Wagner, "Virtue against Vice," pp. 33–38, 44–66; and Otto Wilson, *Fifty Years' Work with Girls, 1883–1933*, pp. 17–28. For a survey and analysis of the traffic in women in contemporary times, see Kathleen Barry, *Female Sexual Slavery*.

2. U.S. Department of Commerce and Labor, *Reports*, 1908, "The White-Slave Traffic," pp. 19–20; Stanley W. Finch, *The White Slave Traffic* (1912); Jane Addams, *A New Conscience and an Ancient Evil* (1912), p. 145; Edwin Sims, "The White Slave Trade of Today" and "The Menace of the White Slave Trade," originally published in 1909 in *Woman's World*, reprinted in Ernest A. Bell, ed., *War on the White Slave Trade* (1909), pp. 47–73; Lavinia L. Dock, *Hygiene and Morality* (1910), pp. 66–67, 104–22, 154; John Hund, *The Physician and the Social Evil* (1911), pp. 24–25; Denslow Lewis, "What Shall We Do with the Prostitute?" *AJDGUD* (1907), pp. 485–93; R. W. Bingham, "Cost of Venereal Infection as Viewed from the Standpoint of the Lawyer," *KMJ* (1910), pp. 1169–70; Evangeline W. Young, "The Conservation of Manhood and Womanhood," *WMJ* (1910), pp. 51–53; Maude E. Miner, *Slavery of Prostitution* (1916), pp. 88–124; Maude E. Miner, "The Problem of Wayward Girls and Delinquent Women," *PAPS* (1912), pp. 604–12.

3. "The White Slave Films," *O* (1914), pp. 120–22; "The White Slave Films: A Review," *O* (1914), pp. 345–50.

4. The Rockefeller grand jury investigation is discussed in Wagner, "Virtue against Vice," pp. 128–31; and "The Rockefeller Grand Jury Report," *MM* (1910), pp. 471–73. The Senate investigation of the international white-slave trade is discussed above in Chapter 3; the Mann Act is discussed below.

5. The incident arose when the son of Anthony Caminetti, Wilson's commissioner of immigration, was arrested and charged under the Mann Act with transporting a woman across state lines for immoral purposes. The elder Caminetti, evidently without ulterior motive, wished to have his son's trial delayed because of his own pressing duties. To this effect, Attorney General McReynolds interceded on Caminetti's behalf by asking John McNab, the U.S. attorney in California (where the incident occurred), to postpone the trial. McNab resigned in a huff, citing improper interference. The affair was made public, and President Wilson was put in a somewhat delicate position when he defended McReynolds'

actions. For a detailed account, see "Woodrow Wilson and the Caminetti Scandal," CO (1913), pp. 76–79; and "Tomlinson and Diggs," S (1913), p. 655.

6. Almost all of the white-slave tracts include discussion of the plight of immigrant white slaves, who are treated quite sympathetically. But the main emphasis of the tracts—the total impression that a reader would draw from the illustrations and the text—is on the native American girl. Efforts on behalf of the immigrant girl are discussed in Egal Feldman, "Prostitution, the Alien Woman and the Progressive Imagination, 1910–1915," pp. 192–206.

7. Jean Turner Zimmermann, *America's Black Traffic in White Girls* (1912), pp. 4–5; Robert J. Moorehead, *Fighting the Devil's Triple Demons* (1911), p. 49. See also Mrs. C. I. Harris, *Modern Herodians or Slaughterers of Innocents* (1909), pp. 20–21; Bell, *War on the White Slave Trade* (1909), pp. 32–33, 57, 68, 108, 119–20, 201–3, 306–8; Clifford G. Roe, *The Great War on White Slavery* (1911), pp. 5–6, 96, 102–3, 189; Clifford G. Roe, *The Girl Who Disappeared* (1914), pp. 19–20, 71–72, 153–54, 183, 199–234; E. Norine Law, *The Shame of a Great Nation* (1909), pp. 152–53; and Virginia Brooks, *My Battles with Vice* (1915), pp. 11–13, 15–16, 26, 72, 97, 235–36. For the conspiratorial mentality in American life, see Richard Hofstadter, *The Paranoid Style in American Politics*; and David Brion Davis, ed., *The Fear of Conspiracy*.

8. Law, *The Shame of a Great Nation* (1909), pp. 5, 70–71.

9. For some examples, see Roe, *The Great War on White Slavery* (1911), pp. 261–62, 372; Roe, *The Girl Who Disappeared* (1914), pp. 264–65; and Moorehead, *Fighting the Devil's Triple Demons* (1911), pp. 17, 39, 79, 95–96, 104–5, 150, 153.

10. For the Indian captivities, see Richard Slotkin, *Regeneration through Violence*, pp. 57–145; and David T. Haberly, "Women and Indians," pp. 431–33. The analogy between the Indian captivities and the white-slave tracts is not perfect. Many of the Indian captivity narratives, for example, concerned not colonists who were captured and rescued but rather colonists who upon capture adopted Indian ways, thus becoming "white Indians." See James Axtell, "The White Indians of Colonial America," pp. 55–88.

11. See David Brion Davis, "Some Themes of Counter-Subversion," pp. 205–24.

12. Zimmermann, *America's Black Traffic in White Girls* (1912), p. 29. Also see pp. 12–13, 20–24, 26, 37; Theodore A. Bingham, "The Girl That Disappears," HM (1910), p. 565. For similar beliefs, see Bell, *War on the White Slave Trade* (1909), pp. 16, 71–72, 145, 187–89, 260; Roe, *The Girl Who Disappeared* (1914), pp. 211–17; Law, *The Shame of a Great Nation* (1909), pp. 92–98; and Moorehead, *Fighting the Devil's Triple Demons* (1911), pp. 120–21.

13. Reginald Wright Kauffman, *The House of Bondage* (1910), p. 19.

14. Roe, *The Great War on White Slavery* (1911), pp. 63, 196–202. Elsewhere, Roe declares that "It should be clearly understood that girl slavery is not a Jewish problem alone, neither is it a French nor an Italian problem. . . . Jews and Gentiles alike have contributed to the great army of panders which now floods the entire earth" (p. 202). Similar qualifications appeared in many of the

other white-slave narratives. The overall message of the tracts, however, was that one of the most odious aspects of the white-slave conspiracy was its control by the "new" immigrants.

15. Harris, *Modern Herodians* (1909), p. 5. See also Roe, *The Great War on White Slavery* (1911), p. 176; and Finch, *The White Slave Traffic* (1912), p. 3.

16. The projection of sexual and racial fears in other contexts is discussed in Davis, "Some Themes of Counter-Subversion," pp. 216–21; Charles A. Cannon, "The Awesome Power of Sex," pp. 61–82; Wayland Young, *Eros Denied*, pp. 288–99; and Winthrop D. Jordan, *White over Black*, pp. 32–43, 136–78.

17. Roe, *The Great War on White Slavery* (1911), p. 157.

18. Bell, *War on the White Slave Trade* (1909), p. 303; Roe, *The Great War on White Slavery* (1911), pp. 186, 306, 310, 311; Zimmermann, *America's Black Traffic in White Girls* (1912), p. 19. As an interesting, and psychologically revealing, side note, some organizations dedicated to rescuing white slaves set up headquarters in buildings that had formerly been brothels. See Bell, *War on the White Slave Trade* (1909), pp. 400, 408.

19. Chicago, *The Social Evil in Chicago* (1911), p. 34; Zimmermann, *America's Black Traffic in White Girls* (1912), p. 17.

20. For the belief in the rural origins of prostitutes, see Addams, *A New Conscience and an Ancient Evil* (1912), pp. 145, 150; "A Philadelphia Warning to Girls," *LD* (1913), p. 234; Clara E. Laughlin, "Girls Who Go Wrong," *PM* (1910), p. 384; Mrs. William Falconer, "The Relation of the Graduate Nurse to the Problem of Social Hygiene," *AJN* (1917), pp. 1076–77; L. Weiss, "The Prostitution Problem in Its Relation to Law and Medicine," *MPCG* (1907), p. 15; S. Adolphus Knopf, "Some Thoughts on the Etiology, Prophylaxis, and Treatment of the Social Ill," *NYMJ* (1908), p. 824; Finch, *The White Slave Traffic* (1912), p. 3; Ralph Beaton, *The Anti-Vice Crusader and Social Reformer*, (1918), pp. 147, 161–62, 184–85; Miner, *Slavery of Prostitution* (1916), pp. 63–64; and Ernest R. Groves, "Psychic Causes of Rural Migration," *AJS* (1916), p. 626. It is interesting to note that when, in the 1920s, Walter Reckless investigated sixty-three white-slavery cases prosecuted in Chicago between 1910 and 1913, he found that twenty-seven (43 percent) of the young women came from Chicago and that fifteen (24 percent) came from other large cities. Only seventeen (27 percent) came from small towns. See Reckless, *Vice in Chicago*, p. 44.

21. Roe, *The Great War on White Slavery* (1911), pp. 27–41, 28, 42. Although Roe presented Mildred's story as factual, it was probably highly embellished. See Reckless, *Vice in Chicago*, pp. 36–40, for an instructive comparison between a similar white-slavery story published by Roe and the actual statement given by the young women involved in the case upon which the story purportedly was based. The actual statement bears little resemblance to the highly emotional and sentimental tales that appeared in the white-slave tracts by Roe and others.

22. Moorehead, *Fighting the Devil's Triple Demons* (1911), pp. 27–37. For similar tales, see Bell, *War on the White Slave Trade* (1909), pp. 48–61, 68–69, 70–71, 105–9; Roe, *The Girl Who Disappeared* (1914), pp. 11–33, 138, 237, 240, 243; Brooks, *My Battles with Vice* (1915), p. 16; and Zimmermann, *America's Black Traffic in White Girls* (1912), p. 18.

23. Clyde Griffen, "The Progressive Ethos," pp. 144–45; Woodrow Wilson, *The New Freedom* (1913), p. 26. For changing conditions and attitudes in rural America in the period, see Richard Hofstadter, *The Age of Reform*, pp. 23–130.

24. Martha Foote Crow, *The American Country Girl* (1915), pp. xii–xiii, 20–21, 25. It is instructive to remember that this paean to the country girl appeared the same year as H. L. Mencken's article "The Flapper," *SS* (1915), pp. 1–2, which announced the debut of a quite different vision of young women.

25. Roe, *The Great War on White Slavery* (1911), pp. 156, 169; Harris, *Modern Herodians* (1909), p. 20; Bell, *War on the White Slave Trade* (1909), pp. 68, 71; Moorehead, *Fighting the Devil's Triple Demons* (1911), p. 31; Law, *The Shame of a Great Nation* (1909), p. 150. This fear of young women leaving home was a manifestation of the general conservative attitudes toward women in the period, which are discussed in Filene, *Him-Her Self*, pp. 5–68; and in Aileen S. Kraditor, *The Ideas of the Woman Suffrage Movement, 1890–1920*, pp. 82–104.

26. Eugene Arden, "The Evil City in American Fiction."

27. See William G. McLoughlin, *The Meaning of Henry Ward Beecher*, pp. 87–88.

28. C. Wright Mills pointed out that the greatest literary interest in the "white collar girl" occurred in the period ten years before and ten years after the First World War (Mills, *White Collar*, pp. 198–204).

29. Roe, *The Great War on White Slavery* (1911), p. 361; Bingham, "The Girl That Disappears," *HM* (1910), pp. 559–60. Similar rumors of disappearing girls, with their latent sexual content, often preceded anti-Semitic outbursts in Europe and lynchings in the American South.

30. Roe, *The Girl Who Disappeared* (1914), pp. 11–15; Bell, *War on the White Slave Trade* (1909), pp. 165, 230–34; H. M. Lytle, *Tragedies of the White Slave* (1909), pp. 59–76. It is significant that these discussions of "stage struck" girls—a condition that at least implies discontent, unfulfillment, or boredom—are always treated in the context of a happy familial situation. Kauffman's *The House of Bondage* (1910) was an exception to this pattern; it was made clear in the novel that the young woman was leaving an unhappy home.

31. Miner, *Slavery of Prostitution* (1916), pp. 271–74. Despite its title, this work, which was presented as a Ph.D. thesis to the Columbia University Sociology Department, was not a white-slave narrative but an analysis by a social worker of wide experience with the problem of urban prostitution.

32. "A Sculptress Who Has Caught the American Rhythm," *CO* (1913), pp. 124–25.

33. The letters to the editor and an editorial rebuttal are in "White Slave," *S* (1913), pp. 311–13, 381–83, 507–10.

34. Christina Merriman, "New Bottles for New Wine," *S* (1913), pp. 196–98. Eberle's sculpture was also in the tradition of William Stead's exposé of child prostitution in Britain in 1885, which is discussed from different points of view in Deborah Gorham, "The 'Maiden Tribute of Modern Babylon' Re-Examined," pp. 353–79; and in Ronald Pearsall, *The Worm in the Bud*, pp. 289–305.

35. Chicago, *The Social Evil in Chicago* (1911), pp. 166–69; Massachusetts, *Report of the Commission for the Investigation of the White Slave Traffic, So*

Called (1914), pp. 31–33. See also Walter Reckless's analysis of the age distribution of the young women involved in the most celebrated white-slavery cases in Chicago between 1910 and 1913. Of forty-six women who gave their ages, two were fifteen, nineteen (41 percent) were either sixteen or seventeen, and twenty-five (54 percent) were between the ages of eighteen and twenty-five. Reckless comments: "This age distribution should not be taken as indicative of the ages of prostitutes in Chicago at the time but merely as indicative of the cases which anti-white-slavery forces gave greatest attention to—namely young girls. We notice, however, that even with this extreme selection of cases there are none under 15 years in spite of what the public believed about girls scarcely in their 'teens' being lured into prostitution" (Reckless, *Vice in Chicago*, p. 43).

36. Jane Deeter Rippin's "Municipal Detention of Women," *PNCSW* (1918), pp. 132–40, deals with a group of 1,205 women detained in the House of Detention for Girls and Women in Philadelphia. Of the 545 of these women held on prostitution charges, 202 (37 percent) were between twenty and twenty-four years of age, and 142 (26 percent) were between twenty-five and twenty-nine years of age. V. V. Anderson's "The Immoral Woman as Seen in Court," *BMSJ* (1917), pp. 899–903, is a profile of 100 women, randomly selected, who appeared in the Municipal Court of Boston in January and February of 1917. Anderson found that 74 of the 100 were under thirty years of age and that the average was twenty-six. Clinton P. McCord's "One Hundred Female Offenders," *JAIC* (1915), pp. 385–407, reported that the average age of the prostitute in his group was twenty-seven years.

37. For the photographs see *E. J. Bellocq: Storyville Portraits* (1912). Additional Bellocq photographs are given throughout Al Rose's *Storyville, New Orleans*.

38. U.S., *Statutes at Large*, vol. 36 (1910), pp. 825–26.

39. For the view that the act infringed on the police powers of the states, see the critical minority report accompanying the Mann Act, U.S. House of Representatives, Committee on Interstate and Foreign Commerce, *White Slave Traffic* (1909), pt. 2. The problem of blackmail is discussed in O. J. Smith, "The Mann White Slave Law," *MLJ* (1916), pp. 4–7; and in "'White-Slave' Law and Blackmail," *LD* (1917), p. 178.

40. U.S. House of Representatives, *Congressional Record*, 61st Cong., 2d sess., 1910, 45, 1: 811.

41. Roe, *The Great War on White Slavery* (1911), pp. 353–54.

42. *Hoke and Economides v. United States*, 227 U.S. 308 (1913); *Athanasaw v. United States*, 227 U.S. 308 (1913); *United States v. Holte*, 236 U.S. 140 (1915); *Caminetti v. United States*, 242 U.S. 470 (1917). There is favorable contemporary response in "The White-Slave Decision," *LD* (1913), pp. 500–502; "The White Slave Traffic before the Supreme Court," *CO* (1913), p. 273; "White Slavers Routed," *O* (1913), pp. 569–70; "Morals and Inter-State Commerce," *O* (1913), pp. 570–71; "Supreme Court Upholds the 'White Slave' Law," *S* (1913), pp. 799–804; and "The Meaning of the White Slave Act as Shown by the Federal Decision," *JCL* (1914), pp. 738–40. For a discussion of these and later cases arising from the Mann Act, see Morris Ploscowe, *Sex and*

the Law, pp. 260–63; Edward H. Levi, *An Introduction to Legal Reasoning*, pp. 33–54; and William Seagle, "The Twilight of the Mann Act," pp. 641–47. Levi argues that the law was early interpreted to apply to noncommercial forms of sexual immorality. Seagle argues that the attorney general usually prosecuted only cases involving commercial or organized prostitution.

43. For federal prosecutions, see U.S. Department of Justice, *Annual Report of the Attorney General of the United States*, 1913, pp. 50–51, 361; 1914, p. 46; 1915, p. 43; 1916, p. 52; 1917, pp. 79–80; 1918, p. 102; 1919, p. 79; 1920, p. 128. For state legislation, see Seagle, "The Twilight of the Mann Act," p. 646.

44. Roe, *The Great War on White Slavery* (1911), p. 171; Bell, *War on the White Slave Trade* (1909), pp. 141, 435; Roe, *The Girl Who Disappeared* (1914), p. 81.

45. "The White Slaves and the Social Evil," *Ch* (1909), pp. 332–33.

46. Ada Elliot Sheffield, "The Written Law and the Unwritten Double Standard," *IJE* (1910), pp. 477–78. For a similar distinction, see "Is White Slavery Nothing More Than a Myth?" *CO* (1913), p. 348; and Charles Reed Zahniser, "A Constructive Program of Sex Control," *HahM* (1918), pp. 550–59.

47. An important impetus for the formation of the grand jury was George Kibbe Turner's exposé of white slavery in New York City, published in *McClure's Magazine* in 1909. For the background and proceedings of the investigation, see Wagner, "Virtue against Vice," pp. 128–31; Pamela Ann Roby, "Politics and Prostitution," pp. 137–40; and James F. Gardner, Jr., "Microbes and Morality," pp. 201–9.

48. Jau Don Ball and Hayward G. Thomas, "A Sociological, Neurological, Serological and Psychiatrical Study of a Group of Prostitutes," *AJI* (1918), pp. 656, 661–62.

49. Ethel M. Watters, "The Problem of the Women Venereal Disease Carrier," *CJM* (1919), p. 285.

50. C. E. Smith, Jr., "Some Observations on Public Health and Morality," *SPMJ* (1912), p. 195; W. Ray Jones, "Prostitution in Seattle," *NM* (1918), p. 240; W. Ray Jones, "Seattle Prostitution from inside the Quarantine," *NM* (1919), p. 186; Illinois, *Report of the Senate Vice Committee* (1916), p. 30; Paul H. Hass, "Sin in Wisconsin," p. 148; Massachusetts, *Report of the Commission for the Investigation of the White Slave Traffic, So Called* (1914), pp. 21–23; Minneapolis, *Report of the Vice Commission of Minneapolis* (1911), p. 75; Syracuse, *The Social Evil in Syracuse* (1913), p. 102.

51. Teresa Billington-Greig, "The Truth about White Slavery," *ER* (1913), p. 429. For American comment see "Is White Slavery Nothing More Than a Myth?" *CO* (1913), p. 348; and Brand Whitlock, "The White Slave," *F* (1914), p. 201.

52. Billington-Greig, "The Truth about White Slavery," *ER* (1913), pp. 431–32, 443, 434, 444–45.

53. Roe, *The Girl Who Disappeared* (1914), pp. 217–18.

54. Whitlock, "The White Slave," *F* (1914), pp. 193, 195, 197, 200. This essay was synopsized as "The Futility of the White Slave Agitation as Brand Whitlock Sees It" in *CO* (1914), pp. 287–88.

55. *Madeleine: An Autobiography* (1919), pp. 321, 322, 324. This auto-biography, which provides interesting insights into the subculture of prostitution in the late nineteenth and early twentieth centuries, was written in a most re-served style, but it nevertheless aroused the ire of the vice societies that operated throughout the progressive era. See Paul S. Boyer, *Purity in Print*, pp. 49–52.

56. The white-slave tracts did discuss the problem of venereal disease but generally with the intent of instilling fear in the reader. See Bell, *War on the White Slave Trade* (1909), pp. 280–304; and Roe, *The Great War on White Slavery* (1911), pp. 405–41.

57. See Bell, *War on the White Slave Trade* (1909), pp. 48, 51, 59, 62, 67–68, 109–10, 115, 117, 173, 239; Roe, *The Girl Who Disappeared* (1914), pp. 36, 46, 53, 68–69, 76, 127, 148, 201; Harris, *Modern Herodians* (1909), pp. 24–25; Law, *The Shame of a Great Nation* (1909), pp. 187–91, 192–99; Moorehead, *Fighting the Devil's Triple Demons* (1911), pp. 43, 46; Zimmermann, *America's Black Traffic in White Girls* (1912), pp. 82–86; and Lytle, *Tragedies of the White Slave* (1909), pp. 4, 6, 97.

58. [Mencken], "The Flapper," *SS* (1915), pp. 1–2. For Jack Johnson and the Mann Act see Wunsch, "Prostitution and Public Policy," pp. 136–37; for Frank Lloyd Wright, see Robert C. Twombly, *Frank Lloyd Wright*, pp. 141, 151.

59. Young, *Eros Denied*, pp. 132–33.

60. Agnes Repplier, "The Repeal of Reticence," *AtM* (1914), p. 301. See also "The White Slave Films: A Review," *O* (1914), pp. 345–50; "Sex O'Clock in America," *CO* (1913), pp. 113–14; and Anna Garlin Spencer, "A World Cru-sade," *F* (1913), p. 193. The writers of the white-slave tracts also realized the possible double-edged effect of what they were doing and therefore emphasized that they used "plain words—not coarse or vulgar, but chaste and true," and that the good effects of their exposés would vastly outweigh the bad. See Bell, *War on the White Slave Trade* (1909), p. 9.

Chapter 7

1. The material in this paragraph is based on Frederic L. Paxson, *America at War, 1917–1918*, pp. 1–19; Edward M. Coffman, *The War to End All Wars*, pp. 5–53; and John Garry Clifford, *The Citizen Soldiers*, pp. 30–54.

2. For Baker's prewar career see C. H. Cramer, *Newton D. Baker*, pp. 13–75. The war years are covered in Daniel R. Beaver, *Newton D. Baker and the American War Effort, 1917–1919*. Fosdick's early years are covered in Raymond B. Fosdick, *Chronicle of a Generation* (1958), pp. 1–141.

3. Fosdick, cited in Frederick Palmer, *Newton D. Baker*, 1: 299, 301. For Baker and Fosdick's collaboration in the Mexican border situation, see Fosdick, *Chronicle of a Generation* (1958), pp. 135–41; and Palmer, *Newton D. Baker*, 1: 297–305.

4. Fosdick, cited in Palmer, *Newton D. Baker*, 1: 302.

5. Fosdick, *Chronicle of a Generation* (1958), pp. 140–41.

6. Baker, cited in Palmer, *Newton D. Baker*, 1: 307.

7. Baker, cited in Fosdick, *Chronicle of a Generation* (1958), p. 143. See also Bascom Johnson, "Eliminating Vice from Camp Cities," *AAAPS* (1918), p. 61.

The major secondary source on the CTCA is Fred Davis Baldwin, "The American Enlisted Man in World War I," pp. 4–49, 92–142. The work of the CTCA is also discussed in Fosdick, *Chronicle of a Generation* (1958), pp. 142–86; Coffman, *The War to End All Wars*, pp. 76–81; Weldon B. Durham, "'Big Brother' and the 'Seven Sisters,'" pp. 57–60; and Richard F. Knapp, "The Playground and Recreation Association of America in World War I," pp. 27–31, 110–12.

8. Baker, cited in Fosdick, *Chronicle of a Generation* (1958), p. 145; Baldwin, "The American Enlisted Man in World War I," pp. 31–44. The government's authority to repress prostitution in the training camp zones was upheld by the Supreme Court in *McKinley et al.* v. *United States*, 249 U.S. 397 (1919).

9. Johnson, "Eliminating Vice from Camp Cities," *AAAPS* (1918), p. 63; Baldwin, "The American Enlisted Man in World War I," p. 113. Also see James F. Gardner, Jr., "Microbes and Morality," p. 372.

10. See Baldwin, "The American Enlisted Man in World War I," pp. 112, 115.

11. Edward Frank Allen (with the cooperation of Raymond B. Fosdick), *Keeping Our Fighters Fit* (1918), p. 127. For a similar comment see Raymond B. Fosdick, "The Commission on Training Camp Activities," *PAPS* (1918), p. 821. The educational and recreational programs are discussed in Baldwin, "The American Enlisted Man in World War I," pp. 116–24, 125–33; and Allen, *Keeping Our Fighters Fit*, pp. 156–68, 40–137.

12. Fosdick, for example, claimed that the CTCA was responsible for the closing down of 110 red-light districts. See *Chronicle of a Generation* (1958), p. 147.

13. See Joseph Mayer, *The Regulation of Commercialized Vice* (1922), p. 11.

14. Baldwin, "The American Enlisted Man in World War I," pp. 37–38. For the wartime activities of the American Social Hygiene Association, see Willoughby Cyrus Waterman, *Prostitution and Its Repression in New York City, 1900–1931*, pp. 88–89; and Gardner, "Microbes and Morality," p. 372.

15. Johnson, "Eliminating Vice from Camp Cities," *AAAPS* (1918), p. 61. See also Allen, *Keeping Our Fighters Fit* (1918), pp. 191–207. For earlier opposition to the military regulation of prostitution by purity forces, see David J. Pivar, *Purity Crusade*, pp. 218–24; Jane Addams, *A New Conscience and an Ancient Evil* (1912), pp. 201–2; and Lavinia L. Dock, *Hygiene and Morality* (1910), pp. 131–32.

16. For the AEF in France, see Palmer, *Newton D. Baker*, 2: 299–303; Baldwin, "The American Enlisted Man in World War I," pp. 199–224, 230–32; Fred Davis Baldwin, "The Invisible Armor," pp. 432–44; Donald Smythe, "Venereal Disease," pp. 65–74; and Edward H. Beardsley, "Allied against Sin," pp. 189–202. It is interesting to note that the venereal disease rate among the U.S. military police, who picketed the French red-light districts, was sometimes ten times as high as among adjacent units. See Baldwin, "The American Enlisted Man in World War I," p. 214.

17. Walter Lippmann, *A Preface to Politics* (1913), p. 105. For the playground movement, see Allen F. Davis, *Spearheads for Reform*, pp. 60–63; and Paul Boyer, *Urban Masses and Moral Order in America, 1820–1920*, pp. 242–51.

For a comment on the work of the CTCA in the context of progressive social work, see Davis, *Spearheads For Reform*, pp. 225–26.

18. The clearest contemporary account of the detention and treatment of suspected women during the war is given in C. C. Pierce, "The Value of Detention as a Reconstruction Measure," *AJO* (1919), pp. 624–36. Pierce states that "history sheets" were collected from nine thousand of the thirty thousand women. There is a brief and uncritical account of this program in Charles Winick and Paul M. Kinsie, *The Lively Commerce*, pp. 246–52, and Fosdick briefly mentions it in *Chronicle of a Generation* (1958), pp. 147–48. See also Ethel S. Dummer's Foreword to William I. Thomas, *The Unadjusted Girl* (1923), pp. v–xvii. Thomas's 1923 study, which in many ways marked a new direction in the study of female delinquency, made use of some of the data collected in studies of women arrested during the war. This domestic aspect of World War I deserves further and more detailed study.

19. The text of the Chamberlain-Kahn Act is in U.S., *Statutes at Large*, vol. 40 (1918), pp. 886–87. See also C. C. Pierce, "Progress of Venereal Disease Control," *JAMA* (1919), pp. 417–18; and B. H. Mason, "Compulsory Reporting and Compulsory Treatment of Venereal Diseases," *BMSJ* (1919), pp. 36–37.

20. Pierce, "The Value of Detention as a Reconstruction Measure," *AJO* (1919), pp. 625–28. See Fosdick, *Chronicle of a Generation* (1958), pp. 147–48, for a brief description of the crowded condition of one of these facilities.

21. See Baldwin, "The American Enlisted Man in World War I," p. 200; Smythe, "Venereal Disease," p. 65; and Coffman, *The War to End All Wars*, p. 132.

22. Isaac W. Brewer, "The Incidence of Venereal Diseases among 6086 Men Drafted into the Service Who Reported at Camp A. A. Humphreys, Va., between September 4 and September 18, 1918," *BMSJ* (1919), p. 123. See also E. R. Beckwith, "Venereal Diseases," *AJN* (1918), pp. 1136–41; and V. C. Pederson, "Venereal Problems of the War," *MdR* (1919), pp. 60–65, 104–10.

23. For references to "uniform crazy" girls see J. H. Harris, "The Prostitute in Relation to Military Camps," *WMJ* (1918), p. 125; and Robert M. Mennel, *Thorns and Thistles*, p. 172.

24. "Fighting Prostitution in Michigan," *S* (1918), pp. 70–71. For local attempts to release detained women, see ibid., p. 71; and W. F. Draper, "The Detention and Treatment of Infected Women as a Measure of Control of Venereal Diseases in Extra-Cantonment Zones," *AJO* (1919), p. 643. For the general problem of prostitution, venereal disease, and civil rights, see William J. Curran, "Venereal Disease Detention and Treatment," pp. 180–81; and Marilyn G. Haft, "Hustling for Rights," pp. 8–26.

25. Newton D. Baker, *Frontiers of Freedom* (1918), p. 94.

26. Cited in Fosdick, *Chronicle of a Generation* (1958), p. 144.

27. Frank Tannenbaum, "The Moral Devastation of War," *D* (1919), pp. 335–36.

28. Ibid., p. 335.

29. Woodrow Wilson, Special Statement, in Allen, *Keeping Our Fighters Fit* (1918), unpaged.

30. Ernest Hemingway, *A Farewell to Arms*, pp. 184–85, 233.

Epilogue

1. *Hoke and Economides* v. *United States*, 227 U.S. 308, 322. The *Dagenhart* decision and its background are discussed in Stephen B. Wood, *Constitutional Politics in the Progressive Era*, especially pp. 139–76.

2. *Hammer* v. *Dagenhart*, 247 U.S. 280 (1918).

3. Walter Lippmann, *A Preface to Politics* (1913), p. 96.

4. William E. Leuchtenburg, *Franklin D. Roosevelt and the New Deal*, p. 339. For the Seabury investigations see Pamela Ann Roby, "Politics and Prostitution," pp. 173–224. For World War II see Francis E. Merrill, *Social Problems on the Home Front*, pp. 97–144.

BIBLIOGRAPHY

Primary Sources

Acton, William. *Prostitution*. 1857. Reprint. Edited by Peter Fryer. New York: Frederick A. Praeger, 1968.

Addams, Jane. "A Challenge to the Contemporary Church." *Survey* 28 (1912): 195–98.

——. *A New Conscience and an Ancient Evil*. New York: Macmillan Co., 1912.

"An Advertising Campaign against Segregated Vice." *American City* 9 (1913): 3–4.

Akin, C. V. "Venereal Disease Control in South Carolina." *International Journal of Surgery* 33 (1920): 109–14.

Allen, Annie W. "How To Save Girls Who Have Fallen." *Survey* 24 (1910): 684–96.

Allen, Edward Frank (with the cooperation of Raymond B. Fosdick). *Keeping Our Fighters Fit: For War and After*. New York: Century Co., 1918.

Allen, Irvin O. "Sex Problems." *Lancet-Clinic* 111 (1914): 716–22.

"An Ancient Evil." *Outlook* 101 (1912): 103–5.

Anders, J. M. "The Role of the Medical Profession in Combatting the Social Evil." *Medicine* 12 (1906): 821–25.

Anderson, V. V. "The Immoral Woman as Seen in Court: A Preliminary Report." *Boston Medical and Surgical Journal* 177 (1917): 899–903.

Anderson, Winslow. "The Social Evil." *Pacific Medical Journal* 54 (1911): 141–46.

"Antenuptial Examination of Males for Venereal Infection." *Public Health Reports* 35 (1920): 1401.

"Anti-Vice Program of a Woman's Club." *Survey* 33 (1914): 81.

"Are Low Wages Responsible for Women's Immorality?" *Current Opinion* 54 (1913): 402.

Aronstam, N. E. "The Prevention of the Venereal Peril: A Sociologic Study." *Indianapolis Medical Journal* 15 (1912): 189–97.

Ashburn, P. M. "Factors Making for a Low Venereal Record in the Army of the United States." *Military Surgeon* 47 (1920): 208–13.

——. "Venereal Prophylaxis." *Journal of the American Medical Association* 74 (1920): 1314.

Athanasaw v. United States. 227 U.S. 308 (1913).

Atkinson, D. T. *Social Travesties and What They Cost*. New York: Vail-Ballou Co., 1916.

Atlanta, Ga. Atlanta Vice Commission. *Report of the Vice Commission*. 1912.

Bachman, Robert A. "Venereal Prophylaxis: Past and Present." *Medical Record* 84 (1913): 602–6.

———. "Venereal Prophylaxis: Past and Present." *Providence Medical Journal* 14 (1913): 231–44.

———. "Venereal Prophylaxis: Why It Sometimes Fails." *Journal of the American Medical Association* 60 (1913): 1610.

Baker, F. H. "The Control of Venereal Diseases by Health Departments." *American Journal of Public Health* 5 (1915): 290–96.

Baker, Newton D. *Frontiers of Freedom*. New York: George H. Doran Co., 1918.

Baldy, J. M. "The Most Effective Methods of Control of Venereal Diseases." *American Journal of Obstetrics* 78 (1918): 238–42.

———. "The Most Effective Methods of Control of Venereal Diseases." *Transactions of the American Gynecological Society* 43 (1918): 194–200.

Ballenger, E. G. "The Social Evil." *Atlanta Journal-Record of Medicine* 9 (1907): 6–13.

Ball, Jau Don, and Thomas, Hayward G. "A Sociological, Neurological, Serological and Psychiatrical Study of a Group of Prostitutes." *American Journal of Insanity* 74 (1918): 647–66.

Barnett, A. M. "The Quarantine and Treatment of Venereally Diseased Persons in Louisville." *Urologic and Cutaneous Review* 23 (1919): 451–54.

Barry, Richard. "Who Betrays the Working Girl?" *Pearson's Magazine* 25 (1911): 175–81.

Baton Rouge, La. Baton Rouge Purity League. *The Social Evil in Baton Rouge*. 1914.

Bay City, Mich. Social Purity Committee. *The Social Evil in Bay City*. 1914.

Bayly, H. W. "The Prevention of Venereal Disease by Immediate Self-Disinfection." *International Journal of Surgery* 33 (1920): 213–18.

Beard, Mary Ritter. *Woman's Work in Municipalities*. New York: D. Appleton & Co., 1915.

Beaton, Ralph. *The Anti-Vice Crusader and Social Reformer: A Treatise on the Social Evil*. Dallas: Southwestern Printing Co., 1918.

Beavers, J. L. "Suppression Preferable to Segregation." *American City* 9 (1913): 22–24.

Bebel, August. *Women under Socialism*. Translated by Daniel De Leon. New York: New York Labor News Co., 1904.

Beckwith, E. R. "Venereal Diseases." *American Journal of Nursing* 18 (1917–18): 1136–41.

Bell, Ernest A., ed. *War on the White Slave Trade: A Book Designed to Awaken the Sleeping and to Protect the Innocent*. Chicago: Charles C. Thompson Co., 1909. Also published as *Fighting the Traffic in Young Girls; or, War on the White Slave Trade*. New York: Nichols, 1910. (This edition was also published in Chicago, with no publisher indicated, twice in 1910 and once in 1911. An abbreviated version was published in 1911 by the National Bible House, Chicago.)

———. *White Slavery Today.* Chicago: Darrow Printing Co., 1917.

Bieberbach, Walter D. "Venereal Disease and Prostitution." *Boston Medical and Surgical Journal* 172 (1915): 201–8.

Bierhoff, F. "Concerning the Protest, by the Committee Representing Women's Clubs, against Paragraph 79 of the Bill Relating to the Procedures of the Lower Courts of the City of New York." *New York Medical Journal* 92 (1910): 1107–12.

———. "Concerning the Sources of Infection in Cases of Venereal Diseases in the City of New York." *New York Medical Journal* 92 (1910): 949–51.

———. "Further Notes on the Sanitary Control of Prostitution in Some European Cities." *New York Medical Journal* 96 (1912): 569–74, 627–33.

———. "The Page Bill and Regulation of Prostitution." *Medico-Pharmaceutical Critic and Guide* 13 (1910): 437–42.

———. "Police Methods for the Sanitary Control of Prostitution in Some of the Cities of Germany." *New York Medical Journal* 86 (1907): 298–305, 354–59, 400–406, 451–56.

———. "The Problem of Prostitution and Venereal Diseases in New York City." *New York Medical Journal* 93 (1911): 557–61, 618–22.

———. "Venereal Diseases: A Sanitary and Social Problem." *New York Medical Journal* 96 (1912): 1009–13.

Biggs, H. M. "Venereal Diseases: The Attitude of the Department of Health in Relation Thereto." *New York Medical Journal* 97 (1913): 1009–12.

Billington-Greig, Teresa. "The Truth about White Slavery." *English Review* 14 (1913): 428–46.

Bingham, R. W. "Cost of Venereal Infection as Viewed from the Standpoint of the Lawyer." *Kentucky Medical Journal* 8 (1909–10): 1169–70.

Bingham, Theodore A. "The Girl That Disappears." *Hampton's Magazine* 25 (1910): 559–73.

———. *The Girl That Disappears: The Real Facts about the White-Slave Traffic.* Boston: Gorham Press, 1911.

Birtwell, Charles W. "Sex Hygiene." *Survey* 28 (1912): 525–26.

"The Blacker Plague." *Independent* 74 (1913): 275–76.

Blackmer, R. C. "Sexual Ethics: Inquiry into the Causes and Growth of Sexual Vice." *American Journal of Dermatology and Genito-Urinary Diseases* 15 (1911): 317–26.

Blake, Mabelle B. "The Defective Girl Who is Immoral." *Boston Medical and Surgical Journal* 117 (1917): 492–94.

Bloedorn, W. A. "The Control of Venereal Diseases." *Military Surgeon* 39 (1916): 599–607.

Bogart, G. H. "The Menace of Clandestine Prostitution." *Medical Herald* 30 (1911): 490–96.

———. "One Bane of Prudery." *Texas Medical Journal* 27 (1911–12): 165–75.

Bolduan, C. F. "Venereal Diseases: The Relation of the Public Health Authorities to Their Control." *American Journal of Public Health* 3 (1913): 1087–93.

Bowen, Louise de Koven. "Women Police." *Survey* 30 (1913): 64–65.

Brann, H. A. "Social Prophylaxis and the Church." *Medical News* 87 (1905): 74–75.

Brewer, Isaac W. "The Incidence of Venereal Diseases among 6086 Men Drafted into the Service Who Reported at Camp A. A. Humphreys, Va., between September 4 and September 18, 1918." *Boston Medical and Surgical Journal* 180 (1919): 122–24.

Bridgeport, Conn. Bridgeport Vice Commission. *The Report and Recommendations of the Bridgeport Vice Commission.* 1916.

Brockman, D. C. "What Can We Do to Prevent the Sacrifice of the Innocents?" *Iowa Medical Journal* 10 (1904): 431–36.

Brockway, Z. R. "Communications." *Survey* 24 (1910): 841.

Brooks, P. B. "The Relation of the General Practitioner to Prevention of Venereal Diseases." *New York State Journal of Medicine* 13 (1913): 101–3.

―――. "The Result of a Campaign against Venereal Diseases by a Physicians' Organization." *New York State Journal of Medicine* 15 (1915): 322–23.

Brooks, Virginia. *My Battles with Vice.* New York: Macaulay Co., 1915.

Bryant, William Cullen. "The Social Evil." *Pittsburgh Medical Journal* 1 (1913–14): 35–48.

Bulkley, L. Duncan. "Should Education in Sexual Matters Be Given to Young Men of the Working Classes?" *Interstate Medical Journal* 13 (1906): 300–304.

―――. "Syphilis as a Disease Innocently Acquired." *Journal of the American Medical Association* 44 (1905): 681–84.

Bunting, M. H. L. "The White Slave Traffic Crusade." *Contemporary Review* 103 (1913): 49–52.

"The Bureau of Social Hygiene." *Outlook* 103 (1913): 287–88.

Burnham, Edmund Alden. "Abatement of the Social Evil." In *Recent Christian Progress: Studies in Christian Thought and Work during the Last Seventy-five Years*, edited by Lewis Bayles Paton, pp. 477–82. New York: Macmillan Co., 1909.

Burr, Albert H. "The Guarantee of Safety in the Marriage Contract." *Journal of the American Medical Association* 47 (1906): 1887–89.

Cabot, Hugh. "Syphilis and Society." *Journal of Social Hygiene* 2 (1915–16): 347–62.

Cabot, Richard C. "Observations regarding the Relative Frequency of the Different Diseases Prevalent in Boston and Its Vicinity." *Boston Medical and Surgical Journal* 165 (1911): 155–70.

"California Dux." *Independent* 74 (1913): 1064–65.

"California Red-Light Law Still in Doubt." *Survey* 33 (1914): 167.

"California Women and the Abatement Law." *Survey* 31 (1914): 739–40.

"California Women and the Vice Situation." *Survey* 30 (1913): 162–64.

Call, M. "A Plan for the Prevention of Venereal Disease." *Virginia Medical Semi-Monthly* 9 (1904–5): 294–97.

Caminetti v. *United States.* 242 U.S. 470 (1917).

"The Campaign against Vice." *Outlook* 66 (1900): 874–76.

"The Care of Vicious Women." *Outlook* 104 (1913): 101–2.

Carleton, Sprague. "The Prostitute." *Hahnemannian Monthly* 43 (1908): 824–28.

Carrier, Albert E. "What Shall We Teach the Public regarding Venereal Diseases?" *Journal of the American Medical Association* 47 (1906): 1250–52.

Carrington, C. V. "An Analysis of the Report of Abraham Flexner on the Regulation of Prostitution in Europe." *Virginia Medical Semi-Monthly* 21 (1916–17): 11–16.

Carstens, C. C. "The Rural Community and Prostitution." *Journal of Social Hygiene* 1 (1914): 539–44.

Carstens, J. H. "Education as a Factor in the Prevention of Criminal Abortion and Illegitimacy." *Journal of the American Medical Association* 47 (1906): 1889.

"A Changed Problem and the Committee of 14." *Survey* 28 (1912): 412–13.

Chargin, L. "The Reporting and Control of Venereal Diseases." *American Journal of Public Health* 5 (1915): 297–304.

Charleston, S.C. Law and Order League. *Special Report of the Law and Order League of Charleston.* 1913.

Chase, J. Frank. "The Suppression of the Drug Vice Considered from the Demand Side." *American Journal of Public Health* 6 (1916): 814–21.

Chassaignac, C. "Etiology of the Social Evil." *Journal of the American Medical Association* 47 (1906): 2075.

Chicago, Ill. Vice Commission of Chicago. *The Social Evil in Chicago.* 1911.

"Chicago's 'Morals Court.'" *Literary Digest* 46 (1913): 1228–29.

"The Chicago Vice Commission." *Survey* 26 (1911): 215–18.

Christian, H. M. "The Social Evil from a Rational Standpoint." *Pennsylvania Medical Journal* 15 (1912): 788–91.

"The Church and the Magdalen." *Literary Digest* 44 (1912): 992.

"Church Crusade on the Barbary Coast." *Survey* 37 (1917): 694–95.

Clark, J. B. "Systematic Care in the Sexual Diseases." *Journal of the American Medical Association* 72 (1919): 1205–11.

Clarke, Walter. "Prostitution and Alcohol." *Journal of Social Hygiene* 3 (1917–18): 75–90.

———. "Prostitution and Mental Deficiency." *Journal of Social Hygiene* 1 (1914): 364–87.

———. Review of *The Report and Recommendations of the Wisconsin Vice Committee. Journal of the American Institute of Criminal Law and Criminology* 6 (1915–16): 149–52.

"Clause 79 Is Held Unconstitutional." *Survey* 25 (1910): 416–17.

"Clause 79 of the Page Law." *Survey* 25 (1910): 276–80.

"Clause 79 of the Page Law: Symposium." *Survey* 25 (1910): 435–38.

Cleaves, Margaret A. "Education in Sexual Hygiene for Young Working Women." *Interstate Medical Journal* 13 (1906): 304–9.

Cleveland, Ohio. Cleveland Baptist Brotherhood. *Report of the Vice Commission of the Cleveland Baptist Brotherhood.* 1911.

Cleveland, Ohio. Committee on Vice Conditions, Federated Churches of Cleveland. *Vice Conditions in Cleveland.* 1916.

"Closing a Vice District by Strangulation." *Survey* 35 (1915): 229.

Cobb, J. O. "Psychopathic Control of Prostitution." *New York Medical Journal* 108 (1918): 758–61.

Coffee, Rabbi Rudolph I. "Pittsburgh Clergy and the Social Evil." *Survey* 29 (1913): 815–16.

_____. "Pittsburgh Underworld at Bay." *Survey* 29 (1913): 173–74.

Coolidge, Mary Roberts. "California Women and the Abatement Law." *Survey* 31 (1914): 739–40.

Coplin, W. M. L. "Departmental Influence in the Suppression of Social Disease." *New York Medical Journal* 85 (1907): 1204–6.

Cosson, George. "Why an Injunction and Abatement Law?" *American City* 16 (1917): 44–45.

"Courses on Sex Hygiene." *Survey* 30 (1913): 124.

Crane, Frank. "The Lure." *Forum* 51 (1914): 115–18.

Creel, Herr Glessner. *Prostitution for Profit: A Police Reporter's View of the White Slave Traffic.* St. Louis: National Rip-Saw Publishing Co., 1911.

Crothers, T. D. "Some Relations of Alcohol to Venereal Diseases." *American Journal of Dermatology and Genito-Urinary Diseases* 16 (1912): 183–85.

_____. "Some Scientific Conclusions concerning the Vice Problem." *Texas Medical Journal* 29 (1913–14): 381–92.

Crow, Martha Foote. *The American Country Girl.* New York: Frederick A. Stokes Co., 1915.

Cunningham, J. H. "The Importance of Venereal Disease." *Boston Medical and Surgical Journal* 168 (1913): 77–83.

"Damaged Goods." *Lancet-Clinic* 110 (1913): 450.

"A Danger Signal." *Outlook* 94 (1910): 426–27.

"'Daughters of the Poor' One Year After." *McClure's Magazine* 36 (1910): 120.

Davis, J. E. "Clinical, Pathological and Sociological Observations upon Ninety Interned Venereal Patients." *American Journal of Obstetrics and Diseases of Women and Children* 79 (1919): 40–46.

Davis, M. M. "Efficient Dispensary Clinics a Requisite for Adequate Coping with Venereal Diseases." *Journal of the American Medical Association* 65 (1915): 1983–86.

_____. "Evening Clinics for Syphilis and Gonorrhea." *American Journal of Public Health* 5 (1915): 305–11.

_____. "Evening Clinics for Venereal Disease." *Journal of Social Hygiene* 1 (1914): 331–43.

"The Deeper Reason." *Texas Medical Journal* 29 (1913–14): 394–95.

deForest, H. P. "Prostitution: Police Methods of Sanitary Supervision: Personal Observation of Police Methods of Dealing with Prostitution in Germany with Conclusions as to Their Sanitary Value." *New York State Journal of Medicine* 8 (1908): 516–35.

_____. "Soliloquy of a Fallen Woman." *American Journal of Obstetrics and Diseases of Women and Children* 61 (1910): 90–94.

Deland, Margaret. "The Change in the Feminine Ideal." *Atlantic Monthly* 105 (1910): 290–91.

Demeritt, C. L. "Venereal Prophylaxis from a Practical Standpoint." *American Journal of Dermatology and Genito-Urinary Diseases* 14 (1910): 422–26.

Denver County, Colo. Morals Commission of the City and County of Denver. *Report of the Morals Commission of the City and County of Denver concerning Licensed Cafes and Restaurants.* 1913.

Desmond, M. A. "The Prophylaxis of Venereal Diseases." *St. Paul Medical Journal* 14 (1912): 616–20.

"Despair of Our Efforts to End Vice." *Literary Digest* 48 (1914): 494–95.

"Difficulties of Sex Teaching." *New York Medical Journal* 101 (1915): 960–61.

"Discussing the Social Evil." *Nation* 93 (1911): 308–9.

"The District Leaders' Bill." *Survey* 25 (1911): 819–20.

Dock, Lavinia L. "Communications." *Survey* 24 (1910): 868–69.

————. *Hygiene and Morality: A Manual for Nurses and Others, Giving an Outline of the Medical, Social, and Legal Aspects of the Venereal Diseases.* New York: G. P. Putnam's Sons, 1910.

————. "In the Night Court." *Survey* 25 (1910): 304–5.

"A Doctor's Use of a Drama." *Independent* 75 (1913): 424–25.

Dodson, George R. "The Black Plague and the Educational Remedy." *Bulletin of the American Academy of Medicine* 11 (1910): 490–95.

Dorland, W. A. Newman. "The Social Aspect of Gonococcal Infection of the Innocent." *Bulletin of the American Academy of Medicine* 11 (1910): 465–73.

Dorr, Rheta Childe. "Reclaiming the Wayward Girl." *Hampton's Magazine* 26 (1911): 67–78.

————. *What Eight Million Women Want.* Boston: Small, Maynard & Co., 1910.

Dowling, Oscar. "The Marriage Health Certificate, A Deeply Rooted Social Problem." *American Journal of Public Health* 5 (1915): 1139–45.

Draper, W. F. "The Detention and Treatment of Infected Women as a Measure of Control of Venereal Diseases in Extra-Cantonment Zones." *American Journal of Obstetrics and Diseases of Women and Children* 80 (1919): 642–46.

Dreuw, Wilhelm. "The Modern Examination of Prostitutes." *Urologic and Cutaneous Review* 18 (1914): 182–91.

"Duty of the Profession to Womankind." *Journal of the American Medical Association* 47 (1906): 1886–96, 1947–49.

Eaton, G. L. "Venereal Prophylaxis in Large Cities." *Pacific Medical Journal* 54 (1911): 665–69.

E. J. Bellocq: Storyville Portraits—Photographs from the New Orleans Red-Light District, circa 1912. Edited by John Szarkowski. New York: Museum of Modern Art, 1970.

Elder, W. "The Reporting of Venereal Diseases by Physicians." *Journal of the American Medical Association* 74 (1920): 1764–67.

Eliot, Charles W. "The Main Points of Attack in the Campaign for Public

Health." *American Journal of Public Health* 5 (1915): 616–25.

Ellis, H. "The Conquest of the Venereal Diseases." *Medical Record* 74 (1908): 45–51.

Ellis, Mrs. Havelock. "The Puritan and the Prodigal." *Forum* 50 (1913): 577–87.

Elmira, N.Y. Women's League for Good Government. *A Report on Vice Conditions in Elmira, Being a Report of an Investigation of the Moral Conditions of the City.* 1913.

"The End of Clause 79." *Survey* 26 (1911): 552–53.

Evans, W. A. "The Attack upon Venereal Diseases through Education and Publicity." *Medical Review of Reviews* 21 (1915): 539–41.

Everett, Ray H. "The Cost of Venereal Disease to Industry." *Journal of Industrial Hygiene* 2 (1920–21): 178–81.

————. "Publicity and the Campaign against Venereal Disease." *American Journal of Public Health* 9 (1919): 854–58.

Eytinge, E. O. J. "A System of Venereal Prophylaxis and Its Results." *Military Surgeon* 25 (1909): 170–71.

Falconer, Mrs. William. "The Relation of the Graduate Nurse to the Problem of Social Hygiene." *American Journal of Nursing* 17 (1916–17): 1073–77.

"Fighting Prostitution in Michigan." *Survey* 41 (1918): 70–71.

"Fighting Vice Segregation in Chicago." *Literary Digest* 45 (1912): 848.

"Financing a City by Returns from Vice." *Survey* 31 (1914): 512–14.

Finch, Stanley W. *The White Slave Traffic.* U.S. Senate, 62d Cong., 3d sess., 1912, doc. 982.

Finn, A. H. "Detroit Sex Hygiene Campaign." *Survey* 25 (1910): 460–61.

Fisher, George J. "Sex Education in the Young Men's Christian Association." *Journal of Social Hygiene* 1 (1914): 226–30.

"Five 'White Slave' Trade Investigations." *McClure's Magazine* 35 (1910): 346–48.

Flexner, Abraham. *I Remember: The Autobiography of Abraham Flexner.* New York: Simon & Schuster, 1940.

————. "Next Steps in Dealing with Prostitution." *Journal of Social Hygiene* 1 (1914): 529–38.

————. *Prostitution in Europe.* 1914. Reprint. Montclair, N.J.: Patterson Smith, 1969.

"For Social Purity." *Independent* 70 (1911): 533.

"For the Control of Venereal Diseases." *Journal of the American Medical Association* 69 (1917): 1088.

Fosdick, Raymond B. *Chronicle of a Generation: An Autobiography.* New York: Harper & Brothers, 1958.

————. "The Commission on Training Camp Activities." *Proceedings of the Academy of Political Science* 7 (1917–18): 819–26.

Foster, William Trufant, ed. *The Social Emergency: Studies in Sex Hygiene and Morals.* Boston: Houghton Mifflin Co., 1914.

Fulton, John S. "The Medical Statistics of Sex Hygiene: Such as They Are." *American Journal of Public Health* 3 (1913): 661–76.

"The Futility of the White Slave Agitation as Brand Whitlock Sees It." *Current Opinion* 56 (1914): 287–88.

"Gaining Control over Vice in New York." *Survey* 33 (1914): 572.

Gans, Howard S. "Some Consequences of Unenforceable Legislation." *Proceedings of the Academy of Political Science* 1 (1911): 563–89.

Gardner, D. E. "The Relation of the General Practitioner to the Treatment of Venereal Diseases." *American Journal of Dermatology and Genito-Urinary Diseases* 14 (1910): 263–65.

Gartman, L. N. "Is the Prostitute a Criminal?" *American Journal of Urology and Sexology* 10 (1914): 146–53.

Gates, M. F. "The Prophylaxis of Venereal Disease." *Pennsylvania Medical Journal* 14 (1910–11): 255–59.

Gerrish, F. H. "A Crusade against Syphilis and Gonorrhea." *Boston Medical and Surgical Journal* 163 (1910): 1–12.

———. "A Crusade against Syphilis and Gonorrhea." *Medical Communications of the Massachusetts Medical Society* 21 (1910): 723–60.

Giddings, H. G. "The Evils of Drug Store Prescribing in Venereal Diseases." *Rhode Island Medical Journal* 1 (1917): 154–58.

Gilman, Charlotte Perkins. *Women and Economics.* 1898. Reprint. Edited by Carl N. Degler. New York: Harper & Row, 1966.

Glasgow, Maude. "On the Regulation of Prostitution with Special Reference to Paragraph 79 of the Page Bill." *New York Medical Journal* 92 (1910): 1320–23.

———. "Side Lights on the Social Peril." *New York Medical Journal* 93 (1911): 1186–90.

Goler, George W. "The Municipality and the Venereal Disease Problem." *American Journal of Public Health* 6 (1916): 355–59.

Goodman, H. "The Prostitute in Jail: An Opportunity for Public Health Work That Gives Results." *Medical Record* 97 (1920): 483–86.

———. "Prostitution and Community Syphilis." *American Journal of Public Health* 9 (1919): 515–20.

"Gorrell Act for Repression of Prostitution." *Ohio Public Health Journal* 10 (1919): 278–80.

Gotto, Sybil. "The Changing Moral Standard." *Nineteenth Century* 84 (1918): 717–30.

Grand Rapids, Mich. Public Welfare Council. *Report on the Social Evil.* 1913.

Grand Rapids, Mich. Vice Committee of Forty One. *Report on the Investigation of the Committee of Forty One.* 1913.

Greer, Joseph H. *The Social Evil: Its Cause, Effect and Cure.* Chicago: The Author, 1909.

Griffith, F. "Observations upon the Protective Value of the Inspection of Public Women as Carried Out in Paris." *Medical Record* 65 (1904): 651–52.

Groves. Ernest R. "Psychic Causes of Rural Migration." *American Journal of Sociology* 21 (1916): 623–27.

Grubbs, Robert B. "Venereal Prophylaxis in the Military Service." *Military Surgeon* 25 (1909): 756–71.

Gulick, Dr. Luther H. "Recreation and Youth." *Proceedings of the Academy of Political Science* 2 (1912): 592–96.

Guthrie, D. Clinton. "Race Suicide." *Pennsylvania Medical Journal* 15 (1911–12): 855–59.

Guy, W. H. "Analysis of the Venereal Situation with Particular Reference to the Diagnosis and Treatment of Syphilis." *Urologic and Cutaneous Review* 23 (1919): 512–14.

Guyer, Michael F. "Review of Wisconsin 'Eugenics Legislation.'" *American Journal of Obstetrics and Diseases of Women and Children* 77 (1918): 485–92.

Hager, J. H. "Cost of Venereal Infection." *Kentucky Medical Journal* 8 (1910): 1172–75.

Hall, Fred S., and Brooke, Elizabeth. *American Marriage Laws in Their Social Aspects*. New York: Russell Sage Foundation, 1919.

Hall, Winfield S. "Adolescence and the Sex Problem." *Bulletin of the American Academy of Medicine* 11 (1910): 455–64.

_____. "Intoxicants and the Social Evil." *Missionary Review of the World* 42 (1919): 335–36.

_____. "The Relation of Education in Sex to Race Betterment." *Journal of Social Hygiene* 1 (1914): 67–80.

Hamilton, Alice. "Prostitutes and Tuberculosis." *Survey* 37 (1917): 516–17.

Hammer v. Dagenhart. 247 U.S. 251 (1918).

Hancock, F. H. "Regulation of Prostitution in the City of Norfolk, Virginia." *Virginia Medical Semi-Monthly* 17 (1912–13): 559–61.

Harland, Robert O. *The Vice Bondage of a Great City; or, the Wickedest City in the World*. Chicago: Young People's Civic League, 1912.

Harris, Abram W. "The Social Evil." *Journal of the American Institute of Criminal Law and Criminology* 3 (1912–13): 804–5.

Harris, J. H. "The Prostitute in Relation to Military Camps." *Woman's Medical Journal* 28 (1918): 125–27.

Harris, Mrs. C. I. *Modern Herodians or Slaughterers of Innocents*. Portland, Oreg.: Wallace Printing Co., 1909.

Hartford, Conn. Vice Commission of Hartford. *Report of the Vice Commission of Hartford*. 1913.

Harwood, W. E. "A Practical Lesson in Reglementation." *Journal of the American Medical Association* 47 (1906): 2076–78.

Hazzard, Alida B. "In the Night Court." *Survey* 25 (1910): 304–5.

Healy, W. "Contributory Causes of Social Vice." *Chicago Medical Recorder* 35 (1913): 85–89.

"Hearing on the Page Bill." *Survey* 24 (1910): 193–94.

Heidingsfeld, M. L. "The Control of Prostitution and the Prevention of the Spread of Venereal Diseases." *Journal of the American Medical Association* 42 (1904): 305–9.

Hemingway, Ernest. *A Farewell to Arms*. New York: Charles Scribner's Sons, 1929.

Hepburn, Katharine Houghton. "Communications." *Survey* 24 (1910): 637–38.

_____. "The Page Bill." *Survey* 25 (1910): 79–80.

Hepburn, T. N. "Demand for an Open Change of Attitude toward the Social

Evil." *Yale Medical Journal* 14 (1907–8): 167–73.

Herdman, W. J. "The Duty of the Medical Profession to the Public in the Matter of Venereal Diseases, and How To Discharge It." *Journal of the American Medical Association* 47 (1906): 1246–48.

Herzog, A. W. "A Plan to Regulate Prostitution." *Medical Brief* 33 (1905): 381–83.

Hetherington, Clark W. "Play Leadership in Sex Education." *Journal of Social Hygiene* 1 (1914): 36–43.

Hill, Alice M. "Social and Environmental Factors in the Moral Delinquency of Girls Committed to the Kansas State Industrial Farm." *Public Health Reports* 35 (1920): 1501–36.

Hodder, Alfred. "The Alliance between Puritan and Grafter." *Outlook* 73 (1903): 251–60.

Hodge, C. F. "Instruction in Social Hygiene in the Public Schools." *Bulletin of the American Academy of Medicine* 11 (1910): 506–17.

Hoff, J. Van R. "Is There a Venereal Peril for Us?" *Medical Record* 76 (1909): 896–900.

Hoke and Economides v. United States. 227 U.S. 308 (1913).

Holcomb, Richard C. "Has Our Propaganda for Venereal Prophylaxis Failed?" *Military Surgeon* 38 (1916): 30–43.

———. "Letter to the Editor." *Military Surgeon* 38 (1916): 342–47.

Holliday, Carl. "The Motion Picture and the Church." *Independent* 74 (1913): 353–56.

Holmes, Bayard. "The Physical and Evolutionary Basis of Marriage." *Journal of the American Medical Association* 47 (1906): 1886–87.

Holmes, J. D. "Vice and Wages." *Survey* 26 (1911): 701–2.

Holt, W. L. "The American Society of Sanitary and Moral Prophylaxis." *Boston Medical and Surgical Journal* 154 (1906): 168–69.

Holton, Henry D. "The Duty of the State toward Venereal Diseases." *Journal of the American Medical Association* 47 (1906): 1248–49.

"Honolulu's Complicated Vice Problem." *Survey* 32 (1914): 627.

Hooker, D. R. "Communications." *Survey* 24 (1910): 596–97.

———. "The Page Bill." *Survey* 24 (1910): 710–11.

"A Hopeful Book on the Social Evil." *Outlook* 106 (1914): 293–94.

Hopwood, Eric C. "The Opportunity of the Press as a Moral Educator." *Journal of Social Hygiene* 2 (1915–16): 21–36.

Howard, George Elliott. "Alcohol and Crime: A Study in Social Causation." *American Journal of Sociology* 24 (1918): 61–80.

Howard, William Lee. "The Daughters of the Moabites and Our Soldiers." *New York Medical Journal* 107 (1918): 394–95.

———. "The Havoc of Prudery." *Pearson's Magazine* 24 (1910): 589–98.

———. "A Plain Explanation of the Greatest Social Evil." *Pearson's Magazine* 24 (1910): 640–47.

———. "The Protection of the Innocent." *Journal of the American Medical Association* 47 (1906): 1891–94.

"How Atlanta Cleaned Up." *Literary Digest* 46 (1913): 1012–13.

Howe, Frederic C. *The Confessions of a Reformer*. 1925. Reprint. Chicago: Quadrangle Books, 1967.

Hubbard, Elbert. "The Abolition of Vice." *Hearst's Magazine* 23 (1913): 663–64.

Huici, J. "The Necessity of Isolating Prostitutes Who Suffer from Syphilis." *American Journal of Public Hygiene* 6 (1909–10): 523–30.

Hund, John. *The Physician and the Social Evil: A Study of the Medical Science under Religious Influence with Special Reference to the Social Evil*. Milwaukee, Wis.: Enterprise Printing Co., 1911.

Hunt, Milton B. "The Housing of Non-Family Groups of Men in Chicago." *American Journal of Sociology* 16 (1910): 145–70.

Illinois, General Assembly. Senate Vice Committee. *Report of the Senate Vice Committee*. 1916.

Irons, J. C. "The Social Evil: What Shall We Do with It?" *West Virginia Medical Journal* 2 (1907–8): 345–48.

Irvine, H. G. "The Venereal Disease Campaign in Retrospect." *Journal of Cutaneous Diseases Including Syphilis* 37 (1919): 748–53.

———. "The Venereal Disease Problem in California." *Journal of the American Medical Association* 70 (1918): 150–52.

"Is It Crime As Well As Sin?" *Independent* 74 (1913): 176.

Israels, Mrs. Belle Lindner. "Regulation of Public Amusements." *Proceedings of the Academy of Political Science* 2 (1912): 597–600.

"Is White Slavery Nothing More Than a Myth?" *Current Opinion* 55 (1913): 348.

Jacobi, Abraham. Discussion of W. F. Snow, "The Preventive Medicine Campaign against Venereal Diseases." *American Medical Association Bulletin* 9 (1914): 195–96.

Jacobson, A. C. "An Old Evil in a New Light." *Medical Times* 43 (1915): 333–34.

Janney, O. Edward. *The White Slave Traffic in America*. New York: n.p., 1911.

Jenkinson, C. "Social Evil in Vera Cruz." *Survey* 33 (1914): 136–38.

Jewitt, R. A. "How the Industrial Physician Can Help in the Campaign against Venereal Disease." *Pennsylvania Medical Journal* 22 (1918–19): 679–81.

Johnson, Alvin. *Pioneer's Progress: An Autobiography*. New York: Viking Press, 1952.

Johnson, Bascom. "Eliminating Vice from Camp Cities." *Annals of the American Academy of Political and Social Science* 78 (1918): 60–64.

Johnson, Fred Robert. *The Social Evil in Kansas City*. Kansas City, Mo., 1911.

Jones, W. R. "Prostitution in Seattle." *Northwest Medicine* 17 (1918): 239–42.

———. "Seattle Prostitution from inside the Quarantine." *Northwest Medicine* 18 (1919): 184–87.

———. "A Successful Venereal Prevention Campaign." *Journal of the American Medical Association* 71 (1918): 1297–98.

Kauffman, Reginald Wright. *The Girl That Goes Wrong*. New York: Moffat, Yard & Co., 1911.

———. *The House of Bondage*. New York: Moffat, Yard & Co., 1910.

————. *The Sentence of Silence*. New York: Moffat, Yard & Co., 1912.

————. *Spider's Web*. New York: Moffat, Yard & Co., 1913.

Keller v. United States, Ullman v. United States. 213 U.S. 138 (1909).

Kelley, E. R. "The State Clinics for the Treatment of Venereal Diseases." *Boston Medical and Surgical Journal* 181 (1919): 309–13.

Kelley, Florence. "Communications." *Survey* 24 (1910): 646.

————. Review of Jane Addams, *A New Conscience and an Ancient Evil*. *American Journal of Sociology* 18 (1912): 271–72.

Kellogg, Paul V. "The Spread of the Survey Idea." *Proceedings of the Academy of Political Science* 2 (1912): 475–91.

Kellor, Frances A. *Out of Work: A Study of Unemployment*. Rev. ed. New York: G. P. Putnam's Sons, 1915.

————. "Psychological and Environmental Study of Women Criminals." *American Journal of Sociology* 5 (1900): 527–43, 671–82.

Kelly, Howard A. "The Best Way to Treat the Social Evil." *Medical News* 86 (1905): 1157–63.

————. "The Protection of the Innocent." *American Journal of Obstetrics and Diseases of Women and Children* 55 (1907): 477–81.

————. "The Regulation of Prostitution." *Journal of the American Medical Association* 46 (1906): 397–401.

————. "What Is the Right Attitude of the Medical Profession toward the Social Evil?" *Journal of the American Medical Association* 44 (1905): 679–81.

Kelsey, Carl. Review of Abraham Flexner, *Prostitution in Europe*. *Journal of the American Institute of Criminal Law and Criminology* 5 (1914–15): 143–45.

Kendall, Sidney C. *The Soundings of Hell*. Los Angeles: Charlton Edholm, 1903.

Keyes, Edward L., Jr. "Can the Law Protect Matrimony from Disease?" *Journal of Social Hygiene* 1 (1914–15): 9–14.

————. "Morals and Venereal Disease." *Journal of Social Hygiene* 2 (1915–16): 49–55.

————. "The Need of Sexual Education." *Medical News* 86 (1905): 1165–67.

————. "The Prenuptial Sanitary Guarantee." *New York Medical Journal* 85 (1907): 1201–4.

————. "Protection of the Innocent." *Journal of the American Medical Association* 47 (1906): 1895–96.

————. "Report on the Work Accomplished by the French Society of Social and Moral Prophylaxis." *Journal of Cutaneous Diseases Including Syphilis* 23 (1905): 529–34.

————. "The Sexual Necessity." *Medical News* 87 (1905): 72–74.

Kiefer, G. L., and Kober, G. W. "Report of Committee on Control of Venereal Disease by a Municipality." *Journal of the American Medical Association* 57 (1911): 1052–56.

Kneeland, George J. *Commercialized Prostitution in New York City*. 1913. Reprint. Montclair, N.J.: Patterson Smith, 1969.

————. "Commercialized Vice." *Proceedings of the Academy of Political Science* 2 (1912): 601–3.

Knopf, S. Adolphus. "Medicine and Law in Relation to the Alcohol, Venereal Disease, and Tuberculosis Problems." *Medical Record* 69 (1906): 857–62.
_____. "Some Thoughts on the Etiology, Prophylaxis, and Treatment of the Social Ill." *New York Medical Journal* 87 (1908): 819–26.
Konkle, W. B. "The Roots of Evil." *Medical Record* 98 (1920): 179–81.
Lack, C. E. "The Physician's Duty regarding the Prophylaxis of Venereal Diseases." *Medical Times* 37 (1909): 46–48.
Lafayette, Ind. *Report on Vice Conditions.* 1913.
Laidlaw, Harriet Burton. "My Little Sister." *Survey* 30 (1913): 199–202.
Lancaster, Pa. *Report on Vice Conditions in the City of Lancaster.* 1913.
_____. *A Second Report on Vice Conditions in the City of Lancaster.* 1915.
Landis, J. H. "The Social Evil in Relation to the Health Problem." *American Journal of Public Health* 3 (1913): 1073–86.
_____. "What Health Departments Can Do to Solve the Venereal Problem under Existing Conditions." *Medical Review of Reviews* 21 (1915): 535–38.
Lanphear, Emory. "Gonorrhea and Race Suicide." *The Medico-Pharmaceutical Critic and Guide* 8 (1907): 7–8.
Laughlin, Clara E. "Girls Who Go Wrong." *Pearson's Magazine* 23 (1910): 377–87.
_____. "A Single Standard." *Pearson's Magazine* 31 (1914): 728–38.
Law, E. Norine. *The Shame of a Great Nation: The Story of the "White Slave Trade."* Harrisburg, Pa.: United Evangelical Publishing House, 1909.
Lawrence, J. S. "Recent Legislation in New York State, Relating to the Control of Venereal Disease." *Medical Record* 95 (1919): 669–70.
Lecky, William Edward Hartpole. *History of European Morals.* 2 vols. New York: D. Appleton Co., 1870.
Lederer, M. "The Value of the Gonorrheal Complement Fixation Test and the Wassermann Reaction in Determining the Fitness of a Person to Marry." *Long Island Medical Journal* 7 (1913): 102–4.
Lewis, Bransford. "What Shall We Teach the Public regarding Venereal Diseases?" *Journal of the American Medical Association* 47 (1906): 1253–55.
Lewis, Denslow. "The Need of Publicity in Venereal Prophylaxis." *Medical Record* 69 (1906): 863–65.
_____. "The Prophylaxis and Management of Prostitution." *Pennsylvania Medical Journal* 10 (1906–7): 24–30.
_____. "The Social Evil." *Buffalo Medical Journal* 62 (1906): 249–57.
_____. "What Shall We Do with the Prostitute?" *American Journal of Dermatology and Genito-Urinary Diseases* 11 (1907): 485–93.
Lexington, Ky. Vice Commission of Lexington. *Report of the Vice Commission of Lexington.* 1915.
Lies, Eugene T. "Minneapolis Vice Commission's Report." *Survey* 26 (1911): 694–95.
Lippmann, Walter. *A Preface to Politics.* 1913. Reprint. Ann Arbor: University of Michigan Press, Ann Arbor Paperbacks, 1965.

Litchfield, L. "A Plea for the Establishment of an American Association for the Prevention of Social Diseases." *Journal of the American Medical Association* 54 (1910): 692–95.

Little Rock, Ark. Little Rock Vice Commission. *Report of the Little Rock Vice Commission.* 1913.

"A Living Wage for Women." *Independent* 74 (1913): 851.

Locke, Charles Edward. *White Slavery in Los Angeles.* Los Angeles: Times Mirror Co., 1913.

Lockwood, C. D. "Venereal Diseases in Children: Their Causes and Prevention." *Bulletin of the American Academy of Medicine* 11 (1910): 478–82.

"London's Campaign against Vice." *Literary Digest* 53 (1916): 1177–78.

Louisville, Ky. Louisville Vice Commission. *Report of the Vice Commission.* 1915.

Lydston, G. Frank. *The Diseases of Society: The Vice and Crime Problem.* Philadelphia: J. B. Lippincott Co., 1904.

―――. "The Regulation of the Social Evil in Our Large American Cities." *Texas Medical Journal* 24 (1908–9): 183–87.

―――. "The Social Evil and Its Remedies." *American Journal of Clinical Medicine* 16 (1909): 18–23, 155–59, 278–83.

Lytle, H. M. *Tragedies of the White Slave.* Chicago: Charles C. Thompson Co., 1909.

Mabbott, J. M. "The Duties of the Gynecologist in Relation to the State Control of Vice." *American Journal of Obstetrics and Diseases of Women and Children* 64 (1911): 227–37.

McClure, S. S. "The Tammanyzing of a Civilization." *McClure's Magazine* 34 (1909): 117–28.

McCord, Clinton P. "One Hundred Female Offenders: A Study of the Mentality of Prostitutes and 'Wayward' Girls." *Journal of the American Institute of Criminal Law and Criminology* 6 (1915–16): 385–407.

McGrady, Jane R. "Courses on Sex Hygiene." *Survey* 30 (1913): 124–25.

McKinley et al. v. United States. 249 U.S. 397 (1919).

McLaughlin, A. J. "Pioneering in Venereal Disease Control." *American Journal of Obstetrics and Diseases of Women and Children* 80 (1919): 636–42.

McMurtrie, D. C. "Further Note on Prostitution in Japan; Abolition of the Slavery System; Early History of the Yoshiwara: Illicit Prostitution, Medical Inspection and Statistics, Jurisprudence." *New York Medical Journal* 98 (1913): 76–80.

―――. "The Primitive Origins of Prostitution." *Lancet-Clinic* 110 (1913): 457–60.

―――. "Prostitution and Homosexuality in Persia." *Medical Times* 42 (1914): 246.

―――. "Prostitution in Japan." *New York Medical Journal* 97 (1913): 278–81.

―――. "Prostitution in New York City: A Study in Social Hygiene." *Medical Record* 83 (1913): 970–74.

―――. "A Study of Prostitution in Europe." *Medical Record* 85 (1914): 325–28.

Madeleine: An Autobiography. New York: Harper & Brothers, 1919.

"Mann Law Upheld." *Outlook* 115 (1917): 179–80.

"Mann White Slave Traffic Act." *Journal of Social Hygiene* 3 (1917): 278–82.

"Man's Commerce in Women: Mr. Rockefeller's Bureau of Social Hygiene Issues Its First Report." *McClure's Magazine* 41 (1913): 185–89.

Marcy, Henry O. "Education as a Factor in the Prevention of Criminal Abortion and Illegitimacy." *Journal of the American Medical Association* 47 (1906): 1889–91.

―――. "Gonococcal Infections in Women." *Bulletin of the American Academy of Medicine* 11 (1910): 474–77.

Marks, Jeannette. "The Curse of Narcotism in America: A Reveille." *American Journal of Public Health* 5 (1915): 314–22.

Marks, Margurite. "Paul Ehrlich: The Man and His Work." *McClure's Magazine* 36 (1910): 184–200.

"Marriage Laws and Wisconsin's Experience." *Texas Medical Journal* 29 (1913–14): 395–96.

Mason, B. H. "Compulsory Reporting and Compulsory Treatment of Venereal Diseases." *Boston Medical and Surgical Journal* 181 (1919): 34–39.

Massachusetts. *Report of the Commission for the Investigation of the White Slave Traffic, So Called*. Commonwealth of Massachusetts, 1914.

Mayer, Joseph. *The Regulation of Commercialized Vice: An Analysis of the Transition from Segregation to Repression in the United States*. New York: n.p., 1922.

"May the United States Prevent the Importation of Vice." *Outlook* 92 (1909): 250–51.

"The Meaning of the White Slave Act as Shown by the Federal Decision." *Journal of Criminal Law* 4 (1914): 738–40.

Mears, J. Ewing. "The Problem of the Social Evil Considered in Its Social and Medical Aspects and in Its Relation to the Problem of Race Betterment." *Medical Record* 84 (1913): 231–36.

"The Meeting at Memphis: 41st National Conference of Charities and Correction." *Survey* 32 (1914): 232–39.

[Mencken, H. L.] "The Flapper." *Smart Set* 45 (1915): 1–2.

"Merger of Social Hygiene Societies." *Survey* 31 (1914): 485–86.

Merrill, G. V. R. "Supervision of the Venereally Diseased." *New York State Journal of Medicine* 11 (1911): 136–40.

Merriman, Christina. "New Bottles for New Wine: The Work of Abastenia St. Leger Eberle." *Survey* 30 (1913): 196–98.

Mertz, Paul A. "Mental Deficiency of Prostitutes: A Study of Delinquent Women at an Army Port of Embarkation." *Journal of the American Medical Association* 72 (1919): 1597–99.

Miner, Maude E. "One Section of the Inferior Courts Law." *Survey* 25 (1910): 172–75.

―――. "The Problem of Wayward Girls and Delinquent Women." *Proceedings of the Academy of Political Science* 2 (1912): 604–12.

————. "Relation between Occupation and Criminality of Women." *Survey* 30 (1913): 731–32.

————. "Report of Committee on Social Hygiene." *Journal of Social Hygiene* 1 (1914): 81–92.

————. *Slavery of Prostitution: A Plea for Emancipation.* New York: Macmillan Co., 1916.

————. "Two Weeks in the Night Court." *Survey* 22 (1909): 229–34.

"Minimum Wage Discussed by Retail Association." *Survey* 30 (1913): 260–61.

Minneapolis, Minn. Minneapolis Vice Commission. *Report of the Vice Commission of Minneapolis.* 1911.

Mitchell, Lucy Sprague. "School Children and Sex Idealism." *Survey* 32 (1914): 327–28.

Moore, J. E. "The Value of Prophylaxis against Venereal Diseases." *Journal of the American Medical Association* 75 (1920): 911–15.

Moorehead, Robert J. *Fighting the Devil's Triple Demons—The Traffic in Innocent Girls—Rum's Ruinous Ruin—The Sins of Society: Three Books in One.* Philadelphia: National Book Publishing Co., 1911.

"The Moral Havoc Wrought by Moving Picture Shows." *Current Opinion* 56 (1914): 290.

"Morals and Inter-State Commerce." *Outlook* 103 (1913): 570–71.

"More Syphilis Than Tuberculosis." *Survey* 26 (1911): 878.

Morison, Elting E., ed. *Letters of Theodore Roosevelt.* 8 vols. Cambridge, Mass.: Harvard University Press, 1951–54.

Morrow, Prince. "Education within the Medical Profession." *Medical News* 86 (1905): 1153–56.

————. "Eugenics and Venereal Diseases." *Dietetic and Hygienic Gazette* 27 (1911): 11–16.

————. "The Frequency of Venereal Diseases: A Reply to Dr. Cabot." *Boston Medical and Surgical Journal* 165 (1911): 520–25.

————. "Health Department Control of Venereal Diseases." *New York Medical Journal* 94 (1911): 129–33.

————. "A Plea for the Organization of a 'Society of Sanitary and Moral Prophylaxis.'" *Medical News* 84 (1904): 1073–77.

————. "Prophylaxis of Social Diseases." *American Journal of Sociology* 13 (1907): 20–33.

————. "Publicity as a Factor in Venereal Prophylaxis." *Journal of the American Medical Association* 47 (1906): 1244–46.

————. "The Relations of Social Diseases to the Family." *American Journal of Sociology* 14 (1909): 622–35.

————. "Report of Progress in Sanitary and Moral Prophylaxis." *New York Medical Journal* 95 (1912): 577–82.

————. "Results Achieved by the Movement for Sanitary and Moral Prophylaxis: Outlook for the Future." *Medical Record* 76 (1909): 1061–65.

————. "Results of the Work Accomplished by the Society of Sanitary and

Moral Prophylaxis." *New York Medical Journal* 86 (1907): 1108–13.
_____. "Sanitary and Moral Prophylaxis." *Boston Medical and Surgical Journal* 154 (1906): 674–77.
_____. "The Sanitary and Moral Prophylaxis of Venereal Diseases." *Journal of the American Medical Association* 44 (1905): 675–79.
_____. "The Sanitary Supervision of Prostitutes." *Interstate Medical Journal* 18 (1911): 98–108.
_____. *Social Diseases and Marriage, Social Prophylaxis*. New York: Lea Brothers & Co., 1904.
_____. "Social Prophylaxis and the Medical Profession." *American Journal of Dermatology and Genito-Urinary Diseases* 9 (1905): 264–72.
_____. "The Society of Sanitary and Moral Prophylaxis: Its Object and Aims." *American Medicine* 9 (1905): 317–21.
_____. "Venereal Diseases and Their Relation to Infant Mortality and Race Deterioration." *New York Medical Journal* 94 (1911): 1315–17.
"Mr. Rockefeller, Jr.'s War on the Social Evil." *Literary Digest* 46 (1913): 283–84.
Mulvy, T. H. "The Report of the Louisville Vice Commission." *Kentucky Medical Journal* 14 (1916): 493–99.
Muren, G. M. "A Contribution to the Prophylaxis of Venereal Diseases." *American Medicine* 6 (1903): 480–81.
Nascher, J. L. "Prostitution." *New York Medical Journal* 88 (1908): 260–62.
Nasher, I. L. "Prostitution in 1886 and in 1916." *American Journal of Urology and Sexology* 12 (1916): 501–7, 541–51.
"National Dental Association Cooperating in Venereal Disease Control." *Public Health Reports* 35 (1920): 186.
"National Merger to Fight White Slavery." *Survey* 27 (1912): 1991–92.
"Nation-wide Attention to Vice and Low Wages." *Survey* 29 (1913): 897–98.
"Needed: A Scientific Study of Prostitution." *Current Opinion* 54 (1913): 6.
Neisser, A. "Is It Really Impossible to Make Prostitution Harmless As Far As Infection Is Concerned?" *American Journal of Urology and Sexology* 12 (1916): 289–99.
"Never Told Tales." *American Journal of Clinical Medicine* 16 (1909): 255–56.
Newark, N.J. Citizen's Committee on Social Evil. *Report of the Social Evil Conditions of Newark*. 1914.
"New Methods of Grappling with the Social Evil." *Current Opinion* 54 (1913): 308–10.
New York City. Committee of Fifteen. *The Social Evil: With Special Reference to Conditions Existing in the City of New York*. New York: G. P. Putnam's Sons, 1902.
New York City. Research Committee of the Committee of Fourteen for the Suppression of "Raines Law Hotels" in New York City. *The Social Evil in New York City. A Study in Law Enforcement*. New York: Andrew H. Kellogg Co., 1910.
"No Dirty Compromise." *Independent* 74 (1913): 1117.

Norcross, G. E. "The Regulation of Prostitution." *Massachusetts Medical Journal* 25 (1905): 335–40.

"Nostrums for Vice." *Independent* 52 (1900): 2942–43.

Owens, W. D. "Proposed Methods of Venereal and Hygienic Educational Prophylaxis." *Military Surgeon* 39 (1916): 265–72.

Owings, Chloe. *Women Police*. New York: F. H. Hitchcock, 1925.

Paducah, Ky. Paducah Vice Commission. *Report of the Paducah Vice Commission*. 1916.

Park, Robert E. "The City: Suggestions for the Investigation of Human Behavior in the City Environment." *American Journal of Sociology* 20 (1915): 577–612.

Patterson, J. "An Economic View of Venereal Infections." *Journal of the American Medical Association* 62 (1914): 668–71.

"Paying the Price of Publicity." *Survey* 27 (1912): 1665–66.

Pederson, V. C. "Venereal Problems of the War." *Medical Record* 96 (1919): 60–65, 104–110.

Persons, Charles E. "Estimates of a Living Wage for Female Workers." *Publications of the American Statistical Association* 14 (1914–15): 567–77.

———. "Women's Work and Wages in the United States." *Quarterly Journal of Economics* 29 (1914–15): 201–34.

Peterkin, G. S. "A System of Venereal Prophylaxis That Is Producing Results." *American Medicine* 10 (1905): 326–30.

———. "Use and Limitation of Law in Dealing with Prostitution or the Social Evil." *American Journal of Dermatology and Genito-Urinary Diseases* 16 (1912): 402–7.

Philadelphia, Pa. Vice Commission of Philadelphia. *Report of the Vice Commission of Philadelphia*. 1913.

"A Philadelphia Warning to Girls." *Literary Digest* 46 (1913): 234.

"The Physical and 'Social' Havoc of the Social Plague." *Bulletin of the American Academy of Medicine* 11 (1910): 455–523.

Picton-Turbervill, Edith. "America and the Social Evil." *Nineteenth Century* 86 (1919): 153–63.

Pierce, C. C. "The Nurse as a Factor in the Prevention and Control of Venereal Disease." *American Journal of Nursing* 19 (1918–19): 923–30.

———. "Progress of Venereal Disease Control." *Journal of the American Medical Association* 73 (1919): 416–21.

———. "The Value of Detention as a Reconstruction Measure." *American Journal of Obstetrics and Diseases of Women and Children* 80 (1919): 624–36.

———. "Venereal Disease Control in Civilian Communities." *American Journal of Public Health* 9 (1919): 340–45.

———. "Venereal Disease Control: Methods, Obstacles and Results." *American Journal of Public Health* 10 (1920): 132–37.

Pittsburgh, Pa. Morals Efficiency Commission. *Report and Recommendations of the Morals Efficiency Commission*. 1913.

"Pittsburgh's Housecleaning." *Literary Digest* 47 (1913): 1232.

Platt, P. S. "The Efficiency of Venereal Clinics: Suggested Remedies for Present Defects." *American Journal of Public Health* 6 (1916): 953–56.

Pollack, Flora. "The Acquired Venereal Infections in Children." *American Journal of Dermatology and Genito-Urinary Diseases* 13 (1909): 289–98.

"Popular Gullibility as Exhibited in the New White Slavery Hysteria." *Current Opinion* 56 (1914): 129.

Portland, Maine. Citizens' Committee of Portland to Investigate the Social Evil. *First Report of the Citizens' Committee of Portland to Investigate the Social Evil.* 1914.

Portland, Oreg. Portland Vice Commission. *Report of the Portland Vice Commission to the Mayor and City Council of the City of Portland.* 1913.

Post, Abner. "What Should Be the Attitude of Boards of Health toward Venereal Diseases?" *American Journal of Public Hygiene* 9 (1907–8): 46–51.

Potter, Marion C. "Venereal Prophylaxis." *American Journal of Nursing* 7 (1906–7): 340–51.

──────. "Venereal Prophylaxis." *Woman's Medical Journal* 18 (1908): 230–41.

Powell, Aaron M., ed. *The National Purity Congress: Its Papers, Addresses, Portraits.* New York: American Purity Alliance, 1896.

Powers, A. H. "Prostitution and Venereal Disease." *New England Medical Gazette* 40 (1905): 559–61.

"Prevent Crime to Reduce Poverty." *Survey* 25 (1911): 648–49.

"Probation for Girls Who Err." *Survey* 23 (1909): 349–50.

"The Problem of Vice and Graft." *Literary Digest* 46 (1913): 61–62.

"Prostitution." *Encyclopedia Britannica.* 11th ed.

"Prostitution Banished in One New York Town." *Survey* 30 (1913): 158–59.

"Prostitution in Europe: Abraham Flexner's Study of Supply, Demand, Regulation." *Survey* 31 (1914): 471–73.

"Protecting New York Children." *Survey* 30 (1913): 269.

"Protection of the Home." *Independent* 52 (1900): 2647.

"Provisions of the Page Bill." *Survey* 24 (1910): 499–503.

"The Punishment of a White Slave Trader." *Outlook* 98 (1911): 567–68.

Purrington, W. A. "Professional Secrecy and the Obligatory Notification of Venereal Diseases." *New York Medical Journal* 85 (1907): 1206–10.

Rathbun, N. P. "The Control of Social Disease." *Long Island Medical Journal* 2 (1908): 21–25.

Ravogli, A. "Education and Instruction in Sexual Relations as a Prophylaxis against Venereal Diseases." *New York Medical Journal* 91 (1910): 1218–22.

──────. "Syphilis as a Cause of Pauperism." *Interstate Medical Journal* 18 (1911): 88–97.

"Reaction against Sex Talk." *Survey* 31 (1914): 682–83.

"Real Estate Agent Convicted in Disorderly Case." *Survey* 31 (1913): 341.

"A Real Social Evil Treatise." *Nation* 98 (1914): 75–76.

Reeder, R. R. "Post Graduates of the Hired Man." *Survey* 29 (1913): 816–18.

"Reorganization in New York Courts." *Survey* 24 (1910): 823–25.

"Report of Chicago Vice Commission." *Survey* 26 (1911): 99.

Repplier, Agnes. "The Repeal of Reticence." *Atlantic Monthly* 113 (1914): 297–304.

"Responsibility Put Up to Department of Health." *Survey* 25 (1911): 621.

Reynolds, James Bronson. "Commercialized Vice." *Survey* 31 (1913): 354.

————. "Prostitution in Europe: The Failure of Licensing and Medical Inspection." *American City* 10 (1914): 155–56.

Rippey, Sarah Cory. "The Case of Angeline." *Outlook* 106 (1914): 252–56.

Rippin, Jane Deeter. "Municipal Detention of Women." *Proceedings of the National Conference of Social Work* 45 (1918): 132–40.

Robins, Margaret Dreier. "One Aspect of the Menace of Low Wages." *Journal of Social Hygiene* 1 (1914): 358–63.

Robinson, D. E., and Wilson, J. G. "Tuberculosis among Prostitutes: Report of an Investigation Made in Connection with a Study of the Disease in Cincinnati, Ohio." *American Journal of Public Health* 6 (1916): 1164–72.

Robinson, W. J. "Venereal Disease as a Retribution for Illicit Intercourse." *American Journal of Urology and Sexology* 12 (1916): 24–29.

"The Rockefeller Grand Jury Report." *McClure's Magazine* 35 (1910): 471–73.

"Rockefeller Report on Commercialized Vice." *Survey* 30 (1913): 257–59.

Rockland County, N.Y. Committee of Fifty. *Report of the Survey Made in Rockland County.* 1915.

Roe, Clifford G. "The American Vigilance Association." *Journal of the American Institute of Criminal Law and Criminology* 3 (1912–13): 806–9.

————. *The Girl Who Disappeared.* Chicago: American Bureau of Moral Education, 1914.

————. *The Great War on White Slavery; or, Fighting for the Protection of Our Girls.* N.p.: Clifford G. Roe and B. S. Steadwell, 1911. Also published as *Horrors of the White Slave Trade: The Mighty Crusade to Protect the Purity of Our Homes.* New York: n.p., 1911; and as *The Prodigal Daughter: The White Slave Evil and the Remedy.* Chicago: L. W. Walter Co., 1911.

————. "Letters to the Editor." *American City* 7 (1912): 573.

————. *Panders and Their White Slaves.* New York: Fleming H. Revell Co., 1910.

Rogers, P. F. "The Sociologic Aspect of the Venereal Diseases." *Wisconsin Medical Journal* 8 (1909–10): 253–62.

Roloff, Bernal C. "The Eugenics Marriage Laws of Wisconsin, Michigan, and Indiana." *Journal of Social Hygiene* 6 (1920): 227–54.

Roosevelt, Theodore. "An Achievement for Humanity." *Outlook* 103 (1913): 116.

————. *Autobiography.* Vol. 22 *The Works of Theodore Roosevelt: Memorial Edition.* New York: Charles Scribner's Sons, 1925.

————. "The Cause of Decency." *Outlook* 98 (1911): 569–71.

Rosenstirn, J. "The Municipal Clinic of San Francisco." *Medical Record* 83 (1913): 467–76.

————. "The Notification of Venereal Disease." *Medical Record* 86 (1914): 343.

————. "Should the Sanitary Control of Prostitution Be Abandoned?" *Medical Record* 85 (1914): 1066–71.

Ross, E. A. *Sin and Society: An Analysis of Latter-Day Iniquity.* 1907. Reprint. New York: Harper & Row, Harper Torchbooks, 1973.

Ruck, Carl von. "Tuberculosis an Excitant to Sexual Excess." *American Journal of Dermatology and Genito-Urinary Diseases* 14 (1910): 119–21.

Ruggles, E. W. "The Physician's Relation to the Social Evil." *New York Medical Journal* 85 (1907): 159–61.

Sanger, William W. *The History of Prostitution: Its Extent, Causes, and Effects throughout the World.* 1858. Reprint. New York: Eugenics Publishing Co., 1937.

Satterthwaite, T. E. "Venereal Disease Peril." *New York Medical Journal* 112 (1920): 172.

Saunders, Jessie C. "Communications." *Survey* 24 (1910): 637.

Scherck, H. J. "Venereal Disease and the Social Evil." *St. Louis Medical Review* 4 (1910): 39–41.

Schevitz, Jules. "Are We Controlling Venereal Disease?" *Modern Medicine* 2 (1920): 507–9.

Scholtz, M. "The Problem of Social Evil in a Large Municipality." *Journal of Sociological Medicine* 18 (1917): 100–114.

Schroeder, Theodore. "Censorship of Sex Literature." *Medical Council* 14 (1909): 91–98.

————. "Mormonism and Prostitution." *Medical Council* 14 (1909): 171–78.

————. "Prostitution as a Social Problem." *Arena* 41 (1909): 196–201.

"Science vs. Romance." *Interstate Medical Journal* 18 (1911): 8–10.

"A Sculptress Who Has Caught the American Rhythm." *Current Opinion* 55 (1913): 124–25.

Seager, Henry Rogers. "The Theory of the Minimum Wage." *American Labor Legislation Review* 3 (1913): 81–91.

Sears, Frederick W. "The Wayward Girl." *Vermont Medical Monthly* 18 (1912): 7–9.

Sedgwick, William T. "Reappearance of the Ghost of Malthus." *American Journal of Public Health* 3 (1913): 1032–39.

"Sex in Education." *Arena* 24 (1900): 206–14.

"Sex O'Clock in America." *Current Opinion* 55 (1913): 113–14.

"Shall Chicago Legalize Hell?" *American City* 7 (1912): 405–6.

Sheffield, Ada Eliot. "Communications." *Survey* 24 (1910): 596.

————. "The Written Law and the Unwritten Double Standard." *International Journal of Ethics* 21 (1910–11): 475–85.

Shreveport, La. Shreveport Vice Commission. *Brief and Recommendations.* 1915.

Simpson, F. T. "The Extent and Importance of the Venereal Diseases in the Social Body." *Virginia Medical Semi-Monthly* 14 (1909–10): 126–29.

Skinner, E. M. "The Work of the Vice Commission." *Chicago Medical Recorder* 35 (1913): 90–93.

"The Slave Traffic in America." *Outlook* 93 (1909): 528–29.

Slosson, Edwin E. "A Dramatist Who Means Something." *Independent* 74 (1913): 749–52.
Smith, Andrew. "The Prophylactic Value of Normal Marriage." *Medical News* 86 (1905): 1163–65.
Smith, C. E., Jr. "Some Observations on Public Health and Morality." *St. Paul Medical Journal* 14 (1912): 194–202.
Smith, G. G. "The Venereal Infirmary at Camp Humphreys, Virginia." *Boston Medical and Surgical Journal* 180 (1919): 270–72.
Smith, O. J. "The Mann White Slave Law." *Medical-Legal Journal* 33 (1916–17): 4–7.
Smith, Theodate L. "Delinquent Girls." *Woman's Medical Journal* 25 (1915): 241–45.
Snow, William F. "Occupations and the Venereal Diseases." *Journal of the American Medical Association* 65 (1915): 2054–55.
———. "The Preventive Medicine Campaign against Venereal Diseases." *American Medical Association Bulletin* 9 (1914): 188–98.
———. "Public Health Measures in Relation to Venereal Diseases." *Journal of the American Medical Association* 66 (1916): 1003–8.
———. "Report of the Committee on Venereal Diseases." *American Journal of Public Health* 6 (1916): 592–93.
———. "Sex Education." *Survey* 31 (1913): 354–55.
———. "The Swing of the Pendulum on Sex Hygiene." *Survey* 32 (1914): 6.
"Social Diseases and the Family." *Outlook* 91 (1909): 233–34.
"The Social Evil." *Medicine* 12 (1906): 614–17, 673–78, 749–52.
"The Social Evil." *Outlook* 70 (1902): 606–8.
"The Social Evil." *Outlook* 101 (1912): 245–48.
"Social Evil in a Smaller City." *Survey* 26 (1911): 212–13.
"The Social Evil in the American Army." *Current Opinion* 54 (1913): 273–74.
"The Social Evil: The Immediate Remedies." *Outlook* 103 (1913): 298–99.
"Social Vice." *Independent* 68 (1910): 109–10.
"The Society of Moral Prophylaxis." *Medical News* 86 (1905): 1175–76.
Southard, M. Madeline. *The White Slave Traffic versus the American Home.* Louisville, Ky.: Pentecostal Publishing Co., 1914.
"Sowing Wild Oats." *Texas Medical Journal* 24 (1913–14): 410–11.
Spargo. *The Bitter Cry of the Children.* 1906. Reprint. Chicago: Quadrangle Books, 1968.
Spaulding, Edith L. "Mental and Physical Factors in Prostitution." *Woman's Medical Journal* 24 (1914): 133–36.
———. "The Problem of Venereal Disease in Its Relation to Penal Institutions." *Medical Record* 103 (1918): 714–19.
Spencer, Anna Garlin. "The Age of Consent and Its Significance." *Forum* 49 (1913): 406–20.
———. "Is the Page Bill All Right?" *Survey* 24 (1910): 354–55.
———. "Josephine Butler and the English Crusade." *Forum* 49 (1913): 703–16.
———. "Josephine Butler and the English Crusade: II." *Forum* 50 (1913): 77–81.
———. Review of *Hygiene and Morality.* *Survey* 24 (1910): 719–22.

_____. "The Scarlet Woman." *Forum* 49 (1913): 276–89.
_____. "Social Nemesis and Social Salvation." *Forum* 50 (1913): 432–44.
_____. "State Regulation of Vice and Its Meaning." *Forum* 49 (1913): 587–606.
_____. "A Word More on the Page Bill." *Survey* 24 (1910): 514–15.
_____. "A World Crusade." *Forum* 50 (1913): 182–95.
Spingarn, Arthur B. *Laws Relating to Sex Morality in New York City*. New York: Century Co., 1915.
Stannard, D. E. "The Crime of Sexual Ignorance, Showing Why the Doctor Is to Blame." *American Journal of Clinical Medicine* 17 (1910): 1167–72.
"The State Vice Report in Massachusetts." *Survey* 31 (1914): 736–37.
Stokes, J. H. "Hospital Problems of Gonorrhea and Syphilis." *Journal of the American Medical Association* 67 (1916): 1960–62.
Stone, Lee Alexander. "The Prostitute: An Ethnological Study." *Urologic and Cutaneous Review* 19 (1915): 609–12.
Stowe, Lyman Beecher. "Vice, Crime, and the New York Police." *American Review of Reviews* 48 (1913): 73–78.
Stoy, Elinor H. "Chinatown and the Curse That Makes It a Plague-Spot in the Nation." *Arena* 38 (1907): 360–65.
Stratton, Mary R. "Social Evil and Its Consequences." *Woman's Medical Journal* 29 (1919): 62–65.
Strong, S. L. "A Symposium on the Reportability and Control of Venereal Diseases." *Boston Medical and Surgical Journal* 169 (1913): 903–7.
Sumner, Walter T. "General Considerations on the Vice Problem." *Chicago Medical Recorder* 35 (1913): 96–107.
"Suppression of Brothels a Valid Health Measure." *Journal of the American Medical Association* 73 (1919): 1158.
"Supreme Court Upholds the 'White Slave' Law." *Survey* 29 (1913): 799–804.
Swayze, George B. H. "Shall Social Evil Infections Be Legally Repressed?" *Medical Times* 34 (1906): 257–62.
_____. "The Social Evil." *Medical Times* 34 (1906): 193–98.
_____. "Social Evil Dilemma." *Medical Times* 34 (1906): 225–29.
"Symposium on the Social Evil." *Kentucky Medical Journal* 8 (1909–10): 1163–78.
"Symposium on the Venereal Peril." *Providence Medical Journal* 6 (1905): 59–78.
"Symposium on Venereal Diseases." *Journal of the American Medical Association* 47 (1906): 1244–58.
Syracuse, N.Y. Committee of Eighteen, Morals Survey Committee. *The Social Evil in Syracuse*. 1913.
Tallant, Alice W. "A Medical Study of Delinquent Girls." *Bulletin of the American Academy of Medicine* 13 (1912): 283–93.
Tannenbaum, Frank. "The Moral Devastation of War." *Dial* 66 (1918–19): 333–36.
Tarbell, Ida M. "Good Will to Woman." *American Magazine* 75 (1913): 45–52.
Taylor, Graham. "Fighting Vice in Chicago." *Survey* 29 (1912): 94–95.

————. "Morals Commission and Police Morals." *Survey* 30 (1913): 62–64.

————. "Police Efficiency the First Test of Vice Inquiries." *Survey* 29 (1912): 136–41.

————. "Recent Advances against the Social Evil in New York." *Survey* 24 (1910): 858–65.

————. "Routing the Segregationists in Chicago." *Survey* 29 (1912): 254–56.

————. "The Story of the Chicago Vice Commission." *Survey* 26 (1911): 239–47.

————. "The War on Vice." *Survey* 29 (1913): 811–13.

"The Teaching of Sex Hygiene." *New York Medical Journal* 101 (1915): 850.

Teats, M. E. "Eugenic Parenthood and Its Relation to Christian and Social Ethics." *Texas Medical Journal* 29 (1913–14): 400–409.

Terrell, F. G. *The Shame of the Human Race–The White Slave Traffic: Commercializing the Sacredness of Sex: Beautiful White Girls Sold into Ruin.* N.p., 1904.

Thomas, William I. *Sex and Society: Studies in the Social Psychology of Sex.* Chicago: University of Chicago Press, 1907.

————. *The Unadjusted Girl: With Cases and Standpoint for Behavior Analysis.* 1923. Reprint. Montclair, N.J.: Patterson Smith, 1969.

Thomas, William I., and Znaniecki, Florian. *The Polish Peasant in Europe and America.* 1918–20. Reprint. 2 vols. New York: Dover Publications, 1958.

Thompson, Loyd, and Bolansny, J. R. "Venereal Disease in the Thirty-Ninth Division." *Journal of the American Medical Association* 71 (1918): 1291–97.

Thomson, A. N. "Attacking the Venereal Peril." *Long Island Medical Journal* 10 (1916): 141–46.

————. "Methods of Controlling Venereal Disease." *American Journal of Nursing* 17 (1916–17): 1068–73.

————. "The Problem of Venereal Disease Control." *New York State Journal of Medicine* 18 (1918): 451–55.

"The Toleration of Vice." *Independent* 53 (1901): 50–51.

Tomkins, F. W. "Sanitary Science and the Social Evil: Social Hygiene." *Pennsylvania Medical Journal* 13 (1909–10): 172–74.

"Tomlinson and Diggs." *Survey* 30 (1913): 655.

"To Reform Courts of Inferior Jurisdiction." *Survey* 24 (1910): 177–79.

"To Rehabilitate Portland Prostitutes." *Survey* 31 (1913): 176.

"The Trade in White Slaves." *American Review of Reviews* 39 (1909): 371–72.

Treadway, W. L. "A Psychiatric Study of Delinquent Women in Lansing, Kansas." *Public Health Reports* 35 (1920): 1197–1210.

————. "Some Constitutional Factors in Prostitution." *Public Health Reports* 35 (1920): 1575–92.

Treadway, Walter L., and Weldon, L. O. "Conclusions and Recommendations." *Public Health Reports* 35 (1920): 1593–96.

"The Trend of Things." *Survey* 26 (1911): 278.

Tuffier, T. "The War against the Venereal Diseases in France." *Journal of the American Medical Association* 47 (1906): 1249–50.

Turner, George Kibbe. "The City of Chicago: A Study of the Great Im-
moralities." *McClure's Magazine* 28 (1907): 575–92.
———. "The Daughters of the Poor: A Plain Story of the Development of New
York City as a Leading Center of the White Slave Trade of the World,
under Tammany Hall." *McClure's Magazine* 34 (1909): 45–61.
———. "The Strange Woman." *McClure's Magazine* 41 (1913): 25–33.
"United against Social Vice." *Independent* 74 (1913): 509–10.
U.S. Department of Commerce and Labor. *Reports*, 1908. "Report of the
Commissioner-General of Immigration."
———. *Reports*, 1908. "The White-Slave Traffic."
U.S. Department of Justice. *Annual Report of the Attorney General of the United
States*. 1913–20.
U.S. House of Representatives. Committee on Interstate and Foreign Commerce.
White Slave Traffic. 61st Cong., 2d sess., 1909, H. Rept. 47.
———. *Congressional Record*. 61st Cong., 2d sess., 1910, 45, pt. 1: 801–23; pt.
2: 1030–41.
U.S. Senate. *Importing Women for Immoral Purposes: A Partial Report from the
Immigration Commission on the Importation and Harboring of Women
for Immoral Purposes*. 61st Cong., 2d sess., 1909, doc. 196, pp. 3–61.
———. *Report on Conditions of Women and Child Wage Earners in the United
States*. Vol. 15. *Relation between Occupation and Criminality of Women*.
61st Cong., 2d sess., 1911, doc. 645.
———. Reports of the Immigration Commission. Vol. 19. *Importation and
Harboring of Women for Immoral Purposes*. 61st Cong., 3d sess., 1910,
doc. 753, pp. 55–124.
U.S. *Statutes at Large*. Vol. 18. Ch. 141. "An Act supplementary to the acts in
relation to immigration." 1875.
———. Vol. 32. Ch. 1012. "An Act to regulate the immigration of aliens into the
United States." 1903.
———. Vol. 34. Ch. 1134. "An Act to regulate the immigration of aliens into the
United States." 1907.
———. Vol. 36. Ch. 128. "An Act to amend an Act entitled 'An Act to regulate
the immigration of aliens into the United States,' approved February
twentieth, nineteen hundred and seven." 1910.
———. Vol. 36. Ch. 395. "An Act to further regulate interstate and foreign
commerce by prohibiting the transportation therein for immoral purposes
of women and girls, and for other purposes." 1910. ("White Slave Traffic
Act").
———. Vol. 40. Ch. 143. "An Act Making appropriations for the support of the
Army for the fiscal year ending June thirtieth, nineteen hundred and
nineteen." 1918.
United States v. *Bitty*. 208 U.S. 393 (1908).
United States v. *Holte*. 236 U.S. 140 (1915).
United States v. *Portale*. 235 U.S. 27 (1914).
Upshur, J. N. "The Limitation and Prevention of Venereal Disease." *American
Journal of Dermatology and Genito-Urinary Diseases* 14 (1910): 348–49.

————. "Venereal Diseases and Marriage, with Remarks upon Other Essential Conditions to the Perpetuation of a Robust Race." *American Journal of Dermatology and Genito-Urinary Diseases* 9 (1905): 13–15.

————. "Venereal Diseases as a Social Menace." *Virginia Medical Semi-Monthly* 9 (1904–5): 292–94.

"Valid Provisions for the Quarantining of Persons with Venereal Diseases." *Journal of the American Medical Association* 74 (1920): 1348.

Vanderveer, A. "In the Relation We Bear to the Public, What Use Shall We Make of Our Knowledge of the Evil Effects of Venereal Disease?" *American Journal of Obstetrics and Diseases of Women and Children* 64 (1911): 1033–42.

Vaught, C. H. "Symposium on the Social Evil: Cost of Venereal Infection as Viewed by the General Practitioner." *Kentucky Medical Journal* 8 (1909–10): 1163–69.

Vecki, V. G. "Can We Abolish, Shall We Ignore, or Must We Regulate Prostitution?" *American Journal of Dermatology and Genito-Urinary Diseases* 14 (1910): 213–20.

Vedder, E. B. "Has Our Propaganda for Venereal Prophylaxis Failed?" *Military Surgeon* 38 (1916): 340–41.

"The Venereal Disease Problem: I." *Journal of the American Medical Association* 68 (1917): 375–77.

"Venereal Prophylaxis after the War." *New York Medical Journal* 109 (1919): 599–600.

"Vice Fought by the 'Golden Rule.'" *Literary Digest* 46 (1913): 234.

"Vice Investigation by the Illinois Senate." *Survey* 29 (1913): 897.

"The Vice Problem in Philadelphia." *Survey* 30 (1913): 259.

"The 'Vice Trust' in New York City." *Current Opinion* 54 (1913): 5–6.

"A Vicious Use of Frankness." *Independent* 75 (1913): 604–5.

Vogt, Paul L. "Rural Morality: A Study in Social Pathology." *Journal of Social Hygiene* 1 (1914): 207–19.

"Voluntary Censorship of Cleveland Movies." *Survey* 30 (1913): 639.

"Votes for Women and Votes to Table the Hartford Vice Report." *Survey* 31 (1913): 73.

"Wages and Sin." *Literary Digest* 46 (1913): 621–24.

Walsh, F. C. "Venereal Diseases and Marriage." *American Journal of Dermatology and Genito-Urinary Diseases* 14 (1910): 225–27.

Warner, A. R. "The Result of Closing the Segregated Vice District upon the Public Health of Cleveland." *American Journal of Urology and Sexology* 12 (1916): 313–16.

————. "The Result of Closing the Segregated Vice District upon the Public Health of Cleveland." *Cleveland Medical Journal* 15 (1916): 171–73.

Watters, Ethel M. "The Problem of the Woman Venereal Disease Carrier." *California State Journal of Medicine* 17 (1919): 284–87.

"The Ways, Wages, and Wherefore of the Scarlet Woman." *Hearst's Magazine* 24 (1913): 147–49.

"Wayward Girls." *Survey* 25 (1911): 690–91.

Weidensall, Jean. "Psychological Tests as Applied to Criminal Women." *Psychological Review* 21 (1914): 370–75.

Weil, A. Leo. "In the Hands of the Police." *Survey* 30 (1913): 203–4.

Weiss, L. "The Prostitution Problem in Its Relation to Law and Medicine." *Journal of the American Medical Association* 47 (1906): 2071–75.

————. "The Prostitution Problem in Its Relation to Law and Medicine." *Medico-Pharmaceutical Critic and Guide* 8 (1907): 8–18.

Weldon, L. O. "A Study of Physical and Mental Conditions of 100 Delinquent White Women in Louisville, Ky." *Public Health Reports* 35 (1920): 1247–69.

"What My Boy Knows." *American Magazine* 75 (1913): 42–46.

Whiteside, George. "What Should We Teach the Public Regarding Venereal Disease?" *Journal of the American Medical Association* 47 (1906): 1252–53.

"White Slave." *Survey* 30 (1913): 311–13, 381–83, 507–10.

"The White-Slave Decision." *Literary Digest* 46 (1913): 500–502.

"The White Slave Films." *Outlook* 106 (1914): 120–22.

"The White Slave Films: A Review." *Outlook* 106 (1914): 345–50.

"'White-Slave' Law and Blackmail." *Literary Digest* 54 (1917): 178.

"White Slavers Routed." *Outlook* 103 (1913): 569–70.

"White Slaves." *Outlook* 94 (1910): 131–32.

"White Slaves and Immigration." *Outlook* 93 (1909): 881–83.

"The White Slaves and the Social Evil." *Chautauquan* 57 (1909–10): 331–33.

"The White Slave Trade." *Contemporary Review* 82 (1902): 735–40.

"White Slave Trade." *Missionary Review of the World* 26 (1903): 149.

"The White Slave Traffic." *Outlook* 95 (1910): 545–46.

"The White Slave Traffic before the Supreme Court." *Current Opinion* 54 (1913): 273.

Whitlock, Brand. "The White Slave." *Forum* 51 (1914): 193–216.

Williams, A. "The Anti-Venereal Campaign: Its Propaganda, Present Status, Future Possibilities." *Detroit Medical Journal* 9 (1909): 39–47.

Williams, E. H., and Brown, J. S. "Venereal Diseases and Practical Eugenics in Small Communities." *Medical Record* 84 (1913): 1018–20.

Wilson, L. T. "A Few Remarks on the Prevalence of Venereal Disease." *American Journal of Public Hygiene* 4 (1907–8): 39–45.

Wilson, Robert N. *The American Boy and the Social Evil: From a Physician's Standpoint*. Philadelphia: J. C. Winston, 1905.

————. "The Economic Relations of Social Diseases." *Pennsylvania Medical Journal* 15 (1911–12): 843–55.

————. "The Eradication of the Social Diseases in Large Cities." *Journal of the American Medical Association* 59 (1912): 924–29.

————. "Judge Not, That Ye Be Not Judged! Does the American Federation for Sex Hygiene Speak the Truth?" *American Journal of Public Health* 3 (1913): 874–81.

————. "The Public Health Problem Twenty-five Years from To-day." *Medical Review of Reviews* 21 (1915): 332–38.

———. "The Relation of the Medical Profession to the Social Evil." *Journal of the American Medical Association* 47 (1906): 29–32.

———. "The Social Evil in University Life: A Talk with the Students of the University of Pennsylvania." *Medical News* 84 (1904): 97–105.

Wilson, Samuel Paynter. *Chicago and Its Cesspools of Infamy.* Chicago: n.p., 1910.

Wilson, W. H. "Report of Venereal Disease at Camp Stutsenburg, Pampanya, R. I." *Military Surgeon* 28 (1911): 162–69.

Wilson, Woodrow. *The New Freedom.* Edited by William E. Leuchtenburg. Englewood Cliffs, N.J.: Prentice-Hall, 1961.

Wisconsin. *Report and Recommendations of the Wisconsin Legislative Committee to Investigate the White Slave Traffic and Kindred Subjects.* Madison, Wis., 1914.

"Wisconsin's Last Segregated District Closed." *Survey* 33 (1914): 328.

Wolbarst, Abraham L. "The Prevalence of Venereal Disease among Recently Arrived Immigrants, with Special Reference to Intermarital Infection." *New York Medical Journal* 90 (1909): 739–41.

———. "The Problem of Venereal Prophylaxis: Some Remedial Suggestions Relating to It." *Boston Medical and Surgical Journal* 155 (1906): 280–86.

———. "Universal Circumcision as a Sanitary Measure." *Journal of the American Medical Association* 62 (1914): 92–97.

———. "The Venereal Diseases: A Menace to the National Welfare." *American Journal of Dermatology and Genito-Urinary Diseases* 14 (1910): 268–76.

———. "The Venereal Diseases: A Menace to the National Welfare." *Medical Review* 62 (1913): 372–80.

Wood, J. C. "The Social Evil: The Duty of the Physician." *Hahnemannian Monthly* 47 (1912): 567–74.

"Woodrow Wilson and the Caminetti Scandal." *Current Opinion* 55 (1913): 76–79.

Woods, R. A. "Banners of a New Army." *Survey* 29 (1913): 813–14.

Woolston, Howard B. *Prostitution in the United States: Prior to the Entrance of the United States into the World War.* 1921. Reprint. Montclair, N.J.: Patterson Smith, 1969.

Young, Evangeline W. "The Conservation of Manhood and Womanhood." *Woman's Medical Journal* 20 (1910): 51–53.

Zahniser, Charles Reed. "A Constructive Program of Sex Control." *Hahnemannian Monthly* 53 (1918): 550–59.

Zimmermann, Jean Turner. *America's Black Traffic in White Girls.* 8th ed. Chicago: n.p., 1912.

Secondary Sources

Abbott, Carl. "Civic Pride in Chicago, 1844–1860." *Journal of the Illinois State Historical Society* 63 (1970): 399–421.

Anderson, Eric. "Prostitution and Social Justice: Chicago, 1910–15." *Social*

Service Review 48 (1974): 203–28.

Anderson, Odin W. *Syphilis and Society: Problems of Control in the United States, 1912–1964.* Center for Health Information Foundation, Research Series, vol. 22. Chicago: University of Chicago Press, 1965.

Arden, Eugene. "The Evil City in American Fiction." *New York History* 35 (1954): 259–79.

Asbury, Herbert. *The Barbary Coast: An Informal History of the San Francisco Underworld.* New York: Alfred A. Knopf, 1933.

————. *The Gangs of New York: An Informal History of the Underworld.* New York: Alfred A. Knopf, 1928.

————. *Gem of the Prairies: An Informal History of the Chicago Underworld.* New York: Alfred A. Knopf, 1940.

Axtell, James. "The White Indians of Colonial America." *Willam and Mary Quarterly* 32 (1975): 55–88.

Baer, Judith A. *The Chains of Protection: The Judicial Response to Women's Labor Legislation.* Westport, Conn.: Greenwood Press, 1978.

Baldwin, Fred Davis. "The American Enlisted Man in World War I." Ph.D. dissertation, Princeton University, 1964.

————. "The Invisible Armor." *American Quarterly* 16 (1964): 432–44.

Banner, Lois. *Women in Modern America: A Brief History.* New York: Harcourt Brace Jovanovich, 1974.

Barker-Benfield, G. J. *The Horrors of the Half-Known Life: Male Attitudes toward Women and Sexuality in Nineteenth-Century America.* New York: Harper & Row, 1976.

————. "The Spermatic Economy: A Nineteenth Century View of Sexuality." In *The American Family in Social-Historical Perspective*, edited by Michael Gordon, pp. 336–72. New York: St. Martin's Press, 1973.

Barnhart, Jacqueline Baker. "Working Women: Prostitution in San Francisco from the Gold Rush to 1900." Ph.D. dissertation, University of California, San Francisco, 1976.

Barry, Kathleen, *Female Sexual Slavery.* New York: Prentice-Hall, 1979.

Baum, Charlotte; Hyman, Paula; and Michel, Sonya. *The Jewish Woman in America.* New York: Dial Press, 1976.

Baylen, Joseph O. "A Victorian's 'Crusade' in Chicago, 1893–1894." *Journal of American History* 51 (1964): 418–34.

Beardsley, Edward H. "Allied against Sin: American and British Responses to Venereal Disease in World War I." *Medical History* [Great Britain] 20 (1976): 189–202.

Beaver, Daniel R. *Newton D. Baker and the American War Effort, 1917–1919.* Lincoln: University of Nebraska Press, 1966.

Benjamin, Harry, and Masters, R. E. L. *Prostitution and Morality.* London: Souvenir Press, 1965.

Berg, Charles. *Fear, Punishment, Anxiety and the Wolfenden Report.* London: George Allen & Unwin, 1959.

Blocker, Jack S., Jr. *Retreat from Reform: The Prohibition Movement in the United States, 1890–1913.* Westport, Conn.: Greenwood Press, 1976.

Boyer, Paul S. *Purity in Print: The Vice-Society Movement and Book Censorship in America.* New York: Charles Scribner's Sons, 1968.

————. *Urban Masses and Moral Order in America, 1820–1920.* Cambridge: Harvard University Press, 1978.

Bremner, Robert. *From the Depths: The Discovery of Poverty in the United States.* New York: New York University Press, 1956.

Brooks, Stewart M. *The V.D. Story.* South Brunswick and New York: A. S. Barnes & Co., 1971.

Brown, E. Richard. *Rockefeller Medicine Men: Medicine and Capitalism in America.* Berkeley: University of California Press, 1979.

Bullough, Vern L. *The History of Prostitution.* New Hyde Park, N.Y.: University Books, 1964.

————. "Problems and Methods for Research in Prostitution and the Behavioral Sciences." *Journal of the History of the Behavioral Sciences* 1 (1965): 244–51.

Bullough, Vern L., and Bullough, Bonnie. *Prostitution: An Illustrated Social History.* New York: Crown Publishers, 1978.

————. *Sin, Sickness and Sanity: A History of Sexual Attitudes.* New York: New American Library, 1977.

Bullough, Vern, and Voght, Martha. "Homosexuality and Its Confusion with the 'Secret Sin' in Pre-Freudian America." *Journal of the History of Medicine and Allied Sciences.* 28 (1973): 143–55.

Burnham, John C. "American Historians and the Subject of Sex." *Societas: A Review of Social History* 1 (1972): 307–16.

————. "Medical Inspection of Prostitutes in America in the Nineteenth Century: The St. Louis Experiment and Its Sequel." *Bulletin of the History of Medicine* 45 (1971): 203–18.

————. "Medical Specialists and Movements toward Social Control in the Progressive Era: Three Examples." In *Building the Organizational Society,* edited by Jerry Israel, pp. 19–30. New York: Free Press, 1972.

————. "The Progressive Era Revolution in American Attitudes toward Sex." *Journal of American History* 59 (1973): 885–908.

————. *Psychoanalysis and American Medicine, 1894–1918: Medicine, Science, and Culture.* New York: International Universities Press, 1967.

————. "The Social Evil Ordinance: A Social Experiment in Nineteenth Century St. Louis." *Bulletin of the Missouri Historical Society* 27 (1971): 203–17.

Burstyn, Joan N. "Images of Women in Text Books, 1880–1920." *Teachers College Record* 76 (1975): 431–40.

Cannon, Charles A. "The Awesome Power of Sex: The Polemical Campaign against Mormon Polygamy." *Pacific Historical Review* 43 (1974): 61–82.

Casidy, James H. "The Registration Area and American Vital Statistics: Development of a Health Research Source." *Bulletin of the History of Medicine* 39 (1965): 221–31.

Chafe, William H. *The American Woman: Her Changing Social, Economic and Political Roles, 1920–1970.* New York: Oxford University Press, 1972.

Chambers, Clarke A. *Paul U. Kellogg and the Survey: Voices for Social Welfare*

    and Social Justice. Minneapolis: University of Minnesota Press, 1971.
Chudacoff, Howard P. *The Evolution of American Urban Society*. Englewood
    Cliffs, N.J.: Prentice-Hall, 1975.
Clark, Norman H. *Deliver Us from Evil: An Interpretation of American Prohibi-
    tion*. New York: W. W. Norton, 1976.
Clarke, Charles Walter. *Taboo: The Story of the Pioneers of Social Hygiene*.
    Washington, D.C.: Public Affairs Press, 1961.
Clifford, John Garry. *The Citizen Soldiers: The Plattsburgh Training Camp
    Movement, 1913–1920*. Lexington: University of Kentucky Press, 1972.
Coffman, Edward M. *The War to End All Wars: The American Military Experi-
    ence in World War I*. New York: Oxford University Press, 1968.
Comfort, Alex. *The Anxiety Makers*. New York: Dell Publishing Co., 1970.
Cominos, Peter T. "Late Victorian Sexual Respectability and the Social System."
    International Review of Social History 8 (1963): 18–48, 216–50.
Cramer, C. H. *Newton D. Baker: A Biography*. Cleveland: World Publishing Co.,
    1961.
Cressey, Paul G. *The Taxi Dance Hall*. Chicago: University of Chicago Press,
    1932.
Curran, William J. "Venereal Disease Detention and Treatment: Prostitution and
    Civil Rights." *American Journal of Public Health* 65 (1975): 180–81.
Davies, Stanley Powell. *Social Control of the Mentally Deficient*. New York:
    Thomas Y. Crowell Co., 1930.
Davis, Allen F. *American Heroine: The Life and Legend of Jane Addams*. New
    York: Oxford University Press, 1973.
————. *Spearheads for Reform: The Social Settlements and the Progressive
    Movement, 1890–1914*. New York: Oxford University Press, 1967.
Davis, Audrey W. *Dr. Kelly of Hopkins: Surgeon, Scientist, Christian*. Baltimore:
    Johns Hopkins Press, 1959.
Davis, David Brion. *Homicide in American Fiction, 1798–1860*. Ithaca: Cornell
    University Press, 1957.
————. "Some Themes of Counter-Subversion: An Analysis of Anti-Masonic,
    Anti-Catholic, and Anti-Mormon Literature." *Mississippi Valley Histori-
    cal Review* 47 (1960–61): 205–24.
————, ed. *The Fear of Conspiracy: Images of UnAmerican Subversion from the
    Revolution to the Present*. Ithaca: Cornell University Press, 1971.
Davis, John Kyle. "The Grey Wolf: Tom Dennison of Omaha." *Nebraska History*
    58 (1977): 25–52.
Davis, Kingsley. "Sexual Behavior." In *Contemporary Social Problems*, edited by
    Robert K. Merton and Robert A. Nisbet, pp. 322–72. 2d ed. New York:
    Harcourt, Brace & World, 1966.
Dedmon, Emmet. *Fabulous Chicago*. New York: Random House, 1953.
Degler, Carl N. "What Ought to Be and What Was: Women's Sexuality in the
    Nineteenth Century." *American Historical Review* 79 (1975): 1476–90.
Ditzion, Sidney. *Marriage, Morals and Sex in America*. New York: Bookman
    Associates, 1953.
Douglass, Mary. *Purity and Danger: An Analysis of Concepts of Pollution and*

Taboo. Baltimore: Penguin Books, 1970.

Dowling, Harry F. *Fighting Infection: Conquests of the Twentieth Century*. Cambridge, Mass.: Harvard University Press, 1977.

Duncan, Hugh Daziel. *Culture and Democracy: The Struggle for Form in Society and Architecture in Chicago and the Midwest during the Life and Times of Louis Sullivan*. Totowa, N.J.: Bedminster Press, 1965.

Durham, Weldon B. "'Big Brother' and the 'Seven Sisters': Camp Life Reforms in World War I." *Military Affairs* 42 (1978): 57–60.

Erikson, Kai T. "Notes on the Sociology of Deviance." *Social Problems* 9 (1961–62): 307–14.

Evans, Richard J. "Prostitution, State and Society in Imperial Germany." *Past and Present* 70 (1976): 106–29.

Faris, Robert E. L. *Chicago Sociology, 1920–32*. San Francisco: Chandler Publishing Co., 1967.

Faulkner, Harold Underwood. *The Quest for Social Justice, 1898–1914*. New York: Macmillan Company, 1931.

Feldman, Egal. "Prostitution, the Alien Woman and the Progressive Imagination, 1910–1915." *American Quarterly* 19 (1967): 192–206.

Felt, Jeremy P. "Vice Reform as a Political Technique: The Committee of Fifteen in New York, 1900–1901." *New York History* 54 (1973): 24–51.

Fiedler, Leslie A. *Love and Death in the American Novel*. Rev. ed. New York: Dell Publishing Co., 1966.

Filene, Peter G. *Him-Her Self: Sex Roles in Modern America*. New York: New American Library, 1975.

———. "An Obituary for 'the Progressive Movement.'" *American Quarterly* 22 (1970): 20–34.

Filler, Louis. *Crusaders for American Liberalism*. Yellow Springs, Ohio: Antioch Press, 1950.

Flegel, Kenneth. "Changing Concepts of the Nosography of Gonorrhea and Syphilis." *Bulletin of the History of Medicine* 48 (1974): 571–88.

Flexner, Eleanor. *Centuries of Struggle: The Woman's Rights Movement in the United States*. Rev. ed. Cambridge, Mass.: Harvard University Press, Belknap Press, 1975.

Forcey, Charles. *The Crossroads of Liberalism: Croly, Weyl, Lippmann and the Progressive Era*. New York: Oxford University Press, 1961.

Gardner, James F., Jr. "Microbes and Morality: The Social Hygiene Crusade in New York City, 1892–1917." Ph.D. dissertation, Indiana University, 1973.

Gibens, T. C. N. "Juvenile Prostitution." *British Journal of Delinquency* 8 (1957): 3–12.

Ginger, Ray. *Atgeld's America: The Lincoln Ideal versus Changing Realities*. Chicago: Quadrangle Books, 1958.

Glaab, Charles N., and Brown, A. Theodore. *A History of Urban America*. New York: Macmillan Company, 1967.

Goodman, H. *Notable Contributors to the Knowledge of Syphilis*. New York: Froben Press, 1943.

Gordon, Linda. *Woman's Body, Woman's Right: A Social History of Birth Control in America*. New York: Grossman, 1976.

Gorham, Deborah. "The 'Maiden Tribute of Modern Babylon' Re-Examined: Child Prostitution and the Idea of Childhood in Late-Victorian England." *Victorian Studies* 21 (1978): 353–79.

Gottlieb, Lois C. "The Perils of Freedom: The New Woman in Three American Plays of the 1900's." *Canadian Review of American Studies* 6 (1975): 84–98.

Griffen, Clyde. "The Progressive Ethos." In *The Development of an American Culture*, edited by Stanley Coben and Lorman Ratner, pp. 120–49. Englewood Cliffs, N.J.: Prentice-Hall, 1970.

Grob, Gerald N. *Edward Jarvis and the Medical World of Nineteenth Century America*. Knoxville: University of Tennessee Press, 1978.

Haberly, David T. "Women and Indians: *The Last of the Mohicans* and the Captivity Tradition." *American Quarterly* 28 (1976): 431–43.

Hackett, C. J. "On the Origin of the Human Treponematoses." *Bulletin of the World Health Organization* 41 (1963): 7–41.

Haft, Marilyn G. "Hustling for Rights." *Civil Liberties Review* 1 (1974): 8–26.

Hale, Nathan G., Jr. *Freud and the Americans: The Beginnings of Psychoanalysis in the United States, 1876–1917*. New York: Oxford University Press, 1971.

Hall, Gladys Mary. *Prostitution in the Modern World: A Survey and a Challenge*. New York: Emerson Books, 1936.

Haller, John S., Jr., and Haller, Robin M. *The Physician and Sexuality in Victorian America*. Urbana: University of Illinois Press, 1974.

Haller, Mark H. *Eugenics: Hereditarian Attitudes in American Thought*. New Brunswick, N.J.: Rutgers University Press, 1963.

―――. "Urban Vice and Civic Reform: Chicago in the Early Twentieth Century." In *Cities in American History*, edited by Kenneth T. Jackson and Stanley K. Schultz, pp. 290–305. New York: Alfred A. Knopf, 1972.

Handlin, Oscar. *Race and Nationality in American Life*. Garden City, N.Y.: Doubleday & Co., 1957.

Hanser, Charles J. *Guide to Decision: The Royal Commission*. Totowa, N.J.: Bedminster Press, 1965.

Harrison, Brian. "Underneath the Victorians." *Victorian Studies* 10 (1967): 239–62.

Harrison, Fraser. *The Dark Angel: Aspects of Victorian Sexuality*. New York: Universe Books, 1978.

Hass, Paul H. "Sin in Wisconsin: The Teasdale Vice Committee of 1913." *Wisconsin Magazine of History* 49 (1965): 138–51.

Haughton, Walter. *The Victorian Frame of Mind, 1830–1870*. New Haven: Yale University Press, 1957.

Hays, Samuel P. *The Response to Industrialism, 1885–1914*. Chicago: University of Chicago Press, 1957.

Heimert, Alan. *Religion and the American Mind: From the Great Awakening to the Revolution*. Cambridge, Mass.: Harvard University Press, 1966.

Henriques, Fernando. *Love in Action: The Sociology of Sex.* New York: E. P. Dutton & Co., 1960.

————. *Prostitution and Society.* 3 vols. Vol. 1, *Primitive, Classical and Oriental.* Vol. 2, *Prostitution in Europe and the Americas.* Vol. 3, *Modern Sexuality.* London: MacGibbon and Kee, 1962–68.

Higham, John. *Strangers in the Land: Patterns of American Nativism, 1860–1925.* 2d ed. New York: Atheneum, 1969.

Hofstadter, Richard. *The Age of Reform.* New York: Alfred A. Knopf, 1955.

————. *Anti-Intellectualism in American Life.* New York: Random House, Vintage Books, 1963.

————. *The Paranoid Style in American Politics and Other Essays.* New York: Random House, Vintage Books, 1967.

Hofstadter, Richard, and Wallace, Michael, eds. *American Violence: A Documentary History.* New York: Alfred A. Knopf, 1970.

Holmes, Kay Ann. "Reflections by Gaslight: Prostitution in Another Age." *Issues in Criminology* 7 (1972): 83–101.

Hopkins, C. Howard. *The Rise of the Social Gospel in American Protestantism, 1865–1915.* New Haven: Yale University Press, 1940.

Howe, Irving. *World of Our Fathers.* New York: Harcourt Brace Jovanovich, 1976.

Hoyt, Homer. *One Hundred Years of Land Values in Chicago: The Relationship of the Growth of Chicago to the Rise of Its Land Values, 1830–1933.* Chicago: University of Chicago Press, 1933.

Hudson, Robert P. "Abraham Flexner in Perspective: American Medical Education, 1865–1910." *Bulletin of the History of Medicine* 46 (1972): 545–61.

Hughes, H. Stuart. *Consciousness and Society: The Reorientation of European Social Thought, 1890–1930.* New York: Random House, Vintage Books, 1958.

Ichioka, Yuji. "Ameyuki-san: Japanese Prostitutes in Nineteenth Century America." *Amerasia Journal* 4 (1977): 1–21.

"Is Prostitution Still a Significant Health Problem?" *Medical Aspects of Human Sexuality* 2 (1968): 39–46.

Jaher, Frederic Cople. *Doubters and Dissenters: Cataclysmic Thought in America, 1885–1918.* London: Free Press of Glencoe, 1964.

James, Jennifer. "The Prostitute as Victim." In *The Victimization of Women*, edited by Jane Roberts and Margaret Gates, pp. 175–201. Beverly Hills: Sage Publications, 1978.

Jeffrey, Kirk, Jr. "The Family as Utopian Retreat from the City: The Nineteenth Century Contribution." *Soundings* 55 (1972): 21–41.

Johnson, Bascom, ed. *Digest of Laws and Regulations Relating to the Prevention and Control of Syphilis and Gonorrhea in the Forty-eight States and District of Columbia.* New York: American Social Hygiene Association, 1940.

Johnson, Claudia D. "That Guilty Third Tier: Prostitution in Nineteenth-Century American Theaters." *American Quarterly* 27 (1975): 575–84.

Johnson, R. Christian. "Anthony Comstock: Reform, Vice, and the American Way." Ph.D. dissertation, University of Wisconsin, 1973.

Jordan, Winthrop D. *White over Black: American Attitudes toward the Negro, 1550–1812.* Baltimore: Penguin Books, 1969.

Kelves, Daniel J. "Testing the Army's Intelligence: Psychologists and the Military in World War I." *Journal of American History* 55 (1968): 565–81.

Kennedy, David M. *Birth Control in America: The Career of Margaret Sanger.* New Haven: Yale University Press, 1970.

————. "Overview: The Progressive Era." *American Quarterly* 37 (1974–75): 453–68.

Kessner, Thomas. *The Golden Door: Italian and Jewish Immigrant Mobility in New York City, 1880–1915.* New York: Oxford University Press, 1977.

Kingsdale, Jon M. "The 'Poor Man's Club': Social Functions of the Urban Working Class Saloon." *American Quarterly* 25 (1973): 472–89.

Kinsey, Alfred C., et al. *Sexual Behavior in the Human Female.* Philadelphia: W. B. Saunders Co., 1953.

————. *Sexual Behavior in the Human Male.* Philadelphia: W. B. Saunders Co., 1948.

Kirschner, Don S. "The Ambiguous Legacy: Social Justice and Social Control in the Progressive Era." *Historical Reflections* 2 (1975): 69–88.

Klein, Alice, and Roberts, Wayne. "Besieged Innocence: The 'Problem' and the Problems of Working Women—Toronto, 1896–1914." In *Women at Work: Ontario, 1850–1930,* pp. 211–60. Toronto: Canadian Women's Educational Press, 1974.

Klein, Maury, and Kanter, Harvey A. *Prisoners of Progress: American Industrial Cities, 1850–1920.* New York: Macmillan Company, 1976.

Knapp, Richard F. "The Playground and Recreation Association of America in World War I." *Parks and Recreation* 7 (1972): 27–31, 110–12.

Kraditor, Aileen S. *The Ideas of the Woman Suffrage Movement, 1890–1920.* New York: Random House, Vintage Books, 1965.

————. *Means and Ends in American Abolitionism: Garrison and His Critics on Strategy and Tactics, 1834–1850.* New York: Random House, 1969.

Krich, Aron. "Before Kinsey: Continuity in American Sex Research." *Psychoanalytic Review* 53 (1966): 233–54.

Kushner, Howard I. "Nineteenth-Century Sexuality and the 'Sexual Revolution' of the Progressive Era." *Canadian Review of American Studies* 9 (1978): 34–49.

Laird, Sydney M. "Prostitution and Venereal Diseases in Manchester." *British Journal of Venereal Diseases* 32 (1956): 181–83.

Lasch, Christopher. *The New Radicalism in America, 1889–1963: The Intellectual as a Social Type.* New York: Alfred A. Knopf, 1965.

————. *The World of Nations: Reflections on American History, Politics and Culture.* New York: Alfred A. Knopf, 1973.

Leab, Daniel J. "Women and the Mann Act." *Amerikastuden/American Studies* [West Germany] 21 (1976): 55–65.

Lerna, Gerda. "The Lady and the Mill Girl: Changes in the Status of Women in the Age of Jackson." *MidContinent American Studies Journal* 10 (1969): 5–15.

Leuchtenburg, William E. *Franklin D. Roosevelt and the New Deal*. New York: Harper & Row, 1963.

Levi, Edward H. *An Introduction to Legal Reasoning*. Chicago: University of Chicago Press, 1948.

Levin, N. Gordon, Jr. *Woodrow Wilson and World Politics*. New York: Oxford University Press, 1968.

Light, Ivan. "The Ethnic Vice Industry, 1880–1944." *American Sociological Review* 42 (1977): 464–79.

————. "From Vice District to Tourist Attraction: The Moral Career of American Chinatowns, 1880–1940." *Pacific Historical Review* 43 (1974): 367–94.

Link, Arthur. "What Happened to the Progressive Movement in the 1920's?" *American Historical Review* 64 (1959): 833–51.

Lomax, Elizabeth. "Infantile Syphilis as an Example of Nineteenth Century Belief in the Inheritance of Acquired Characteristics." *Journal of the History of Medicine and Allied Sciences* 34 (1979): 23–39.

Lubove, Roy. *The Professional Altruist: The Emergence of Social Work as a Career, 1880–1930*. New York: Atheneum, 1972.

————. "The Progressives and the Prostitute." *Historian* 24 (1962): 308–30.

Lundberg, Ferdinand, and Farnham, Marynia F. *Modern Woman: The Lost Sex*. New York: Harper & Brothers, 1947.

McCarthy, Kathleen D. "Nickel Vice and Virtue: Movie Censorship in Chicago, 1901–1915." *Journal of Popular Film* 5 (1976): 37–55.

MacDonald, R. H. "The Frightful Consequences of Onanism: Notes on the History of a Delusion." *Journal of the History of Ideas* 28 (1967): 423–31.

McGovern, James R. "The American Woman's Pre-World War I Freedom in Manners and Morals." *Journal of American History* 55 (1968): 315–33.

————. "David Graham Phillips and the Virility Impulse of Progressives." *New England Quarterly* 39 (1966): 334–55.

————. "'Sporting Life on the Line': Prostitution in Progressive Era Pensacola." *Florida Historical Quarterly* 54 (1975–76): 131–44.

McKelvey, Blake. *The Emergence of Metropolitan America, 1915–1966*. New Brunswick, N.J.: Rutgers University Press, 1968.

————. *The Urbanization of America, 1860–1915*. New Brunswick, N.J.: Rutgers University Press, 1963.

McLoughlin, William G. *The Meaning of Henry Ward Beecher: An Essay on the Shifting Values of Mid-Victorian America, 1840–1870*. New York: Alfred A. Knopf, 1970.

MacPhail, Elizabeth C. "When the Red Lights Went Out in San Diego: The Little Known Story of San Diego's 'Restricted' District." *Journal of San Diego History* 20 (1975): 1–28.

Madge, John. *The Origins of Scientific Sociology.* New York: Free Press, 1962.

Marcus, Steven. *Engels, Manchester, and the Working Class.* New York: Random House, Vintage Books, 1974.

———. *The Other Victorians: A Study of Sexuality and Pornography in Mid-Nineteenth-Century England.* New York: Basic Books, 1966.

Marcuse, Herbert. *Reason and Revolution: Hegel and the Rise of Social Theory.* London: Routledge & Kegan Paul, 1955.

May, Henry F. *The End of American Innocence: A Study of the First Years of Our Own Time, 1912–1917.* Chicago: Quadrangle Books, 1964.

———. *The Protestant Churches and Industrial America.* New York: Harper & Row, 1949.

Mayer, Harold, and Wade, Richard. *Chicago: The Growth of a Metropolis.* Chicago: University of Chicago Press, 1969.

Mennel, Robert M. *Thorns and Thistles: Juvenile Delinquents in the United States, 1825–1940.* Hanover, N.H.: University Press of New England, 1973.

Merrill, Francis E. *Social Problems on the Home Front: A Study of Wartime Influences.* New York: Harper & Brothers, 1948.

Miller, Perry. *The New England Mind: From Colony to Province.* Boston: Beacon Press, 1961.

Miller, Zane L. *Boss Cox's Cincinnati: Urban Politics in the Progressive Era.* New York: Oxford University Press, 1968.

———. *The Urbanization of Modern America: A Brief History.* New York: Harcourt Brace Jovanovich, 1973.

Millett, Kate. *The Prostitution Papers.* New York: Ballantine Books, 1976.

Mills, C. Wright. *White Collar.* New York: Oxford University Press, 1951.

Morton, R. S. *Venereal Diseases.* Baltimore: Penguin Books, 1974.

Mowry, George E. *The Era of Theodore Roosevelt.* New York: Harper & Brothers, 1958.

Myers, Rex C. "An Inning for Sin: Chicago Joe and the Hurdy-Gurdy Girls." *Montana* 27 (1977): 24–33.

Nelli, Humbert S. *Italians in Chicago, 1880–1930: A Study in Ethnic Mobility.* New York: Oxford University Press, 1970.

Noble, David W. *The Progressive Mind, 1890–1917.* Chicago: Rand McNally & Co., 1970.

O'Connell, Lucille. "Travelers' Aid for Polish Immigrant Women." *Polish American Studies* 31 (1974): 15–19.

O'Neill, William L. *Divorce in the Progressive Era.* New Haven: Yale University Press, 1967.

———. *Everyone Was Brave: A History of Feminism in America.* Chicago: Quadrangle Books, 1971.

Palmer, Frederick. *Newton D. Baker: America at War.* 2 vols. New York: Dodd, Mead & Co., 1931.

Parran, Thomas. *Shadow on the Land: Syphilis.* New York: Reynal & Hitchcock, 1937.

Parsons, Gail Pat. "Equal Treatment for All: American Medical Remedies for

Male Sexual Problems, 1850–1900." *Journal of the History of Medicine and Allied Sciences* 32 (1977): 55–71.

Paxson, Frederic L. *America at War, 1917–1918*. Boston: Houghton Mifflin Co., 1939.

Pearsall, Ronald. *The Worm in the Bud: The World of Victorian Sexuality*. Toronto: Macmillan Co., 1969.

Petrie, Glen. *A Singular Inequity: The Campaigns of Josephine Butler*. New York: Viking Press, 1971.

Pickens, Donald K. *Eugenics and the Progressives*. Nashville: Vanderbilt University Press, 1968.

Pivar, David J. *Purity Crusade: Sexual Morality and Social Control, 1868–1900*. Westport, Conn.: Greenwood Press, 1973.

Platt, Anthony M., ed. *The Politics of Riot Commissions, 1917–1970: A Collection of Official Reports and Critical Essays*. New York: Collier Books, 1971.

Ploscowe, Morris. *Sex and the Law*. New York: Prentice-Hall, 1951.

Polsky, Ned. *Hustlers, Beats, and Others*. Garden City, N.Y.: Anchor Books, 1969.

Pomeroy, Wardell B. *Dr. Kinsey and the Institute for Sex Research*. London: Thomas Nelson & Sons, 1972.

Pusey, William Allen. *The History and Epidemiology of Syphilis*. Springfield, Ill.: Charles C. Thomas, 1931.

Ranulf, Svend. *Moral Indignation and Middle Class Psychology*. 1938. Reprint. New York: Schocken Books, 1964.

Reckless, Walter C. *Vice in Chicago*. 1933. Reprint. Montclair, N.J.: Patterson Smith, 1969.

Reed, James. *From Private Vice to Public Virtue: The Birth Control Movement and American Society since 1830*. New York: Basic Books, 1978.

Reiss, Ira L. *The Social Context of Premarital Sexual Permissiveness*. New York: Holt, Rinehart & Winston, 1967.

Riegel, Robert E. "Changing American Attitudes toward Prostitution, 1800–1920." *Journal of the History of Ideas* 29 (1968): 437–52.

Rischin, Moses. *The Promised City: New York's Jews, 1870–1914*. New York: Corinth Books, 1964.

Roby, Pamela Ann. "Politics and Prostitution: A Case Study of the Formulation, Enforcement, and Judicial Administration of the New York State Penal Laws on Prostitution." Ph.D. dissertation, New York University, 1971.

Rose, Al. *Storyville, New Orleans: Being an Authentic, Illustrated Account of the Notorious Red-light District*. University, Ala.: University of Alabama Press, 1974.

Rosebury, Theodor. *Microbes and Morals: The Strange Story of Venereal Disease*. New York: Viking Press, 1971.

Rosen, Ruth. "The Lost Sisterhood: Prostitution during the Progressive Era." Ph.D. dissertation, University of California, Berkeley, 1976.

Rosen, Ruth, and Davidson, Sue, eds. *The Maimie Papers*. Old Westbury, N.Y.: The Feminist Press, 1977.

Rosenberg, Charles E. "Sexuality, Class and Role in 19th-Century America." *American Quarterly* 25 (1973): 131–53.

Rosenkrantz, Barbara Gutmann. *Public Health and the State: Changing Views in Massachusetts, 1842–1936.* Cambridge, Mass.: Harvard University Press, 1972.

Rottenberg, Lori. "The Wayward Worker: Toronto's Prostitute at the Turn of the Century." In *Women at Work: Ontario, 1850–1930,* pp. 37–70. Toronto: Canadian Women's Educational Press, 1974.

Rugoff, Milton. *Prudery and Passion: Sexuality in Victorian America.* New York: G. P. Putnam's Sons, 1971.

Rutman, Darrett B. *Winthrop's Boston: A Portrait of a Puritan Town, 1630–1649.* Chapel Hill: University of North Carolina Press, 1965.

Schorer, Mark. *Sinclair Lewis: An American Life.* New York: McGraw-Hill Book Co., 1961.

Seagle, William. "The Twilight of the Mann Act." *American Bar Association Journal* 55 (1969): 641–47.

Sears, Hal D. *The Sex Radicals: Free Love in High Victorian America.* Lawrence: Regents Press of Kansas, 1977.

Seymour-Smith, Martin. *Fallen Women.* London: Thomas Nelson & Sons, 1969.

Shade, William G. "'A Mental Passion': Female Sexuality in Victorian America." *International Journal of Women's Studies* [Canada] 1 (1978): 13–29.

Shover, Michele J. "Roles and Images of Women in World War I Propaganda." *Politics and Society* 5 (1975): 469–86.

Shryock, Richard Harrison. *The Development of Modern Medicine: An Interpretation of the Social and Scientific Factors Involved.* New York: Alfred A. Knopf, 1947.

———. *Medicine in America: Historical Essays.* Baltimore: Johns Hopkins Press, 1966.

Shumsky, Neil Larry. "The Municipal Clinic of San Francisco: A Study in Medical Structure." *Bulletin of the History of Medicine* 52 (1978): 542–59.

Sigsworth, E. M., and Wyke, T. J. "A Study of Victorian Prostitution and Venereal Disease." In *Suffer and Be Still: Women in the Victorian Age,* edited by Martha Vincinus, pp. 77–99. Bloomington: Indiana University Press, 1972.

Sinclair, Andrew. *The Emancipation of the American Woman.* New York: Harper & Row, 1966.

———. *Era of Excess: A Social History of the Prohibition Movement.* New York: Harper & Row, Harper Colophon Books, 1964.

Slotkin, Richard. *Regeneration through Violence: The Mythology of the American Frontier, 1600–1860.* Middletown, Conn.: Wesleyan University Press, 1973.

Smith, Daniel Scott. "The Dating of the American Sexual Revolution: Evidence and Interpretation." In *The American Family in Social-Historical Perspective,* edited by Michael Gordon, pp. 321–35. New York: St. Martin's Press, 1973.

Smith-Rosenberg, Carroll. "Beauty, the Beast and the Militant Woman: A Case Study in Sex Roles and Social Stress in Jacksonian America." *American Quarterly* 23 (1971): 562–84.

Smith Rosenberg, Carroll. *Religion and the Rise of the American City: The New York City Mission Movement, 1812–1870.* Ithaca: Cornell University Press, 1971.

Smith-Rosenberg, Carroll, and Rosenberg, Charles. "The Female Animal: Medical and Biological Views of Woman and Her Role in Nineteenth-Century America." *Journal of American History* 110 (1973): 332–56.

Smuts, Robert W. *Women and Work in America.* New York: Schocken Books, 1971.

Smythe, Donald. "Venereal Disease: The AEF's Experience." *Prologue: The Journal of the National Archives* 9 (1977): 65–74.

Sochen, June. *The New Woman in Greenwich Village, 1910–1920.* New York: Quadrangle Books, 1972.

Solomon, Barbara Miller. *Ancestors and Immigrants: A Changing New England Tradition.* Cambridge, Mass.: Harvard University Press, 1956.

Sprague, Claire, ed. *Van Wyck Brooks: The Early Years.* New York: Harper & Row, 1968.

Stage, Sarah J. "Out of the Attic: Studies of Victorian Sexuality." *American Quarterly* 27 (1975): 480–85.

Strong, Byran. "Ideas of the Early Sex Education Movement in America, 1890–1920." *History of Education Quarterly* 12 (1972): 129–61.

Taylor, G. Rattray. *The Angel Makers: A Study in the Psychological Origins of Historical Change, 1750–1850.* New York: E. P. Dutton & Co., 1974.

————. *Sex in History.* New York: Vanguard Press, 1954.

Temkin, Owsei. "Therapeutic Trends and the Treatment of Syphilis before 1900." *Bulletin of the History of Medicine* 29 (1955): 309–16.

Thomas, Keith. "The Double Standard." *Journal of the History of Ideas* 20 (1959): 195–216.

Thompson, E. P. "Time, Work-Discipline, and Industrial Capitalism." *Past and Present* 38 (1967): 56–97.

Timberlake, James H. *Prohibition and the Progressive Movement, 1900–1920.* Cambridge, Mass: Harvard University Press, 1963.

Trudgill, Eric. *Madonnas and Magdalens: The Origins and Development of Victorian Sexual Attitudes.* New York: Holmes & Meier, 1976.

Twombly, Robert C. *Frank Lloyd Wright: An Interpretive Biography.* New York: Harper & Row, 1973.

Tylor, Peter L. "'Denied the Power To Choose the Good': Sexuality and Mental Defect in American Medical Practice, 1850–1920." *Journal of Social History* 10 (1976–77): 472–82.

U.S. Public Health Service. *Syphilis: A Synopsis.* Public Health Service Publication no. 1660. Washington, D.C.: Government Printing Office, 1967.

Wade, Louise C. *Graham Taylor: Pioneer for Social Justice, 1851–1938.* Chicago: University of Chicago Press, 1964.

Wagner, Roland Richard. "Virtue against Vice: A Study of Moral Reformers and

Prostitution in the Progressive Era." Ph.D. dissertation, University of Wisconsin, 1971.

Walters, R. G. "Sexual Matters as Historical Problems: A Framework of Analysis." *Societas: A Review of Social History* 6 (1976): 157–75.

Washburn, Charles. *Come into My Parlor: A Biography of the Aristocratic Everleigh Sisters of Chicago*. New York: Arno Press, 1974.

Waterman, Willoughby Cyrus. *Prostitution and Its Repression in New York City, 1900–1931*. New York: Columbia University Press, 1932.

Welter, Barbara. "The Cult of True Womanhood." *American Quarterly* 18 (1966): 151–74.

Wendt, Lloyd, and Kogan, Herman. *Lords of the Levee: The Story of Bathhouse John and Hinky Dink*. New York: Bobbs-Merrill, 1943.

White, Morton. *Social Thought in America: The Revolt against Formalism*. Boston: Beacon Press, 1957.

Whiteaker, Larry Howard. "Moral Reform and Prostitution in New York City, 1830–1860." Ph.D. dissertation, Princeton University, 1977.

Wiebe, Robert H. "The Progressive Years, 1900–1917." In *The Reinterpretation of American History and Culture*, edited by William H. Cartwright and Richard L. Watson, Jr., pp. 425–42. Washington, D.C.: National Council for the Social Studies, 1973.

————. *The Search for Order, 1877–1920*. New York: Hill & Wang, 1967.

Wilcox, R. R. *Textbook of Venereal Diseases and Treponematoses*. 2d ed. Springfield, Ill.: Charles C. Thomas, 1964.

Wilson, Otto (with the collaboration of Robert South Barrett). *Fifty Years Work with Girls, 1883–1933: A Story of the Florence Crittenton Homes*. Alexandria, Va.: National Florence Crittenton Mission, 1933.

Winick, Charles, and Kinsie, Paul M. *The Lively Commerce: Prostitution in the United States*. Chicago: Quadrangle Books, 1971.

Wood, Ann Douglass. "The Fashionable Diseases: Women's Complaints and Their Treatment in Nineteenth Century America." In *Clio's Consciousness Raised*, edited by Mary Hartman and Lois Banner, pp. 1–22. New York: Harper & Row, 1974.

Wood, Stephen B. *Constitutional Politics in the Progressive Era: Child Labor and the Law*. Chicago: University of Chicago Press, 1968.

Wunsch, James L. "Prostitution and Public Policy: From Regulation to Suppression, 1858–1920." Ph.D. dissertation, University of Chicago, 1976.

————. Review of Stephen Longstreet, ed., *Nell Kimball: Her Life as an American Madam*. *Journal of Social History* 6 (1972–73): 121–26.

Wyman, Margaret. "The Rise of the Fallen Woman." *American Quarterly* 3 (1951): 167–77.

Yellis, Kenneth A. "Prosperity's Child: Some Thoughts on the Flapper." *American Quarterly* 21 (1969): 44–64.

Young, Kimball. "Contributions of William Isaac Thomas to Sociology." *Sociology and Research* 47 (1962–63): 3–34, 123–37, 251–72.

Young, Wayland. *Eros Denied: Sex in Western Society*. New York: Grove Press, 1964.

INDEX